Wirtschaftsgeschichte der mittelalterlichen Juden

Fragen und Einschätzungen

Schriften des Historischen Kollegs

Herausgegeben von Lothar Gall

Kolloquien
71

R. Oldenbourg Verlag München 2008

Wirtschaftsgeschichte der mittelalterlichen Juden

Fragen und Einschätzungen

Herausgegeben von
Michael Toch
unter Mitarbeit von
Elisabeth Müller-Luckner

R. Oldenbourg Verlag München 2008

Das Historische Kolleg fördert im Bereich der historisch orientierten Wissenschaften Gelehrte, die sich durch herausragende Leistungen in Forschung und Lehre ausgewiesen haben. Es vergibt zu diesem Zweck jährlich bis zu drei Forschungsstipendien und zwei Förderstipendien sowie alle drei Jahre den „Preis des Historischen Kollegs".
Die Forschungsstipendien, deren Verleihung zugleich eine Auszeichnung für die bisherigen Leistungen darstellt, sollen den berufenen Wissenschaftlern während eines Kollegjahres die Möglichkeit bieten, frei von anderen Verpflichtungen eine größere Arbeit abzuschließen. Professor Dr. Michael Toch (Jerusalem) war – zusammen mit Prof. Dr. Wilfried Hartmann (Tübingen), Prof. Dr. Heinz Schilling (Berlin) und PD Dr. Peter Scholz (Frankfurt a. M.) – Stipendiat des Historischen Kollegs im Kollegjahr 2004/2005. Den Obliegenheiten der Stipendiaten gemäß hat Michael Toch aus seinem Arbeitsbereich ein Kolloquium zum Thema „Wirtschaftsgeschichte der mittelalterlichen Juden. Fragen und Einschätzungen" vom 21. bis 23. Juni 2005 im Historischen Kolleg gehalten. Die Ergebnisse des Kolloquiums werden in diesem Band veröffentlicht.
Das Historische Kolleg wird seit dem Kollegjahr 2000/2001 – im Sinne einer „public private partnership" – in seiner Grundausstattung vom Freistaat Bayern finanziert, seine Stipendien werden gegenwärtig aus Mitteln der Fritz Thyssen Stiftung, des Stifterverbandes für die Deutsche Wissenschaft und eines ihm verbundenen Förderunternehmens dotiert. Träger des Historischen Kollegs, das vom Stiftungsfonds Deutsche Bank und vom Stifterverband errichtet und zunächst allein finanziert wurde, ist nunmehr die „Stiftung zur Förderung der Historischen Kommission bei der Bayerischen Akademie der Wissenschaften und des Historischen Kollegs".

historischeskolleg.de
Kaulbachstraße 15, D-80539 München
Tel.: 49+89 2866 3860 · Fax: 49+89 2866 3863
E-Mail: kontakt@historischeskolleg.de

Bibliographische Information der Deutschen Nationalbibliothek
Die Deutsche Nationalbibliothek verzeichnet diese Publikation in der Deutschen Nationalbibliographie; detaillierte bibliographische Daten sind im Internet über <http://dnb.d-nb.de> abrufbar.

Rosenheimer Straße 145, D-81671 München
Internet: oldenbourg.de

Umschlagbild: Jüdischer Geldleiher im Gespräch mit einem Bauern.
Aus der Handschrift „Memorial der Tugend" von Johann von Schwarzenberg, entstanden um 1530/40. Kantonsbibliothek Appenzell A. Rh. in Trogen, CM Ms. 13: 73r.

Gedruckt auf säurefreiem, alterungsbeständigem Papier (chlorfrei gebleicht)
Satz: Typodata GmbH, München
Druck: Memminger MedienCentrum, Memmingen
Bindung: Buchbinderei Klotz, Jettingen-Scheppach

ISBN 978-3-486-58670-1

Inhalt

Vorwort

Die Wirtschaftsgeschichte der Juden leidet in ihren beiden Verankerungen, der allgemeinen Wirtschaftsgeschichte wie auch der Geschichte der Juden, bis heute an einer mehrfachen Isolierung. Die allgemeine Wirtschaftsgeschichte besitzt keinen Zugang zu den hebräischen Quellen und begnügt sich zumeist mit oberflächlichen, oft aus zweiter und dritter Hand tradierten Allgemeinplätzen. Trotz der einstimmig beteuerten wirtschaftlichen Bedeutung der Juden liegt keine mittelalterliche oder periodenübergreifende Wirtschaftsgeschichte vor, die diesen Aspekt voll integrieren konnte. Der Geschichte der Juden dagegen fehlte oft das Interesse an der allgemein-historischen Relevanz. Sie betrachtete den wirtschaftsgeschichtlichen Aspekt als Ausdruck einer jüdischen Besonderheit, als Phänomen per se, ohne sich mit den Parallelen und Divergenzen zwischen Mehrheitsgesellschaft und Minderheit aufzuhalten. Schwerwiegend ist die Tatsache, daß beide Forschungstraditionen zutiefst von der die Juden und ihre Geschichte umwogenden Polemik und Apologetik des 19. und frühen 20. Jahrhunderts beeinflußt wurden. Darin wurde dem angenommenen Übergewicht von Juden in einigen Wirtschaftssparten eine außerordentliche Rolle eingeräumt. Der „Handels- und Wucherjude" galt nicht nur unverbesserlichen Antisemiten als geradezu zeitlose Essenz des Judentums und des Juden. Mehr als andere historische Probleme diente die Wirtschaftsgeschichte der Juden als Kärrnerin weltanschaulicher Ausrichtungen, sei es wohlwollenden Verbesserern der Sitten der Juden, dem modernen Antisemitismus, den bürgerlichen bzw. sozialistischen jüdischen Emanzipationsbemühungen, oder der zionistischen Idee einer „Normalisierung" jüdischen Lebens. Trotz unverkennbarer Tendenzen zu objektiveren Sichtweisen nach 1945 hat sich in der Öffentlichkeit wie in der historischen Forschung nicht wenig von diesen Zugängen erhalten, oft einfach in unreflektierter Weiterschreibung alter Handbücher, die wiederum alten Vorurteilen entsprachen.

Andererseits hat der allgemeine, in allen europäischen Regionen spürbare Aufschwung in der Erforschung der mittelalterlichen Geschichte der Juden auch auf dem Gebiet der Wirtschaftsgeschichte seine positiven Auswirkungen gezeitigt. Von Spanien bis Osteuropa erscheinen jährlich zahlreiche Neuveröffentlichungen, darunter auch Quelleneditionen, auf deren Grundlage neue Forschungen möglich werden (siehe dazu den Beitrag von Annegret Holtmann in diesem Band). Die Erschließung der Archive, besonders in quellenreichen Ländern wie etwa Italien, bringt neue Einsichten auch zu wirtschaftsgeschichtlichen Fragenstellungen, sichtbar in diesem Band etwa in den Beiträgen von David Jacoby und Reinhold Mueller. Neue methodische Zugänge bereichern auch die Wirtschaftsgeschichte, so etwa die Geschlechtergeschichte wie in diesem Band der Beitrag von Martha Keil. Für gewisse Regionen liegt nunmehr so viel Material vor, daß zusammenfassende Darstellungen möglich sind, wie in diesem Band die Beiträge von David Abulafia und dem Herausgeber.

Die Genesis des vorliegenden Bandes ist eine denkbar einfache. Im akademischen Jahr 2004/2005 war der Herausgeber Forschungsstipendiat des Historischen Kollegs in München, mit dem Forschungsthema „Die Wirtschaftgeschichte der mittelalterlichen Juden". Im Juni 2005 traten in den Räumen des Kollegs Forscher aus Deutschland, Großbritannien, Israel, den Vereinigten Staaten, Italien und Österreich zu einem dreitägigen Kolloquium zusammen, dessen überarbeitete und mit wissenschaftlichem Apparat versehene Vorträge der Band vereinigt. Ziel war, der Bandbreite der wirtschaftlichen Tätigkeiten, also den „Wirtschaftsgeschichten" (im Plural) nachzugehen, sowie einige zentrale Fragenkomplexe wie Geldleihe, Buchhaltung, Armenfürsorge, Frauenarbeit anhand neuerer Forschungserkenntnisse auszuleuchten. Damit war die Struktur der Tagung und dieses Bandes gegeben: Kernfragen wie die Wahrnehmung jüdischen Wirtschaftsverhaltens durch die christliche Mehrheitsgesellschaft; die Stellungnahmen zur Geldleihe an Nichtjuden im innerjüdischen religiösen Denken; eine Reihe von Überblicken zu Byzanz, Sizilien und Süditalien, den venezianischen Besitzungen im Mittelmeer, dem Deutschen Reich. Daneben widmete sich die Tagung und widmet sich der Band einigen wesentlichen Fragenkomplexen: das leidige Problem der Verpfändung von Kirchengegenständen; Probleme der Buchhaltung.

Der vorliegende Band ist weit davon entfernt, eine einzige und das ganze mittelalterliche Europa verpflichtende Wirtschaftsgeschichte der Juden vorlegen zu wollen. Dafür fehlen einige zentrale Bereiche, die angefragt waren, leider jedoch nicht zur Teilnahme kommen konnten: die iberische Halbinsel, Frankreich und England. Gewichtiger jedoch kann als ein Fazit der Tagung und der nunmehr gedruckt vorliegenden Beiträge vermerkt werden: die Wirtschaftsgeschichten der Juden in den verschiedenen Regionen Europas spiegeln die ganze Breite und Vielfältigkeit der europäischen Wirtschaftsgeschichte wider.

Ganz herzlich sei an dieser Stelle dem Historischen Kolleg zu München und Frau Dr. Müller-Luckner gedankt, die dem Herausgeber die denkbar allerbesten Arbeitsmöglichkeiten und den Teilnehmern des Kolloquiums ein angenehmes und zur Reflexion verführendes Ambiente geboten haben. Des weiteren danke ich meinem Forschungsassistenten, Herrn A. L. M. Thoma in München, der an der Organisation der Tagung wesentlichen Anteil hatte, sowie Frau Anna Gutgarts in Jerusalem, die das Register erstellte.

Jerusalem, im März 2008 *Michael Toch*

Verzeichnis der Tagungsteilnehmer

Prof. Dr. David Abulafia, Cambridge, dsa1000@hermes.cam.ac.uk
Rainer Barzen M. A., Trier, barzenr@uni-trier.de
Prof. Dr. Alfred Haverkamp, Trier, haverkamp@uni-trier.de
Dr. Annegret Holtmann, Griesheim, holtmann-mares@t-online.de
Prof. Dr. David Jacoby, Jerusalem, jacobgab@mscc.huji.ac.il
PD Dr. Martha Keil, St. Pölten, martha.keil@injoest.ac.at
Prof. Dr. Reinhold C. Mueller, Venedig, mueller@unive.it
Prof. Dr. Hans-Georg von Mutius, München, hansgeorg@vonmutius.m.uunet.de
Prof. Dr. Joseph Shatzmiller, Durham, USA, joshatz@duke.edu
Prof. Dr. Michael Toch, Jerusalem (Stipendiat des Historischen Kollegs 2004/05); mstoch@mscc.huji.ac.il
Prof. Dr. G. Todeschini, Triest, todeschi@univ.trieste.it
Prof. Dr. J. Markus Wenninger, Klagenfurt, markus.wenninger@uni-klu.ac.at

Giacomo Todeschini

Christian Perceptions of Jewish Economic Activity in the Middle Ages

The most common and long surviving Jewish stereotype elaborated by Christian culture during the Middle Ages is the image of the Jewish usurer. On the double and interconnected subject, the economic activity of the Jews in the Middle Ages and its Christian representation or description, one can read in historical studies or manuals several common places. They are summed up by the idea that usury actually was, still in the high Middle Ages, the more typical economic activity of the European Jews[1]. Before analysing that strange encounter between medieval and historiographical stereotypes[2], I believe it is essential to have in mind the texts regarded as basic by medieval Christian authors when they utilised the word "usury" *usura* to represent Jewish economic activity as a manifestation of greed. In fact, the formation of the Jewish usurious stereotype is deeply rooted in the inner logic and vocabulary of Christian economics. When we read Medieval Latin sources on economic arguments, it is important to understand that these representations of economic activity are in most cases sections of ecclesiastical sources regarding both the real and symbolic representation of Christian society. So they draw on the traditional ecclesiastic language concerning both the earthly and eternal happiness of the Christians. It is well known that medieval Christian authors ignore Jewish economic culture and laws or do not pay attention to them, with the consequence that Christian economic sources represent economic Jewish activities as totally subordinate to the Christian vision of the world[3]. We cannot however deduce from that Christian misrepresentation that Jewish economic culture and laws did not exist or

[1] On this problem, *G. Todeschini*, I mercanti e il tempio. La società cristiana e il circolo virtuoso della ricchezza fra medioevo ed età moderna (Bologna 2002) ch. 6.

[2] *R. Chazan*, Medieval Stereotypes and Modern Antisemitism (Berkeley, Los Angeles 1997).

[3] *W. C. Jordan*, The French Monarchy and the Jews: from Philip Augustus to the Last Capetians (Philadelphia 1989); *G. Todeschini*, La ricchezza degli Ebrei. Merci e denaro nella riflessione ebraica e nella definizione cristiana dell'usura alla fine del Medioevo (Centro Italiano di Studi sull'Alto Medioevo, Biblioteca di "Studi Medievali" XV, Spoleto 1989); *J. Shatzmiller*, Shylock Reconsidered. Jews, Moneylending and Medieval Society (Berkeley 1990); *A. Sapir Abulafia*, Theology and the commercial revolution: Guibert of Nogent, St. Anselm and the Jews of northern France, in: Church and city 1000–1500. Essays in honour of Christopher Brooke, eds. *D. Abulafia, M. Franklin, M. Rubin* (Cambridge 1992) 23–40; *G. Todeschini*, "Usura" ebraica e identità economica cristiana: la discussione medievale, in: Gli Ebrei in Italia, *C. Vivanti* ed., ("Annali" Einaudi, 11/2, Torino 1997) 289–318.

that the economic life of medieval Jews simply consisted in a reiteration of stereotyped behaviours like those depicted by the word "usury". Similarly, when analysing the formation of Christian economic language, it is inappropriate to disregard the theological vocabulary and to separate it from what we, today, conceive as a purely economic vocabulary.

In the books of Deuteronomy and Leviticus as in the Psalms, that is the sources common to the Jewish and Christian traditions, the giving and receiving of interest on a loan is forbidden, especially when the borrower is a poor; loan on interest is admitted when the borrower is a stranger, that is a non-Jew (*nokhri*), that is to say a person not subject to Jewish law. While medieval Christian authors did know these texts in the Greek Septuaginta version or in the Latin version ascribed to Jerome – the so-called *Vulgata* – they generally did not know or disregarded the Hebrew Bible as well as the halakhic definitions of usury and contracts offered by the mishnaic and talmudic treatises on damages. Their lack of familiarity with these sources had important consequences. For instance, the word "nokhri", stranger, which in the Hebrew text indicated the person who could pay interest, in the Septuaginta version became (αλλὸτριος) *allòtrios*, "alien", and then, in the Vulgata, *alienus*. The last step of this semantic transformation was taken by the *Glossa ordinaria*, the medieval commentary to the Bible (standardised in the twelfth century), which established an equivalence between the word *alienus* and the word *infidelis* or *iniquus*[4]. Through these gradual transformations of meaning, the credit relation between residents and outsiders, or between Christians and Jews, began to implicate an economic antagonism previously inexistent.

Later, when the Church Fathers and the Christian doctors interpreted the Gospels, they found two very different representations of usury. A prohibition of interest for loans seemed to be present in Christ's words *date mutuum nihil inde sperantes* ("When you make a loan, you must expect nothing or nothing in addition as restitution")[5]. However, in the celebrated parable of the talents Christ argued explicitly that fructification of wealth produced by the activity of the *trapezites*

[4] *B. Nelson,* The Idea of Usury. From tribal Brotherhood to universal Otherhood (Philadelphia 1948); Glossa ad Dt. 23, 20 (Strassburg 1480/81 = Brepols 1992) f. 406: "Sed alieno. Infideli vel iniquo cui pecuniam damus ad usuram, cum pro verbo predicationis exigimus fidem penitentiam et operationem bonam." See *Ambrosius*, De Tobia 15, 51, in *M. Giacchero*, Ambrosii de Tobia. Saggio introduttivo, traduzione con testo a fronte (Genova 1965): „Sed forte dicas quia scriptum est: *Alienigenae faenerabis* et non consideras quid euangelium dicat, quod est plenius. Sed hoc interim sequestremus: legis ipsius uerba considera. *Fratri tuo non faenerabis* inquit *ad usuram; alienigenam exiges*. Quis erat tunc alienigena nisi Amalech, nisi Amorraeus, nisi hostis ? Ibi, inquit, usuram exige. Cui merito nocere desideras, cui iure inferuntur arma, huic legitime indicuntur usurae. Quem bello non potes facile uincere, de hoc cito te potes centesima uindicare. Ab hoc usuram exige quem non sit crimen occidere. Sine ferro dimicat qui usuram flagitat, sine gladio se de hoste ulciscitur qui fuerit usurarius exactor inimici. Ergo ubi ius belli, ibi etiam ius usurae. Frater autem tuus omnis, fidei primum, deinde Romani iuris est populus: *Narrabo nomen tuum fratribus meis, in medio ecclesiae laudabo te*"; Decretum Gratiani C. XIV q. 3 c. 12, *Friedberg*, ed. 738.

[5] Lc. 6, 35; *S. Piron*, Le devoir de gratitude: émergence et vogue de la notion d'antidora au XIIIe siècle, in: Credito e usura fra teologia, diritto e amministrazione. Linguaggi a confronto, eds. *D. Quaglioni, G. Todeschini, G. M. Varanini* (Ecole Française de Rome, Rome 2005) 73–101.

(that is to say moneychangers or moneylenders) was an appropriate representation of spiritual life. The sense of this parable was supported by a *logion* of Christ, that is a sentence attributed to Christ by the Christian tradition, which began to be quoted in the writings of the Greek and Latin Fathers of the second/third century. This *logion* affirmed the duty for the Christians to be "like expert moneylenders", that is to be able to separate good from evil like the moneylenders are able to separate the good coins from the devalued ones [6].

When historians state that medieval Church forbade without exception any sort of loan on interest and declared the sterility of money, they simplify a structural semantic ambiguity very typical of Christian language and thought on these economic subjects. A glance at the writings of the Church Fathers and at Canon Law as summarized by the monk Gratianus in Bologna around 1140 is sufficient to demonstrate the complexity of the Christian attitude in regard to money affairs and the usefulness of wealth[7]. The semantic ambiguity which characterizes this representation at the end of the Middle Ages was summed up in Erasmus's exegesis of the parable of the talents in the Gospel according to Matthew. Focusing on the apparent contradiction between this parable and Psalm 15, which strictly forbade usury, Erasmus wrote: "No contradiction here: the Lord loves usury that yield him profit, hates usury that a servant takes to his own self."[8]

*

With these premises in mind, one can easily affirm that the subject of medieval usury[9] has been and remains the occasion for many disputable historiographical

[6] *A. Resch*, Agrapha. Aussercanonische Evangelienfragmente (Leipzig 1889, ²1906) n. 87.

[7] On the semantic ambiguity of early Christian attitude towards money and profit, see *M. Herz*, Sacrum Commercium. Eine begriffsgeschichtliche Studie zur Theologie der Römischen Liturgiesprache (Münchener Theologische Studien, II 15, München 1958); *R. Bogaert*, Changeurs et banquiers chez les Pères de l'Eglise, in: Ancient Society 4 (1973) 239–270; *B. Gordon*, The Economic Problem in Biblical and Patristic Thought (Supplements to Vigiliae Christianae IX, Leiden 1989); *G. Todeschini*, "Quantum valet?" Alle origini di un'economia della povertà, in: Bullettino dell'Istituto storico italiano per il Medioevo 98 (1992) 173–234.

[8] Mt. 25, 24-7 (parable of the talents) and Psalm XV, 1, 5 (condemnation of usury): *Erasmus*, Enarratio psalmi XIV Qui est de puritate tabernaculi siue ecclesiae christianae, in: Opera omnia V, 2 Ordinis quinti tomus secundus, eds. *Ch. Béné, S. Dresden, A. Godin* (Amsterdam 1985); see *Erasmus*, Opera (Leiden 1706) vol. 10, c. 306: "Sed hic occurrit scrupulus, cum in Evangelio damnatur servus qui pecuniam sibi creditam non dederat ad usuram, qui convenit ut hic laudetur, qui non dederit ad usuram. Nihil ista pugnant: Dominus amat usuram, quae ipsi Lucrum adfert: odit usuram, quam servus sibi vindicat."

[9] *T. P. McLaughlin*, The Teaching of the Canonists on Usury (XII, XIII and XIV Centuries), in: Medieval Studies 1 (1939) 81–147; 2 (1940) 1–22; *B. Nelson*, The Idea of Usury. From tribal Brotherood to universal Otherhood (Philadelphia 1948); *J. T. Noonan*, The Scholastic Analysis of Usury (Cambridge/Mass. 1957); *O. Langholm*, Economics in Medieval Schools: Wealth, Exchange, Value, Money and Usury according to the Paris Theological Tradition, 1200–1350 (Leiden 1992); *H. Siems*, Handel und Wucher im Spiegel frühmittelalterlicher Rechtsquellen (MGH Schriften 35, Stuttgart 1992).

statements, especially about the role played by the Jews within Christian medieval economy. It is still common to read in textbooks or general histories of the Jews in the Middle Ages that, from the tenth century, usury was the specialized activity of European Jews. This opinion, recently repeated by Kenneth Stow in his book *Alienated Minority*[10], is in each case based on unsubstantiated historical theories regarding the economic role of medieval Jews that are typical of the European historical culture, as can be seen in the studies of Roscher (1875) and Sombart (1911) and the book on the so called "economic revolution of the middle ages" written by Roberto Lopez in the 1970s[11]. From that point of view medieval Jewish society appears as totally conditioned by the economic and political decisions and idiosyncrasies of the majority, namely by the cultural identity of Christian society. Many economists or historians of economic doctrines have also repeated this widespread *idée reçue*, with the obligatory implication that medieval Jews did not have a specific economic vision, but only a daily economic practice, namely usury, imposed both by external powers and by the Jew's lack of a specific economic identity. Derek Penslar, for instance, in his book *Shylock's Children. Economics and Jewish Identity in Modern Europe* quotes Stow who in turn quoted Lopez, saying "the Jews' existence as a dispersed minority, dependent for their economic well-being on external forces in their host societies, discouraged the formation of a comprehensive economic philosophy. Although Rabbinic and Medieval Judaism lacked an economic philosophy, it had identifiable economic sensibilities"[12]. A look at the past and current production of studies on Jewish economic reflections and laws is enough to undermine the common place that medieval Rabbis legitimating medieval Jewish transactions did not possess a specific economic vision. From Boaz Cohen's accurate comparison between Roman and Jewish economic laws to the more recent analysis of the rabbinic conceptions of market and credit transactions by Aaron Kirschenbaum, Hillel Gamoran, Aaron Levine, Richard Ohrenstein, Abraham Weingort and Haym Soloveitchik, the depth and com-

[10] *K. Stow*, Alienated Minority. The Jews of Medieval Latin Europe (Cambridge/Mass. 1992) 215–16.

[11] *W. Roscher*, Die Juden im Mittelalter betrachtet vom Standpunkte der allgemeinen Handelspolitik, in: Zeitschrift für die Gesamte Staatswissenschaft 31 (1875) 503–526; *W. Sombart*, Die Juden und das Wirtschaftsleben (Leipzig 1911); *R. S. Lopez*, The Commercial Revolution of the Middle Ages (Englewood Cliffs/N.J. 1971). See *T. Oelsner*, W. Roscher's Theory of the Economic and Social Position of the Jews in the Middle Ages, in: Yivo Annual of Jewish Social Science 12 (1959) 176–195; *F. Raphael*, Judaisme et capitalisme. Essai sur la controverse entre Max Weber et Werner Sombart (Paris 1982); *G. Todeschini*, Una polemica dimenticata: Sombart e "Die Juden und das Wirtschaftsleben" nella discussione storiografica (1911–1920), in: Società e storia 35 (1987) 139–160; *N. Zemon Davis*, Religion and Capitalism Once Again? Jewish Merchant Culture in the Seventeenth Century, in: Representations 59 (1997) 56–84; *G. Todeschini*, Les historiens juifs en Allemagne et le débat sur l'origine du capitalisme avant 1914, in: Écriture de l'histoire et identité juive. L'Europe ashkénaze XIXe–XXe siècle, eds. *D. Bechtel, E. Patlagean, J.-C. Szurek, P. Zawadzki* (Paris 2003) 209–228.

[12] *D. J. Penslar*, Shylock's Children. Economics and Jewish Identity in Modern Europe (Berkeley 2001) 52.

plexity of Jewish medieval economics becomes totally evident[13]. Indeed, many years ago Jacob Katz was able to recapitulate in his *Tradition and Crisis* the medieval rabbinic conception of credit. He pointed to a distinction "between direct, personal contact and impersonal, economic operations" and to a "progressive rationalization of the economic process in which the traded goods lose their specific character and are considered merely an object for profitable enterprise"[14]. Thus one can conclude that medieval Jewish communities possessed an economic vocabulary and an economic language that had been highly conceptualised by their rabbinical leaders. In the words of A. Gross Schaefer, "the Jewish legal system enumerates rituals to demonstrate contract formation", so that the growth of a "Jewish vocabulary of obligation" is the necessary consequence of the "formal action required under Jewish law ... to reduce the possibility of unintentionally entering into a legally binding agreement"[15].

This well attested existence of a Jewish medieval economic culture is all the more puzzling as almost until the thirteenth century and the rise of Christian banking and commercial companies there is little evidence for usurious practices by Jews beyond simple and direct loans on pledge[16]. By contrast, between the tenth and thirteenth century there is clear evidence of Jewish involvement in all sorts of economic relations or contractual forms; many historians, from Kriegel to Shatzmiller[17] have pointed out that this complex Jewish participation in European economic

[13] *B. Cohen*, Jewish and Roman Law (New York 1966); *A. Kirschenbaum*, Jewish and Christian Theories of Usury in the Middle Ages, in: Jewish Quarterly Review 75 (1985) 270–289; *H. Gamoran*, Talmudic Usury Laws and Business Loans, in: Journal for the Study of Judaism in the Persian, Hellenistic and Roman Period 7 (1976) 129–142; *Idem*, The Talmudic Law of Mortgages in View of the Prohibition against Lending on Interest, in: Hebrew Union College Annual 52 (1981) 153 162, *Idem*, Credit Transactions in Geonic Times in the Light of the Law against Usury, in: Jewish Law Annual 11 (1994) 67 ss.; *Idem*, Investing for Profit. A Study of Iska up to the Time of Rabbi Abraham ben David of Posquieres, in: Hebrew Union College Annual 70–71 (1999–2000) 153 ss.; *A. Gross Schaefer*, Contractual Intent: Is the Reasonable Person Standard Sufficient?, in: Jewish Law Annual 11 (1994) 85–100; *R. A. Ohrenstein*, *B. Gordon*, Economic Analysis in Talmudic Literature. Rabbinic Thought in the Light of Modern Economics (Leiden 1992); *A. Levine*, Economics and Jewish Law (New York 1987); *A. Weingort*, Intérêt et crédit dans le droit talmudique (Paris 1979); *Idem*, Responsabilité et sanction en droit talmudique et comparé (Paris 1998); *H. Soloveitchik*, Pawnbroking: a study in Ribbit and of the Halakhah in exile, in: Proceedings of the American Academy for Jewish Research 38–9 (1970–71) 203–268; *Idem*, The Jewish Attitude in the High and Late Middle Ages (1000–1500), in: Credito e usura fra teologia, diritto e amministrazione. Linguaggi a confronto, eds. *D. Quaglioni*, *G. Todeschini*, *G. M. Varanini* (Ecole Française de Rome, Rome 2005) 115–127; *A. Toaff*, Testi ebraici italiani relativi all'usura dalla fine del XV agli esordi del XVII secolo, ibidem 103–113.

[14] *J. Katz*, Tradition and Crisis. Jewish Society at the End of the Middle Ages (New York 1993) 66.

[15] *A. Gross Schaefer*, Contractual Intent 91.

[16] *M. Toch*, Jews and Commerce: Modern Fancies and Medieval Realities, in: Il ruolo economico delle minoranze in Europa. Secc. XIII–XVIII , *S. Cavaciocchi* ed. (Firenze, Atti della XXXI Settimana di Studi, Istituto Francesco Datini, Prato 2000) 43–58.

[17] *M. Kriegel*, Les Juifs à la fin du Moyen Age dans l'Europe méditerranéenne (Paris 1989); *J. Shatzmiller*, Shylock Reconsidered.

life survived until the fifteenth century. In sum, the factual and intellectual complexity of the Jewish economic presence in the Middle Ages, poses a problem about the formation and sense – in the eleventh and twelfth century – of Christian representations of medieval Jews as usurers and of Jewish wealth as completely derived from usurious transactions. This problem concerns, first, Christian economic language, that is the vocabulary and the categories which enabled Christians, *before* and *during* the economic and monetary revolution of the eleventh and twelfth centuries, to speak and write about the economic attitude or economic practice of aliens or strangers. At the same time, when addressing this subject, we are obliged to revise the historiographical canon constantly repeated by economic historians – on the basis of the historiographical sanctification or trivial reading of De Roover, McLaughlin, Noonan and other historians of medieval economic doctrines – declaring the medieval existence of a compact Christian or ecclesiastic "theory" which prohibited any form of money fructification and stated the sterility of money[18]. In fact, the common notion of a Jewish monopoly in medieval money transactions is strictly connected with the complementary and also unsupported idea that medieval Christian *magistri* were horrified by the concept of credit, interest and, generally, monetary wealth. It is therefore imperative to define the linguistic relation between the "dramatic transformation" (as Cary Nederman has recently called it) of the European economy after 1100 and the representation of this "revolution" by contemporary theologians, canonists and confessors on the basis of their economic culture and vocabulary. It is very difficult to reduce this theological or canonistic attitude to a "distaste for commerce" as Cary Nederman has called it, somewhat hastily, in a paper published in 2002[19]. Similarly, it is impossible to reduce the significance of medieval Christian economics, as Nederman and many others have suggested, to some especially astute medieval thinkers who were able to perceive "systematically and cogently the temporal impact of the technological, commercial and fiscal changes experienced by European society"[20]. Undeniably, Erasmus's interpretation quoted earlier was made possible by centuries of Christian thinking on and representations of economic reality in terms which clearly separated the utility and the needs of churches and Church from the utility and needs of individuals, especially when belonging to the laity. In more specific terms, credit dialectics were analysed as regarding *bonum commune* or *bonum particulare*, common or individual good[21]. Especially from the twelfth century, this attitude found

[18] *T. P. Mc Laughlin*, The Teaching of the Canonists on Usury; *J. T. Noonan*, The Scholastic Analysis of Usury; *R. De Roover*, La pensée économique des Scolastiques (Montréal, Paris 1971); *O. Langholm*, Economics in Medieval Schools.

[19] *C. Nederman*, The virtues of necessity: labour, money and corruption in John of Salisbury's thought, in: Viator 33 (2002) 55–56.

[20] Ibidem 67.

[21] *G. Todeschini*, Il prezzo della salvezza. Lessici medievali del pensiero economico (Roma 1994); *M. Kempshall*, The common good in late medieval political thought (Oxford 1999); *P. Von Moos*, "Public" et "privé" à la fin du Moyen Âge. Le "bien commun" et la "loi de la conscience", in: Studi Medievali s. 3a, XLI/2 (2000) 505–548.

legal expression in the double canonistic and theological vocabulary of *usura* (usury) and *interesse* (interest), forbidden and alien the former, permitted and rational the latter. The way to this opposition however had been very long, and complicated by the fact that the Christian sources on economy in late Antiquity or high Middle Ages used different linguistic techniques. Actually the well known expositions or moral evaluations of contracts so typical of late medieval confessors and scholastics, made use of economic categories shaped by the patristic and monastic approach to economy; an approach synthesized from the eighth to the twelfth century in systematic collections of canons and, finally, in the *Decretum Gratiani* (1140 c.), which was to be recognized by the late medieval popes as the formal basis of Catholic doctrine and law[22]. We can subdivide the Christian sources on contracts and economy from the fourth to the eleventh century into three principal linguistic types, that is three basic or logical styles of exposition and demonstration: exegetical or metaphorical, polemical or political, and juridical[23].

The first one, chronologically and semantically antedating the others, which we can define as exegetical or metaphorical, represents economic relations by commenting on the Scriptures and derives from the scriptural vocabulary terms and concepts which will subsequently be semantically modified and adapted to the problems of specific historical realities. The logical centre of this procedure is metaphorical, and in itself based on what Christianity considered its own principal and founding economic metaphor: the exchange between divine perfection and human finitude or mortality, realized by the divine incarnation. The most renowned Greek and Latin Fathers of the Church, Basil of Caesarea, Ambrose of Milan, Augustine of Hippo, commonly described this exchange (greek: *synallagma*; latin: *commercium*) by means of an image of commercial dialectic operating between divine and human and having its result in Salvation[24]. This central point is the source, in the Patristic writings, of a chain of conceptualisations formulated in the banking and commercial vocabulary, and systematically utilising words and logical connections typical of the market transactions of the late Roman Empire. Credit and usury appear in this context in the form of a double and interconnected verbal representation: a good and virtuous logic of loaning/borrowing even characterised by the exchange between wealth and immaterial values (favour, compassion, protection, patronage) implying right interests, and, on the opposite, usury, that is the selling of real money paid by a concrete amount of coins. In the Ambrosian treatise *De Tobia*[25], in the Augustinian exegesis and in other patristic writings it is possible to

[22] *A. Winroth*, The Making of Gratian's Decretum (Cambridge 2000); *G. Todeschini*, Linguaggi economici ed ecclesiologia fra XI e XII secolo: dai Libelli de lite al Decretum Gratiani, in: Medioevo, Mezzogiorno, Mediterraneo. Studi in onore di Mario del Treppo, *G. Rossetti, G. Vitolo* eds. (Napoli 2000) 59–87.

[23] *G. Todeschini*, Il prezzo della salvezza.

[24] *M. Herz*, Sacrum Commercium; *R. Bogaert*, Changeurs et banquiers chez les Pères de l'Eglise.

[25] *M. F. Barry*, The Vocabulary of the Moral-Ascetical Works of Saint Ambrose. A Study in Latin Lexicography (Washington 1926); *L. M. Zucker*, S. Ambrosii de Tobia. A Commentary, with an Introduction and Translation (Washington 1933); *M. Giacchero*, Ambrosii de Tobia. Saggio intro-

detect some references to the *judaicus populus* as avaricious, and, at the same time, to Judas as vendor of Christ as archetypical representation of the Jews[26]. Nevertheless it is important to stress that these references in no way have to do with a specific definition of Jews as economic subjects, merchants or usurers. The problem, here, is to describe Jewish resistance to Christian conversion by the economic vocabulary of avarice and unjust acquisition, or of an incapacity for the appropriate use of wealth. Ambrose, for instance, writes that Jews possess a Law, which is *like* a devalued coin: they are attached to this useless and fictitious wealth in consequence of their religious obstinacy[27]. This exegetical or metaphorical mode of representing economic and credit transactions, separating good investment from unfruitful speculation, is understood by the high medieval monastic written culture as a basic economic categorization[28]. The long chain of monastic commentaries on Scripture and the treatises on virtues of the high Middle Ages, totally neglected by historians of economic ideas or languages, transmits, on the basis of the patristic economic vocabulary, more than a compact economic doctrine, a linguistic style deeply connecting the notion of fruitfulness to the notion of faith and trust. The church society of the *fideles* must, from this point of view, continually grow and expand its frontiers. Economic morality consists, therefore, in the multiplication of the ecclesiastical patrimony made up both of persons and ecclesiastical goods. A

duttivo, traduzione con testo a fronte (Genova 1965); *M. Mcguire*, S. Ambrosii De Nabuthae. A Commentary with an Introduction and Translation (Washington 1927); *V. R. Vasey*, The Social Ideas in the Works of St. Ambrose. A Study of the De Nabuthae (Roma 1982); *S. Giet*, De Saint Basile à Saint Ambroise. La condamnation du pret à intéret au IVe siècle, in: Recherches de Sciences Religieuse 33 (1944) 95–128.

26 *B. Blumenkranz*, Die Judenpredigt Augustins. Ein Beitrag zur Geschichte der jüdisch-christlichen Beziehungen in den ersten Jahrhunderten (Basel 1946); *Idem*, Les auteurs chrétiens latins du Moyen Âge sur les Juifs et le Judaïsme (Paris 1963); *H. Schreckenberg*, Die christliche Adversus Judaeos-Texte und ihr literarisches und historisches Umfeld (I–XI Jh.) (Frankfurt, Bern 1982); *M. S. Taylor*, Anti-Judaism and Early Christian Identity. A Critique of the Scholarly Consensus (Leiden 1995).

27 *Ambrosius*, De Tobia 19, 64: "Vbi coepit populus Iudaeorum non custodire legem, coeperunt aduenae, hoc est ex populo nationum, qui in Iesum dominum crediderunt, interpretationem scripturarum illi uetusto populo faenerare. Faenerauit Timotheus patre Graeco ortus uerbum Iudaeis , cum sacerdotium recepisset , faeneramus hodieque sacerdotes in ecclesia uerbum Iudaeis, qui de synagoga ad ecclesiam transierunt, faeneramus et nouam et uetustam pecuniam , Etenim quam habuerunt iam non habent; *ocutos habent et non uident, aures habent et non audiun , pecuniam habent et non habent, quia usum eius ignorant, pretium eius nesciunt, figuram eius et formam non cognouerunt*. Nam si cognouissent, numquam auctorem eius pecuniae denegassent dicentes: *Nolumus hunc regnare super nos* . Qui quidem accepto regno rediens iussit uocari seruos suos, quibus dedit pecuniam et eos qui faenerassent pecuniam praedicauit, ei autem qui pecuniam tenuit otiosam domini sui respondit: *Sciebas quod ego austerus homo sum: tollo quod non posui et meto quod non seminaui. Et quare non dedisti pecuniam meam ad mensam? Et ego ueniens cum usuris utique exegissem illam.*"

28 *J.M. Clement*, Lexique des anciennes Règles monastiques occcidentales (Instrumenta Patristica VII B, Steenbrugis 1978); *B. Gordon*, The Economic Problem in Biblical and Patristic Thought (Leiden 1989); *G. Todeschini*, I vocabolari dell'analisi economica fra alto e basso medioevo: dai lessici della disciplina monastica ai lessici antiusurari (X–XIII secolo), in: Rivista Storica Italiana, 110/3 (1998) 781–833.

keyword of this metaphorical economics is *lucrifacere*, that is "to increase the wealth". The mystical and economic concept of divesting the Church of wealth, *res ecclesiarum*, becomes a synonym for heretical perversity. The climax is reached in the ninth century, during the intense collaboration between the Carolingian emperors and their ecclesiastical officials. In fact, it is at this time that the *dispersio rerum ecclesiarum*, the dispersion of the ecclesiastical wealth, becomes a public crime, in consequence of the emperor's legislation, which declares the equivalence of fiscal or public and ecclesiastical goods[29]. Much more than in Justinian's *Corpus Juris*, it is probably from the time of the Carolingian alliance with the Roman bishop, that metaphorical Christian language regarding the sacred augmentation of ecclesiastical wealth becomes effectively a structured component of the public and bureaucratic economic language.

The second type of Christian sources concerning exchange and wealth dynamics, before the twelfth century, can be described as polemic or political. In fact, the source of the misunderstandings regarding the economic role of the Jews in the Middle Ages and the formation of a Christian stereotype of Jewish usury, derives from the devaluation or ignorance of the role played in the formation of a Western economic language by the high medieval conceptualisations about the inalienability of Church goods. From the first collections of conciliar canons in the seventh century to the rapid development and multiplication of these legal compilations after the first half of the ninth century, we can observe inside the European system of ecclesiastical law an ever-increasing attention to the political institutions or subjects which could be perceived as dangerous for the economic-political organization of the churches. A new galaxy of concepts and related words appears to circumscribe even more accurately the semantics of simony (*simonia*), whose depiction and logical delineation is preceding and conditioning the definition of usury in the successive canonical texts, that is during the so called Juridical Renaissance of the twelfth century. The sense of the notion of simony, or rather the sense of the word *simoniacus*, the individual who commits the crime, is intelligible as the concretisation and unification in political and legal terms of the different economic behaviours generically denoted as *infideles*[30]. More than the greed of the *simoniaci*, their lack of understanding of the extraordinary economic nature of the material and immaterial things composing the body of the churches makes of them a group of

[29] *R. Newhauser*, Towards modus in habendo: Transformations in the Idea of Avarice. The early Penitentials through the Carolingian Reform, in: Zeitschrift der Savigny Stiftung für Rechtsgeschichte – Kan. Abt. 106 (1989) 1–22; *H. Siems*, Handel und Wucher im Spiegel frühmittelalterlicher Rechtsquellen (MGH Schriften 35, Stuttgart 1992); *G. Todeschini*, Linguaggi teologici e linguaggi amministrativi: le logiche sacre del discorso economico fra VIII e X secolo, in: Quaderni Storici 102/3 (1999) 597–616.

[30] *B. Szabò-Bechstein*, Libertas ecclesiae. Ein Schlüsselbegriff des Investiturstreits und seine Vorgeschichte. 4.–11. Jh. (Studi Gregoriani XII, Roma 1985); *G. Todeschini*, "Judas mercator pessimus". Ebrei e simoniaci dall'XI al XIII secolo, in: Zakhor. Rivista di storia degli ebrei in Italia I (1997) 11–23; *T. Reuter*, Gifts and simony, in: Medieval Transformations: Texts, Power and Gifts in Context, eds. *E. Cohen, M. B. de Jong* (Leiden 2000) 57–68.

heretics very close to the world of infidels and especially of Jews. Jewish stubbornness, in this context, has nothing to do with usury or a specific illegitimate economic way of conduct; it is, however, the infidelity model to which the heretical deviancy of Simoniacs is compared. The connection between Judas' lack of faith and Judas' greed, that is to say the notion of Judas' untrustworthiness, is obviously and obsessively recounted as exemplification of the mental process which determines the fall of the Simoniac into the abyss of heresy, that is the exit from the even more delimited space of Christian fidelity[31]. Sometimes, at the end of the eleventh century, the antisimoniac texts begin in fact to tell stories of Jews allied with the Simoniacs. The charge to be inside enemies of the Christian world is therefore deepened by the emphasis on the Simoniacs' involvement with the infidels par excellence[32].

Before the twelfth century, the Christian West produces a third type of linguistic procedure, which was suitable for denoting and connoting economic discourse. This textuality, definable as juridical or legal, after the sixth century is composed of a more and more solid interplay between Roman and Canon law. On the particular subject of credit and usury, we can now utilise the fundamental book of Harald Siems, *Handel und Wucher im Spiegel frühmittelalterlicher Rechtsquellen*[33]. Perhaps, the most important aspect of this very accurate book, often regrettably forgotten by economic historians, is the systematic analysis of the semantic fluctuation or undecided sense of the word-concept "usury" in the western Christian legal sources until the twelfth century. This ambiguity appears, in comparison with Roman and Talmudic Law, as a main Christian characteristic. In Roman law as summed up by the Justinian Code, the word, in the plural form *usurae*, denoted interests legally admitted, but not as a specific contractual form. In the Talmudic

[31] See, for instance, *Humbertus de Silvacandida*, Adversus simoniacos libri tres (MGH, Libelli de lite I, 95–253), II 20, 163–4: "Haut secus hos hereticos [scil.: symoniacos] nefandi ambitione commercii dirumpere vincula christianae legis et proicere a se iugum apostolicae disciplinae quaerentes, qui habitat in caelis, irridet et subsannat, ubi impudenter negotiando de Deo nichil inveniunt in manibus suis, nisi quod Iudas et Iudaei in suis, perpetuam scilicet maledictionem et damnationem, qua exemplo Iudae fiunt filii eorum orphani, et uxor vidua, quia sanguis Christi super eos et super filios eorum, ut vindicetur, manet"; on simony from a juridical point of view, see *R. M. Freher*, Preventing Crime in the High Middle Ages: The Medieval Lawyers' Search for Deterrence, in: Popes, Teachers, and Canon Law in the Middle Ages, eds. *J. R. Sweeney, S. Chodorow* (Ithaca, London 1989) 212 ss.

[32] See, for instance, *Gaufridus Vindocinensis*, Libellus II. Goffridus abbas Rainaldo episcopo Andegavensi non canonice electo laicorum investituram haeresim esse demonstrat, (1116–18), in: MGH. Libelli de Lite II, 684: "... illis invitis [the clergy of Angers] et non petentibus arreptus fuistis a vulgo: et quod ibi factum est hoc praesumptuosa et pernitiosa fecit seditio. Quorum iustam reprobationem cum *quidam de genere Iudeorum laicus audisset, qui semper, dum potuit, oppressit aecclesiam* et qui, nullo eum comitante de clero, a latere nostro vos primus arripuerat, turbam vulgi, quam ipse turbaverat, secum adduxit et in medium sancti conventus impudenter prosiluit, clamans: Quis nobis in hoc opere nostro contradicit, eligat unus ex duobus, aut mori statim, aut concedere quod fecimus! Sic grex religiosus abbatum et clericorum, qui ad pastoris electionem convenerat, turbatus est et dispersus ...".

[33] *H. Siems*, Handel und Wucher.

treatises on damages, usury was described as an illicit but clearly defined economic transaction, very different from society contracts as *iska* or from particular forms of economic transgression as *ona'a*[34]. Thereafter – as Haym Soloveitchik has clearly explained – the rabbinic French and German *responsa* from the eleventh century could describe it "simply [as] a way of earning a living"[35]. Since, as we saw, the traditional Christian discourse developed a double and conflicting conceptualisation of credit transactions, the legal definition of usury in the works of Christian jurists, until the great codifier Gratianus, is very incongruous, and in most cases, although the illegality of usury is affirmed, a specific definition of the contractual manifestations of usury is absent. The typical definition of usury in the normative and legal Christian sources from the ninth to the eleventh centuries, or from Charlemagne to Gratianus, is: "usury is when more is requested as restitution than has been given" (*usura est ubi amplius requiritur quam datur*)[36]. Actually, the elusiveness of this definition opened the way to the possibility of differentiating between credit transactions perceived as favourable to increasing churches – as for instance the commerce in rents – and loans and restitutions outside the ecclesiastical public space, by private subjects whose aim, from a clerical perspective, was not to augment institutional wealth, but the private – *carnalis* carnal – prosperity of one's own familiar group[37]. The insistence of this canonical definition on the words "request"-"give" (*requiri-dari*), in fact, established that usury, properly said, could happen only when an individual firmly imposed a specific difference between the loaned and returned value. When the credit transaction took place without this precise quantification of interest, so that the gain derived from the repayment in a different type of value (for instance a sum of money was compensated by periodical land rents), the transaction was no longer considered usurious, principally because this difference of value was granted as correct by the institutional subjects (churches, abbeys, landlords) who normally determined it. It is in the period after Gratianus, in the second half of the twelfth century, that what Haym Soloveitchik has defined as "a dramatic change" occurred[38]. Alternatively, we can say, it is after

[34] *A. Weingort*, Intérêt et crédit dans le droit talmudique.

[35] *H. Soloveitchik*, The Jewish Attitude 126.

[36] Capitulare Niumagae datum, (806), n. 11: Monumenta Germaniae Historica, Capitularia, II p. 132; Decretum Gratiani C. XIV q. 3, c. 4 and 9, *Friedberg* ed. 735 and 737; *Siems*, Handel und Wucher 745 ss.; *Todeschini*, Linguaggi teologici e linguaggi amministrativi; *Idem*, Linguaggi economici ed ecclesiologia.

[37] *F. Veraja*, Le origini della controversia teologica sul contratto di censo nel XIII secolo (Roma 1960); *W. Trusen*, Zum Rentenkauf im Spämittelalter (1971), now in *W. Trusen*, Gelehrtes Recht im Mittelalter und in der frühen Neuzeit (Goldbach 1997); *J. Kirshner*, Storm over Monte Comune: Genesis of the Moral Controversy over the Public Debt of Florence, in: Archivum Fratrum Praedicatorum 53 (1983) 219–276; *J. Hernando*, Quaestio disputata de licitudine contractus emptionis et venditionis censualis cum conditione revenditionis. Un tratado sobra la licitud del contrato de compra-venta de rentas personales y redimibles. Bernat de Puigcercòs, OP (siglo XIV), in: Acta Mediaevalia Barcelona, 10 (1989) 9–87; *L. Armstrong*, Usury and Public Debt in Early Renaissance Florence: Lorenzo Ridolfi on the Monte Comune (Toronto 2003).

[38] *H. Soloveitchik*, The Jewish Attitude 124–25.

1160 that a firm clarification of Christian opinions about usury is clearly evident in the explicit condemnation of usurious contracts. Usury now appears as an even better defined system of contractual typologies. Haym Soloveitchik points out that this new Christian attention to usury is "the real riddle, not the Jewish position on usury but what came to be the Christian one, the why and the how of this major transformation in the mentalité of Western Europe"[39]. I suggest that it is possible to solve the puzzle, and at the same time to understand the rapid formation at the end of the twelfth century of the Jewish usurer stereotype, if this change is viewed in the light of the earlier Christian sources, and particularly from the point of view of their semantics of the double significance of credit. As we saw, it is incorrect to state that Christian juridical tradition, as summed up by Gratianus in 1140, was totally unfavourable to credit transactions; on the contrary, the credit economy was perceived as useful when it revealed a specific ecclesiastical or public meaning. As Amos Funkenstein, Anna Sapir Abulafia, Miri Rubin, Jeremy Cohen[40] and some others have substantiated, is it highly likely that the Christian change of attitude concerning Jews at the end of the twelfth century depended in some measure on the deep doctrinal change which, after the Gregorian Reform and the affirmation of the real eucharistic presence, made Christology the essential reference point for political or religious credibility. To believe the real presence of Christ in the Eucharist, and to recognize as sacred the power of the ecclesiastics, became the fundament of belonging to the human community. From this point of view, the growing ideological and graphical representation of Jews as semi-human monsters menacing Christian women and children has much to do, as Trachtenberg and recently Sara Lipton and Ruth Mellinkoff[41] demonstrated, with the theological representations of infidels as aliens so typical of the last part of the twelfth century Christian thought. This explanation is mostly correct, but my idea is that it is necessary to emphasize the economic and juridical roots of the new hostile Christian attitude against Jews, paying attention to the way the traditional Christian vocabulary of economics was adapted to the changing economic situation of the twelfth and thirteenth centuries. As Violante and Duby have pointed out[42], the accelera-

[39] Ibid.

[40] *A. Funkenstein*, Changes in the Patterns of Christian Anti-Jewish Polemics in the Twelfth Century, in: Zion 33 (1968) 125–144; *Idem*, Basic Types of Anti-Jewish Polemics in the Later Middle Ages, in: Viator 2 (1972) 373–382; *A. Sapir Abulafia*, Christians and Jews in Dispute. Disputational literature and the rise of anti-Judaism in the West (c. 1000–1150) (Aldershot 1998); *Idem*, Christians and Jews in the Twelfth-Century Renaissance (London, New York 1995); *M. Rubin*, Corpus Christi. The Eucharist in Late Medieval Culture (Cambridge 1991); *J. Cohen*, The Friars and the Jews. The Evolution of Medieval Antijudaism (Ithaca, London 1983).

[41] *R. Mellinkoff*, Outcasts: Signs of Otherness in Northern European Art of the Later Middle Ages (Berkeley, Los Angeles 1993); *Idem*, Antisemitic Hate Signs in Hebrew Illuminated Manuscripts from Medieval Germany (Jerusalem 1999); *S. Lipton*, Images of Intolerance: The Representation of Jews and Judaism in the Bible Moralisée (Berkeley, Los Angeles 1999).

[42] *G. Duby*, Les chanoines réguliers et la vie économique des XIe et XII [e] siècles, in: La vita comune del clero nei secoli XI e XII (Milano 1962) 72–81; *C. Violante*, I vescovi dell'Italia centro-settentrionale e lo sviluppo dell'economia monetaria, in: Vescovi e diocesi in Italia nel Medioevo (sec.

tion and the multiplication of money transactions in the eleventh and twelfth centuries was after all not so much the result of a generic new lay enterprise spirit, but on the whole a consequence of the economic rationality of landlords, among whom bishops, abbots and canons were particularly prominent. In France as well as in northern Italy the real problem with this new economic situation was, moreover, that the creation and the increase of markets were accompanied by the multiplication of economic subjects, initially controlled by their lords, but in time even more apt to play the role of entrepreneurs albeit outside the sacred space of political powers. Credit, or the increase of commercial operations founded on delayed payments, was also a consequence of this economic revolution. The general effect was the huge and rapid growth of social and economic relations based on loans and restitutions, but, also, the empowerment of politically unauthorized subjects. In this situation at the middle of the twelfth century, it is possible to detect some new signals of polemic against the wealth of the Jews, though they are not yet systematically designated as usurers. In 1146 Peter the Venerable, abbot of Cluny in Burgundy, writes to the king Louis VII of France with the aim to authorize him to expropriate the wealth of the French Jews in order to finance a crusade. In this letter can we see the beginning of a Christian trend that Jews as infidels and therefore serfs of the landlords and of the Church cannot possess legitimate wealth of their own. Thus the reasoning of Peter of Cluny that their riches are without doubt illegal and fruit of robbery or commercial tricks. Peter declares that the French Jews are normally partners of Christian sacrilegious thieves, that is of Simoniacs[43]. In other words, the participation of Jews, infidels and outsiders par excellence, in the new economic reality troubles, among other charismatic leaders, Peter the Venerable of Cluny, himself an important ecclesiastical landlord, because the new economic play seems to authorize them to acquire power over Christian land, that is to become politically significant. In the same years, the same ecclesiastical fear of the acquisition of wealth and, frequently, of ecclesiastical possessions by lay people, determines the textual spreading of the crucial semantic equivalence between *carnalitas* and *usura*. It will thereafter be common, from Bernard of Clairvaux to Peter the Chanter at the end of the century, to utilise the word *judaisare* to define the activity of Christian usurers[44]. As Sara Lipton has adroitly shown in her analysis of the representations of Jews and Synagogue in the *Bibles Moralisées* of the

IX–XIII) (Padova 1964) 193–217; *Idem*, Monasteri e canoniche nello sviluppo dell'economia monetaria (secoli XI–XIII), in: Istituzioni monastiche e istituzioni canonicali in Occidente, 1123–1215 (Milano 1980) 369–416; *C. Brittain Bouchard*, Holy Entrepreneurs. Cistercian, Knights, and Economic Exchange in Twelfth Century Burgundy (Ithaca, London 1991).

[43] The letters of Peter the Venerable, I, ed. *G. Constable* (Cambridge/Mass. 1978) 327–330; *Y. Friedman*, An Anatomy of Antisemitism: Peter the Venerable's Letter to Louis VII, King of France (1146), in: Bar-Ilan Studies in History (1978) 87–102.

[44] Dictionary of Mediaeval Latin from British Sources (London 1975) I, s. v. "judaizantes"; *Petrus Cantor*, Verbum adbreviatum. Textus conflatus, ed. *M. Boutry* (Turnhout 2004) 325; *J. W. Baldwin*, Masters, Princes and Merchants. The Social Views of Peter the Chanter and his Circle (Princeton 1970).

beginning of the thirteenth century, this semantic equation does not signify that the Christian authors recognize usury as a real and typical Jewish profession, but that the "carnality" traditionally imputed to Jews as logical attribute of their misunderstanding of Scriptures makes them the obvious paradigm of the new Christian economic reality when this reality appears external or dangerous to ecclesiastical economic policy[45]. The point becomes more and more clear when, from the seventies of the twelfth century, the papal power assumes a precise position on the question of the economic and juridical role of the Jews in Christian Europe. Alexander III, Celestine III, and then at the beginning of the thirteenth century, Innocent III, that is from 1160 to 1215, send a series of official letters to many European lords and kings. Their aim is on the one hand to establish that Jews that become possessors of pledged ecclesiastical land must be compelled to pay tithe to the churches, that is to recognize the ecclesiastical jurisdiction as a legitimate fiscal jurisdiction[46]. On the other hand, Jewish witnesses against Christians in economic controversies may not be accepted by Christian tribunals[47]. It is at this moment – the last years of the twelfth century – that the growth of an usurious representation of the economic activity of the Jews becomes gradually observable in some penitential manuals and narrative or hagiographic sources, but also in the pontifical legislation collected and edited by Solomon Grayzel[48]. This stereotyping process can be interpreted as the rhetoric or emotional rendering, and then as the adaptation to a linguistic standard of divulgation, of a more complex situation regarding ecclesiastical territorial power seen as a form of control apparently menaced by the economic initiative of lay individuals. Sara Lipton describes this phenomenon very clearly: "indebtness entails emotional as well as legal obligation. Power over the clerical debtor is conferred upon the lay creditor, and the superiority of clergy ... is consequently undermined. Moreover, if lay power over the clergy was at all times a cause for concern, when the laymen in question were infidels a disturbing religious dimension came into play."[49] The persisting ambiguity of the Christian legal sources on the matter of credit during the development of economic anti-Jewish discourses indicates that representing medieval Jews as usurers and Jewish wealth as completely derived from usurious transactions is, on the whole, a linguistic stereotype signifying the canonistic and theological rejection of the lay economic initiatives when they are perceived as menacing the sacred wealth of the churches. Indeed, the ecclesiastical lawyers of the late twelfth and early thirteenth century developed an even more systematic definition regarding the legitimacy of putting

45 *S. Lipton,* Images of Intolerance 34. *M. Awerbuch*, Christlich-jüdische Begegnung im Zeitalter der Frühscholastik (München 1980).

46 *G. Todeschini*, I mercanti e il tempio 248 ss.

47 *W. Pakter*, Medieval canon law and the Jews (Ebelsbach 1988) 174 ss.

48 *S. Grayzel*, The Church and the Jews in the Thirteenth Century (Philadelphia 1933); *J. Gilchrist*, The Canonistic Treatment of Jews in the Latin West in the Eleventh and Early Twelfth Centuries, in: Zeitschrift der Savigny Stiftung für Rechtsgeschichte – Kan. Abt. 106 (1989) 70–106; *A. Linder*, The Jews in the legal sources of the early middle ages (Detroit, Jerusalem 1997).

49 *S. Lipton*, Images of Intolerance 34–38.

on the market the ecclesiastical rents or *decimae* (tithes), that is the right of churches and abbeys to make credit transactions in the form of buying and selling periodical revenues[50]. In the thirteenth century, growing obsession with usury as a dangerous and destructive economic practice and the accompanying detestation of Jewish economic activities systematically represented as the paradigm of the usurious infidelity, will thereafter be perfectly compatible with the Christian development of a market society, but also of a Christian economics promoted and popularised principally in the writing and preaching of the leading intellectual *magistri* active in the Mendicant Orders[51]. The fourth Lateran Council in 1215 and the second Council of Lyon in 1274 will promulgate inflexible decrees on usury and usurers[52]. However, a close reading of these norms clearly shows that their aim was an accurate differentiation between the sinful economic practice of individuals even depicted as aliens and strangers or heretics, and the economic trend represented in the same years by Christian merchant companies promoted by the popes to the role of bankers and tax collectors of the Apostolic Chamber[53]. The Jews, in this situation, play a strange role: as paradigm of infidelity they embody the usurious avarice daily concretised by the indifference of sectors of the Christian market society to the holiness of Church properties; as an actual economic presence, although in business practice very similar to the Christian one, they appear in legal sources as harshly reproached and sometimes condemned for their determination to participate in economic interplay on a basis of juridical parity with Christians. At the same time, as subjects clearly conscious of possessing a specific economic culture sometimes conflicting with the ecclesiastical one, the Jews are presented in many canonistic or theological writings as arrogant and ungrateful guests (*hostes ingrati*) within Christian society[54]. Finally, the Christian representation of Jewish economic activities as basically reducible to usury, and the interrelated idea that Jewish wealth was the result of an extraordinary capacity to manage money, will give rise to the paradoxical notion of a monetary usefulness of the carnal Jews for the spiritual Christians. Then, from the thirteenth century, the greed and avarice traditionally attributed to the Jews was perceived by Christian economic powers as the occasion for an economic strategy controlled by Christian governments. The Jewish economic evil began to appear as an ambiguous component of the sacred common

50 *G. Constable*, Monastic Tithes from their Origins to the 12th C. (Cambridge 1964); *F. Veraja*, Le origini della controversia teologica sul contratto di censo.

51 *O. Langholm*, Economics in Medieval Schools; *G. Todeschini*, Ricchezza francescana. Dalla povertà volontaria alla società di mercato (Bologna 2004).

52 *T. P. Mc Laughlin*, The Teaching of the Canonists on Usury; *U. Santarelli*, La prohibición de la usura, de canon moral a regla jurídica. Modalidades y éxitos de un "transplante", in: Del Ius mercatorum al derecho mercantil, *C. Petit* ed. (Madrid 1997) 237–256.

53 *E. D. English*, Enterprise and Liability in Sienese Banking, 1230–1350 (Cambridge/Mass. 1988); Gli spazi economici della Chiesa nell'Occidente mediterraneo (Centro italiano di studi di storia e d'arte, Pistoia 1999).

54 For instance: *S. Grayzel*, The Church and the Jews 104, 108; *S. Grayzel*, The Church and the Jews in the Thirteenth Century, II, ed. *K. R. Stow* (Jewish Theological Seminary, New York 1989), 63; *W. Pakter*, Medieval canon law and the Jews 66.

good. In consequence of this evolution of the stereotype, many Italian cities at the end of the Middle Ages could grant a sort of citizenship to the Jews who were willing to play the role of public usurer[55], thereby consenting to exchange wealth, originated by means of a multitude of economic activities, with a civic identity founded on the usurious specialization which in fact was the last embodiment of an ancient religious stereotype: the *perfidia* or *duritia Judaeorum*[56].

[55] Gli ebrei in Italia, I, ed. *C. Vivanti* (Torino 1996); *A. Toaff*, Judaei cives? Gli ebrei nei catasti di Perugia del Trecento, in: Zakhor. Rivista di Storia degli Ebrei d'Italia IV (2000) 11–36.

[56] *B. Blumenkranz*, Perfidia, in: Archivum Latinitatis Medii Aevi-Bulletin Du Cange 22 (1952) 157–70; *Idem*, Juifs et chrétiens. Patristique et Moyen Age (London 1977) VII; *G. Todeschini*, Franciscan Economics and Jews in the Middle Ages: From a Theological to an Economic Lexicon, in: Friars and Jews in the Middle Ages and Renaissance, eds. *S. J. McMichael*, *S. E. Myers* (Leiden, Boston 2004) 99–117.

Hans-Georg von Mutius

Taking Interest from Non-Jews – Main Problems in Traditional Jewish Law

Questions of money lending between Jews and non-Jews and the problems of interest-charged loans can be viewed through the mirror of Jewish law and have been discussed by rabbinical authorities. To begin with the legal sources: All Jewish communities of the Middle Ages in the Mediterranean area and in non-Mediterranean Europe have a common stock of Holy Scriptures constituting the basis of their legal culture and life. Apart from the Hebrew Bible with the Pentateuch as the main law book, they all have in common use a corpus of legal und ritual works written in Palestine and Babylonia during the Late Antiquities: the Mishna compiled at the beginning of the 3rd century C.E. in Northern Palestine, constituting the first comprehensive law-book of normative Judaism after the destruction of the Second Temple with laws and legal discussions mainly from the 2nd century; then a commentary to the Mishna in form of the Babylonian Talmud containing laws and legal discussions from the 3rd to the 6th century; further legal corpora of secondary importance as the Tosefta and the Palestinian Talmud from the 4th and 5th centuries; and the bulk of the so-called Midrashic literature. Midrashic literature, of Jewish Palestinian origin, presents the rabbinical expositions of scriptural verses. Embodied into this literature is a canonical corpus of Midrashim with laws and legal discussions from the 2nd to the 3rd centuries expounding the laws of the Pentateuch. These legal or Halakhic Midrashim were, in addition to the Mishna and the Babylonian Talmud, of obligatory significance for every community in the medieval Jewish world.

As two thirds of the medieval discussions of the leading Jewish scholars are based upon the laws and discussions in the Talmudic and Midrashic literature, it is indispensable to begin with the statements of the rabbis in late antiquity concerning the problem of money lending to non-believers. One main problem and a blue thread in all discussions, from late antiquity and continuing in the Middle Ages, is the correct understanding of the central injunction of Deuteronomy 23, 21: *From a foreigner You may exact interest; from Your brother You shall not exact it, in order that the Lord Your God bless You in all Your enterprises* etc. Already in the early rabbinical literature enumerated above we find a fundamental discord concerning the correct understanding of the treatment of non-Jews in biblical law. Must the text be understood as translated: *From a foreigner You* may *exact interest*, or is the correct understanding of the text as follows: *From a foreigner You* must *exact in-*

terest? At the surface, it is a problem of Biblical Hebrew syntax. The verb of the Hebrew text: *tashik*, uses the so-called preformative conjugation, which is ambiguous in its modal uses, designing inter alia either a possibility or a necessity[1]. The Mishna clearly presupposes the optional solution. In the Tractate Baba Metzi'a V,6 we find the short statement: *One may borrow from non-Jews and lend to them at interest*[2]. Whereas the biblical legislation deals only with the constellation of lending money to a non-Jew, early rabbinical law presents an important enlargement: It is also allowed for a Jew to borrow money from a Gentile and to pay him interest for the loan[3]. And, to look forward into the Middle Ages: In the legal literature of Judaism in Muslim and Christian countries we find beyond the theoretical discussions clear evidence of interest charged loans in everyday life, payable by a Jewish debtor to a Muslim or to a Christian creditor. And when the Jewish disputant in the Sefer ha-Berit of Josef Kimhi, written in Narbonne in the second half of the 12th century, attacks his Christian counterpart, he uses the argument that Christians also are lending money at interest to both Christians and Jews[4]. His reproach must not be a statement devoid of any substance, on the contrary, it may point to economic realities of that time in Southern France and Christian Spain. But let us return to the older rabbinical legislation. The opposite part to the Mishnaic statement is represented by the Midrash Sifre to Deuteronomy, an important Halakhic work of Palestinian Jewry compiled at the end of the 3rd century[5]. In § 263 of this work the decisive words of the Hebrew text: *la-nokri tashik* are expounded by the following short remark: *It is a positive commandment*[6]. Rabbinical hermeneutics divide the laws of the Pentateuch into two parts, positive precepts and negative ones. Negative precepts comprise actions which must be avoided under all circumstances, for example the injunctions: *You shall not commit murder, You shall not bear false testimony against your fellow* etc. Positive commandments, whose performance is absolutely obligatory, are for example: to circumcise a newborn male, to pay a worker his wages on time and so on. On this background, the position of the Midrash Sifre is clear: The biblical words of Deuter. 23,21 must be understood as a duty: A Jew granting a loan to a non-Jew is by divine revelation obliged to demand interest from the foreigner, whenever he lends money to him, a thing absolutely forbidden towards a coreligionist. Mishna and Midrash Sifre contain the two positions that were to be important for the later medieval discussions. But before we analyze the medieval controversy, we must take a short glimpse at the

[1] Compare *B. K. Waltke*, *M. O'Connor*, An Introduction to Biblical Hebrew Syntax (Winona Lake/Indiana 1990) 508ff.

[2] Hebrew text in the edition of *D. Hoffmann*, Mischnajot – Die sechs Ordnungen der Mischna – Part IV: Ordnung Nesikin (Basel [3]1986) 71.

[3] A very convincing analysis of the Mishnaic statement is presented by *J. Rosenthal*, Ribbit min ha-nokri, in: *idem*, Mehqarim umeqorot, vol. 1 (Jerusalem 1967) 257f.

[4] The Book of the Covenant of *Joseph Kimhi*, translated by *F. Talmage* (Toronto 1972) 34f.

[5] Compare *G. Stemberger*, Einleitung in Talmud und Midrasch (Munich [8]1992) 269.

[6] Hebrew text in the edition of *L. Finkelstein*, Sifre al sefer Debarim (New York 1969) 285 (reprint of the edition Berlin 1939).

Talmudic discussion presented in the Tractate Baba Metzi'a fol.70b–71a, based on authorities living in Babylonia during the 4th and 5th century. The main features of the discussions contained in this section are indeed astonishing: The Babylonian Talmud recommends to avoid the granting of interest-charged loans to non-Jews, if possible. Interest taken from non-Jews will bring about unhappiness to the lender according to an opinion of Rav Huna. According to his son, Rav Hiyya, money lending to non-Jews must be limited to the requirements of one's livelihood; but one should not exercise that activity with the intention to gather wealth; and according to yet a third authority, the permission of the Mishna refers only to scholars. They alone are free to engage in money lending to non-Jews without limitations, because they are not in danger to learn from the ways of the non-Jews, in contrast to an ordinary Jew. The Babylonian Talmud adds by citing a fourth authority, that a Jew having the choice to grant a loan without interest to a coreligionist or at interest to a non-Jew, is obliged to give it to his fellow without demanding interest at the time of repayment. The words of the Babylonian Talmud are well understandable on the background of whole regions and complete towns inhabited exclusively or in overwhelming majority by Jews, as in Sassanid Mesopotamia. There, the functioning of an internal Jewish economy and market was, by that reason, more or less possible. Commercial dealings with non-Jews were not absolutely inevitable to secure one's existence. But the Talmudic admonitions were disregarded in the diaspora of post-Talmudic times. Money lending to non-Jews became one important branch of Jewish livelihood, with no difference between scholars and average members of the Jewish communities playing the role of money-lenders. In a famous statement stemming from the middle of the 12th century Rabbenu Tam, living in France, declares the restrictions of the Babylonian Talmud as not applicable any more to the conditions of Jewish life in his time[7]. He points out that Jews of today must pay taxes to the king and to feudal lords, that Jews are living as a minority between the non-Jews, that Jews are totally dependent on non-Jewish clients in all kinds of commercial transactions, and that therefore lending at interest to non-Jews must be allowed to everybody in the Jewish community[8]. Such theoretical discussions took place also in Egypt in the second half of the 12th century, by no inferior scholar than Moses Maimonides, whose legal works received broad acceptance already during his lifetime, not only in oriental Jewry but also in the Jewish communities of Christian Mediterranean countries. In an extremely harsh statement in his "Book of Commandments", written about 1170 in Arabic language, positive precepts § 198, Maimonides says that the words of Deuter. 23,21 concerning the non-Jew are of obligatory nature. One must lend at interest to a non-Jew, "*so that we don't be useful to him nor treat him kindly; on the contrary: that we cause damage to him even in money lending by means of interest,*

[7] Mentioned already by *Rosenthal*, Ribbit min hanokri, op. cit. 263.

[8] Tosafot to Baba Metzia 70b. The edition used here is: Masseket Baba Metzia min Talmud Babli im perush Rashi, Tosafot … (Jerusalem 1981).

which we impose on him by contract"[9]. Maimonides continues, that the words of Deuter. 23,21 contain a command and that no freedom of choice is implied therein; and he adduces the Midrash Sifre to Deuteronomy as the decisive proof for his arguments. In his main legal work written in Hebrew, the Mishneh Torah, Maimonides repeats his injunction in his laws concerning money lending, chapter V § 1, in a non-polemical form by only citing Midrash Sifre without mentioning his source by name[10]. Several Hebrew translations of the Book of Precepts already realised during Maimonides' lifetime secured a broad reception of this work in the other Mediterranean Jewish communities; the same happened to the Mishneh Torah, which did not need a translation and was completed about 1180. The reactions to his theory of interest were negative by the majority of his commentators. The first and most important one was his contemporary Abraham Ben David of Posquières in Southern France, who wrote a commentary to the Mishneh Torah of Maimonides, consisting of very critical glosses and who, by virtue of his personal biography, had no reason to act benevolently towards non-Jews. In his comment to chapter V § 1 of Maimonides' laws concerning money lending he remarks in his short, enigmatic style, that such an exegetical tradition is unknown to him, and that Maimonides misunderstood the Midrash Sifre. The Midrash, says Abraham Ben David, which declares money lending at interest to non-Jews as a positive commandment, intends only to corroborate the prohibition to exact interest from a fellow Jew, and nothing else[11]. Moses Nahmanides (Gerona, middle of the 13th century) follows Abraham Ben David in his commentary to Maimonides' Book of Commandments (chapter 6 in his general introduction) and writes, that Maimonides committed a mistake by classifying Deuter. 23,21 as a commandment. The Midrash Sifre must be interpreted as a mere permission to lend money at interest to a non-Jew, and as a non-permission to lend money at interest to a coreligionist[12]. The position of Abraham Ben David is repeated by Nahmanides' pupil Solomon Ben Adret of Barcelona in his Talmudic commentary to Baba Metzi'a 70b: The Midrash Sifre, classifying the exaction of interest from a non-Jew as a positive commandment, intends only to strengthen the prohibition of demanding interest from a fellow Jew. It is not the intention of the Midrash to obligate Jews to take interest from non-Jews, and Maimonides does not present the correct interpretation of the Midrashic state-

[9] Arabic text in: *Moshe ben Maimon*, Sefer hamitzwot, edited and translated into Hebrew by *D. Kapah* (Jerusalem 1971) 159. *Rosenthal*, Ribbit min hanokri, op. cit. 265, in his Hebrew translation of the text omits the clause on damaging the non-Jew!

[10] Hebrew text in: Mishneh Torah wehu sefer hajad hahazaqah leharab rabbenu Moshe Bar Maimon zal, traditional edition with commentaries, 2nd part (Berlin, New York 1926) 34a in the tractate Hilkot malweh weloweh.

[11] Text of his remark according to the bibliography given in the preceding footnote. The critique of Abraham Ben David is also cited by *Rosenthal*, Ribbit min hanokri, op.cit. 265.

[12] Hebrew text in: Sefer hamitzwot lehanesher hagadol rabbenu *Moshe Ben Maimon* zal wehaholkim alaw – a) Hassagot haRamban (Rabbenu *Moshe Ben Nahman* zal ...), traditional edition (Jerusalem no year) 52a–b.

ment. So far Solomon Ben Adret[13]. Let us again go back for a moment to Nahmanides. In his commentary on the Pentateuch to Deuter. 23,20, Nahmanides writes that according to verse 21, it is allowed to exact interest from a non-Jew, and that no theft or robbery to the disadvantage of the non-Jew is implied in such a deal[14]. With this statement, Nahmanides is apparently dependent upon his early contemporary David Kimhi (1165–1235) of Narbonne, who already wrote this in his own commentary on the Pentateuch. David Kimhi continues there with the remark, that the granting of interest-free loans to Jewish fellows rests on the legal duty of a Jew to act benevolently towards his coreligionists and to benefit them. These obligations must not be observed in dealings with non-Jews, because most of them hate Jews. But if a non-Jew acts benevolently towards a Jew and deals with him in a kind manner, the Jew is reciprocally obliged to a benevolent dealing with his non-Jewish counterpart[15]. Does David Kimhi herewith indicate a moral obligation to grant an interest-free loan to a non-Jew in certain circumstances? I am unable to give a clear answer to this question, but David Kimhi seems to be inclined to such a solution. The opinion of Maimonides found only a few supporters. A certain acceptance of his position was demonstrated by Levi Ben Gershom (Southern France, 14th century). He writes in his commentary to Deuter. 23,21, that it is absolutely obligatory by divine law to demand interest from a non-Jew in the case of granting a loan to him, because he is an idolater and because one must cause damage to him to the possible extent. This does not constitute a deviation from the principle of righteousness[16]. This means that according to his opinion the religious duty to take interest from a borrowing non-Jew must be fulfilled by demanding a not too excessive percentage of interest[17]. But the vast majority of the Jewish scholars living in the western Mediterranean area during the later Middle Ages regarded the biblical words of Deuter. 23,21 only as a possibility. The final decision of the matter was prepared by the monumental law-code "Arba'a ha Turim" of Jacob Ben Asher from Toledo (1st half of the 14th century). In the section Yoreh Deah § 160, Jacob Ben Asher remarks laconically that according to the word of the Torah it is allowed to lend to a non-Jew at interest[18]. The Shulhan 'Arukh of the Spaniard Josef Caro, though written in Ottoman Palestine about the middle of the 16th century, defi-

[13] Digitalized text in the following edition: Hiddushe haRashba al masseket Baba Metzia fol.70b, in: Hataqlitor hatorani leshas im rishonim (Jerusalem 1999). The statement of Solomon Ben Adret is reproduced by *Rosenthal*, Ribbit min hanokri, op. cit. 267.

[14] Hebrew text in: Perushe hatorah lerabbenu *Moshe Ben Nahman* (haRamban), edited by *Ch. D. Chavel*, 2nd volume (Jerusalem 1960) 461.

[15] Hebrew text in: Perushe rabbi *David Qimhi* (Radaq) al hatorah, edited by *M. Kamelhaar* (Jerusalem 1970) 282.

[16] Hebrew text in: *Levi Ben Gershom*, Perush al hatorah al derek beur (Venice 1547) fol. 234a. The statement of Levi Ben Gershom is presented by *Rosenthal*, Ribbit min hanokri, op. cit. 274 in a totally mutilated form without any mention of the damage to be caused to the non-Jew!

[17] I think that this interpretation of Levi Ben Gershom's statement in the article "Moneylending" in the Encyclopedia Judaica, vol. 12 (Jerusalem 1971) col. 250, is correct.

[18] Text in: Arbaah Haturim – Yoreh Deah, 2nd part, traditional edition with supercommentaries, reprint of the edition from Warsaw 1861 (Jerusalem no year) fol. 1a.

nitely puts an end to the discussion by quoting Jacob Ben Asher verbatim in the section Yoreh Deah § 159[19]. Both authorities silently reject Maimonides in this way; they represent the predominant opinion.

But at the end of these expositions, we must try to trace the rationale of the legal discussions presented here. First, Maimonides is quite correct in interpreting the Midrash Sifre as he does. His opponents, not daring to disregard the authority of that old work, were forced to interpret it against its literal meaning and to squeeze the Midrash in favour of their optional interpretation of the biblical text itself. Furthermore, the Midrash Sifre and Maimonides as its follower represent the most authentic and original Jewish tradition of interpreting Deuter. 23,21. Already the Greek Bible of Alexandrinian Jewry in the 3rd century B.C.E. translated the Hebrew Text as a double commandment: *Upon the stranger You must impose interest; upon Your brother You shall not impose interest* (τω αλλοτριω εκτοκιεις , τω δε αδελφω σου ουκ εκτοκιεις)[20], using the indicative of the future tense as a circumscription of a strong jussive typical for negative and positive injunctions in the legal texts of Septuaginta[21]. Let us return to the Middle Ages. The problem is that for a Christian client borrowing from a Jew it does not make any difference whether the payment of interest imposed on him is the result of an optional interpretation of the biblical law or not within the Jewish community. The internal Jewish discussion remains undisclosed to the non-Jew; and he has to pay, on the basis of non-Jewish contract-law in general and of non-Jewish Jewry law in special, which rendered a Jew's title enforceable before a Christian court of law. The reason for the controversy described above must have been another one. If money lending at interest to a non-Jew is allowed, a Jew is also free to grant to a non-Jew a loan without interest, treating him as a Jewish coreligionist. If money lending to a non-Jew is not allowed without demanding interest, the second possibility is obstructed *ab initio*. The distinction between Israel and the peoples of the world is drawn sharply by the old exegetical tradition in the Midrash Sifre and its medieval recipient Moses Maimonides. The opponents of Maimonides with their more lenient interpretation of Deuter. 23,21 apparently intended to open the possibility to a Jew to grant an interest-free loan to a non-Jewish friend, in order to corroborate existing ties of good neighbourhood, friendship or something like that. Were loans without interest from a Jew to a non-Jew granted anywhere in the medieval world? Gershom Ben Jehudah of Mainz mentions such a case in early 11th century Germany, but without linking it to the discussion presented here[22]. Nevertheless, the presumably rare oc-

[19] Hebrew text in: Shulhan Arukh – Yoreh Deah mehagaon moharar *Josef Qaro* zal, traditional edition (Wilna 1925) 367.

[20] Greek text according to the edition of *J. W. Wevers*, Septuaginta – Vetus Testamentum Graecum ... vol. III,2: Deuteronomium (Göttingen 1977) 263.

[21] Compare *C. Conybeare*, *G. Stock*, Grammar of Septuagint Greek (no location ^{2}1995) 72.

[22] See *H. G. von Mutius*, Rechtsentscheide rheinischer Rabbinen vor dem 1. Kreuzzug, I, (Judentum und Umwelt 13/I, Frankfurt a. M. and elsewhere 1984) 105. The case is mentioned also by *J. Shatzmiller*, Shylock reconsidered – Jews, Moneylending and Medieval Society, (Berkeley and elsewhere 1990) 100.

currence of interest free loans granted by a Jew to a non-Jew shows that the mainstream of legal discussions: *You may* or *You must lend at interest to a foreigner* does not necessarily reflect frequent occurrences in daily live; and that is the main result of the reflections on the matter presented here.

David Jacoby

The Jews in Byzantium and the Eastern Mediterranean: Economic Activities from the Thirteenth to the Mid-Fifteenth Century*

The geographic range of this study requires a short explanation. Byzantium suffered successive territorial losses in the period following the Fourth Crusade (1202–1204), and before its fall in 1453 it was more or less limited to Constantinople and the Peloponnesus. The Latin conquests of the early thirteenth century were followed by the restructuring of commercial networks and a partial re-orientation in the flow of goods in the eastern Mediterranean, which deeply affected Byzantium in the long-run[1]. The investigation of the late Byzantine economy, therefore, cannot be limited to the shrinking territorial framework of the Empire. It must be examined within the context of the broader region within which that economy integrated, primarily in relation to Latin Romania, the former Byzantine lands occupied by the Latins after the Fourth Crusade.

This approach is also indispensable with respect to the Jews in the late Empire for yet another reason, namely, the paucity and nature of the sources bearing on their economic activities. I have recently traced the continuous presence of the

* The following abbreviations are used below: ASV = Archivio di Stato di Venezia, cited for unpublished documents; Badoer = *Umberto Dorini* e *Tommaso Bertelè* (eds.), Il libro dei conti di Giacomo Badoer (Costantinopoli, 1436–1440) (Il Nuovo Ramusio III Roma 1956); BB = *Raimondo Morozzo della Rocca* (ed.), Benvenuto de Brixano, notaio in Candia (1301–1302) (Venezia 1950); LM = *Mario Chiaudano* e *Antonino Lombardo* (eds.), Leonardo Marcello, notaio in Candia, 1278–1281 (Venezia 1960); PP = *Salvatore Carbone* (ed.), Pietro Pizolo, notaio in Candia (1300, 1304–1305) (Venezia 1978–1985); PS = *Antonino Lombardo* (ed.), Imbreviature di Pietro Scardon (1271) (Documenti della colonia veneziana di Creta I, Torino 1942); Taqqanoth = *Elias S. Artom* et *Humbertus M. D. Cassuto* (eds.), Taqqanoth Qandya ve-Zichronoteha (Statuta Iudaeorum Candiae eorumque memorabilia) (Jerusalem 1943) [Hebrew]; ZF = *Antonino Lombardo* (ed.), Zaccaria de Fredo, notaio in Candia (1352–1357) (Venezia 1968). BB, LM, PP and ZF have been edited by the Comitato per la pubblicazione delle Fonti relative alla Storia di Venezia, in the series Fonti per la storia di Venezia, Sez. III – Archivi notarili. For the sake of uniformity known Jewish names cited in documents are reproduced below in their Hebrew version.

1 *David Jacoby*, Changing Economic Patterns in Latin Romania: The Impact of the West, in: *Angeliki E. Laiou* and *Roy Parviz Mottahedeh* (eds.), The Crusades from the Perspective of Byzantium and the Muslim World (Washington, D.C. 2001) 220–229, repr. in *David Jacoby*, Commercial Exchange across the Mediterranean: Byzantium, the Crusader Levant, Egypt and Italy (Aldershot 2005) no. IX.

Jewish community in Thessalonica from the twelfth to the second half of the fifteenth century, yet without finding any indication regarding the economic occupations in which its members engaged[2]. The sources illustrating the strong impact of western maritime powers in the eastern Mediterranean provide the bulk of evidence regarding the Jews of Byzantium and of Latin Romania in the period covered here. Among these sources notarial charters, of primary importance, are particularly abundant for Crete, ruled by Venice from the early thirteenth century onward, and somewhat less for Chios, occupied by the Genoese from 1346 to 1566. Yet for many other localities the sources offer at best only scattered and isolated data regarding individual Jews and their economic pursuits, or else clusters of relevant information covering short periods. Therefore, any attempt to reconstruct the role of the Jews in the economy of the eastern Mediterranean and to assess its degree of continuity also requires an occasional return to an earlier period and reliance upon circumstantial evidence.

With few exceptions Jews were an exclusively urban element in the eastern Mediterranean of the late Middle Ages[3]. Their economic activities primarily took place within cities or in relation to them, even if they held or owned rural property[4]. These activities, as in other regions, displayed some distinctive features. The production, marketing and consumption of specific commodities among Jews were governed by religious precepts and by strict control and, therefore, were carried out under particular conditions differing from those customary in Christian or Muslim societies. Jews maintained an internal economic network, specific to their communities and exclusively geared toward Jewish customers. This network warrants a separate treatment in view of its economic importance.

The choice and slaughter of animals for meat consumption according to ritual requirements was generally performed in cities. On the other hand, as urban residents Jews depended upon farmers for the supply of grapes and milk, respectively for the production of wine and the consumption of milk, butter and cheese. We have no information regarding the internal Jewish network in Byzantium, whether in the centuries preceding the Fourth Crusade or following it. Yet the evidence regarding kasher wine and cheese produced in Venetian Crete, apparently more abundant than for any other group of medieval Jewish communities, offers an insight into its nature and operation. The set of ordinances issued in 1228 by the Jewish leaders in Crete points to well-structured communities and implies the existence of a Jewish economic network in the island in the preceding Byzantine period[5].

In Venetian Crete the purchase of agricultural and pastoral products, mainly wine, cheese and grain, was often tied to advance payments for the delivery of an

[2] Except in the 1160s. See *David Jacoby*, Foreigners and the Urban Economy in Thessalonike, c. 1150 – c. 1430, in: Dumbarton Oaks Papers 57 (2003) 123–129.

[3] A Jew living in the Cretan village of Pala in 1352 was clearly an exception: ZF no. 43.

[4] On which see below, pp. 45–46.

[5] Taqqanoth 3–6, no. 2.

agreed quantity of produce at a specific date or within a specific period. This sale credit system, with its concealed loans, is illustrated by numerous contracts, the exact terms of which widely varied. It was presumably far more common in the Venetian period than in the preceding Byzantine era[6]. For Jews sale credit was not just an option. It was indispensable to ensure constant and close supervision according to rabbinical precepts over wine and cheese directly ordered from the producer.

Kasher wine was in constant demand for Jewish ritual functions, yet was also purchased as beverage. In Crete Jews used sale credit before the grape harvest to ensure the delivery of wine fit for consumption. By contracts of May and August 1271 a Greek woman residing in Candia, the capital of Venetian Crete, promised to deliver a total of 175 *mistati* or 2,252 liters wine from her vineyard in the village of Catalagari to a Jew of the city[7]. Jewish seasonal workers were sent to the countryside to clean the wine press, wine cellar, vats and casks, press the grapes, and supervise the transportation of the must or the wine to Candia[8]. In 1357 the wealthy Moses son of Yehudah instructed that grapes sufficient for the production of 150 *mistati* or 1,930 liters wine be brought to his house in order to have them pressed in the city[9].

Ever larger volumes of cheese were being traded over long distances in the Mediterranean from the eleventh century onward, as illustrated by Byzantine, Arabic, Jewish and western sources. Exports of Cretan cheese to Constantinople are attested from the 1020s and to Alexandria from the 1060s. An eleventh or twelfth-century Jewish letter written in Alexandria apparently deals with the import of Cretan cheese. By the second half of the twelfth century Venetian involvement in the import of high-grade Cretan cheese to Constantinople was so extensive that the Venetian quarter had become the major market for that commodity in the city[10]. We may safely assume, therefore, that kasher cheese produced in the island also reached Constantinople and other Byzantine cities in that period.

All stages of production and distribution of kasher cheese were conducted under close supervision, as for wine. Various precepts applied to milking, the use of rennet from a ritually slaughtered animal to curdle the milk, as well as to the processing, storage, transportation and marketing of the cheese. Religious consid-

[6] *Jacoby*, Changing Economic Patterns 218, on the background and effects of that system.

[7] PS nos. 319, 429. The *botte* of Candia, also used for shipments to Constantinople and Alexandria, contained 540. 70 liters equivalent to 42 *mistati*: see *Ugo Tucci*, La *botte* veneziana, in: Studi veneziani 9 (1967) 213–217, esp. 215–216. It follows that the *mistatus* held 12.87 liters.

[8] Taqqanoth 22–25, no. 33.

[9] ZF no. 93.

[10] *David Jacoby*, Byzantine Crete in the Navigation and Trade Networks of Venice and Genoa, in: *Laura Balletto* (ed.), Oriente e Occidente tra medioevo ed età moderna. Studi in onore di Geo Pistarino (Università degli Studi di Genova, Sede di Acqui Terme, Collana di Fonti e Studi 1/1, Acqui Terme 1997) 519–523, 525–529, 535–536, repr. in *David Jacoby*, Byzantium, Latin Romania and the Mediterranean (Aldershot 2001) no. II. For the Jewish letter, see *Shlomo D. Goitein*, A Mediterranean Society. The Jewish Communities of the Arab World as Portrayed in the Documents of the Cairo Geniza, vol. I (Berkeley and Los Angeles 1967–1993) 429, n. 66.

erations, in addition to economic incentives, prompted some Jews to commission cheese directly from producers rather than purchase it from Jewish merchants. In a notarial contract of 1304, a Jewess of Candia undertook to send a Jewish worker to produce 68.7 kg ripe Jewish cheese she had ordered from a Greek living at Belvedere, in southern Crete[11]. The latter promised transportation and delivery of the cheese at the market place of Candia[12]. In 1301 a Greek of the Cretan city of Canea undertook to bring to the home of a resident of Candia 180 Cretan gross pounds or some 94 kg Jewish cheese[13]. Jews buying cheese molds from merchants made sure that they had been properly produced, stamped and handled[14].

Laxity in supervision induced the leaders of the Jewish community of Candia to state in greater detail the rules to be applied to the production, transportation and marketing of Jewish products. In 1363 they issued an ordinance regarding kasher wine, incidentally allowing the sale of improperly handled wine to Christians[15]. They also prohibited at several occasions the purchase of milk, butter and cheese they considered unfit for Jewish consumption. In 1363 they dealt with cheese bought by Jews of Castelnuovo in southern Crete from local Christian producers and marketed as kasher produce[16].

Some contracts between Cretan Jews and non-Jews provided for the delivery of rather small amounts of wine or cheese. In 1301 a Jew ordered 34 *mistati* or 437 liters must[17]. A Greek peasant promised the delivery of some 52 kg cheese in April 1272 to Salomon son of Shabbetai[18]. As in the case of the Jewess mentioned earlier, these consignments were intended for private consumption or for local retail trade. Yet other transactions involved Jewish merchants acting as entrepreneurs, who commissioned the production of large volumes of wine and cheese that they handled in bulk, selling the produce to local retailers or other wholesale merchants or else exporting it.

[11] The quantity mentioned was 2/15 of one *milliarium* of Candia. The latter weighed 1,100 Venetian *libre grosse* of 0.476 kg, hence 523 kg. For this ratio, see *Francesco Balducci Pegolotti*, La pratica della mercatura, ed. by *Allan Evans* (Cambridge, Mass. 1936) 106. The gross pound of Candia or 1/1000 of the *milliarium* thus weighed 0.523 kg.

[12] PP no. 850: *de bono caseo Cretensi bene conducto* [sic for *condicto*] *et sasionato iudaico* (…) *Et tu debes mittere Iudeum ad faciendum ipsum caseum*. On this 'hard' cheese, which could travel over long distances, see *David Jacoby*, Cretan Cheese: A Neglected Aspect of Venetian Medieval Trade, in: *Ellen E. Kittel* and *Thomas F. Madden* (eds.), Medieval and Renaissance Venice (Urbana and Chicago 1999) 50–51, repr. in *Jacoby*, Commercial Exchange no. VIII. A Jewish ordinance issued in Candia in 1363 refers to Jewish workers 'freezing' the cheese in the rennet: Taqqanoth 27, no. 37, lines 17–18. The rennet is also mentioned ibid. 55, no. 55, lines 21–22.

[13] BB no. 420.

[14] A stamp is mentioned in 1399: Taqqanoth 55, no. 55, line 38, and see commentary 54. On stamped cheese molds in Egypt, see *Goitein*, A Mediterranean Society, vol. IV, 251 and 444, n. 188.

[15] See above, n. 15.

[16] On milk, butter and cheese in 1363: Taqqanoth 27–28, no. 37, and 52–53, no. 53, a case of unaccompanied milk sold by a Christian to Jewish customers; in 1399: ibid. 54–56, no. 55.

[17] BB no. 50.

[18] PS no. 438. Shabbetai appears as Sambatus in Venetian notarial documents.

We have already noted two contracts for some 2,000 liters and more wine[19]. Within less than four months in 1280–1281 Jeremiah Nomico made advance purchases of 600 *mistati* or 7,722 liters of Jewish wine, sufficient for the yearly consumption of at least 25 people[20]. As we shall see below, some Jews exported even larger volumes. Wine production in Crete was furthered by a substantial expansion of vineyards from the fourteenth century onward in response to a growing foreign demand, especially for high-grade brands[21]. Similarly, there was an increasing Jewish demand for Cretan wine, both locally and abroad, as illustrated by later documents adduced below.

As for wine, some Jewish entrepreneurs handled large volumes of cheese. A Jew of Candia, Shabbetai son of Moses, ordered in three contracts concluded from April to August 1271 a total of 628 kg cheese[22]. Moses the dyer was expecting 784 kg, partly in April and the rest in May 1272 at the latest[23]. Two Jews of Rethymno, Salomon son of Lazar and Moses Capsali, made considerable advance purchases of cheese before 1402, although such purchases with or without payments had been prohibited in 1393 since they led to the indebtedness and flight of peasants and herd owners[24]. The two Jews were heavily fined in 1402, respectively 7,219 and 3,971 hyperpers, sums that imply large amounts of cheese obviously intended for export, in the first case well above 100 metric tons[25].

Kasher cheese and wine produced in Venetian Crete were widely distributed throughout the eastern Mediterranean. The earliest explicit reference in this respect appears in a contract concluded in 1300 between two Jews of Candia for trade in kosher cheese *per terram et per aquam*. Incidentally, the contract also refers to the

[19] See above, p. 27.

[20] LM nos. 323, 452. In the fourteenth century, the average yearly consumption of wine in Venice, Genoa and Florence was between 250 and 300 liters: *John Day*, Prix agricoles en Méditerranée à la fin du XIVe siècle, in: Annales. Économies, sociétés, civilisations 16 (1961) 638. I have used that average here in the absence of a similar study for the eastern Mediterranean.

[21] *Jacoby*, Changing Economic Patterns 219.

[22] PS nos. 218, 280, 436.

[23] PS nos. 421 and 448. Prices varied between 12 and 16 Cretan hyperpers per *milliarium* of Candia.

[24] Prohibition of 1393: *Hippolyte Noiret*, Documents inédits pour servir à l'histoire de la domination vénitienne en Crète de 1380 à 1485 (Paris 1892) 55. The Jews got hold of the herds belonging to defaulting debtors: see ibid., 59–60. The officials who condemned the two Jews and the fines are mentioned in a decision of 1403 by which the doge's council overturned the verdict: ed. by *Freddy Thiriet*, Délibérations des assemblées vénitiennes concernant la Romanie, vol. II (Paris 1966–1971) 308, no. 1042. These officials had left Venice in 1402: *Constantin N. Sathas*, Documents inédits relatifs à l'histoire de la Grèce au Moyen Age, vol. II (Paris 1880–1900) 56–59.

[25] The fine comprised the value of the cheese and, in addition, 50 hyperpers for each purchase. A purely hypothetical calculation illustrates the magnitude of the business deals. If in the first case we assume fifty purchases entailing fines (50 x 50 hyperpers = 2,500), the remaining 4720 hyperpers would have covered purchases over several years totaling 277 *milliaria* or 144.871 metric tons at the rate of 17 hyperpers per *milliarium*. For the sake of comparison, in 1300 the Venetian Andrea Corner ordered a total of 30 *milliaria* or 15.690 metric tons at the same rate from two merchants, one in Canea and the other in Candia, obviously for export, the total cost reaching 510 hyperpers: PP nos. 170, 332.

shipping of ritual ram horns or *shofars*, clearly intended for export[26]. In 1352 a Jew of Candia purchased the fourth part of a *griparia*, a small ship, which regularly sailed from the Cretan port to Famagusta in Cyprus, Syria, Cilician Armenia, Rhodes and Alexandria. The Jewish merchant obtained a maritime loan from the Greek partner, and enjoyed free transportation and board. The reimbursement of the loan was to take place within one month after arrival at Famagusta or Rhodes[27]. The whole business arrangement was clearly related to the shipping of Jewish commodities. This was presumably also the case in 1411, when a Jew of Candia sailing to Rhodes suffered losses inflicted by a Sicilian merchant[28].

Jewish wine and cheese were also shipped from Crete to more distant ports. They were most likely included among the goods belonging to a Venetian Jew yet carried by a Genoese ship, which were confiscated some time before April 1343 by the authorities of Pera, the Genoese suburb of Constantinople[29]. In 1370 a Jew of Candia concluded a contract with a local Greek for the transportation of ten casks containing 5,407 liters wine as well as cheese to Constantinople[30]. In 1403 or 1404 the Genoese authorities in Pera seized 23 casks holding 12,436 liters kasher Cretan wine[31]. Lazar son of Isaac de Alemania shipped wine from Candia to the Byzantine capital in 1418[32].

As attested in 1320, Venetian merchants went from Constantinople to the countryside at the time of the grape gathering to buy must[33]. There is good reason to believe that some Jews of Constantinople acted similarly and proceeded like Cretan Jews to ensure their basic supply of kasher wine. The Jewish wine from Crete was nevertheless competitive, as suggested by its import. It was sold in the Venetian quarter of Constantinople, as well as in the Genoese quarter, as implied by its occasional confiscation in Pera. The Byzantine authorities strongly opposed its sale to Byzantine Jews, like that of Cretan non-kasher wine to other imperial

[26] PP no. 554, modeled after the *collegancia* contract no. 553. On that type of contract, see below, p. 44. The formula *per terram et per aquam* sometimes covered trade in Crete and along its coast, as explicitly stated in BB nos. 237 and 421.

[27] ZF nos. 61, 66, 71, 72. That sailing to Egyptian ports was common is implied by a clause prohibiting it on that specific occasion: ibid. no. 71.

[28] *Noiret*, Documents 211.

[29] ASV, Senato, Misti, reg. 21, fol. 24v–25r.

[30] *Silvano Borsari*, Ricchi e poveri nelle communità ebraiche di Candia e Negroponte (secc. XIII–XIV), in: *Chryssa A. Maltezou* (ed.), Plousioi kai ftochoi sten kononia tes ellenolatinikes Anatoles (= Ricchi e poveri nella società dell'Oriente grecolatino) (Biblioteca dell'Istituto ellenico di Studi bizantini e postbizantini di Venezia 19, Venezia 1998) 216, 217.

[31] *Noiret*, Documents 179–180. The case, discussed in 1406, occurred while Tommaso Mocenigo was duke of Crete, an office to which he had been elected in 1403: ibid. 147 and n. 1.

[32] *Nicolas Iorga*, Documents concernant les Grecs et les affaires d'Orient tirés des registres des notaires de Crète, in: Revue historique du sud-est européen 14 (1937) 93.

[33] *Georg Martin Thomas* (ed.), Diplomatarium veneto-levantinum, vol. I (Venetiis 1880–1899) 164 lines 2–3 from below; see also *David Jacoby*, Les Vénitiens naturalisés dans l'Empire byzantin: un aspect de l'expansion de Venise en Romanie du XIIIe au milieu du XVe siècle, in: Travaux et mémoires 8 (1981) 224–225, repr. in *David Jacoby*, Studies on the Crusader States and on Venetian Expansion (Northampton 1989) no. IX.

subjects, since Venetian citizens and subjects enjoyed full tax exemption[34]. Some time before 1450 they established a special office, called *scribania vegetum Judeorum Venetorum*, which collected a tax of one half of a hyperper on each imported cask. Emperor Constantine XI promised to abolish the tax when Venice protested against this infringement of its privileges[35].

Jews were legally barred from permanently residing in Venice until 1513, except for the years 1382–1397. Some Jews nevertheless lived in the city in the fourteenth century, clearly with the knowledge of the Venetian authorities[36]. The Cretan shipments of kasher wine and cheese were intended for local Jews, as well as for the Jewish communities in the neighboring continental territories of northeastern Italy. However, Alexandria appears to have become the main foreign market for these commodities in the fourteenth century. Wine was in high demand in Egypt, in which it was not always easily available due to restrictions imposed by the Muslim authorities[37]. Liachus or Elijah Capsali, a Cretan Jew from Rethymno apparently established in Alexandria, traded in kasher Cretan wine on a very large scale. In April 1421, he imported 70 casks containing 37,849 liters[38]. In the following year he concluded in Alexandria an agreement for the transportation of 50 or 60 casks of Jewish wine as well as cheese from Rethymno to Alexandria on board a small vessel belonging to a resident of his home city[39]. He had hired or acquired in Alexandria a warehouse that also served as tavern to store kasher wine and engage in its retail trade, handled by a Jewish servant[40]. In 1428 other Cretan Jews imported Jewish wine that was to be delivered in Alexandria to two Jewish agents of a Jew of Rethymno or sold in retail, *ad minutum sive ad spinam*[41].

Kasher cheese and wine were exclusively handled by Jews within a closed Jewish production, distribution and marketing network requiring and affording constant

34 Ibid. 225–226.

35 *Thomas*, Diplomatarium, vol. II, 379–380.

36 *David Jacoby*, Les Juifs à Venise du XIVe au milieu du XVIe siècle, in: *Hans-Georg Beck*, *Manoussos Manoussacas*, *Agostino Pertusi* (eds.), Venezia, centro di mediazione tra Oriente e Occidente (secoli XV–XVI): aspetti e problemi (Atti del II Convegno internazionale di storia della civiltà veneziana, Venezia 1973) vol. I (Firenze 1977) 163–216, repr. in *David Jacoby*, Recherches sur la Méditerranée orientale du XIIe au XVe siècle. Peuples, sociétés, économies (London 1979) no. VIII; *David Jacoby*, I Greci ed altre comunità tra Venezia e oltremare, in: *Maria Francesca Tiepolo* ed *Eurigio Tonetti* (eds.), I Greci a Venezia (Atti del Convegno Internazionale di Studio, Venezia, 5–7 novembre 1998) (Istituto Veneto di Scienze, Lettere ed Arti, Venezia 2002) 67–79.

37 For instance in 1428: *Eliyahu Ashtor*, New Data for the History of Levantine Jewries in the Fifteenth Century, in: Bulletin of the Institute of Jewish Studies 3 (1975) 78–79, repr. in *Eliyahu Ashtor*, The Jews and the Mediterranean Economy, 10th–15th Centuries (London 1983) no. VIII.

38 Ed. by *Ashtor*, New Data 93–94, no. I.

39 Ed. by *Charles Verlinden*, Marchands chrétiens et juifs dans l'Etat mamelouk au début du XVe siècle d'après un notaire vénitien, in: Bulletin de l'Institut historique belge de Rome 51 (1981) 72–73. On the technical expressions *de firmo* and *de respectu*, see *Ashtor*, New Data 78, n. 2.

40 Ed. by *Ashtor*, New Data 95–96, doc II, and see also 77–78; *Eliyahu Ashtor*, Ebrei cittadini di Venezia?, in: Studi veneziani 17–18 (1975–76) 151–152.

41 ASV, Cancellaria inferiore, Notai, b. 211, Nicolo Turiano, IV, fol. 50v–51r. *Ashtor*, New Data 78–79, failed to note the retail trade. On Liachus Capsali and other Jewish traders in Egypt in the 1420s, see ibid. 75–79; *Ashtor*, Ebrei cittadini 147–148, 150.

supervision. Since Jews accompanied these commodities on land and sea, it is hardly surprising that they took advantage of their business trips and connections to extend the range of their transactions to unsold kasher surpluses, products rendered unfit for Jewish consumption, and non-kasher wine and cheese. This offshoot of the internal Jewish traffic further promoted the integration of Jewish merchants within the broader trade patterns of the eastern Mediterranean, beyond their use of land and maritime transportation provided by Christians and Muslims.

The sale of wine rendered unfit for Jewish consumption was permitted by the leaders of the Jewish community of Candia[42]. On 2 August 1280 the Jew Lignaco concluded an agreement with two Christian residents of Candia by which he offered them 400 *mistati* or 5,148 liters of wine, in return for the same quantity of must delivered at his home in the following month from the vineyard cultivated by one of the two Christians. The must would have obviously been kasher. At first glance the transaction appears to be an exchange, yet in fact it was a loan for somewhat more than a month, as explicitly stated in the contract. It is likely that the concealed interest paid by the Christian traders consisted in transportation costs, which they covered both for the wine they received and the one they were to deliver[43]. In the first half of the fifteenth century some Cretan Jewish merchants also dealt with wine unfit for Jewish consumption in Alexandria. In 1422 Elijah Capsali from Rethymno sold 60 casks containing 32,442 liters wine imported from his home city to the consul of Naples and to two Venetian tavern-keepers[44].

Similar transactions are attested for cheese. In October 1280 Shabbetai Callamiti of Candia transferred some 80 *milliaria* or around 38 metric tons cheese to a Greek of Belvedere, as a loan in kind until Lent of the following year[45]. We have already noted the large volume of cheese handled by Salomon son of Lazar. His business was clearly not limited to kasher cheese. Around 1382 he obtained for himself and his descendants permission to maintain shops for retail trade outside the Jewish quarter of Rethymno. The grant was revoked in 1412, when prominent Latin residents of the city complained that the Jews dominated the local retail market. It was decided, therefore, that in Rethymno, as in Candia and Canea, the Jews should have shops exclusively within the boundaries of their quarters. However, they were allowed to maintain storehouses outside their quarter, in view of the large volume of cheese, wine and other commodities they handled[46].

[42] See above, p. 28.

[43] LM no. 156. Lignacus concluded a similar deal with another Christian in March 1281: ibid. no. 535.

[44] Ed. by *Ashtor*, New Data 94–97, no. II, and see also 77–78; *Ashtor*, Ebrei cittadini 151–152. Jews also sold non-kasher wine in Venice in the sixteenth century: *Jacoby*, Les Juifs à Venise 202.

[45] LM no. 293. For cheese from that region, see above, p. 28.

[46] *Noiret*, Documents 213–214. The grant was made by Marco Marcello, governor of Rethymno, who held that office in 1382: *Elisabeth Santschi*, Régestes des arrêts civils et des mémoriaux (1363–1399) des archives du duc de Crète (Bibliothèque de l'Institut hellénique d'études byzantines et post-byzantines de Venise 9, Venise 1976) 82, no. 319. In Candia the leasing of storehouses to Jews outside their quarter was authorized in 1391 and 1406: see *Maria Georgopoulou*, Venice's Mediterranean Colonies. Architecture and Urbanism (Cambridge 2001) 200 and 334–335, n. 52.

It is time to examine Jewish involvement in manufacture. When Benjamin of Tudela visited Constantinople around 1160, he noted three occupational groups within the Jewish community residing in the suburb of Pera: tanners, silk workers and merchants[47]. The Jewish neighborhood in the suburb of Pera was gutted by fire in 1203, and most surviving Jews established themselves in Constantinople proper. It is unclear whether they immediately and spontaneously settled in the region of Vlanga, or whether Michael VIII Palaeologus resettled the Jews in that area after 1261 in the framework of his policy to promote the city's economy. Jewish tanners are documented in that urban region around 1300. The neighboring harbor of Kontoskalion served as sewer for the dirty waters of the tanning[48].

Jewish involvement in the tanning of hides in Constantinople increased in the following decades. This development was furthered by Venetian entrepreneurs. They engaged local craftsmen and apparently attracted others to process skins imported from the Black Sea, which after being tanned were shipped to Venice with added value. In order to further reduce the cost of the hides, Venice granted Venetian status to an unknown number of Jewish craftsmen, who thus enjoyed full exemption from imperial taxes. The cooperation between Venetian and Byzantine Jews in tanning, which also enabled evasion from imperial taxation, generated tension between Emperor Andronicus II and Venice from 1319 to 1324. Since only Jews are mentioned in that context, it is likely that they were dominant in tanning in Vlanga at that time. The Venetian Jews were compelled to resettle in the Venetian quarter in 1324 or shortly afterwards[49].

The Jewish neighborhood of Vlanga survived until the Ottoman conquest of 1453[50]. Jewish tanners presumably pursued their activity in its midst. One of them appears in the account book of the Venetian merchant Giacomo Badoer, who resided in Constantinople from 1436 to 1440. In 1438 Elijah Chanazi delivered to him wool from 200 sheep hides, which he had tanned and were sent to Venice[51]. Later in the same year he tanned and bleached one batch of 272 and another of 200 hides, also shipped to Venice[52]. The Jew Elijah Dedimari, who traded in pepper and silk[53], stored in his warehouse 300 salted hides of castrated horses imported from

[47] *Marcus N. Adler* (ed. and trans.), The Itinerary of Benjamin of Tudela (London 1907), Hebrew text 16–17, English trans. 14. New dating of his visit by *David Jacoby*, Benjamin of Tudela and his "Book of Travels", in: *Klaus Herbers* and *Felicitas Schmieder* (eds.), Venedig im Schnittpunkt der Kulturen. Außen- und Innensichten europäischer und nicht-europäischer Reisender im Vergleich (Venezia incrocio di culture. A confronto le percezioni dall interno e dall esterno di viaggiatori europei e non) (Roma 2008), in press.

[48] *David Jacoby*, The Jewish Community of Constantinople from the Komnenan to the Palaiologan Period, in: Vizantijskij vremennik 55/2 (80) (1998) 31–40, repr. in *Jacoby*, Byzantium no. V.

[49] *David Jacoby*, Les quartiers juifs de Constantinople à l'époque byzantine, in: Byzantion 37 (1967) 191–194, 196–207, repr. in *David Jacoby*, Société et démographie à Byzance et en Romanie latine (London 1975) no. II.

[50] Ibid. 194–196.

[51] Badoer 395 lines 2–9, 435 lines 14–18.

[52] Badoer 434 lines 20–21, 582 lines 23–24.

[53] Badoer 188 lines 32–36, 803 lines 20–21.

the Black Sea for Badoer[54]. It is unclear whether he was involved in the tanning business.

Jewish tanners are also attested in several ports of the eastern Mediterranean under Venetian rule in the late medieval period. In Candia the tanneries were situated outside the western city gates along the Bay of Dermata or 'Bay of hides'[55]. The location of the Jewish quarter along that bay was clearly related to the exercise of tanning among Jews, attested in 1228, although there was no Jewish monopoly in the field[56]. The ritual slaughter of animals provided skins, and Jewish butchers acted as middlemen between the owners of herds and tanners, both Jewish and Christian. Yet Jews also bought dried and salted skins from Christian merchants and butchers, as in 1271[57]. In 1305 a Cretan Jew commissioned the construction of a mill for the grinding of various materials, including acorn cups providing tannin used in the tanning process[58]. The leather produced by Jews was not always of good quality, as attested in 1342[59]. Incidentally, in 1396–1398 the governor of Canea, Pietro Nani, bought a large quantity of skins at the slaughterhouse. Once they had been tanned he took advantage of his position to compel Jewish cobblers and other craftsmen to produce for him a substantial number of shoes, which he obviously intended to export. As a result, there was a shortage of shoes on the local market[60]. A contract of 1419 between two Jews of Candia provided for the tanning of skins by one of the partners[61]. Cretan Jews participated in the import of skins from the Turkish emirates of Asia Minor, which were tanned in Crete. In 1371 Salomon Astrigo entrusted 22 ducats to Elkanah son of Elkanah for the import of hides from Palatia (ancient Miletos), in the emirate of Menteshe[62]. In 1370 Shemaryah of Negroponte and Mordechay son of Yehudah de Medico of Candia

54 Badoer 394 lines 2–3, 7–13, 17–21. The salting preserved the hides until the tanning was performed.

55 The name appears in 1352: *Sally McKee* (ed.), Wills from Late Medieval Crete, 1313–1420, vol. I (Washington, D. C. 1998) 247.

56 Ordinance of 1228 against the soaking of skins in the water of the ritual bath: Taqqanoth 8, no. 15.

57 PS nos. 37, 72.

58 *Charalambos Gasparis*, He ge kai oi agrotes sten mesaionike Krete, 13os–14os ai. (= Land and Peasants in Medieval Crete, 13th –14th c) (National Hellenic Research Foundation, Institute for Byzantine Research, Monographs 4, Athens 1997) 105.

59 *Spyridon M. Theotokes* (ed.), Thespismata tes benetikes gerousias, 1281–1385 (= Decrees of the Venetian Senate, 1281–1385) vol. I (Athens 1937) 225–226, no. 543.

60 ASV, Avvogaria di Comun, Raspe, V/II, fol. 49r, 16 March 1402. Nani was also accused of other misdeeds: *Noiret*, Documents 126–127. For his tenure of office, see ibid. 91–92.

61 *Chryssa Maltezou*, Métiers et salaires en Crète vénitienne (XVe siècle), in: Byzantinische Forschungen 12 (1987) 329–330.

62 The deal concerned hides and not leather, as stated by *Silvano Borsari*, I movimenti del porto di Candia AA. 1369–1372 (*Dal repertorio del notaio Giorgio Aymo*), in: Università di Macerata, Annali della Facoltà di Lettere e Filosofia 30–31 (1997–1998) 335. On the import of hides from Asia Minor, see *Elizabeth A. Zachariadou*, Trade and Crusade. Venetian Crete and the Emirates of Menteshe and Aydin (1300–1415) (Library of the Hellenic Institute of Byzantine and Post-Byzantine Studies 11, Venice 1983) 264, s. v. skins.

jointly traded in hides in Negroponte, the main city of the island of Euboea and an important transit port in which Venice had a quarter from 1211 onward[63]. It is unclear whether they also dealt with tanning.

Jewish tanners were active in Coron and Modon, two ports of the southwestern Peloponnesus under Venetian rule from 1207 onward. In 1357 Moses son of David from Coron and another Jew, both residents of Candia, shipped skins to Coron and promised to pay for them after their return from that city[64]. The former resident of Coron must have been acquainted with local Jewish tanners there and assumed that tanning would be cheaper than in Candia. Fourteenth and fifteenth-century Venetian ordinances and several travelers refer to tanners among the Jews living in a suburb of Modon[65]. In 1464 only Jewish tanners appear to have been available in the city[66]. Interestingly, Jews owning sheep and goats in the vicinity are attested in 1483[67]. It is unclear since when this was the case.

As noted earlier, Benjamin of Tudela encountered Jewish silk workers in Constantinople around 1160. High-grade silk manufacture collapsed in the city in the wake of its fall to the Latins in 1204, and the local silk workers moved to Asia Minor to pursue the exercise of their craft. Silk was later traded in Constantinople, yet the production of silk textiles was not revived until the Ottoman period[68]. There is some evidence suggesting the pursuit of silk manufacturing in Thessalonica in the fourteenth century. However, as noted above, we have no information regarding the economic activity of the city's Jews. Benjamin of Tudela was especially impressed by Jewish participation in the silk branch of Thebes, whether as weavers or tailors[69]. Thebes pursued the production of silk textiles in the thirteenth and fourteenth century[70]. The continuous existence of the local Jewish community is attested in that period[71]. However, whether Theban Jews participated then in local silk manufacture remains an open question, in view of the lack of evidence in that respect.

63 *Borsari*, Ricchi e poveri 211, n. 3. On the quarter, see *David Jacoby*, La consolidation de la domination de Venise dans la ville de Négrepont (1205–1390): un aspect de sa politique coloniale, in: *Chryssa A. Maltezou* e *Peter Schreiner* (eds.), Bisanzio, Venezia e il mondo franco-greco (XIII–XV secolo) (Atti del Colloquio Internazionale organizzato nel centenario della nascita di Raymond – Joseph Loenertz o. p., Venezia, 1–2 dicembre 2000) (Venezia 2002) 151-187.

64 ZF no. 104; see also no. 120, which relates to the same journey.

65 *Joshua Starr*, Romania. The Jewries of the Levant after the Fourth Crusade (Paris 1949) 64, 66-67.

66 *Sathas*, Documents, vol. IV, 33-34.

67 Ibid. 127

68 *David Jacoby*, The Jews and the Silk Industry of Constantinople, in: *Jacoby*, Byzantium no. XI, 1-20; *David Jacoby*, The Silk Trade of Late Byzantine Constantinople, in: *Sümer Atasoy* (ed.), 550th Anniversary of the Istanbul University. International Byzantine and Ottoman Symposium (XVth century) (30-31 May 2003) (Istanbul 2004) 129-144.

69 *David Jacoby*, Silk in Western Byzantium before the Fourth Crusade, in: Byzantinische Zeitschrift 84/85 (1991/1992) 466, 485-487, repr. in *Jacoby*, Trade no. VII.

70 *David Jacoby*, The Production of Silk Textiles in Latin Greece, in: Technognosia ste latinokratoumene Ellada (= Technology in Latin-Occupied Greece) (Athens 2000) 24-27, repr. in *Jacoby*, Commercial exchange no. XII.

71 *Steven B. Bowman*, The Jews of Byzantium, 1204-1453 (Tuscaloosa, Alabama 1985) 269-270, no. 60a; 287, no. 92; 296, no. 108 note; 302-303, no. 117.

In any event, some of them were acquainted with its sources of raw materials and its operation. This was certainly the case of Moses son of Shabbetai Galimidi, who in 1260–1263 left Thebes for Negroponte. His knowledge regarding silk was undoubtedly one of the reasons that prompted David Kalomiti, a rich merchant of Negroponte involved in silk transactions, to recruit him in his service. In the 1290s Kalomiti entrusted Galimidi's sons with the collection of silk. It is unclear whether the reference is to raw material, silk textiles, or both, yet the operations must have taken place in Euboea and presumably also in neighboring territories. After David Kalomiti's death the relations between his sons and those of Galimidi soured, and some of these fled. It is not coincidental that one of them who had resided for some time in Corinth settled in Thebes after the earthquake of 1303, while another established himself in Andros, an island producing both raw silk and silk textiles in that period[72].

Jewish silk weaving was practiced in Candia on a modest scale. The purchase of small quantities of raw silk, in one case by a woman in 1373, suggests the domestic manufacture of small pieces such as girdles, hoods, veils and kerchiefs, similar to those produced by Jewish women in Modon in the late fifteenth century[73]. Yet there were also Jewish silk weavers who produced larger pieces[74]. Their sendals did not always meet the required quality standard, as reported in 1342[75]. Some Jews of Chios traded in silk, as attested in 1398 and in 1408, yet presumably on a small scale[76]. In 1408 Aharon Lachano and Elijah Fogiano jointly operated a dyeing workshop in the city. Another Jewish dyer is recorded in Chios in 1456[77].

Jews also practiced crafts other than tanning or silk weaving. A large number of cobblers worked in Candia in the fourteenth century, in addition to those attested in Canea around 1400[78]. In 1420 a Jewish mason and his Christian partner undertook to build a cistern for a Jewish physician in Candia[79]. A dagger was commissioned in 1394 from a blacksmith in Chios. Salomon Spagnoli and his son Joste

[72] The case is reported in an anonymous and undated Hebrew letter, translated by *Bowman*, The Jews of Byzantium 234-240, no. 30. It has been discussed by several authors. I shall return to the issue and justify the dates mentioned here in a forthcoming study. On silk in Andros, see *Jacoby*, Silk in Western Byzantium 460-462; *Jacoby*, The Production of Silk Textiles 29.

[73] For Crete: *Borsari*, Ricchi e poveri 220; for Modon: *Starr*, Romania 64.

[74] *Borsari*, Ricchi e poveri 220-221.

[75] *Theotokes*, Thespismata, vol. I, 226, no. 544.

[76] *Domenico Gioffrè*, Atti rogati in Chio nella seconda metà del XIV secolo, in: Bulletin de l'Institut historique belge de Rome 34 (1962) 393; *Michel Balard*, La Romanie génoise (XIIe - début du XVe siècle) (Bibliothèque des Écoles françaises d'Athènes et de Rome 235, Rome 1978) 283.

[77] *Philip P. Argenti*, The Occupation of Chios by the Genoese and their Administration of the Island, 1346-1566, vol. I (Cambridge 1958) 442-443, 647, and vol. III, 743-745, no. 32. Fogiano is also recorded earlier as Foihano, yet without indication of his occupation: *Paola Villa*, Documenti sugli Ebrei a Chio nel 1394, in: Atti della Società Ligure di Storia Patria, n. s. 5 (79) (1965) 128, no. 4.

[78] *Sally McKee*, Uncommon Dominion. Venetian Crete and the Myth of Ethnic Purity (Philadelphia 2000) 94-95, and see above, p. 34.

[79] *Maltezou*, Métiers et salaires 326.

pursued the same occupation in Candia before 1424[80]. A shipwright was active in Chios in 1456[81]. However, commerce and moneylending were clearly the main Jewish activities in the eastern Mediterranean of the late Middle Ages.

The range of goods Jews handled in local retail and wholesale trade extended beyond those mentioned above, as illustrated for Crete. In 1276 a Jew of Canea was robbed of wax, silk and grain while trading in the countryside to the east of the city along the bay of Suda[82]. Various sources mention women's finery, ironware, haired skins and tanned hides of domestic origin[83], as well as imported textiles, from western woolens of rather modest quality to luxury velvet[84]. Diversity in local Jewish trade is also found elsewhere[85].

The number of Jewish residents of Crete and Negroponte engaging in regional maritime trade appears to have been quite substantial by the last decades of the thirteenth century. The volume of their operations induced Venice to enhance its fiscal revenue by imposing a discriminatory tax of 5% upon goods imported or exported by its Jews, similar to that imposed upon foreigners. This tax, initially collected in Crete before 1290, was extended in that year to Negroponte, as well as to other Venetian colonies and outposts except for Tyre[86]. The Jews evaded that high rate by arriving at agreements with Venetian citizens, who presumably in return for a payment declared the formers' commodities as their own. In September 1290 Venice threatened those defrauding its treasury by that device with the confiscation of half their goods[87].

The large geographic range and complex ramifications of Jewish maritime trade is amply illustrated from the second half of the thirteenth century onward. To the cases adduced above we may add a few others. In 1273 or somewhat later a Cretan Jew and his Christian associates returning from Thessalonica were robbed of their goods by pirates based in Monemvasia, the main port of the Byzantine Pelopon-

80 *Gian Giacomo Musso*, Gli Ebrei nel Levante genovese: ricerche di archivio, Berio – Bollettino bibliografico quadrimestriale 10/2 (1970) 19; ASV, Notai di Candia, b. 25, Giorgio Candachiti, fol. 224r.-v., deals with Joste Spagnoli's widow.

81 *Argenti*, The Occupation of Chios, vol. I, 443, 648.

82 *Gottlieb L. Fr. Tafel* und *Georg M. Thomas* (eds.), Urkunden zur älteren Handels- und Staatsgeschichte der Republik Venedig, vol. III (Wien 1856–1857) 257; dating by *Gareth Morgan*, The Venetian Claims Commission of 1278, in: Byzantinische Zeitschrift 69 (1976) 431, no. 137.

83 Taqqanoth 5, no. 10, of 1228; *Noiret*, Documents 253–254, 269, respectively of 1416 and 1419.

84 *Silvano Borsari*, Il mercato dei tessuti a Candia (1373–1375), in: Archivio veneto, 5th. ser. 143 (1994) 8, 13, 19–26.

85 For details, see below.

86 *Roberto Cessi* (ed.), Deliberazioni del Maggior Consiglio di Venezia, vol. III (Bologna 1931–1950) 274, § 94. See also *David Jacoby*, Venice and the Venetian Jews in the Eastern Mediterranean, in: *Gaetano Cozzi* (ed.), Gli Ebrei e Venezia (secoli XIV–XVIII) (Milano 1987) 40, repr. in *Jacoby*, Studies no. X; *David Jacoby*, The Demographic Evolution of Euboea under Latin Rule, 1205–1470, in: *Julian Chrysostomides*, *Charalambos Dendrinos*, *Jonathan Harris* (eds.), The Greek Islands and the Sea (Proceedings of the First International Colloquium held at the Hellenic Institute, Royal Holloway, University of London, 21–22 September 2001) (Camberley, Surrey 2004) 160. For Tyre, see following note.

87 *Cessi*, Deliberazioni, vol. III, 283, § 124.

nesus[88]. In Negroponte the tax of 5% was presumably related to the export of raw silk, silk textiles, or both to Venice[89]. In 1286 a Jew from crusader Acre granted a piece of samite apparently bought in Negroponte and woolens to two Venetians in return for a loan[90]. Jewish merchants from the Aegean traded with Acre and Tyre before 1291[91]. Cretan Jews were regularly traveling to Alexandria before 1301[92]. They pursued that activity in the following decade, as implied by the complaints of the Dominican inquisitor Andreas Doto against them, voiced in 1314 or somewhat earlier and reproduced by the canonist Oldrado de Ponte[93]. Cretan Jews continued to do so even after Venice imposed a ban on trade with Egypt in 1323. Jewish and foreign merchants claimed that it did not apply to them since they paid the dues levied from aliens in Crete. In response Doge Giovanni Soranzo extended the ban to all the island's inhabitants in July 1324[94]. The resumption of direct trade between Venice and Egypt in 1345 reduced the role of Crete as intermediary until 1374[95]. Yet in 1357 a Jew and a Greek of Candia jointly exported to Damietta copper imported from an unknown western source[96].

In 1318 Venice changed its policy in Negroponte and abolished the discriminatory rate it had imposed on Jewish maritime trade, in order to promote an increase in the number of its Jews in the city[97]. In 1321 two Jewish partners of Negroponte involved in regional maritime trade reported a loss of 1,544 hyperpers and a third Jew a loss of 42 hyperpers, both inflicted by Byzantine pirates operating in the Aegean[98]. There is no indication about the commodities they handled. On the other hand, around 1340 some Venetian Jews were trading in samites, most likely collecting them from weaving workshops in Euboea and Andros and exporting them to Venice. In 1340 a group of Jews who had recently obtained Venetian status complained that Jewish tax collectors in the service of the feudal lords of Euboea con-

[88] *Tafel* und *Thomas*, Urkunden, vol. III, 160–161; dating by *Morgan*, The Venetian Claims Commission 429, no. 79.
[89] On this export, see below, next paragraph.
[90] *David Jacoby*, L'expansion occidentale dans le Levant: les Vénitiens à Acre dans la seconde moitié du treizième siècle, in: Journal of Medieval History 3 (1977) 248–249, repr. in *Jacoby*, Recherches no. VII.
[91] See previous note and for Tyre, above, n. 87.
[92] As implied by BB no. 354.
[93] *David Jacoby*, Venice, the Inquisition and the Jewish Communities of Crete in the early 14th Century, in: Studi veneziani 12 (1970) 128–129, 138–141, repr. in *Jacoby*, Recherches no. IX. Translation of Doto's arguments by *Norman Zacour*, Jews and Saracens in the Consilia of Oldradus de Ponte (Pontifical Institute of Mediaeval Studies, Studies and Texts 100, Toronto 1990) 36–37.
[94] *David Jacoby*, Creta e Venezia nel contesto economico del Mediterraneo orientale sino alla metà del Quattrocento, in: *Gherardo Ortalli* (ed.), Venezia e Creta (Atti del Convegno internazionale di studi, Iraklion-Chanià, 30 settembre – 5 ottobre 1997) (Venezia 1998) 97–98.
[95] Ibid. 99.
[96] ZF 67, no. 91.
[97] *Jacoby*, The Demographic Evolution of Euboea 161. The rate was maintained in Crete: see above, n. 94.
[98] *Thomas*, Diplomatarium, vol. I, 183–184.

tinued to collect from them the trade tax on behalf of these lords. They requested Venice to intervene in order to ensure them the same fiscal exemption as that enjoyed by the *Judei antiqui* of Venice. Leo Psoma of Negroponte presented the petition in Venice, where he must have been involved in trade[99]. Some twenty years later he was importing raw silk to Venice on a large scale. In 1361 the verdict inflicting upon him the huge fine of 4,000 hyperpers or more than 1,000 ducats for illegal dealings was quashed and he was exceptionally allowed to transfer that sum or its equivalent in goods on board a state galley sailing to Negroponte. In 1440 the Venetian Senate stressed the importance of the state revenue deriving from Jewish trade in Negroponte. A petition submitted by the Jews of Negroponte in 1452 mentions commercial journeys to Genoese Chios, Turkish Asia Minor, Rhodes, ruled by the Hospitallers, and other destinations[100].

We have already noted some commercial operations of Cretan Jews directed toward Constantinople. These operations were undoubtedly furthered by the presence of Venetian Jews established in the Venetian quarter of the Byzantine capital, among them immigrants from Crete who retained links with their family in the island[101]. In 1350 the Venetian Jew David Yalomati, who resided in Constantinople, gave power of attorney to Samuel son of Samson to collect in his name in Crete money owed by Moyse Casani, a resident of Candia, transfer it to David's son Elijah, who obviously would be there, and appear before the Venetian authorities in the island if necessary[102].

As noted above, Jewish trade between Crete and Venice was not limited to kasher goods. A decree issued in 1402 exceptionally allowed some Jews undoubtedly living in Venetian colonies to send money from Venice to Corfu, Coron, Modon and Crete on board state galleys in return for a fee of two percent[103]. A Jewish merchant and his wife from Candia resided in Venice some time before 1414[104]. Isaiah son of Hayyim was a Cretan merchant who often traveled to that city. In Alexandria Elijah Capsali gave him power of attorney in 1420 to obtain in Venice a loan of 130 ducats and transfer the sum to the Egyptian port or to Candia[105]. In 1422 he entrusted the same Jew, another one of Candia and a resident of Venice to

[99] Ed. by *François-Xavier Leduc* (ed.), Venezia – Senato. Deliberazioni miste, Registre XIX (1340–1341) (Istituto veneto di scienze, lettere ed arti, Venezia – Senato. Deliberazioni miste VI, Venise 2004) 18, no. 36. See *Jacoby*, The Demographic Evolution of Euboea 161–162.

[100] Ibid. 164–165.

[101] *Jacoby*, Les quartiers juifs de Constantinople 205–214.

[102] *Angeliki E. Laiou*, Un notaire vénitien à Constantinople: Antonio Bresciano et le commerce international en 1350, in: *Michel Balard, Angeliki E. Laiou, Catherine Otten-Froux*, Les Italiens à Byzance (Byzantina Sorbonensia 6, Paris 1987) 125–126, no. 27.

[103] *Jacoby*, Venice and the Venetian Jews 48–49 and 57, n. 81.

[104] ASV, Avvogaria di Comun, Miscellanea civil, b. 31, fasc. 27, ed. by *David Jacoby*, Inquisition and Converts in Candia and Negroponte in the 14th and 15th Centuries, in: *Sefunoth*, Annual for Research on the Jewish Communities in the East 8 (1964) 314–316, no. 2, with commentary ibid. 308–310 [Hebrew].

[105] Ed. by *Verlinden*, Marchands chrétiens et juifs 53.

obtain for him in that city full Venetian citizenship[106]. In 1428 a Jew of Candia engaged a Majorcan Jew as servant for the duration of his round-trip to Venice[107].

Jews also conducted local, regional and long-distance trade in and around Genoese Chios. Moses Cohen together with some Jews of Pera imported foodstuffs such as grain, flour, chickpeas and figs, the dyestuff orchil, as well as skins, cloth, carpets and blankets from the island of Mytilene (Lesbos) to Chios[108]. Jews bought imported goods, such as silks in 1408, pearls and precious stones in 1413, and fustians in 1414[109]. In 1450 or somewhat earlier the Christian Lazarus Catalanus entrusted a Jew with the purchase of grain[110]. Elijah Calaihi traded in Pera before 1394[111].

It is noteworthy that in Chios Jews handled two commodities, grain and mastic, that were closely supervised by the local authorities. The *Officium provisionis*, apparently composed of wealthy residents, namely two Latins, two Greeks and one Jew, was responsible for the supply of grain to Chios. It concluded agreements with merchants undertaking to import specific quantities of grain from Apulia, Sicily, or Phocea on the coast of Asia Minor, found the necessary capital to finance the deals, and guaranteed minimum prices it would pay[112]. In 1404 the Jew Benjamin was member of that office, and the Jew Nathan undertook to bring in the same year 200 modia grains to Chios[113]. The gross sale of mastic was a monopoly of the Maona of Chios, the body composed of Genoese settlers governing the island[114]. In 1386 this institution promised mastic to a Jew in return for a loan. In 1394 the Jew ceded his right to obtain the remainder of the mastic to two Genoese, who were to sell it in Cyprus, Damascus or Alexandria[115]. In 1403 Elijah Cohen concluded in Chios a contract with a Turk of Bursa by which he undertook to deliver him thirteen cases of mastic either in Pergamon or in Iasmati (Ayiasmatin-Hagiasmatin, presently Altun-ova), situated on the coast of Asia Minor between Chios and Mytilene[116]. All three localities were then under Ottoman rule.

[106] Ed. by *Ashtor*, Ebrei cittadini 147–148, and commentary ibid. 152–153. Ashtor was completely mistaken about the issue of Jews and Venetian citizenship, for which see *Jacoby*, Venice and the Venetian Jews 34–38.

[107] Ed. by *David Jacoby*, Quelques aspects de la vie juive en Crète dans la première moitié du XVe siècle. Actes du Troisième Congrès international d'études crétoises (Rethymnon 1971) vol. II (Athènes 1974) 115, n. 39, and commentary ibid. 114–115, repr. in *Jacoby*, Recherches no. X.

[108] *Gioffrè*, Atti rogati in Chio 348–349, 389–390.

[109] *Musso*, Gli Ebrei 16.

[110] *Argenti*, The Occupation of Chios, vol. III, 629, no. 215.

[111] *Villa*, Documenti sugli Ebrei 126–127, no. 3.

[112] On the operation of the office, see *Balard*, La Romanie génoise 388–389, 392, and the following note.

[113] *Paola Piana Toniolo* (ed.), Notai genovesi in Oltremare. Atti rogati a Chio da Gregorio Panissaro (1403–1405) (Accademia Ligure di Scienze e Lettere, Serie Fonti 2, Genova 1995) 176–177, no. 126; and 180–181, no. 131.

[114] *Michel Balard*, Le mastic de Chio, monopole génois (XIVe–XVIe s.), in: *Raoul Curiel* et *Rika Gyselen* (eds.), Itinéraires d'Orient. Hommages à Claude Cahen (Bures-sur-Yvette 1994) 223–228.

[115] *Villa*, Documenti sugli Ebrei 138–144, nos. 9–10.

[116] *Piana Toniolo*, Notai genovesi 105–106, nos. 52–53. My thanks to Elizabeth Zachariadou for identifying and locating Iasmati.

The Jews residing in Constantinople engaged in regional maritime commerce, yet they appear to have been primarily involved in local trade. Two Jews bought respectively a garment and a piece of cotton cloth from a Genoese merchant in Pera around 1390[117]. In 1389 the physician Baronus living in that suburb willed a quarter of his movable wealth to his son-in-law Ismael from Chios, also a physician, yet on condition that his investments would be limited to trade from the island of Tenedos northward and in the Black Sea[118]. In 1394 Shemaryah, a nephew or grandson of Baronus, and a Jew of Candia, settled their business accounts in Chios[119]. In 1398 two Jews of Pera traded in Mytilene and Chios[120]. In 1437-1438 Baron, most likely a grandson of the physician Baronus mentioned above, acted jointly with *magister* Elijah, who appears to have been a Venetian Jew, buying silken veils from the Venetian Giacomo Badoer[121]. The two, as well as Barona, surely a relative of Baron, appear in 1443 among the creditors of Gabriele Catacalo, a Greek of Candia who served as notary and interpreter at the court of the Venetian bailo in Constantinople between 1434 and 1449. The verdict issued by the bailo Marino Soranzo in 1443 was transcribed ten years later in Pera at the request of a Genoese creditor[122]. The cooperation of Venetian Jews with other merchants in Constantinople is illustrated in 1418. Emperor Manuel II accused Venetian citizens, subjects and Jews of defrauding the imperial treasury by declaring at the customs goods belonging to imperial subjects and to Turks as their own[123].

The Venetian Giacomo Badoer conducted business with thirty Jews during his stay in Constantinople from 1436 to 1440. Most transactions involved Jews selling high-grade silk from the region of the Caspian Sea, requested by silk weavers in Venice, and purchasing western textiles or bartering the silk for these goods. In one

[117] *Michel Balard*, Péra au XIVe siècle: Documents notariés des archives de Gênes, in: *Balard, Laiou, Otten-Froux*, Les Italiens à Byzance 63, no. 139. Another customer, Lodixio Portonario, is attested in documents of 1389 and 1390 and thus provides an approximate date for the leaf from the merchant's account book on which the Jews are recorded: ibid. 31, no. 59; 34, no. 71; and 42, no. 102.

[118] Ibid. 35, no. 75, and see also no. 74. Similar restrictions appear in charters drafted in Black Sea ports limiting trade to the region extending as far as Abydos in the Dardanelles: *Nicolas Oikonomidès*, Hommes d'affaires grecs et latins à Constantinople (XIIIe–XVe siècles) (Montréal-Paris 1979) 39.

[119] *Villa*, Documenti sugli Ebrei 148–149 no. 12.

[120] See above, note 76.

[121] Joint operations in Badoer, 174 lines 17, 21; 219 lines 24–25; 287 lines 10–11; 340 lines 25–26, 28; 348 lines 18–20; 349 lines 18–19; 368 lines 28; 409 lines 2–3; 466 lines 4–5. Magister Elijah was a relative of a Venetian Jewess, mentioned in a letter of the bailo Pietro Contarini written in 1424: ed. by *Jacoby*, Les quartiers juifs de Constantinople 224, no. II.

[122] *Ausilia Roccatagliata*, Notai genovesi in oltremare. Atti rogati a Pera (1453), in: Atti della Società ligure di Storia patria, n. s. 39 (CXIII) (1999) 136–142, no. 11. For the tenure of office of Catacalo, see *Chryssa Maltezou*, O thesmos tou en Konstantinoupolei Benetou bailou (1268–1453) = The Institution of the Venetian Bailo in Constantinople, 1268–1453) (Athens 1970) 184 no. 33; 186–188 no. 37; 206 no. 53; 207–209 no. 58.

[123] *Julian Chrysostomides*, Venetian Commercial Privileges under the Palaeologi, in: Studi veneziani 12 (1970) 354–355, no. 19.

case Daniel de Anastaxo sold more than 1,385 pounds of silk worth 6,237 hyperpers, which he exchanged for silk cloth, silken veils and woolens of various qualities[124]. Several Jews bought western gold thread used in embroidery[125]. These commodities were partly intended for re-export to Ottoman territories and to Black Sea ports. Such was certainly the case of the woolens bought in 1438 by a Jew from Adrianople/Edirne, the Ottoman capital at that time[126]. There was a large demand for Italian silks and woolens among the Ottoman elite[127]. Yet Jews also handled other commodities. Wax imported from the Black Sea, especially from the region of Zagora in Bulgaria, was shipped to Venice on a large scale[128]. While two local Jews sold wax bought from importers[129], Jacob of Sofia arrived in 1438 in Constantinople with a large consignment of wax that he sold directly to Venetian merchants, in one case in exchange for woolens from Maiorca[130]. Elijah Flaflama and Elijah Dedimari bought pepper imported from Caffa in the Crimea, which they sold to Venetians[131]. On the other hand, the Jew Zechariah purchased tin brought from Venice[132].

Jewish trade in the eastern Mediterranean was furthered by two factors: Jewish mobility across political and cultural boundaries, more extensive than for other ethnic, religious or cultural groups, and linguistic aptitudes. Negroponte attracted Jewish immigrants from the Greek mainland and Crete in the thirteenth and fourteenth century, yet there was also emigration from Negroponte to Candia. Spanish and Oriental Jews appear in that city by the mid-fourteenth century, as well as in Constantinople. Cretan Jews established in Constantinople and Alexandria have already been mentioned[133]. Some Jews from Genoese Chios settled in Pera[134]. Connections between family members and partners dispersed throughout the eastern Mediterranean and beyond were an important asset in business.

The use of Hebrew facilitated connections and transactions between Jews living in different cultural milieus. The extensive business of Cretan Jews in Alexandria in the 1420s was undoubtedly furthered by their meeting with Jews from other Christian and from Muslim countries in the *funduq* or *fondaco* for foreign Jews, attested in 1405[135]. In addition, migration across the Mediterranean created polyglot Jewish communities. Polyglot Jews acted as middlemen and interpreters, functions that enabled the collection of precious commercial information. Jews appear as official

[124] Badoer, 792 lines 1–18, 793 lines 2–9.

[125] Badoer, 197 lines 4–5,10–11,15–18, 21–22; 229 lines 25–31, 35–37.

[126] Badoer, 511 lines 11–13.

[127] *Jacoby*, The Silk Trade of Late Byzantine Constantinople 134–140, 142–144.

[128] *Giovanni Bertelè*, Il Libro dei conti di Giacomo Badoer (Costantinipoli 1436–1440). Complemento e indici (Padova 2002) 161–163, s. v. Zera.

[129] Badoer 30 lines 27–29; 55 lines 18–20; 97 lines 43–44; 170 lines 2–4.

[130] Badoer 740 lines 20–38; 743 lines 37–40; 745 lines 12–13.

[131] Badoer 745 line 25; 759 line 11; 760 lines 2–5, 18–19.

[132] Badoer 74 lines 25–27; 75 lines 18–19.

[133] *Jacoby*, The Demographic Evolution of Euboea 159-162, 165–167; *Jacoby*, Quelques aspects 108–112.

[134] See below, note 154.

[135] See *Ashtor*, New Data 81. The authorities would not have established a *funduq* for local Jews.

and private middlemen in Crete until 1433, when Venice prohibited their employment in that capacity in transactions between Christians[136]. On the other hand, private Jewish brokers are attested in fifteenth-century Constantinople[137], and official ones operated in Alexandria[138]. In this city the Mamluk authorities and some foreign consuls employed Jews as official interpreters[139].

Jewish moneylending is often attested by notarial and official documents, since it generated lawsuits, legislation and taxation. However, it is important to note that its nature differed widely. We have already mentioned advance payments for the delivery of cheese, wine and grain, as well as loans in kind, such as wine, cheese and grain, the latter to be sown in return for the entire product of the harvest to be delivered at the creditor's home[140]. Jewish retailers in Rethymno and undoubtedly also in other Cretan cities sold various commodities on credit[141]. All these transactions, which often resulted in heavy indebtedness among peasants, were prohibited in 1393[142]. From the thirteenth century onward many urban residents in Crete, including Venetian fiefholders, prominent Greeks, as well as some of the duke's councilors and members of their staff took consumption loans or bought goods on credit[143]. The treaty concluded by the Cretan archon Alexios Kallergis with Venice in 1299 contains a provision allowing Jews to reside wherever they wish[144]. His intervention on their behalf was presumably related to loans obtained from them during his rebellion. In the years 1360–1381 Yehudah de Medego son of Elijah granted in Candia loans to members of the Venetian and Greek aristocracy of Crete, 1,440 hyperpers in one case and 8,038 hyperpers in another[145]. In 1408 Cassani of Candia loaned 500 ducats to the local authorities for the equipment of the galley of Crete[146]. David Kalomiti lent money to the feudal lords of Euboea in the second half of the thirteenth century, as implied by the Hebrew letter referring to

136 *Jacoby*, Venice, the Inquisition and the Jewish Communities 128–138; *Noiret*, Documents 359–361.

137 *Giovanni Bertelè*, Il Libro dei conti di Giacomo Badoer 173, s. v. Cain; 196–197, s. v. Pulixoto; 198, s. v. Samaria zudio sanser.

138 *Verlinden*, Marchands chrétiens et juifs 69; *Ashtor*, New Data 89.

139 Ibid. 88–89.

140 Grain: LM no. 358. On loans in wine and cheese, see above, p. 32.

141 See above, note 24.

142 See above, p. 29.

143 See below, p. 45; *Johannes Jegerlehner* (ed.), Beiträge zur Verwaltungsgeschichte Kandias im XIV. Jahrhunderts, in: Byzantinische Zeitschrift 13 (1904) 450, § 64: prohibition of 1369 regarding officials.

144 Ed. by *Konstantinos Mertzioș*, He syntheke Eneton-Kalerge kai oi sunodeuontes auten katalologoi (= The Venetian-Kallergis Treaty and the Adjunct Lists), in: Kretika Chronika 3 (1949) 272, § 22. On the long rebellion of Kallergis and the treaty, see *Silvano Borsari*, Il dominio veneziano a Creta nel XIII secolo (Napoli 1963) 51–66.

145 *Borsari*, Ricchi e poveri 212 and n. 4.

146 *Freddy Thiriet*, La Romanie vénitienne au Moyen Âge. Le développement et l'exploitation du domaine colonial vénitien (XIIe–XVe siècles) (Bibliothèque des Écoles françaises d'Athènes et de Rome 193, Paris 1959) 408.

him, and possibly also to the Venetian authorities in Negroponte[147]. It is likely that David of Negroponte was granted Venetian status in 1268 after loaning a substantial sum to these same authorities[148]. Local Jews lent money to prominent men in the Catalan Duchy of Athens around 1370, and in the 1390s to the count of Cephalonia, Carlo Tocco, who had taken hold of Corinth, in this case in return for jewels as security[149]. In February 1389 two Jews of Chios jointly loaned 2,669 ducats for about two and a half months to the Maona of Chios[150]. Geronimo da Camoglio, bishop of Chios, claimed in the 1470s that his predecessors had been compelled to obtain loans burdened with heavy interest from Jews, since the Maona had failed to transfer to them the entire yearly amount it had promised[151].

Credit was an indispensable tool in local and especially regional trade. Jews around the eastern Mediterranean granted and received commercial, exchange and maritime loans and concluded unilateral *collegancia* contracts binding a sedentary investor to a traveling manager, who obtained one third of the profit. In 1301 the Jew Belus concluded two contracts by which Matteo Beaqua, like him a resident of Candia, invested capital in a *societas terre* for trade in Crete during three months and in a *cambium maritimum* with repayment of the loan in Alexandria in local currency[152]. Moses son of Yehudah of Candia granted 31 maritime loans totaling 1,002 hyperpers with interest within the second half of 1369, the rate of interest varying according to destination and the presumed length of the roundtrip, which included ports of the Aegean, Cyprus, Alexandria, Constantinople, Venice and Pisa. Within the years 1369–1372 he extended such loans amounting to more than 7,700 hyperpers[153]. In 1391 the Jewish physician Yishmael of Chios granted in Pera a commercial loan to Francesco Giustiniani de Campis, which had not been repaid by 1394[154]. In that year the Jew Raffael Catalano received in Chios a loan of 350 ducats from Giovanni Giustiniani, who acted on behalf of Domenico Cataneo of Genoa[155]. In 1400 the patriarchal court in Constantinople dealt with a commercial loan granted by a Jew to a Greek in the previous year[156]. In 1418 Elijah of Rethymno loaned in Candia 2,200 hyperpers to Niccolò Taiapetra of that city, a sum not yet repaid in 1421[157], and in 1414 Lazar Todescho granted 1,082 hyperpers to Bernardo Balbi and his brothers,

[147] See above, n. 72.
[148] *Jacoby*, The Demographic Evolution of Euboea 160–161.
[149] Ibid. 164.
[150] *Enrico Basso* (ed.), Notai genovesi in Oltremare. Atti rogati a Chio da Giuliano de Canella (2 Novembre 1380–31 Marzo 1381) (Accademia Ligure di Scienze e Lettere [Serie Fonti] 1, Athena 1993) 101–102 no. 45.
[151] *Argenti*, The Occupation of Chios, vol. I, 655. Geronimo, bishop from 1470, negotiated a new settlement with the Maona after the intervention of Pope Sixtus IV, elected in 1471.
[152] BB, nos. 353–354.
[153] *Borsari*, Ricchi e poveri 213–214; *Borsari*, I movimenti del porto di Candia 327–329, 338.
[154] Ed. by *Villa*, Documenti sugli Ebrei 145–147 no. 11.
[155] Ibid. 127–129 no. 4.
[156] *Franz Miklosich* et *Joseph Müller* (eds.), Acta et diplomata graeca medii aevi sacra et profana, vol. II (Wien 1860–1890) 313–314 no. DXXX.
[157] Ed. by *Verlinden*, Marchands chrétiens et juifs 61–62.

residents of Venice[158]. The will of Bartolomeo Zane de Visdanelis, drafted in Patras in 1430, provided for the reimbursement of two commercial loans granted by Jews. One of the creditors was to obtain 1,000 pounds of iron, to be brought from Lepanto, in addition to a sum of money, the other a sum corresponding to the debt recorded in the testator's account book[159]. By the early fifteenth century the Jews of Rethymno were investing money in *colleganze* on a large scale, besides exporting cheese and wine to Egypt. In 1412 prominent Latin residents of the city pointed to the considerable profit the Jews enjoyed from these investments, in addition to money-lending[160]. We may safely assume that this was also the case in Candia.

Jews conducted maritime trade with the assistance of agents or acted as agents and operated as partners in joint ventures. Jews appear as agents of Jews in Alexandria in 1428 and in Constantinople in 1437[161]. Around 1300 some Cretan Jews served as agents or partners of Christian Catalans on their way with western woolens to Cyprus, Rhodes, the Levant and Egypt. Partnerships between Cretan Jews and Venetian citizens residing in Venice or elsewhere, some of them belonging to the city's social elite, are attested in the first half of the fifteenth century. They involved the transfer of capital between Venice, Venetian colonies and Venetian outposts[162]. In 1394 Elisha of Chios jointly with several Latins insured the cargo on board the ship of Bernabò Dentuto sailing to Altoluogo (also called Theologo, ancient Ephesos), in the emirate of Aydin[163]. In 1404 Elijah Cohen of Chios contributed 300 ducats to a joint venture with a capital of 8,800 ducats involving a sailing to Sicily and trade in that island[164].

Credit operations resulted in various cases in the transfer of rural land and dependent peasants into Jewish hands as acquisition from insolvent debtors, whether temporarily as security for loans or permanently, at least in principle. In the second half of the thirteenth century David Kallomiti of Negroponte had fields and vineyards in Euboea[165]. In 1370 four rich Jews of Negroponte held rural property belonging to the Latin patriarchate of Constantinople[166]. In 1402 Venice, alarmed by the increase in Jewish rural property in Euboea, ordered the Jews to relinquish all assets located outside the old Jewish quarter of Negroponte and prohibited further acquisitions[167]. Verdicts issued by the dukes of Crete in 1364 and 1372 illustrate Venice's strong opposition to the transfer of a specific category of property to Jews,

158 ASV, Notai di Candia, b. 26, Gasparino Cocco, fol. 88v.

159 Ed. by *Ernst Gerland*, Neue Quellen zur Geschichte des lateinischen Erzbistums Patras (Leipzig 1903) 213 and 215 no. 17.

160 *Noiret*, Documents 213. See also above, p. 44.

161 See respectively above, n. 41, and Badoer 179 lines 15–16, 188 lines 32, 40.

162 *Jacoby*, Venice and the Venetian Jews 48.

163 *Villa*, Documenti sugli Ebrei 149–151 no. 13.

164 *Piana Toniolo*, Notai genovesi 118–119 no. 65.

165 See above, note 72.

166 *Borsari*, Ricchi e poveri 219–220. In 1314 Pope Clement V united the functions of bishop of Negroponte and Latin patriarch of Constantinople, whose seat was since then in Negroponte: *Giorgio Fedalto*, La chiesa latina in Oriente, vol. I (Verona ^{2}1981) 281, 443.

167 *Sathas*, Documents, vol. II, 83–84 no. 303; also in *Noiret*, Documents 131–133.

namely, fiefs and sergeantries entailing military service granted by the state to Latins and some Greeks[168]. A verdict of 1414 ordered the immediate sale of real estate serving as collateral to a loan to Venetians capable of performing the required service[169]. In 1423 Venice issued a general ban on Jewish acquisitions of property outside the Jewish quarters in its overseas territories, and enjoined the Jews to sell the property they held within two years[170]. The decree was repeated in the following year with additional clauses to prevent transgressions[171]. Jews nevertheless continued to acquire property outside their quarters. Thus in 1450 the Jew Theodoro Cresto of Candia obtained a vineyard in the region of Bonifacio in southern Crete from a Greek peasant, as partial repayment of a loan[172].

There was apparently no limitation to Jewish rural property in the eastern Mediterranean outside the Venetian territories. In 1394 a Genoese judge in Chios allocated to Elijah Cohen a sum of money, a fruit garden, a field and part of a vineyard in compensation for a loan to Niccolò Tilano[173]. In 1398 the Jewess Ihera Melicha of Chios owned fruit gardens in the city's suburb and vicinity and other vineyards in the countryside[174]. Jews must have been eager to obtain rural land with their villeins as security for loans, for such lands' yield of revenue and, more importantly, for enabling close supervision over the production of kosher produce. Not surprisingly, therefore, Jews also leased land, like Salomon son of Abraham, a resident of Patras in the Peloponnesus, who for many years before 1436 had held a plot of rural land turned into a garden in the city's vicinity[175].

This brief survey is far from exhaustive. It covers only some major fields of Jewish economic activity and fails to deal extensively with various Jewish occupations such as those of rabbis, physicians, pharmacists, lawyers, teachers and scribes, as well as communal and ritual officers, which were often combined with trade and moneylending. Shopkeepers, servants and seasonal workers have been mentioned in passing only. The picture emerging from the evidence, overwhelmingly found in Venetian and Genoese sources, is necessarily fragmented and biased. It nevertheless allows some conclusions.

[168] *Maria K. Chairete*, Anekdota benetika eggrafa peri ton Ebraion en Krete (= Unpublished Venetian Documents regarding the Jews in Crete), in: Epeteris Etaireas byzantinon spoudon 33 (1964) 171–179, nos. 1-5: *exceptis tamen feudis que remanentur in dispositione ducalis dominii* and similar formulations. On the illegal transfer of a fief to a Jew in 1341, see *McKee*, Uncommon Dominion 71 and 184–187.

[169] *Chairete*, Anekdota benetika eggrafa 180–182 no. 6.

[170] *Noiret*, Documents 297–298. For Corfu, see *Jacoby*, Venice and the Venetian Jews 53, n. 26, and the study by Reinhold Mueller in this volume.

[171] *Eliyahu Ashtor*, Gli inizi della Comunità ebraica a Venezia, in: La Rassegna Mensile di Israel 44 (1978) 689–690, repr. in *idem*, The Jews and the Mediterranean Economy, Tenth to Fifteenth Centuries (London 1983) n. IV.

[172] ASV, Notai di Candia, b. 2, Francesco Avonal, fol. 3v. See also *Jacoby*, Venice and the Venetian Jews 37–38.

[173] *Villa*, Documenti sugli Ebrei 122–126, no. 2.

[174] *Gioffrè*, Atti rogati in Chio 379–381.

[175] *Gerland*, Neue Quellen 218–220, no. 19.

Jews operated within two distinct, though partly overlapping and strongly interwoven economic networks. Indeed, the internal network dealing with Jewish goods was a closed circuit, yet required close cooperation with non-Jews. It largely, though not entirely conformed to the features of the broader eastern Mediterranean economy within which it was integrated with respect to capital investment, business patterns, production, transportation, distribution and sale. It was also similarly subject to state regulation and taxation. However, the geographic range and orientations of its distribution pattern, especially for wine, were far more extensive than for non-kasher commodities since they were determined by the wide Jewish dispersion in the Mediterranean region and beyond. Some Jewish communities could not ensure the production of kasher food and wine, either because of their small size, unfavorable economic conditions in their region, or the absence of a rabbinical authority sanctioning the fitness of the commodities. As a result, these communities and scattered individual families depended upon provisioning from larger or well-supplied centers. However, the diffusion of kasher goods was also determined by a demand for alternative qualities, as for instance wine in Constantinople[176]. The three main ports of destination of Cretan products in the eastern Mediterranean acted as distribution centers. Constantinople supplied Jews in neighboring European and Asian territories and around the Black Sea[177]. Alexandria acted similarly with respect to provincial cities in Egypt[178], and Venice to northeastern Italy. Kasher commodities were clearly more expensive than others, as a result of the added cost of supervision, the special arrangements related to it, and a less competitive market than for other goods. In 1422 the wholesale price of a cask of Cretan wine in Alexandria was 12 ducats, whereas that of kasher wine was 14 1/2 ducats. In addition, the profit margin for the kasher wine was undoubtedly much larger, since its retail sale was expected to yield at least 23 ducats per cask[179].

There was no economic activity exclusively carried out by Jews, expect for ritual and communal functions, no legal impediments to the exercise of occupations, nor was any occupation imposed upon them, as often argued with respect to tanning in Byzantium. The Jews were firmly integrated within the production, manufacture and trade networks of Byzantium and Latin Romania, though to varying degrees determined by local and regional conditions. Their financial and actual involvement in maritime trade appears to have been more important than generally assumed, yet its extent and volume was restricted by two factors. Jews were entirely barred from the lucrative trans-Mediterranean trade in precious commodities, monopolized by the Venetian and Genoese social elites, and could only participate in it at the local or intermediate level, as illustrated for Crete and Constantinople. In addition, Jews lacked transportation facilities of their own, were reluctant to invest

[176] See above, pp. 30–31.

[177] Wine exported from Candia reached Tana at the mouth of the river Don: *Pegolotti*, La pratica 24: We may safely assume a similar transfer of kasher wine.

[178] As attested for Sicilian cheese: *Goitein*, A Mediterranean Society, vol. IV, 251–252.

[179] *Ashtor*, New Data 95–96, no. II.

in them, and only seldom acquired a share in small vessels[180]. As a result, they were totally absent from the large-scale trade and transportation of grain, alum and cotton across the Mediterranean.

Some developments were specific to the Jewish communities in the Venetian colonies. The growing fiscal burden upon them in the fourteenth and fifteenth centuries limited the capital available for investment in trade[181], and the restrictions on the acquisition of real estate undoubtedly enhanced the involvement of Jews in moneylending. In terms of capital, this appears to have been the largest sector of Jewish economic activity in Venetian Crete.

[180] The religious restrictions on sailing on Sabbath and Jewish holidays were clearly an indirect, though important factor in that respect and also account for the absence of Jewish sailors.

[181] *Thiriet*, La Romanie vénitienne 406–407; *Jacoby*, Venice and the Venetian Jews 40–41.

David Abulafia

The Jews of Sicily and Southern Italy: Economic Activity

The aim of this paper is to make a series of comparisons: between the economic activities of the Jews in Sicily and southern Italy in the early Middle Ages and the late Middle Ages; between the economic activities of the Jews on the mainland and on the island of Sicily (as well as its dependent territory of Malta). We are fortunate in the survival of a large range of sources – the Cairo Genizah letters for the early period, notarial acts and government decrees for the later period – and at first sight it seems a straightforward task to compare the evidence of these different groups of sources. However, some caution is needed. The Cairo Genizah letters document the activity of international merchants, in the main, with connections to Spain in the west, Tunisia in the south, Egypt and even Yemen and India in the east. Notarial evidence, on the other hand, tends to illuminate local communities with often quite restricted networks of trade and credit. Even bearing this in mind, it does seem possible to draw a broad distinction between an early period in which Jews played a leading role in the long-distance trade of the Mediterranean that passed through Sicily, and a later period in which their role as artisans and small traders was more confined, now that others – Genoese, Tuscan or Catalan Christians – dominated the longer distance networks of trade. Jews thus came to play the role of retail merchants, of distributors on a local scale. But it was precisely in this role that they were able to participate alongside local Christians in the economic recovery of the Italian South during the fifteenth century.

If we turn to the tenth and eleventh centuries, we are struck by the contrast between the wealth of documentation concerning the economic life of the Sicilian Jews and the lack of information concerning the economic life of the much larger communities of Muslims and Greeks on the island during the period of Islamic rule. The miraculous survival of the Cairo Genizah documents has resulted in this imbalance[1]. It is therefore hard to be sure whether the Jews were distinctive in their commercial interests; occasional references to partnerships with Muslims or even Christians suggest that others shared their interests, but it is possible that the Jewish merchants were able to exploit family connections right across the Mediterranean, and that they thus occupied a more prominent position in long-distance trade

[1] *S. D. Goitein*, A Mediterranean Society, vol. 1, Economic Foundations (Berkeley, Los Angeles 1967).

than their mere numbers would warrant. They seem to have been uninterested in some commodities, such as grain, which undoubtedly were being traded in massive quantities out of both Egypt and Sicily. Their speciality was the luxury trade, though they were also very interested in the cheese trade out of Syracuse, exporting kosher cheese as far as Egypt, and remaining involved in the cheese business right up to the fifteenth century. Dietary requirements certainly had a significant impact on the range of goods Jews produced and traded. Among notable imports handled by Sicilian Jews are found dyestuff such as brazil wood and lapis lazuli; silk was both imported and exported, and it was normal to bank one's spare cash in investments of silk. These were commodities which were traded along the much extended trade routes that carried Jews from Sicily and Tunisia all the way down the Red Sea to Yemen, and in some cases as far as India. However, the Jews of Sicily also took a significant interest in the export of unprocessed or semi-processed raw materials such as hides, as well as Sicilian cloths in the form of turbans, blankets and shawls[2].

One important feature of the trade of the Sicilian Jews in the Islamic and early Norman period is the fluidity of the community itself; Egyptian Jews would come to settle in Palermo, buying houses, marrying and, of course, making business deals with fellow Jews. Among notable arrivals were important Spanish Jews, such as Khalaf bar Ya'aqub *ha-Sefardi* ['the Spaniard'] in the early eleventh century, who retained a distinctive identity, but also possessed a magical ability to seize positions of leadership in the island[3]. Thus an intimate relationship with Spain long precedes the Catalan-Aragonese conquest of 1282, for in the open Islamic Mediterranean movement between al-Andalus and Sicily was constant and fluent. There was also a large community of north African settlers, who were to be a consistent feature of Sicilian Jewries: the political troubles that wracked north Africa in the mid-eleventh century acted as a stimulus to immigration, though occasionally it was Sicily that suffered local wars, with the result of net emigration. It was with Tunisia that the Sicilian Jews not surprisingly entertained the most intense relations, with Mazara (later to be superseded by Trapani) functioning as the major jumping-off point for Tunis or al-Mahdiyyah, termini of the Saharan gold caravans. Assuming that the Genizah merchants were a dominant force in the eleventh century, it then follows that by 1150 they had ceded control of the key trade routes, including that towards Sicily, to competitors better placed to service demand in the hinterland of an expanding western Europe: the Genoese, Pisans, Venetians[4]. They also lost con-

[2] *S. D. Goitein*, Sicily and southern Italy in the Cairo Genizah documents, in: Archivio storico per la Sicilia orientale 67 (1971) 9–33; see also *M. Gil*, The Jews in Sicily in the light of the Geniza documents, in: Italia Judaica. Atti del I Convegno internazionale (Rome 1983) 87–134.

[3] *M. Ben-Sasson*, The Jews of Sicily 825–1068. Documents and Sources (Oriens Judaicus, ser. 1, vol. 1, Jerusalem 1991) doc. 20, 107–110 [= Cambridge University Library, T-S 24.6].

[4] *David Abulafia*, The Two Italies: economic relations between the Norman Kingdom of Sicily and the northern communes (Cambridge 1977); *E. Ashtor*, Gli Ebrei nel commercio mediterraneo nell'alto medioevo (sec. X–XI), in: Gli Ebrei nell'alto medioevo (Settimane di studio del Centro italiano di studi sull'alto medioevo vol. 26, Spoleto 1980) 447–50.

trol of the spice trade linking Egypt, via Yemen, to the Indies, which fell into the hands of the Muslim merchants known as the *karimi*, or merchants of the caravan[5]. The Jews were squeezed out of the role as middlemen between the markets of the western Mediterranean and those of the Orient. And the arrival first of Norman conquerors in Sicily (still quite benign to the Jews) and then of crusaders in the Levant confirmed that hegemony in the Mediterranean, political as well as economic, belonged henceforth to Christendom.

On the mainland around 1150, the image is different. Long-range Jewish merchants comparable to those living in Palermo seem relatively rare. The Jewish population consisted primarily of artisans. All the evidence suggests that it was Christian merchants from Amalfi, Ravello and neighbouring centres, who dominated the internal trade of southern Italy in the twelfth century, including the exchange of money[6]. Pursuing regrettable stereotypes, some historians have searched all too eagerly for signs of Jewish involvement: the great Salernitan businessman Solomon, who in any case lived mainly in Genoa, was clearly not a Jew, despite common assumptions[7]. The preparation, especially dyeing, of cloth, including silk, dominated the economic life of the Jewish communities at such towns as Salerno, but the subsequent marketing of these cloths does not seem to have been a Jewish speciality. In fact, the Jews, though economically specialised, were well integrated in the wider structure of the south Italian economy. Within the towns, Jews often sought out a monopoly over the slaughtering of animals; this was apparently conceded because it was a messy business, but also because of the Halakhic requirements about the way beasts should be slaughtered and about which parts of the animal could be eaten. What the Jews rejected was regularly added to the wider meat stock. Similarly, there was an interest in wine production, for the rabbis forbade the consumption of wine produced or handled by non-Jews. By 1250, the economic character of the Jewish communities in Sicily seems to have been similar to that on the mainland; in Sicily, the Jewish artisans famously included a number of Greek Jewish silk weavers, kidnapped from Thebes by King Roger II to boost his luxury silk production.

Frederick II, in his *Constitutions of Melfi*, attempted to regulate Jewish money lending; and it is easy to assume, as Bresc does, that this was a reality; in fact, the emperor was simply imitating papal legislation of the Lateran councils, and his provisions seem rather theoretical[8]. In both territories, Jews were not particularly deeply involved in money lending at this period – no more than were Christian businessmen. Indeed, they served for the south Italian Thomas Aquinas as a model for the smaller north European communities, for whom lending at interest had

[5] *David Abulafia*, Asia, Africa and the trade of medieval Europe, in: Cambridge Economic History of Europe, vol. 2, 2nd edition, ed. *M. M. Postan* et al. (Cambridge 1987).
[6] *G. Imperato*, Amalfi e il suo commercio (Salerno 1980); *M. del Treppo* and *A. Leone*, Amalfi medioevale (Naples 1977).
[7] *Abulafia*, Two Italies.
[8] *H. Bresc*, Arabes de langue, juifs de religion (Paris 2001).

become the sole significant occupation, or rather the sole occupation Christian rulers and artisan competitors would permit the Jews to have. Aquinas, in his famous letter to the duchess of Brabant *De regimine Judaeorum,* expresses the view that it is better for Jews to work productively *sicut in partibus Italiae faciunt* than to let them indulge in the easy and fraudulent life of usurers[9]. Thus the Jews of southern Italy, to his knowledge, were involved in a wide variety of economic tasks; while in reality lending of money was practised on a moderate scale by anyone, Jew or Christian, who had money in his pocket in the Mediterranean world of the thirteenth century. If anyone dominated the handling of money in southern Italy at this period, it was the Amalfitans and, increasingly, non-native merchants from Tuscany and the north of Italy. Only at the end of the Trecento did the south Italian Jews become heavily involved in money lending. Meanwhile, it was their involvement with silk production and cloth dyeing that was of most interest to Frederick II, as we can see from his edict of June 1231 in which he decrees that silk produced in Val di Crati, Apulia and Calabria must be sold to a Jewish factory in Trani, which will produce silk goods for him *ad opus curie*. Thus he seems to have continued the methods of Roger II, using Jewish silkworkers to fabricate fine vestments, which may well include those that now hand in the Vienna Schatzkammer. A Jewish firm from Capua was commissioned with oversight of the cloth dyeing industry, as well, though here we should note again the encouragement to Jews to carry out 'messy' economic activities such as dyeing, slaughtering and leather-making[10].

Clearly these economic activities must have been disrupted by the anti-Jewish measures of 1290, which led to mass conversion, emigration and the impoverishment of some communities in Apulia. But there is little evidence for a radical change in the position of the south Italian Jews until the early fifteenth century. Joanna I, queen of Naples in the late fourteenth century, confirmed the right of the Jews to trade freely with Christians; but King Ladislaus, at the start of the fifteenth century, offered the family of Ligucio di Dattolo the right to open a pawnshop and to trade in the Abruzzi. This coincides with the spread of Jewish pawnbroking in northern and central Italy, and it is hardly surprising that the northernmost territory of the kingdom of Naples should have opened its door to Jewish *banchieri*, especially since there was a need for credit following the destructive internal wars of the late Angevin period[11]. The availability of Jewish credit no doubt had a beneficial effect on the economy, despite the lurid image presented not so long ago by the modern Neapolitan historian Silvestri of rapacious Jewish usurers feeding off the southern economy. Further similar privileges followed from 1420 onwards in Abruzzo, Molise and nearby areas, in the face of the bitter disapproval of Queen Joanna's II charismatic confidant, Fra Giovanni di Capestrano[12]. In the end, the

[9] *Thomas Aquinas*, De regimine Judaeorum.
[10] *Winckelmann*, Acta imperii no. 796; *Abulafia*, Lo Stato 165–87.
[11] *Nicola Ferorelli*, Gli Ebrei nell'Italia meridionale dall'età romana al secolo XVIII, 2nd edition, ed. *F. Patroni Griffi* (Naples 1990) 73–4.
[12] *Ferorelli*, Gli Ebrei nell'Italia meridionale 74–5.

queen ignored the friar, and thus laid the basis for the Aragonese relationship with the Jews of southern Italy[13].

The arrival in 1442 of Alfonso of Aragon as conqueror of Naples, unlike the arrival of Charles of Anjou, posed little threat to the Jews of southern Italy[14]. Alfonso and his successor Ferrante retained the awareness of the financial utility of protecting the Jews that had long been practised in their native Spain. What did change, however, was the level of involvement by the crown in the control and taxation of Jewish moneylending, and here royal fiscal needs combined with long-term changes in the character of the Jewish community. The arrival of Jewish moneylenders from central Italy shifted the emphasis in royal taxation of the Jews; moreover, the Aragonese monarchy had for centuries exacted fees and fines from the Jews in Spain in return for permission to lend at interest. Thus as early as June 1452 Alfonso confirmed the right of the Jews to lend at interest, following the payment of a fee of 1,000 ducats by the south Italian Jews[15]. On the other hand, it would be a serious mistake to imagine that moneylending rapidly came to dominate what remained communities of artisans; we should distinguish between the native Jews and the newcomers, such as the pawnbroker Mosé de Gauy of Cesena, who settled in the far south, in Cosenza.

There also existed Jewish élites: as now, medicine was a traditional Jewish occupation. But new technology was not ignored. Southern Italy became a major home of Hebrew printing. Reggio di Calabria already had a Hebrew press in 1475. Naples itself rapidly became a highly productive, pioneering centre of Jewish publishing, attracting to the city Spanish and German rabbis who could work as correctors of the proof texts (note again the presence of newcomers). The monarchy recognised the profitability of the printing industry; in 1491 Davit Bono, Jew of Naples, received a royal privilege allowing him to export books, without liability for customs duties[16].

[13] *Ferorelli*, Gli Ebrei nell'Italia meridionale 75.

[14] The best general account of southern Italy in this period is *G. Galasso*, Il Regno di Napoli, t. 1, Il Mezzogiorno angioino e aragonese, Storia d'Italia diretta da *G. Galasso*, vol. 15 (Torino 1992) 561–775.

[15] In addition to *Ferorelli's* Gli Ebrei nell'Italia meridionale 89–198, see for the Aragonese period *V. Bonazzoli*, Gli ebrei del regno di Napoli all'epoca della loro espulsione, I parte, Il periodo aragonese, 1456–99, in: Archivio storico italiano 137 (1979) 495–559.

[16] *N. Ferorelli*, Tipografi e librai ebrei nel Napoletano verso la fine del secolo XV, repr. in: *Ferorelli*, Gli Ebrei nell'Italia meridionale 279–83, with a valuable bibliographical aggiornamento by *F. Patroni Griffi*, ibid. 282–3; also, *Ferorelli*, 133. Of note are *R. Frattarolo*, Tipografi e librai, ebrei e non, nel Napoletano alla fine del secolo XV, in: Biblioteca degli eruditi e dei bibliofili 23 (Firenze 1956); *M. Fava* and *G. Bresciano*, La stampa a Napoli nel XV secolo, 2 vols. (Sammlung bibliothekswissenschaftlicher Arbeiten, vol. 32, Lipsia 1911–12); *J. Bloch*, Hebrew printing in Naples, in: New York Public Library Bulletin (1942) repr. in Hebrew printing and bibliography. Studies by *J. Bloch* and others, ed. *C. Berlin* (New York 1976); *M. Santoro*, La Stampa a Napoli nel Quattrocento (Napoli 1984); to be added to her list is *A. K. Offenberg*, Hebreeuwse Incunabulen in de Bibliotheca Rosenthaliana, in: Studia Rosenthaliana. Tijdschrift voor Joodse Wetenschap en Geschiedenis in Nederland 14 (1980) 176–90, especially the long section from 178 onwards on 'Hebreeuwse drukkers in Napels' (Hebrew printers in Naples); and *C. Roth*, A Hebrew printer in Naples, 1477, in: Bulletin of the John Rylands Library 39 (1956) 188–95, repr. in: *C. Roth*, Studies in books and booklore. Essays in Jewish bibliography and allied subjects (Farnborough 1972).

After 1494 Hebrew printing ceased at Naples, though it continued in the Venetian lordship of Monopoli[17]. Alongside these professionals, Jews were involved still in the widest range of economic activities, industrial and agrarian. In Apulia, Jewish advance purchases lubricated the trade in cereals and oil; Jews acted as intermediaries with Florentines and Venetians[18]. A Jew of German origin was involved, in 1446, in a partnership with the aim of setting up a dye workshop; in 1470 some Jews of Lecce, experts in the leather industry, made a deal with a Florentine merchant, who was to finance the purchase of raw skins but who proved to be an unreliable partner[19]. Thus the traditional involvement of Jews in leather and dyeing continued even as money lending became more a significant activity.

Increasingly, however, Jews were seen as a source of credit, and so valued for this that in the Abruzzi Jews who did not lend money were exempt from taxes on the grounds, apparently, that they must be indigent[20]. As early as 1409 the citizens of Brindisi thanked the crown for permitting Jews to lend at 40% interest[21]. A major factor in demand for loans was the periodic shortage of specie in western Europe, which affected the Regno as much as elsewhere; once an important source of silver coinage, merchants in southern Italy now occasionally adopted barter as a means to overcome the bullion famine[22]. Loans from Jews could stimulate the economy and restore the rate of transactions to more familiar levels. Economic recovery in the 1470's did not render the Jews superfluous, but only served to underline their fundamental importance[23]. King Ferrante anticipated these events. As early as 20 April 1491 he assured newly arrived Spanish Jews that they could enjoy the same privileges as the *antiqui*, and that they would be treated exactly as if they were natives of the Regno. Perhaps the most revealing part of these orders is the king's insistence that his officials should record not merely how many Jews had arrived and from where their ship had come, but *de che artificio o mercancia sia* the head of each household. Once on south Italian soil, these Jews must be free to choose a place to live, so that they could buy food, conduct trade and produce goods without hindrance. He saw the Spanish and Sicilian Jews who arrived *en masse* in 1492–3

[17] *Bonazzoli*, Gli Ebrei pt. 2, 226.

[18] *Bonazzoli*, Gli Ebrei pt. 1, 551–5.

[19] *Ferorelli*, Gli Ebrei nell'Italia meridionale 135.

[20] *Ferorelli*, Gli Ebrei nell'Italia meridionale 137: "quillo iudio che non prestasse dinari, né havesse modo de tenere banco".

[21] *Ferorelli*, Gli Ebrei nell'Italia meridionale loc. cit.

[22] *Petralia*, op. cit.; *J. Day*, The medieval market economy (Oxford 1986).

[23] But King Ferrante probably appreciated the Jews primarily as artisans, not moneylenders: *David Abulafia*, The Crown and economy under Ferrante I of Naples, 1458–1494, in: *T. Dean*, *C. Wickham* (eds.), City and Countryside in late medieval and early Renaissance Italy. Studies presented to Philip Jones (London 1990) 125–46, here 137. Even so, Jews did not appear in the ranks of the great merchant bankers at court, as *Bonazzoli*, Gli Ebrei pt. 1, 556, observes. Their individual role was on a much smaller scale than, say, the millionnaire Strozzi. For data on Jewish loans in Salerno, see *A. Silvestri*, Il commercio a Salerno nella seconda metà del Quattrocento (Salerno 1952) 30–6.

as a further source of economic benefit to a kingdom whose industries and (not least) finances he was attempting to encourage[24].

1492 saw one dramatic change, the doubling (probably) of Jewish numbers in southern Italy following the expulsions of Ferdinand and Isabella. Ferdinand's conquest of Naples in 1503, after nine years of chaos within the kingdom, marked another dramatic change. Some Jewish communities had fallen on very hard times during the Italian wars; but Ferdinand was only interested in two things: their eventual expulsion, and in the meantime the maximisation of his income from those Jews who could produce funds for him, the moneylenders. Therefore in 1510 he broke his golden rule and allowed some Jews to remain in one of his kingdoms: 200 of the richest south Italian Jews. In fact, there seems even to have been a trickle of Jewish immigrants after 1510, many of whom were simply returning home; and in 1520, at Naples, the citizens tried to explain to the crown *il bisogno grandissimo che teneno de li hebrei*[25]. In Apulia, it became obvious that without Jewish moneylenders, Christian usurers filled the gap; but they showed far less consideration to their clients. The main factor delaying final expulsion, which after postponements took place in 1541, was the economic climate: *secondo le carestie sono state in lo regno et la povertà in che la gente al presente se trova, saria grandissima ruina ai populi quando se desse materia che li hebrei uscessero dal regno*. A reflection of the continuing economic importance of the Apulian Jews can be found in the 400 entries in six notarial registers from Bari between January 1540 and August 1541. A group of Jewish moneylenders, including several of German descent, are seen making a multiplicity of small loans to Christians, often to help with purchases of cloth. But by early 1541 the main item of business was the recovery of debts, as the Jews of Bari gave up hope of remaining any longer[26]. What was perhaps surprising was that after forty years of failing to decide to expel the Jews, expulsion was firmly and irrevocably decreed in 1541[27]. Even this was not the absolute end of a Jewish presence in southern Italy: the Lanciano fairs were again being visited by Jews in 1543[28]. But even before the death of Ferrante I the centre of gravity of Italian Jewry had begun to shift northwards, to the loan banks of Tuscany, Umbria, the Marche, to Rome and to Venice, to Ferrara and Mantua.

We must now retrace our steps to the mid-thirteenth century, to see how this image of Jewish economic activity compares with that of Sicily; here we now have the additional help of Henri Bresc's study of the Sicilian Jews, 'Jews by religion, Arabs by language', as he describes them, and Nadia Zeldes' helpful examination of the communities at the time of the expulsion[29]. A sense of the rather 'provincial',

[24] *Ferorelli*, Gli Ebrei nell'Italia meridionale 93–4.

[25] *Ferorelli*, Gli Ebrei nell'Italia meridionale 220; *Bonazzoli*, Gli Ebrei pt. 2, 204.

[26] *Ferorelli*, Gli Ebrei nell'Italia meridionale 228; Presenza ebraica in Puglia 91–167.

[27] *Bonazzoli*, Gli Ebrei pt. 2, 281.

[28] *Ferorelli*, Gli Ebrei nell'Italia meridionale 237; *C. Marciani*, Ebrei a Larciano dal XII al XVIII secolo, in: Archivio storico per le provincie napoletane, n. s., vol. 2 (1962).

[29] *Bresc*, Juifs de religion; *Nadia Zeldes*, The former Jews of this kingdom. Sicilian converts after the expulsion 1492–1516 (Leiden 2003).

almost archaic, character of Sicilian Jewry in the later Middle Ages emerges from the fourteenth and fifteenth century documentation in other ways than the survival of Arabic speech among the Sicilian Jews: Bresc remarks that, whereas once the use of Arabic had been a signal of integration into the wider world, it now became a signal of isolation. The situation of late medieval Sicilian Jewry is best appreciated through a series of case studies, for there is still much to be discovered about their legal status, about their tax arrangements, about their demography and internal organisation, and recent research on the individual communities has only brought this out more clearly. Maybe, indeed, it is precisely the fragmented, localised character of the Jewish communities of Sicily that needs to be stressed in this period, for certain changes, such as seclusion in reserved areas of the towns, occurred more rapidly in some cities than in others. This is not to deny the importance of local trade networks, managed by Jews, linking the smaller towns across the island. The major common theme is the largely artisan identity of the Jewish communities (with a good sprinkling, however, of physicians), as on the mainland; but it will also be possible to identify several successful Jewish merchants.

The first case to examine is the Jewish community of Erice or Monte San Giuliano, on the steep hill overlooking Trapani in western Sicily, the economic activities of which are amply recorded in a notarial register of the years around 1300[30]. Among the Jews of Erice, who may have numbered as many as 400, up to 5% of the total population of the territory, there are artisans, shopkeepers and agricultural labourers, but no obvious professional moneylenders. When Jews advance money to Christians it is in the form of improvement grants for land, often vineyards; these Jewish investments are no different in character from investments made by Christian inhabitants of the town. Indeed, the community leader Chilfa de David not merely lived next door to Catalans and other Christians, but he owned lands of his own outside the town walls, which he decided in 1298 to put to good use, by having a Christian workman plant trees, construct walls and irrigation ducts, and harvest the produce under terms quite similar to those of the contemporary north Italian *mezzadria* contracts. It was normal for Jews with a professional interest in, say metalworking, such as the prominent figure Azaronus de Sydica, also to maintain additional interests in wine production. The same applied to one of the town's Jewish physicians, Iacobus Rude de Rumen, who commissioned a non-Jew to work on his land beyond the town walls, and provided him with an improvement grant made explicitly 'without profit or usury' in order to get the work started. A survey of the professions mentioned in the major source for the history of the Erice Jews, the cartulary of the notary Giovanni Maiorana of

[30] *David Abulafia*, Una communità ebraica della Sicilia occidentale: Erice 1298–1304, in: Archivio storico per la Sicilia orientale 80 (1984) 7–39, repr. in: *David Abulafia*, Commerce and Conquest in the Mediterranean, 1100–1500 (Aldershot 1993); also published in Hebrew as Jehudei Erice (Monte San Giuliano) shebeSitsiliah, 1298–1304, in: Zion: a quarterly for research in Jewish history 51 (1986) 295–317; the key text is: Il registro del notaio ericino Giovanni Maiorana (1297–1300), ed. *A. Sparti*, 2 vols. (Palermo 1982); older edition: Il registro notarile di G. Maiorana (1297–1300), ed. *A. de Stefano* (Palermo 1943).

1297–1300, indicates that eight were described as metalworkers (*fabri*), including one goldsmith. There were also a couple of butchers, a carpenter and some clothworkers. In other words, they were a well-rounded community, of modest standing.

Less rich is the documentation concerning Jews in the notarial registers of Palermo from the same period, but many of the prime features observable in Erice are there too. Some activities were more characteristic of a big city, such as the sale of slaves, and joint enterprises with Christians in silk production[31]. At Palermo, as at Erice, wine production was a special concern of the Jews, not simply in order to provide wine that was ritually fit, but also as a reliable form of investment: wine and grapes were bought from Christians (there was no bar on buying and selling non-kosher wine, since the rabbinic injunction forbade consumption only, and was probably much honoured in the breach). Moneylending by Jews is not mentioned in the notarial documents of this period, even though it remained the subject of so much restrictive legislation, much of which (once again) was theoretical rather than practical. Indeed, the Palermitan notaries preserve one document in which a Jew receives a loan from someone who seems to be a Tuscan Christian. It was to a Christian of Palermo that the kosher butchers of Palermo in 1299 consigned the fleeces and skins of the sheep they expected to slaughter over the next three or four years. This suggests that the activities of the Jews of Palermo as tanners were quite limited by comparison with mainland southern Italy, Catalonia or Byzantium. On the other hand, the Sicilian Jews, like those of southern Italy, do appear to have continued to dominate the dyeing industry right up to the expulsion of 1492. Other areas of the textile industry in which they worked (though not alone) included the production of silken cloths, for instance in eastern Sicily, but this was not a specifically Jewish craft.

Jews were not absent from involvement in the overseas trade of Palermo in the early Aragonese period, as witnessed by an act of 1287 revealing links between a Jew and a Christian of Messina for trade as far as Genoa. But the major area of interest in overseas trade appears to have been the slave market, for Palermo, along with Barcelona and Majorca, was one of the key centres of exchange of Muslim slaves. Even so, the Jews appear in the documentation as purchasers rather than as international slave dealers; and the indications are that Christian Catalan and north Italian merchants completely dominated the Mediterranean slave trade through Sicily, as one would expect of those who owned ships and fought aggressively against Muslim and even Christian foes. Increasingly strict legislation (especially under Frederick III from 1310 onwards) to ensure that Jews did not possess Chris-

[31] *David Abulafia*, Le attività economiche degli Ebrei siciliani attorno al 1300, in: Italia Judaica 5: Gli Ebrei in Sicilia sino all'espulsione del 1492. Atti del V Convegno internazionale, Palermo, 15–19 giugno 1992 (Rome 1995) 89–95. This discussion is based on *P. Burgarella*, Le imbreviature del notaio Adamo de Citella a Palermo (1° Registro: 1286–1287) Fonti e Studi del Corpus membranarum italicarum, ser. 3, 1 (Roma 1983); summaries in: *P. Burgarella*, Il protocollo del notaio Adamo de Citella dell'anno 1286–7, in: Archivio storico per la Sicilia orientale 75 (1979) 435–553.

tian slaves meant that the Muslim slave was the object of special demand in Jewish households; many of them came from the Monte Barca region of Cyrenaica.

Palermo was certainly the most substantial Jewish community in Sicily at the start of the fifteenth century, with about 850 families in 1487, according to the traveller Obadiah of Bertinoro[32]. Although there was a traditional focus for Jewish settlement close to the Martorana convent, they had shops and houses all over the city, in the Kalsa, in Seralcadio, and close to the shore, where the physician Moses Chazen owned a tannery. The impression is that the Jews remained well integrated into the structure of Palermitan society during the fifteenth century. A wide range of professions attracted them: there were sugar planters, much in demand in a period when the island's sugar industry was undergoing a dramatic Renaissance, and some were involved in oil production and of course viticulture; Palermo was something of a 'garden city', with plots of land within and outside the walls, and a sizeable proportion of the population engaged in specialist agriculture. In 1239–40 Frederick II had already encouraged the settlement in Palermo of north African Jews, who were invited to restore the cultivation of henna, indigo and other specialised crops which had flourished under Muslim and early Norman rule; this community even had its own synagogue. Artisan crafts included not just dyeing and tanning, but metalworking, carpentry, cloth production, shoemaking. There were also Jewish tunny fishermen alongside the many Christian and occasional Muslim ones. The presence of such a wide range of skills was cited as an argument against the expulsion of 1492[33]. Indeed, the impression is that the Jews were performing virtually every conceivable economic function, while they preserved their traditional interests in cloth-dyeing and metalwork, crafts traditionally assigned to Jews in some parts of the Islamic world. But in some areas Jews were forced to perform demeaning tasks such as the execution of criminals, if Rabbi Obadiah of Bertinoro (1488) is to be believed: 'the labour imposed upon them by the government weighs heavily upon them, for they are compelled to go into the service of the king whenever any new labour project arises; they have to drag ships to the shore, to construct dykes and so on'.

Palermo's Jews also included successful merchants, handling Catalan cloths for re-export to the east. This is not to say that they could compete with the large-scale import-export businesses of the Genoese, Catalans and Tuscans. But the Jews may have played an important role in the internal market as purveyors of goods, where Henri Bresc has found them to be increasingly active, across the island, by the late fifteenth century (a similar role, on a smaller scale, can be posited in Malta). There

[32] *E. Ashtor*, Palermitan Jewry in the fifteenth century, in: Hebrew Union College Annual 50 (1979) 219–251.

[33] On the expulsion, see now *F. Renda*, La fine del giudaismo siciliano (Palermo 1993) and *Zeldes*, The former Jews of this kingdom; older studies of value include *E. Ashtor*, La fin du Judaisme sicilien, in: Revue des études juives 142 (1983) 323–47, a critique of *C. Trasselli*, Sull'espulsione degli ebrei della Sicilia, in: Annali della Facoltà di economia e commercio, Università di Palermo 8 (1954) and C. Trasselli's lecture Gli ebrei di Sicilia printed in his: Siciliani fra Quattrocento e Cinquecento (Messina 1981) 135–57.

is an interesting comparison to be made here with the contemporary Jewish merchants of Castile, Valencia and Granada. As in the days of the Genizah, there were also north African Jewish businessmen who maintained a base in Palermo, Syracuse, or Trapani, and regularly traded across the straits towards Tunis and Tripoli. The powerful Sala family of Trapani was involved in the wheat trade towards north Africa at the start of the fifteenth century. Jews purchased such goods as English and French cloth, which they passed on to customers such as the royal court and Sicilian bishops. What this evidence reveals is once again the broad similarity between the economic function of the Jews and that of the Christian merchants, even though the Jews were small fry compared to the Genoese, Catalans and Tuscans. Certainly, there is very little evidence even in the last years of Sicilian Jewry for the involvement in money lending which characterised the Jews of northern and central, and, increasingly, southern Italy. Some measures were taken at the start of the fifteenth century against Jewish usury; but this policy was so heavily moulded by Catalan experience that it provides no proof that excessive interest was being regularly charged.

From Malta to Messina the Jewish élite practised medicine, as in southern Italy; well over a hundred and fifty Jewish physicians are recorded in late fourteenth and fifteenth-century Sicily. The *dienchelele*, the head of the Jewish communities appointed by the Crown, assumed the right to grant licences to practice medicine. Access to universities remained extremely difficult for Jewish students of medicine, though Padua in the north became willing to admit a few Jews, even a Sicilian. Attempts to establish Jewish centres of medical and other studies, comparable to the universities, are recorded, notably a grant from the Crown in 1466, but there were no long-lasting results.

A smaller community such as that of Sciacca in the south of the island displays many features in common with the *giudecca* of Palermo[34]. First heard of in 1295, when Sant'Alberto da Trapani was at work converting Jews of Sciacca, the community was concentrated in the area of the town known as La Cadda, but there were Jewish properties in other parts of town, and Christian house-owners in La Cadda. In 1435 187 male Jews voted in an election of the *proti* or syndics of the community, which would produce a total figure of anything from 500 to 1,000 Jews in the town, perhaps ten per cent of the total town population of somewhere around 10,000. A distinctive feature of the community was that it was granted to a secular lord, Antonio de Luna Peralta, in 1457; around the same time the Jewry of Agrigento was granted to another great baron. The count of Luna could prove obdurate in his attitude to the Jews, so that on one occasion the Viceroy Ximenes d'Urrea had to intervene to secure the release of some Jews the count had illicitly imprisoned. In this respect, the Jewries of the middle-ranking towns were no dif-

[34] *A. Scandaliato* and *M. Gerardi*, La Giudecca di Sciacca tra XIV e XV secolo (documenti inediti) (Castelvetrano 1992), reprinting their article of similar title from the book Sciacca città degna (Sciacca 1990) and an additional study by *A. Scandaliato*, La donna ebrea siciliana nel Medioevo, first published in: Fardelliana 1991.

ferent from other royal assets, on which the money-famished Alfonso the Magnanimous was always ready to capitalise. In fact, the *giudecca* of Sciacca was careful to make handsome contributions to Alfonso's war funds, such as fifty onze in 1436; *una cifra non indifferente*, as two accomplished historians of Sciacca's Jews point out. This did not release the Jews from the familiar but vexatious humiliation of having to wear a *rotella rossa* one palm's breadth broad; in 1427 the priest Giovanni Planellario travelled to Sciacca to ensure that this law was being respected. Moreover, there were outbreaks of violence against the Jews, who were subjected to the usual vigorous attempts at conversion.

A final example of a Jewish community in the Sicilian kingdom is provided by Malta[35]. Here the Jews were to all intents treated as citizens of the archipelago's small towns, and in the fifteenth century even the *angaria* or corvées traditionally imposed on the Jews had been very largely relaxed. The status of the Jews as *servi* of the Crown was in fact cited by the Jews themselves, in 1492, to escape intrusion in their affairs by the local Church[36]. The Maltese community enjoyed especially close links to Syracuse, whose Jewish community was active in trade towards not just Malta but north Africa, sending such objects as coral, spun cotton (perhaps grown in Malta), raw silk and cheese to the Maghreb, and olive oil to Malta. Malta was a valued part of the kingdom, despite its physical separation from Sicily and its cultural separation, expressed in the remarkable survival of an Arabic vernacular not just among the Jews but among the general population. Moreover, the Maltese community is well documented for the fifteenth century. They were landowners, petty merchants and retailers, rarely big businessmen, not especially involved in money lending. Bahyuni Mehyr and his wife Zambite possessed fourteen fields and thirteen smaller portions of arable land in Malta and Gozo, and even some property near Syracuse in Sicily. The easiest way for propertied Jews to participate in the exploitation of such scattered estates was through *mezzadria* agreements with farmers, Jewish or Christian. The Maltese historian Wettinger believes that most of the Jewish land was acquired from Christian owners who effectively mortgaged it in return for loans[37]. It is true that Maltese Jews made rather little effort to consolidate their estates, in the way typical of many Maltese Christians; but there is really no evidence that the Jews of Malta were heavily involved in moneylending, and such mortgage practices were as frequent among Christians as they were among Jews. The image preserved in English literature of Christopher Marlowe's *Jew of Malta* simply cannot be substantiated in the late medieval evidence. Wettinger points out, in fact, that land mortgages were even more common among Christians than they were among Jews[38].

Malta was pre-eminently famous as a source of raw cotton, and Jews, sometimes working closely with partners from Syracuse, were active in the exploitation of this

[35] *G. Wettinger*, The Jews of Malta in the late Middle Ages (Valletta 1985).
[36] *Wettinger*, Jews of Malta 16; cf. 262.
[37] *Wettinger*, Jews of Malta 34–42.
[38] *Wettinger*, Jews of Malta 24.

resource: in 1487 Ximxon Ketib promised to supply the Christian Pero Caruana with a substantial quantity of cotton; the very same day another Maltese Jew arranged for the delivery of cotton from the fields. Once again, the Jews had no special place in this day-to-day business; they were active alongside native and Sicilian Christians and foreign merchants such as the Catalans. The sale of foreign cloths was, however, an area where the Jews were particularly active, and Jewish petty traders were sometimes the target of hostility in the villages (there were also attempts to create a ghetto in Mdina). It has to be remembered, though, that the Jews were generally transmitting goods acquired on the international trade routes by big-time foreign merchants with whom they could in no way compete. Their function lay in the distribution of these goods out of the medieval capital of Malta, Mdina. Yet there was a Jewish involvement in trade between Sicily and Malta, which slotted into the existing medium-range trade network linking Tripoli and Tunis to Syracuse: in 1442–3 Jews are found exporting chick-peas to Malta; one of the exporters came from Tripoli in Cyrenaica. In 1482 a Syracusan Jew supplied Malta with some coal. Another speciality was metalwork: in the late fifteenth century a group of Jews probably from Syracuse functioned as the main blacksmiths on the island; and they were so valued that Hauad Cussu the Jew received exemption from the *corvée* normally imposed on Jews and from certain taxes; his work included the repair of the cathedral bells in Mdina. This speciality in metalwork has parallels with the practice in parts of the Islamic world, from Morocco to Yemen, where metal production was often assigned primarily or exclusively to Jews. Thus Maltese Jewry seems to consist of a microcosm of that of Sicily, excepting only the linguistic convergence between Jews and Christians; but that too was largely a thing of the past in Sicily before 1492.

In both Sicily and southern Italy, then, there is plentiful evidence that the presence of Jews was seen as economically valuable, and it should be emphasized that historians increasingly see the fifteenth century as a period of gathering economic recovery in both southern Italy and Sicily, a recovery in which the Jews played a part. This was not simply a fiscal question, that is, a matter of using the Jews as a fruitful source of taxation. In southern Italy the Crown, in Sicily the cities, insisted on the usefulness of the Jews as artisans in the years around 1492. Later, in southern Italy, there is evidence that Jews were often regarded as a preferable source of small-scale credit to unregulated Christians. On the mainland, it appears that the shift to pawnbroking was more noticeable than in Sicily, under the impetus of wider changes taking place in the Jewish demography of Italy and in the economy of the region; even Ferdinand the Catholic recognised this when he permitted some Jews to remain in Naples after 1510. And, despite popular agitation against the Jews, there was no overwhelming pressure to expel them from within these territories; the decision was made by the Crown – by Ferdinand in respect of Sicily, in 1492; and by Charles V and his Viceroy Pedro de Toledo in respect of Naples, in 1541. It is also clear that the Jewish communities of the end of the Middle Ages could show far fewer powerful business families than appear in the age of the Genizah. Locally such families as the Sala of Trapani exercised influence, and there was a tradition in several Sicilian noble houses of employing Jewish major-domos; but, until the Abravanels arrived in Naples from Castile, few Jews possessed close links to the viceregal courts in the way that the Iberian Jewish élites had enjoyed ready access to the royal courts in Spain and Portugal. Cumulatively, however, as highly productive artisans and local traders, the Jews played an important role in the economic recovery of the Italian South, only to be forced out when that recovery was well under way.

Reinhold C. Mueller

The Status and Economic Activity of Jews in the Venetian Dominions during the Fifteenth Century

Recent studies on the history of Jews in the Venetian Terraferma in the last century of the Middle Ages have expanded our knowledge considerably. An excellent collection of studies by the late Daniel Carpi on Jews in Padua appeared in 2002. A seminar held in Verona in 2003 was dedicated to the cases of Treviso, Verona, Vicenza, Feltre and, beyond the borders of Venice but in its sphere of influence, Rovigo (part of the Veneto only from 1484) and Trieste (in the empire); most of the participants were young scholars who had devoted laurea and doctoral theses to specific cities and areas of the Terraferma[1]. As regards the social and economic history of Jews in the maritime provinces, the Venetian *Stato da mar*, the single historian who has contributed most is unquestionably David Jacoby, many of whose articles have been collected in readily available volumes. The largest of the provinces, Crete, as Jacoby affirmed already in 1983, remains even today – for the history of the Jews – the least-studied area with the most voluminous documentation[2]. The present contribution considers the social status and the economic activity of Jews in both regions under the direct governance of Venice.

The status of Jews in Venetian territories

The conventional vocabulary of the majority reflects at first glance the social and legal status of a minority, in Venice as anywhere else. The terms *subditus* and *servus*

[1] *Daniel Carpi*, L'individuo e la collettività. Saggi di storia degli ebrei a Padova e nel Veneto nell'età del Rinascimento (Florence 2002); Ebrei nella Terraferma veneta del Quattrocento, Atti della Giornata di studio (Verona, 14 novembre 2003), edited by *Gian Maria Varanini* and *Reinhold C. Mueller* (Florence 2005) 149–50 (available also on-line in Reti Medievali – Rivista, VI, 2005, 1: www.dssg.unifi.it/_RM/rivista/atti/ebrei.htm). My own contribution to that volume, Lo *status* degli ebrei nella Terraferma veneta del Quattrocento: tra politica, religione, cultura ed economia. Saggio introduttivo, ibid. 1–22, constitutes a first attempt to deal with some of the themes of this paper as well as other, wider, issues. My thanks to David Jacoby for his careful reading of an earlier version of the present essay and for his helpful suggestions.

[2] The best overview is still *David Jacoby*, Venice and the Venetian Jews in the Eastern Mediterranean, in: *Gaetano Cozzi* (ed.), Gli Ebrei e Venezia, secoli XIV–XVIII (Milan 1987) 29–58, reprinted in: *David Jacoby*, Studies on the Crusader States and on Venetian Expansion (Northampton 1989), art. X. See also *idem*, Recherches sur la Méditerranée orientale du XIIe au XVe siècle (London 1979).

had widely different connotations. Letters addressed by the doge to the council in Verona in the later fifteenth century, as reported in a recent study, refer to the Jews residing in that city as Venetian subjects: "*Iudaei subditi nostri*". The phrase was probably understood to mean that the Jews were subject in the first place directly to the government of the capital city, secondly to the Venetian governors serving *in loco*, and thirdly to local authorities[3]. It meant that the state assumed the obligation of providing protection for Jews resident in its territories and as such was a sought-after condition. It was very different from the concept of "servitude of the Jews" commonly invoked by medieval kings and emperors, a concept not without an echo in Venice, albeit in expressions not originating from the organs of the republican government.

That the status of the Jews as a minority in the states of medieval Christian Europe was often given expression by calling them *servi regis* or *servi regie camerae* or *servi camerae nostre* (*unsere Kammerknechte*) is well known. It was long thought that the concept was introduced by Frederick II in 1236 but David Abulafia, in his search for the origin and meaning of such proprietary terms in different places and times, has found that the roots in the Mediterranean world lie considerably further back – at least as early as 1176, date of the statute of a town in Aragon – and that France, England and German lands had laws with similar formulations antedating Frederick II. He has shown that the concept involved a kind of "apertaining" to the royal treasury or fisc, a direct (Latin: *immediate*) subjection or dominion that was intended to guarantee protection to the Jews. *Servus*, he affirms, did not mean serfdom or slavery and the unfreedom of the Jew concerned only his relationship to the king or the emperor; at the same time, the term and the reality behind it became more pejorative in the later Middle Ages, beginning with the Angevins in Naples and the Aragonese in Sicily[4].

Perhaps closer to Venetian experience was the Byzantine tradition, about which, however, very little is known. One particular diplomatic exchange between emperor Andronicus II and doge Giovanni Soranzo in 1319–20 sheds some light on the issue, even if the original Greek texts are not extant. According to the surviving Latin texts, the emperor wrote of the Jews of the Vlanka quarter of Constantinople

[3] Gian Maria Varanini mentions the phrase *concitare populos contra Iudaeos subditos nostros* in a warning prohibiting any action in the Terraferma city that would incite the people against the Jews, "our subjects"; see his Società cristiana e minoranza ebraica a Verona nella seconda metà del Quattrocento. Tra ideologia osservante e vita quotidiana in Ebrei nella Terraferma veneta, in: *idem, Reinhold C. Mueller (eds.),* Ebrei nella Terraferma veneta (above, note 1) 149–50. It is worth noting that *lettere ducali* merely transmitted to the authorities of subject territories relevant decisions of the state's legislative organs.

[4] *David Abulafia*, The Servitude of Jews and Muslims in the medieval Mediterranean: origins and diffusion, in: Mélanges de l'École Française de Rome – Moyen Âge 112 (2000) 687–714; *idem*, Nam Iudei servi regis sunt, et semper fisco regio deputati: Los Judíos en el Fuero municipal de Teruel (1176–7), in: El món urbà a la Corona d'Aragó del 1137 als Decrets de Nova Planta, XVII Congrès d'Història de la Corona d'Aragó, 3 vols., vol. 2 (Barcelona 2003) 1–10; *idem*, The first Servi Camere Regie in Sicily, in: Mediterraneo, Mezzogiorno, Europa. Studi in onore di Cosimo Damiano Fonseca (Bari 2004) 1–13 – publications kindly provided by the author.

as "our Jews, legitimate property of the Empire (*nostri Iudei quedam appropriata possessio sunt Imperij*)". The seemingly "proprietary" relationship was emphasized in connection with the rank trade of tanning hides, in which Jews under both imperial and Venetian jurisdictions were heavily involved. The point of contention was the right of Jews of the Venetian quarter to live where they wished and ply the trade they wished, including tanning, while profitting from the exemption from imperial taxes as Venetians. The contending parties referred to the Jews as "*vestri*" and "*nostri*": the imperial chancery wrote of those of the Venetian quarter as "*vestri Iudei ut Veneti*" and the Venetians insisted upon imperial recognition that "*Iudei nostri vel alij nostri subditi*" be free to ply the trade of their choice. The possessive pronouns used did not imply servility and the exchange concerned who was *subditus* of whom; the Venetian side gave expression to its obligation to protect its subjects and their interests, which obviously coincided with the interests of the state[5].

So far only three cases reflecting a certain currency of terms of servitude have been uncovered in Venetian documents. Two are in petitions made to the Venetian government, while the third comes from a sermon. The first was directed in 1441 to doge Francesco Foscari by the Jews of Treviso regarding the tax paid by their banks, in which they refer to themselves as "your most faithful servants (*fedelissimi*

[5] The texts can be found in translation in *Steven B. Bowman*, The Jews of Byzantium, 1204–1453 (University of Alabama 1985) 244–247, docs. 37-39; they are discussed on 22–24. In the Latin texts, in *Georg M. Thomas*, Diplomatarium veneto-levantinum, vol. I (Venice 1880), the wording on the emperor's side of the dispute is ... *sic respondemus, quod nostri Iudei quedam appropriata possessio sunt Imperij*; ... *aliqui de vestris Iudeis Venetis ad eos concordati sunt* ... *cum ipsis nostris Iudeis* ... (142). The doge responded – and had his ambassadors respond – with the same terminology of "ours" and "yours": ... *quod [dominus imperator] dictos nostros Iudeos permittat ibi stare, sicut steterunt hucusque, et laborare curamen et pellamen ad suam liberam voluntatem, nullam eis propterea molestiam faciendo* (153); ... *quod Iudei nostri vel alij nostri subditi laborent de suis artibus, quicquid volunt* (129). It should be noted that Bowman already in his introduction (7) warns against falling into the temptation "to draw parallels" between the condition of Jews in Byzantium and "the much-discussed question of Jewish status or Jewish serfdom in the Latin West" and he continues: "The Jews, for their part, were citizens (albeit second class) of the Byzantine Empire from its inception and thus were entitled to the rights and privileges of Rhomaioi (Romans), even though they were subject to various restrictions as Jews." See also *Joshua Starr*, Romania. The Jewries of the Levant after the Fourth Crusade (Paris 1949) 27–32, where the Jewish quarter is called *pelamina*, that is, corresponding to the area of the tanners. For the context and analysis of this controversy, see *David Jacoby*, Venice and the Venetian Jews in the Eastern Mediterranean 38–39; on the status of Venetian Jews in Byzantium, see *idem*, Les Vénitiens naturalisés dans l'Empire Byzantin: un aspect de l'expansion de Venise en Romanie du XIIIe au milieu du XVe siècle, in: Travaux et mémoires, Centre de recherche d'histoire et civilisation de Byzance, 8 (1981), reprinted in: *idem*, Studies, esp. 227–228. Starr remarked that in 1414 it was reported to the Senate that the Jews of Negroponte were too poor to pay the tax of 1250 yperperi, *nam pro maiori parte sunt servi sive vilani*, probably meaning only that some worked on the land (*Starr*, Romania 53). Finally, it is worth mentioning a parallel; according to Abulafia the archbishop of Capua had received from Constance, mother of Frederick II, the grant of the *judaica* of Capua, which guaranteed him tax revenues from the dye-shops of the Jews, a trade not dissimilar from that of tanning; see: The Servitude of Jews and Muslims 701.

servitori vostri; … vostri fedel Hebrei)". The second, less equivocal, was made by Salomoncino, the wealthy Jewish moneylender of Piove di Sacco ten kilometers from Padua, when – in 1477 – he called himself, more than once in the same document, "slave and servant of this illustrious government (*schiavo e servidore de questa Illustrissima Signoria*)"[6]. In both cases the petitioners were probably being a bit obsequious, while stating the favor they asked of the government, but they could not have afforded to use such unambiguous language if it did not reflect an understood legal concept, cognizance of which they, as Ashkenazi Jews, might have acquired from their German ancestors. The final case comes from the Lenten sermon preached by a Franciscan, fra Giovan Maria d'Arezzo, at the conventual church of S. Maria dei Frari in 1515, during the discussions about what to do with the many Jews who had taken refuge in Venice from the invading armies of the League of Cambrai. The account comes from Marin Sanudo, in the context of an invective of his own against the Jews who, during Holy Week, were supposed to disappear from sight; that year, he noted, they had not and no one did anything about it, because during this war the state needed them ("*hanno bisogno di loro*"). The preacher, he writes, spoke out against them "concluding that they could be dispossessed and all their goods used for the defence of the state *because they are our servants* (*perchè sono servi nostri*)"[7]. The Franciscan was probably not a jurist

[6] *Angela Möschter*, Juden im venezianischen Treviso, 1389–1509, unpublished doctoral thesis (University of Trier 2004) Quellen, no. 29, 433–434. Salomoncino's petition, kindly brought to my attention by Ariel Toaff, was published by *Franz Babinger*, Ja'aqûb-Pascha, ein Leibarzt Mehmeds II., Leben und Schicksal des Jacopo aus Gaeta, in: Rivista degli Studi Orientali 26 (1951) 87–113, at 196–197, reprinted in his Aufsätze und Abhandlungen zur Geschichte Südosteuropas und der Levante, vol. 2 (Munich 1966). On Salomoncino see also *David Jacoby*, Les Juifs à Venise du XIVe au milieu du XVIe siècle, in: *Hans-Georg Beck, Manoussos Manoussacas, Agostino Pertusi* (eds.), Venezia, centro di mediazione tra Oriente e Occidente (secoli XV–XVI): aspetti e problemi. Atti del II Convegno internazionale di storia della civiltà veneziana, Venezia 1973 (Florence 1977) vol. I, 163–216, reprinted in: *idem*, Recherches, art. VIII, at 185, 197–198, 201; and *idem*, New Evidence on Jewish Bankers in Venice and the Venetian Terraferma (c. 1450–1550), in: The Mediterranean and the Jews. Banking, Finance and International Trade, XVI–XVIII Centuries (Ramat Gan, Tel Aviv 1989) 154–159.

[7] *Marino Sanuto* (also *Marin Sanudo*), Diarii, *Rinaldo Fulin* et al. (eds.), 58 vols. (Venice 1879–1903) vol. 20, col. 98: … *concludendo si pol tuor tutto il suo haver e meterlo a defension dil Stato, perchè sono servi nostri*. Cited first by *Ennio Concina*, Parva Jerusalem, in: *Ennio Concina, Ugo Camerino, Donatella Calabi*, La città degli ebrei. Il Ghetto di Venezia: architettura e urbanistica (Venice 1991) 33 and note 38 (and cf. 34, 43). Other friars in their Lenten sermons had in previous years already insisted on a right to sack the Jews; Sanudo wrote in April 1511 of Dominicans, Franciscans and parish priests who railed against the Jews: *Et atento che in questi zorni fra Rufin Lovato, qual predicha sul campo di San Pollo, havia dito contra li zudei 'et saria bon tuorli tutto quello che hanno et ponerli a sacho', perchè questa terra è piena di zudei fuziti qui, et eri [1 April] predicoe assai, e dubitando di novità contra di lhoro, in questa matina Anselmo et Viviam, bancheri, fonno a li capi di X, dolendossi di questo. I qual capi andono a la Signoria et fo terminato admonir dito predichador, et cussì quel di frati menori et di San Cassam, che predichano tal cosse, acciò non segui contra ditti zudei qualche cossa*: Diarii, vol. 12, col. 98–99 (2 April 1511). For the origins in Augustine of the right assumed by Christians to dispossess infidels, especially Jews, see *Giacomo Todeschini*, I mercanti e il tempio. La società cristiana e il circolo virtuoso della ricchezza fra Medioevo ed Età moderna (Bologna 2002) 239–45.

but he knew both his legal sources and what his audience would understand and Sanudo considered it important to report the phrase that underscored the servitude of the Jews.

If a direct bond between the republican government of Venice and "its" Jews is surprising at first sight, it is the only legal relationship that can explain a series of otherwise anomalous situations. It explains why the charters (*condotte*) negotiated between local authorities and Jewish moneylenders had to be approved by the Senate[8], as did requests for expelling Jewish moneylenders or the Jews *tout court*, even over the head of the Venetian governor *in loco*. It explains why the charters had almost universally to guarantee exemption of the Jews from local taxes, in order that they could be taxed centrally and as a single community despite the fact that its members operated in many centers. The same holds true for forced loans, both gratuitous and interest-bearing, that could be – and were – requested at any time by the Senate in favor of the central treasury, especially in times of war; even local authorities often had to borrow from Jews in order to meet taxes levied by the next-higher administration. It explains why in so many smaller localities the banks and sometimes the houses of Jewish lenders were located within the castle, a place by definition owned and defended by the government, with a centrally-chosen castellan and a garrison of soldiers, for the protection of the Jews in the interests of the state. This was the case in Mestre, Piove di Sacco, Monselice, Montagnana, Villafranca and yet more fortified towns in the Terraferma[9]. It would explain why many decrees of expulsion of the Jews concerned only the major urban centers, whereas the banks were licensed to operate in localities of the periphery so as to keep alive for the state a vital source of taxes and loans, even though credit in the small towns was more costly to urban clients who were considered foreigners outside their city of residence and whose pawns had to be transported, at further risk and cost[10]. Fi-

[8] Already in the year 1400 a Jew, whose services were requested by the local Wool Guild, agreed to lend in Treviso but only if he received a special license from Venice (Archivio di stato di Venezia, hereafter ASV, Senato misti, reg. 45, fol. 13r, 14 maggio). But it was only in 1424, in a period of heavy pressure against the Jews, concomitant and in the wake of Bernardino da Siena's preaching in the Veneto, that the Senate, having refused confirmation of the charter negotiated by rectors in Verona with three Jewish bankers, decreed that thenceforth no charter could be made with Jewish lenders without confirmation by the Senate itself: ibid., reg. 55, fol. 7v (30 marzo 1424). It should be noted that this latter provision was signalized in the margin, exceptionally, by some notary or scribe in the chancery with the words, in large letters, *JUDEORUM MORSUS* and a large "O", in obvious reference to the yellow sign Jews were once again required to wear. An attempt to rescind the law because of the *tedium* it involved was defeated five years later by a large majority: ibid., reg. 57, fol. 123r (1 July 1429).

[9] For the transfer of banks from cities to nearby towns, see *Carpi*, L'individuo e la collettività 33–34, 64. The counts of Porcia and Brugnera in Friuli (part of the Venetian Terraferma since 1420) negotiated charters, approved by the Senate, with Jews who seem to have both lived and lent money in the family's castles in the fifteenth century. The charter of 1580 explicitly states that the count was to *accettarmi [Abram ebreo] nel predetto suo castello di Brugnara et fenerar et mercantar*: *A. de Pellegrini*, Banchi di pegno degli ebrei nei castelli di Porcia e Brugnera (1451-1604), Sposalizio Fanny dei conti Porcia e Brugnera con E. Collarini, Venezia 1920 (Pordenone 1920) 24, kindly brought to my attention by Benny Arbel.

[10] *Carpi*, L'individuo e la collettività 63–64.

nally, the direct subjection was underscored also when litigation involving Jews was withdrawn from the jurisdiction of local courts and reserved for the court of the Venetian governor, as a ducal letter addressed to the podestà of Padua in 1434 shows[11]. In brief, direct subjection of Jews to the central government guaranteed them protection in return for the chance to tax them and extract loans from them. Whether that status as subjects involved any aspect of "servitude" is less important, although it remains interesting that the latter term was used at all in some contexts.

Citizenship

In spite of the positive elements entailed in the status of *subditi*, it is not surprising that Venice did not grant citizenship privileges to individual Jews, as it did to immigrant Christians, even during those periods when they legitimately resided and kept banks in the city of Venice (1382–1397, 1516–1797). In Romania, the status of *fidelis* and *Venetus albus* for Jewish residents was recognized, but it was useful for protection and for the privileges it entailed only there, not outside of the Romania[12]. Even after the onslaught of the Black Death when Venice invented incentives to repopulate not only the capital city but also the maritime colonies and offered citizenship privileges in 1353 to inhabitants and new immigrants to Negroponte, Coron, Modon, Candia, Canea, Rethimno, Sitia and their suburbs, the Senate underscored the exclusion of Jews from the provision: "*non intelligendo in hoc Iudeos*"[13].

Even though the exclusion was peremptory, Jews occasionally attempted to obtain some kind of privilege that would improve their ability to compete as interregional merchants, attempts that involved mere wishful thinking. Eliyahu Ashtor reported a notarial document of 1422 written in Alexandria in which Elia Capsali of Rethimno (Crete), a hosteller and wholesaler of wine, asked a Venetian nobleman and two Jewish merchants to petition the Venetian government in his name to get "some kind of special citizenship privilege (*de gratia spetiali … quoddam citadinantie privilegium*)", with clauses similar to those conceded to other faithful citizens ("*sicut aliis fidelibus civibus*") and with the seal of San Marco. Capsali promised to pay any and all expenses incurred, but he probably never received what he was looking for, that is, treatment as a local citizen as regards customs charges and the law of reprisals. It is a second case that makes one seriously doubt it[14].

Only three years later a countryman of Capsali, "*Cressonus judeus de Rethimno filius Solomonis Lazari de Meir*" was prosecuted and sentenced for having acquired

[11] *Antonio Ciscato*, Gli ebrei in Padova (1300–1800) (Padua 1901, repr. Bologna 1985) 179. Appeals, whether involving Jews or Christians, were heard in Venice by the *Avogadori di comun*.
[12] See *Jacoby*, Les Vénitiens naturalisés dans l'Empire Byzantin.
[13] ASV, Commemoriali, reg. 5, fol. 3r; Senato Misti, reg. 26, copia, fols. 245v–246v (21 June 1353).
[14] *Eliyahu Ashtor*, Ebrei cittadini di Venezia?, in: Studi veneziani 17–18 (1975–76) 145–156.

a false privilege, forged by a notary of the Venetian chancery for a fee of 40 ducats. He had told the notary he needed the letter patent as an international merchant: "*quia erat grossus mercator in partibus Crete et quod tractaretur pro cive in partibus Crete, quia Iudei tractantur pro forensibus*". The forged patent contained the following phrases:

> *quod dictus Cressonus, civis, subditus et habitator Rethimi, ad diversas mundi partes se conferat et mittat suos factores cum mercationibus et aliis rebus per mare et per terram; quod ipse Cressonus mercationes et res sue in mari et quolibet loco tractentur et expediantur secure, favorabiliter et benigne,*

that is, with the protection and favorable conditions owed to citizens of Rethimno (he did not aspire to Venetian citizenship – it was enough to be proven a citizen of Rethimno). But Cressono was sentenced for having procured a forgery, which means that he knew he could not aspire to the privilege legally. In fact, the forgery said he was a citizen, whereas he himself had admitted that Jews, even if *habitatores* of a city of the Venetian maritime dominion, were treated as *forenses*. Sentenced *in absentia*, he escaped incarceration and seems later to have been quite rehabilitated in Crete[15].

In Italy individual urban governments had the right to grant citizenship even to Jews when they saw fit to do so, as was the case in Perugia, whereas princes simply issued decrees. In Carrara Padua, for example, Francesco I il Vecchio around 1377 granted Paduan original citizenship (*quemadmodum cives originarii Patavii*) via a *decretum civilitatis* to a Jewish medical doctor and banker Abraham and his son. This privilege was renewed by Francesco II Novello in 1394 and again by the new overlord of Padua, Venice, in 1406. But two details characterize the privilege to be *scribantur in numero civium Padue* ...: first of all, normally a grant of citizenship to a Christian did not have to be renewed, as was this one, although it may well be that the Jews had requested the renewal in order to strengthen their position; secondly, the relevant clause in the charter reads that the lender, his employees and his family were "to be had, treated and reputed in all matters just as other citizens of Padua and Piove di Sacco", with the right to purchase real estate and the obligation

[15] ASV, Avogaria di comun, reg. 3647/II, f. 114 (13 May 1427). In December 1434 Venetian authorities "refused to prosecute Cressone (Gershon), a Jew of Rethymno, for thefts and exactions apparently attributed to him out of malice": *Zvi Ankori*, The Living and the Dead: the Story of Hebrew Inscriptions in Crete (Part I, The Lost Record) in: Proceedings of the American Academy for Jewish Research 38–39 (1970–71) 83. The same man, supplier to Venice of almonds, malmsey wine and other Cretan products, was bankrupt in 1450. A civil case regarding him mentions a sentence by the *Provveditori di comun* in 1426 and another case of 1432; see ASV, Giudici di petizion, Sentenze a giustizia, reg. 112, fols. 96v–99v (22 May 1450); the case of 1432 was actually an arbitration by which *Acresone hebreus qd. Salomonis* received *damnum* owed him by Marco di Pietro Muazzo: ibid., reg. 64, fols. 35v–36 (12 Feb. 1432, more veneto). For the case of a notorious spy working for Venice who was to receive tax-exemption in Crete "like Venetian citizens" (he also petitioned successfully for license to purchase real estate in Candia), see *David Jacoby*, Un agent Juif au service de Venise: David Mavrogonato de Candie, in: Thesaurismata 9 (1972) 79–80.

to pay taxes on it[16]. What Abraham received, at the same time as he opened his banking operation in Piove di Sacco in 1377, was probably a kind of temporary citizenship, according to the category defined by the jurist Onofrio Bartolini of Perugia in 1397, that is, he was to be treated "as other citizens" were treated for the duration of the charter by which he was licensed to lend at usury[17].

In exactly the same years but in a city long under Venetian rule, Treviso, Jews included under the provisions of a charter insisted on their being treated as citizens: *quod per formam ipsorum pactorum debent tractari tamquam alii cives Tarvisii* (1396). This privilege meant protection and some level of equal treatment under the law. In a document of 1409 the relevant clause promising quasi-citizenship read: *ceu proprie alios cives Tarvisini haberetis et prout in similibus vestros homines et cives pertractari*, that is, again they are to be "treated like other citizens and as you treat your citizens". If this phrase is ambiguous, taken literally, a little further on, when the charter is discussed as a document negotiated *inter cives et ipsos* the ambiguity vanishes: the *cives* are the Christian representatives, while *ipsi* are the other party, the Jews. As Angela Möschter writes, this kind of "citizenship" was not equatable with that of Christians because it was temporary and because it made possible neither employment in the government bureaucracy nor participation in the religious and civic rituals of the city, which were limited to Christians, that is, to *fideles*[18]. Even this temporary and incomplete kind of citizenship, however, was no longer offered to the Jews of Treviso after that and studies of other cities of the Terraferma have not brought to light examples of similar treatment. Finally, the nexus between citizenship and the right – or even obligation – to purchase real

[16] *Ciscato*, Gli ebrei in Padova 229–230: ...*habeantur, tractentur et reputentur in omnibus velut allij cives Padue et Plebis Sachi*. Also *Carpi*, L'individuo e la collettività 197–198, and *Francesca Zen Benetti*, Prestatori ebraici e cristiani nel Padovano fra Trecento e Quattrocento, in: *Cozzi* (ed.), Gli ebrei e Venezia 635–636. Ciscato pointed out that the *toscani*, the Christian moneylenders who operated in Padua before the arrival of the Jews, were obliged by the statutes to purchase a house and a terrain, whereby they became citizens of Padua. When Venice in 1423 gave Jews in all subject territories two years to sell any real estate they owned, the capital city took away any chance to become citizens in this traditional manner: *Ciscato*, Gli ebrei in Padova 17–18, 39. Under Venice, the Jews lost their single most important depositor, the Carrara lords. Francesco il Vecchio, for example, made a deposit of £ 90000 – some 25000 ducats – with one Jewish banker in 1372: *Benjamin G. Kohl*, Padua under the Carrara, 1305–1405 (Baltimore, London 1998) 140.

[17] The comune of Perugia had asked Bartolini for an opinion about the legal status of a Jew, who he said could be either *forensis*, *civis per tempus*, or *civis in perpetuum*. See *Ariel Toaff*, Judei cives? Gli ebrei nei catasti di Perugia del Trecento, in: Zakhor 4 (2000) 11–36. Abraham's son Joseph, who, as we will see below, was tried before several courts in Padua and Venice on charges of lending illegally, could defend himself against the interference of yet another judge on the basis that the latter did not have jurisdiction *inter cives*; see *Philippe Braunstein*, Le prêt sur gages à Padoue et dans le Padouan au milieu du XVe siècle, in: *Cozzi* (ed.), Gli ebrei e Venezia 661.

[18] *Angela Möschter*, Gli ebrei a Treviso durante la dominazione veneziana, in: Ebrei nella Terraferma veneta 75, and her Juden im venezianischen Treviso, Quellen, nos. 21–22, 426–427. For the "extraneousness" of the Jews in the *civitas christiana*, see, for example, *Giacomo Todeschini*, Spiritum non habentes: appunti sulla 'bestializzazione' degli ebrei nell'alto medioevo, forthcoming in: Studi in onore di Enzo D'Alessandro (Palermo 2006) (my thanks to the author for having made the text available to me prior to publication).

estate, as was normal for Christian immigrants and *novi cives*, was eliminated by the Venetian Senate in 1423 when it prohibited Jews from owning real property[19]. This development probably came about under the influence of minorite preaching. However, it may not have constituted a serious limitation to the freedom of Jews to invest money, since in the fifteenth century Jewish bankers had to invest in several and dispersed banking enterprises and keep their investments as liquid and mobile as possible, both by choice and per force, given the increased insecurity and the constant vacillation of the authorities between renewal and termination of licenses to lend.

In brief, in Venetian subject cities and towns, as in Europe generally, the *civitas* was in the essence *christiana*; the *infideles* were *extranei* and could at best be accepted *pro tempore* as *hospites*.

Taxation and forced loans

Most historians would agree with Michael Toch's metaphor comparing the Jews, especially the bankers, to "milk cows", to be taxed almost at will[20]. In economic terms, however, the concept has to be rendered more precise. First of all, ability to pay an annual tax imposed by the central government depended both on the exemption from local direct taxes and on the mix between the capital meant to be made available in a given locality and the ceilings placed on legal rates of interest. Both were essential elements of negotiation prior to agreement on a new charter. This is clear from the simple arithmetical option offered by the government to the Jews in Venice at the time of the renewal of their charter in 1385. The choice was between maximum interest rates of 10% on collateral and 12% on written instruments (chirographs) plus a tax of 4 000 ducats, or rates respectively of 8% and 10% with no tax. The Jews calculated that the higher rates would not produce the amount asked as an annual tax and opted therefore to lend at the lower rates, on the edge of profitability but unquestionably providing a service for the needy, as the Senate had requested. In 1397, the year of the expulsion of Jews from Venice, the Senate tried to tax the Jews in the province of Treviso for 3 000 ducats. The local governor called in representatives of all the centers involved in order to discuss the matter and the bankers showed, locality by locality, that with the capital they were required – by charter – to make available for loans and the limits imposed on interest rates, they would be unable to raise the requested tax. Figures at hand, they showed that the tax constituted 13.6% of the capital they were required to make

[19] ASV, Senato misti, reg. 54, fol. 147v (26 September 1423). The decree was published various times, not always completely. See *Sime Ljubić* (ed.), Listine o odnošajih izmedju Južnoga Slavenstva Mletačke republike, 10 vols. (Zagreb 1868–91) vol. 8 (1886) 253, and *Hippolyte Noiret* (ed.), Documents inédits pour servir à l'histoire de la domination vénitienne en Crète de 1380 à 1485 (Paris 1892) 297–98.

[20] *Michael Toch*, Die Juden im Mittelalterlichen Reich (Enzyklopädie Deutscher Geschichte 44, Munich 1998) 49–51.

available in loans, whereas in the major population centers of Treviso and Mestre, which served Venice, the maximum interest rate was only 14 or 15% on collateral. Table 1 makes this clear.

Table 1. Capital in the Jewish banks of the podesteria of Treviso in 1397 and the respective maximum rates of interest

Locality	capital (ducats)	maximum interest rates
Treviso	12300	14% on pawns (previously 15%)
Mestre	7400	14% on pawns
Conegliano	1000	20% on pawns and 25% on chirographs
Castelfranco	700	20% on pawns and 25% on chirographs
Serravalle	700	20% on pawns and 25% on chirographs
total:	22100	

Note to Table 1: Tax requested: 3000 ducats, divided by 22100 ducats = 13.6%.

By negotiation, the amount of the tax requested of the Jews, who asserted they would not be able to continue to lend if that level of taxation were imposed, was reduced[21].

A further clarification concerns the lowest links of the credit chain which are sometimes overlooked. Loans by Jews to individuals were often necessary to enable them to pay their local taxes, part of which in turn went to the central government (or to the local Venetian *Camera fiscale*). The following example of 1445 is enlightening. The administrators of Legnago in the district of Verona – the Veronese *podestà* and the Venetian *provveditore* of the fortress – seeing that the tax farmer was impounding the belongings of insolvent tax-payers, dispatched the town's unnamed Jew ("*el zudìo*") to Padua to find the liquid capital necessary to keep his lending bank supplied with money and the commune itself afloat (*de tegnir fornido el so bancho de denari, massime per satisfar ai debiti de comun*). The Jew was threatened by the two officials that if he were unsuccessful in finding funds he would be terminated, expelled and replaced – hopefully – by another Jew who would promise to meet local fiscal needs (*perchè speremo de atrovar zudìo servirà de denari abastanza*)[22]. At the top end of the credit chain was Venice, the ultimate beneficiary.

Finally, forced loans, generally at interest, paralleled the outright taxes owed by the Jews. So constant was the pressure of taxes and the recourse to loans that the

[21] The initial document was published by *Giampaolo Cagnin*, Cittadini e forestieri a Treviso nel Medioevo (secoli XIII–XIV) (Studi e fonti di storia locale, 7 Sommacampagna, Verona 2004) 152–154 and doc. 74, 485–487, while *Möschter*, Juden im venezianischen Treviso 162–166 and the respective Quellen, nn. 10–15, 408–417, puts it in the context of the continued discussion.

[22] *Gian Maria Varanini*, Appunti per la storia del prestito e dell'insediamento ebraico a Verona nel Quattrocento. Problemi e linee di ricerca, in: *Cozzi* (ed.), Gli ebrei e Venezia 620 and 627, n. 27, and in: *idem*, Comuni cittadini e stato regionale. Ricerche sulla Terraferma veneta nel Quattrocento (Verona 1992) 287–288.

Jewish pawn bankers of Mestre were permitted to rent houses in Venice in order to facilitate their business with the state, that is, for the payment of their debts to the Signoria and for the collection of credits owed them by the state, a presence permitted nominally for only twenty days per year[23].

Clearly, the expansion of Venice on the Terraferma in 1404–06 brought the capital city suddenly in touch with several Jewish communities, which they learned quickly to "milk" (some of whose members had previously lent in Venice, up to the expulsion of 1397). In 1406 the annual tax levied on the Jews in Padua was raised from 700 to 1 000 ducats[24]. In 1409 an annual tax of £1 000 (*di piccoli*) was levied on the lenders of both Mestre and Treviso who had been paying no taxes despite earning big profits (*magna utilitas et lucrum*)[25]. Less than a decade later additional dues of 500 and 1 000 ducats respectively were asked of Jews at the same banks because they were "very wealthy" and did not pay taxes on their patrimony; the Jews of Treviso, also "very numerous", were said to "have beautiful palaces, real estate and personal property"[26]. In 1432 the rent for the banks of Mestre, set at £2 000 in the condotta, was raised to £3 000, at which the Jews refused to continue lending; a compromise was attempted at £2 500[27]. During the war of Ferrara in 1483 the rent on those banks – then £600 each – was farmed out to three noblemen who collected the rents, which became for them a kind of annuity[28].

Beginning with Venice's expansion on the Terraferma, ordinary and extraordinary taxes and forced loans alternated, especially according to military needs, levied sometimes on individuals, sometimes on Jews of a specific city, sometimes on those of the Terraferma or on those of the dominions as a whole. The war against Milan provides various examples. In 1434 a surtax (*ultra illud quod presentialiter solvunt*) of 3 000 and 2 000 ducats was levied on Jews of the Terraferma and those *a parte maris* respectively[29]. In 1438 a tax of 4 000 ducats had been subdivided arbi-

[23] ASV, Collegio, Notatorio, reg. 10, fol. 112 (28 November 1464), which clearly states that the rented apartments were to be used for those Jews *huc venientibus pro taxatione et modis dandis circa recuperationem solvendarum pecuniarum nostro dominio* etc., as permitted by chapters 14, 19 and 23 of their concession. Almost immediately it was added, however, that the permission to have a *hospitium hebreorum* did not mean that complete synagogue services could be held in Venice – citing a bull of Pius II; ibid., fol. 113. The fiscal intent of the provision does not mean that the accommodations were not also used to facilitate the Jews' business with private clients living in Venice.

[24] ASV, Senato Misti, reg. 47, f. 54 (13 July).

[25] Ibid., reg. 48, f. 59 (21 March 1409).

[26] Ibid., reg. 52, fol. 2v (18 March 1417) for Treviso, whose Jews *sunt multi numero et valde divites et habent pulcerimas domos in Tarvisio et alias possessiones et bona multa et numquam sustenent aliquas factiones reales nec personales in casibus necessitatis*; for Mestre: ibid., fol. 88v (18 April 1418).

[27] Ibid., reg. 58, fols. 153v (31 October 1432) and 162v (9 December).

[28] Biblioteca del Museo Correr, Venice, Cod. Cicogna, 2835 II/2, parchment copy dated 22 September 1483, with an "appendix" of later Senate deliberations. The beneficiaries promoted the important renewal of the charter of Mestre in 1503: *Reinhold C. Mueller*, Charitable institutions, the Jewish community, and Venetian society, in: Studi veneziani 14 (1972) 67–68.

[29] Bilanci generali della Repubblica di Venezia, *Fabio Besta* (ed.), vol. I (Venice 1912) 105.

trarily by the Signoria among the areas closest to Venice, which prompted the Jews of the towns of Feltre and Belluno to petition the Senate to apply a proper *estimo* or calculation of ability to pay, a suggestion that was promptly accepted. The next imposition, of 9900 ducats, was consequently subdivided as follows: Padua and Treviso 3500 ducats each; Vicenza 1500; Istria and Bassano 500 each; and Feltre and Belluno 200 ducats each, which also gives an idea of the relative size of the communities[30]. Again, in 1439 the Jew Moses of Mestre was forced to lend to the Signoria 4000 ducats at 12% interest in order that it could pay arrears due to the mercenary captain Gattamelata[31]. In late 1453 the Senate imposed a tax of 16000 ducats, half on the Jews of the Terraferma (including Istria), half on those of the *Stato da mar*, due in two payments in the following year[32].

Given delays by the state in paying its mercenary captains, the *condottieri* themselves were often forced to take loans from Jews in order to keep their armies together. Anastasio di S. Angelo, one of the captains killed in a battle against Turkish invaders in Friuli in 1477, turned out to have debts of 545 ducats with Jews, a sum which the Signoria offset (*excomputa*) from the annual tax owed by the Jews, but required restitution of the pawns[33]. Late in the century Jewish pawn bankers lent much money to the *condottiere* Tuzio da Costanza to maintain his army; at a certain point he asked that his payments of "usury" be suspended to help him redeem his "many belongings"; a moratorium of seven months was negotiated by the Senate with Samuel of Mestre and Isopo of Castelfranco (where he had his fief) so that the pawns could be redeemed for the principal alone[34].

Shortly thereafter, at the start of the maritime war with the Turks in 1499, diplomatic sources learned that the imposition of a tax of 25000 ducats on the Jews was hoped to serve as guarantee for a quick and much-needed advance from the Pisani bank on the Rialto, itself pressed by its depositors during the banking crisis of that year[35]. A decade later, the war of the League of Cambrai caused many hundreds of Jews of the Terraferma to take refuge in Venice, where some also transferred their

[30] See *Matteo Melchiorre*, Gli ebrei a Feltre nel Quattrocento. Una storia rimossa, in: Ebrei nella Terraferma veneta 89.

[31] *Michael E. Mallett* and *John R. Hale*, The Military Organization of a Renaissance State: Venice ca. 1400 to 1617 (Cambridge 1984) 129, n. 123.

[32] ASV, Senato terra, reg. 3, fol. 89v (7 December 1453), passed unanimously; cf. *Besta* (ed.), Bilanci generali, 125n. The end of the war did not bring the Jews immediate relief: in 1455 an annual surtax for five years was levied, 2000 each from Jews of the Terraferma and from Crete, 1000 from those elsewhere in the maritime provinces (ibid. 130); in 1463 at the outbreak of the war with the Turks a new surtax of 5000 ducats was levied (ibid. 138–139).

[33] ASV, Senato terra, reg. 8, fol. 31r–v (14 December 1478); cf. *Mallet* and *Hale*, Military Organization 49, n. 122.

[34] ASV, Collegio, Notatorio, reg. 14, fol. 140 (9 June 1496); cf. *Mallet* and *Hale*, Military Organization 199.

[35] The Milanese ambassador wrote of the imposition on 25 May, adding *et si crede ne sarà servita dal bancho de' Pisani sopra questo assignamento*: Archivo di stato di Milano, Sforzesco, cart. 1271. Two weeks later representatives of the Jews complained that they were having trouble collecting from all the Jews, whether bankers or not: ASV, Collegio, Notatorio, reg. 15, fol. 5v (5 June 1499). For the crisis and the involvement of Mestran Jews as straw men for illegal loans on pawns by

banks. At one point in the year 1512 the Jews were taxed for 10 000 ducats but they refused to pay, saying that they "had pawns but no money" – to which the government replied by imprisoning two bankers and five other heads of the community[36].

As we have already seen, forced loans and taxes were extracted also from the Jewish communities in Crete, in an entirely different context, however, since those Jews were not bound by charters, but were permanent residents, some few active as moneylenders but most as artisans and merchants. The extent to which there were formal pawn banks at all in Crete is not completely clear[37]. But there were enough wealthy Jews to prompt the government to levy taxes and forced loans. In 1408 the Jew Cassano, *habitator Candide* but at that moment present in Venice, a man described as *dives et potens*, agreed to lend 500 ducats to enable the state to get the Candia galleys off. He lent the money *ad cambium*, that is, via a draft on the Venetian government of Crete, payable at term in Candia[38]. A huge loan of 20 000 ducats was levied on Jews of Crete in 1431, which the government of Crete was prohibited from repaying without specific approval from the Senate[39]. In 1441 the Jews of Crete taken together were to advance 4 000 ducats necessary to pay the interest due on Venice's public debt, a loan at 10% interest to meet the 3–4% interest due on the state's own obligations in the portfolios of its citizens. Quick repayment of the loan, presumably by remittance from the capital city, was called for later so as to limit the accumulation of interest (*usura*) that the state would have to pay to the Jews[40]. After a few years the Jews of Candia, said to be *multi et potentes*, were called upon, as the Jews of the Terraferma had been, to lend 5 000 ducats to expedite the departure of a convoy of seven heavily armed galleys up the Po river against the army of Milan. In order to have the money rapidly, it was gotten by a draft on the government of Crete but payable by the Jews within one month of presentation of the bill of exchange, with penalties – in case of refusal – for all concerned[41]. One way or another, by taxes or by loans, funds made available by the Jews of

Florentine bankers, see *Reinhold C. Mueller*, The Venetian Money Market: Banks, Panics and the Public Debt, 1200–1500 (Baltimore and London 1997) chapter 6, 240–241.

36 *Sanuto*, Diarii, vol. 14, col. 255, 258, 291, 304 (May–June 1512).

37 The wording of two deliberations is not completely unequivocal. In 1447 a loan of 5 000 ducats was requested from *Judei civitatis Candide fenerantes*, and in 1462 there was an accusation against Jews of Candia for exploiting Christians who left pawns as collateral for loans (… *circa factum pignerum que ipsi [Iudei] habent a Christianis in mutuo fenerationis* …): *Noiret*, Documents 417–18, 479. As regards merchants, it is noteworthy that the Senate reiterated papal threats of automatic excommunication of anyone who took aboard any ship "perfidious Jews" or their goods (1429) or allowed them to serve as brokers (1433), but it is doubtful that such declarations actually impeded commercial transactions between Christians and Jews: ibid. 329, 359–61.

38 ASV, Senato misti, reg. 48, fol. 44 (14 November 1408).

39 *Noiret*, Documents 372 (the prohibition to repay is dated 1435).

40 ASV, Senato mar, reg. 1, fol. 12v (21 January 1441): … *restituendo autem subito predictos denarios suprascriptis Judeis ut minus damnum usuarum curat dominio nostro*; the loan seems to have been made two years earlier (see *Noiret*, Documents 387).

41 Ibid., reg. 3, fol. 37v (27 December 1447), in: *Noiret*, Documents 417–18; cf. also ibid. 436, 530.

Venice's dominions constituted an important lubricant for the gears of the machines of war.

Economic activity

The topic of economic activity calls for a premise. There was a fundamental difference between the condition of Jews in the Terraferma – some of Italian or Roman heritage, others decendents of immigrants from Germany[42] – and those in the Venetian maritime provinces, who were largely members of communities that originated from Byzantine settlements of centuries earlier, even though many Jews of Candia were Ashkenazi. The leaders of the communities in the Terraferma were generally the bankers, whose licenses to lend corresponded to their permission to reside – for the time span defined by the charter – in a given locality. The right to ply other arts and trades was generally subservient to the role of the bankers and often tied to the limitations of the same. We know little about most trades, aside from shops dealing in second-hand goods, which will be touched upon below; mere mentions are often the best we can do. For example, in Mestre, among the 27 Jews and their families who rented houses between 1466 and 1507 from the Confraternity of S. Maria dei Battuti, which administered the local hospital, we find one registered as dyer and hat-maker, one was a *scriptor*, one a weaver, one a goldsmith, and the hospital occasionally called in a Jewish doctor to care for the sick[43]. The much larger community in Treviso had an inn, with an innkeeper (and a *famulus in hospitio*), a stall for the horses (and a *famulus ad stallam*), a carter, a paper maker, a cook, as well as a medical doctor; there are mentions of transporters to Venice of goods, especially perishables (perhaps kosher foods); because of the existence of a jeshiva, besides a rabbi there were other *magistri*, a scribe and a school teacher[44].

By contrast, Jews in the maritime dominions were active in nearly all private walks of life. They could be long-distance merchants, retailers and artisans – from tanners to goldsmiths; among them there were some professional moneylenders but they were not necessarily leaders of the community; the right of Jews to reside in a given city was therefore not delimited by charters or *condotte*. Although, as we have seen, they were not – with the notable exception of Corfu – considered citizens, Jews were recognized as Venetian *fideles* simply by reason of their residence in a Venetian territory. On the other hand, even that somewhat privileged status

[42] *Ariel Toaff*, Convergenza sul Veneto di banchieri ebrei romani e tedeschi nel tardo Medioevo, in: *Cozzi* (ed.), Gli ebrei e Venezia 595–613.

[43] *Alessandra Checchin*, La scuola e l'ospedale di S. Maria dei Battuti di Mestre dalle origini al 1520 (Centro Studi Storici Mestre, Quaderno di studi e notizie 6, Mestre 1996) 59, 100 (table 14); the confraternity also took a small loan from a Jew that allowed them to finish the sacristy of the church.

[44] *Möschter*, Juden im venezianischen Treviso 128–136. The author identified numerous *famuli*, mostly Jews themselves (128, n.98).

did not relieve them of the requirement – imposed by Venice around 1325 but harking back to a much earlier situation in Constantinople – to live in defined areas, *ebraiké, judaiche* or *giudecche*, which was not the case in the cities of the Terraferma[45].

Pawn banking is the economic activity of Jews in the Terraferma about which we know most, in part from the charters but also from notarial contracts and testaments unearthed in recent investigations. Three factors seem worth underscoring: a) the relatively small numbers of Jews making up even the largest communities, such as those of Treviso and Padua (with some 150 members each in the early 15th century); b) the fact that their permanence in a given locality was continually at the whim of the authorities, the preachers and the populace; c) the endogamy of this religious and ethnic minority, which protected patrimonies and directed dowries within a small circle of families – all these factors brought the economic leaders among the Jews to resort to what seems to be the most extensive mobility known in medieval Italian entrepreneurship of both human capital and money capital, irregardless of political boundaries, through complex networks that can be only partially reconstructed. The active economic role of especially Ashkenazi women, not only as investors but also as owners and managers of banks, is part of the picture[46]. The examples are myriad but I will limit myself – using extreme oversimplification – to only two families revolving initially around Padua during the transition from Carrara lordship to Venetian dominion, without naming the numerous other Jewish partners and investors in each bank and their diverse places of origin[47].

The Finzi brothers of Ancona, Salomone, Gaio and Manuele, recent immigrants to Padua, dissolved two banking partnerships in 1380, one of them with the very considerable capital of 12000 ducats, and contemporaneously established a new

[45] *Jacoby*, Venice and the Venetian Jews 43, 37.

[46] See *Miriam Davide*, Il ruolo delle donne nelle comunità ebraiche dell'Italia nord-orientale (Padova, Treviso, Trieste e Friuli), in: Ebrei nella Terraferma veneta 31–43, from which it is clear that women of German origin were freer to become directly involved in banking activity than were those of Italian or Roman origin, because of their distinctly different mores. See also the article by Keil in this volume.

[47] In general on the mobility of Jews and on the familial character of their networks, see especially *Michele Luzzati*, Banchi e insediamenti ebraici nell'Italia centro-settentrionale fra tardo Medioevo e inizi dell'Età moderna, in: Storia d'Italia, Annali, 11, Gli ebrei in Italia, ed. *Corrado Vivanti* (Turin 1996) 175–238, and *Möschter*, subchapter entitled "Netzwerke: Verbindungen trevisanischer Bankiers in andere Städte und Regionen", in her Juden im venezianischen Treviso 128–133. The movement of not only principals but also factors and lesser employees should be kept in mind. Among the Jewish witnesses called to testify about the operations of the banker Joseph di maestro Abraamo, discussed immediately below, Bonaiuto di Bonaiuto said that in the last decade he had not been employed by a bank; Salomon *strazarolus* said that he had worked for Beniamino Finzi up to four years before; Salomon di Abraam that he was *olim factor in bancho Michaletis*; Abraam de Mele that he was *ad presens factor in bancho Beniamini [Finzi] et olim in bancho Bovis*; Mandolin that he was factor in the bank at S. Lorenzo, while previously he had been factor in that at the Volto de' Negri; Mele Vitale, finally, said he was at the time *famulus* in the bank at S. Lucia, but *olim famulus in nonnullis aliis banchis Hebreorum*: Biblioteca Marciana, Venice, Mss. lat., cl. XIV, 290 (= 4261), fasc. III, fol. 4v (March 1449).

company in Padua – with a capital of 9000 ducats – together with other partners, none of whom were resident there. In the same act the partners founded a new bank in nearby Montagnana, with a capital of 3800 ducats. In 1389 they purchased a half interest in a bank in Lendinara (for 2420 ducats). In the 1390s they invested in banks in Badia Polesine, Rovigo, and Este, while maintaining principal ownership and management of the bank in Padua. Even though Salomone, a medical doctor, moved to Bologna where he opened a bank in 1418 and lent money to the commune, in Padua – a city subject to Venice after 1405 – he, Gaio and the heirs of Manuele continued to invest in banks there and outside of the city. Benjamino and Consiglio, sons of Manuele, ran a bank in Vicenza, where Benjamino, who seems to have learned the business at a bank in Rovigo, resided for almost thirty years. He also invested heavily in a second bank in Vicenza, one in Cologna Veneta and one in Modena, until 1445, before returning to Padua to manage yet another bank. At the same time, Gaio and Benjamino remained partners initially in the bank in Lendinara, then in that of Rovigo, managed by yet other partners from nearby Ferrara. Around 1426 Gaio followed his brother and an uncle to Bologna where he obtained the license for a lending bank in 1428, leaving his sons to represent his interests in Padua and Montagnana. Beginning in 1437, after Gaio's death, the latter's sons took over the banks of Lendinara, where Joseph resided, and Rovigo, where Leuccio resided, till 1462 – all the while maintaining interests in banks in Bologna and Ferrara, where the third son, Consiglio, resided[48].

The second case involves a single person, the above-mentioned medical doctor *maestro Abraham di maestro Aleuccio da Roma*, formerly doctor to pope Innocent VII and "original citizen" of Padua. By 1377 he had a bank in Piove di Sacco, by 1392 he was head also of a bank in Padua in which he, together with a partner, had already invested 6000 ducats in 1380; both concessions were renewed by Venice in 1406. Before 1401 he had partnerships in six further banks: Este, Bagnocavallo, Soave, Cittadella, Monselice and an unnamed location "in the Trevigiano or Lombardy". Between 1406 and his death about 1420 Abraham maintained his role in both banks in Piove di Sacco and in Padua and had partnerships in another bank in Padua as well as in banks in Vicenza, Bologna, and Siena[49].

Abraham's son Joseph (*Joseph quondam magistri Abraam da Roma quondam Aliuzzo*) continued the business as licensed titular head of banks in the small centers of Piove di Sacco and Este, run by factors, while he himself resided in Padua – after 1423 in rented houses – where it seems he invested in one or more local banks. His taxable patrimony was estimated at 10500 ducats in 1434, 8000 in 1442

[48] *Carpi*, L'individuo e la collettività, chap. 1; for Salomone and Gaio Finzi in Bologna, see *Maria Giuseppina Muzzarelli,* I banchieri e la città, in: Banchi ebraici a bologna nel XV secolo, ed. by *eadem* (Bologna 1994) 105–106; also *Rachele Scuro*, La presenza ebraica a Vicenza e nel suo territorio nel Quattrocento, in: Ebrei nella Terraferma veneta 110–113; *Elisabetta Traniello*, Tra appartenenza ed estraneità: gli ebrei e le città del Polesine di Rovigo nel Quattrocento, in: Ebrei nella Terraferma veneta 163–168; and *eadem*, Gli ebrei e le piccole città. Economia e società nel polesine del Quattrocento (Rovigo 2004) 72–81, 90–111.

[49] *Carpi*, L'individuo e la collettività 195–204. Cf. *Kohl*, Padua 272.

and 1445. By comparison, the Paduan *condotta* of 1437 shows an unexplained drop in capital to be made available by the five banks from 25 000 to 15 000 ducats. We know about Joseph's operations because he was accused by a coreligionist of lending illegally in Padua, practically as an interloper, to which he countered a) that the *condotta* permitted lending by more than the five licensed banks, and b) that he had a secret agreement with a licensed banker to begin lending when that bank found itself illiquid. The tension during the court procedure, which lasted years, must have been considerable, also within the Jewish community itself: both the accuser, promised a cut of any eventual fine, and the accused were Jews, and the translator for the court of entries from his account books was a baptised Jew and *strazarolo*. Some witnesses accused Joseph of mistreating the poor and the peasants, but all of them were themselves wealthy[50].

In light of such widespread and rapidly changing investments in moneylending operations, involving several Jewish partners and investors even from distant regions and across political boundaries, it is understandable that the head of a bank named in a charter might at a given moment move elsewhere. In other words, whole banks could be bought and sold, as could shares in them, even during the validity of a charter. On at least one occasion, in 1447, the municipal council of Padua tried to simplify matters by making an agreement with a single Jewish banker, in this case a Iacop *de Florentia seu de Perusio*, charging him with the task of finding interested parties for the five other banks of the city, as *conductor omnium bancorum Padue*. At the same time, limits might be set in order to promote competition among the banks; in 1435 the charter for Vicenza, which specified that four banks make available 20 000 ducats, stated that they were to be *divisi et separati*, although that might have been wishful thinking[51]. If in the larger cities the matter of licensing operations could be rather flexible, so that it was not always necessary to be specifically named in a *condotta*, by contrast, in smaller towns the charter often contained a specific clause granting the chartered bank monopoly rights, to protect the owner or operator from unwelcome competition in a limited market.

Little that is new can be said about the daily operation of banks, given the paucity of accounting documents, but since two known fragments of accounts regarding cities of the Terraferma are extant, it is worth reviewing them briefly.

The above-mentioned legal prosecution of Joseph son of master Abraham of Padua, last studied by Philippe Braunstein, produced extracts from his accounts[52].

[50] *Braunstein*, Le prêt sur gages à Padoue 653–663; for the identification of Joseph as son of the medical doctor Abraham, see *Carpi*, L'individuo e la collettività 31.

[51] *Carpi*, L'individuo e la collettività 31, 62, 115–123, 125.

[52] *Braunstein*, Le prêt sur gages à Padoue; almost all the accounts were published by *Antonio Medin* and *G. Tolomei*, Per la storia aneddotica dell'università di Padova nel secolo XVI, in: Atti e memorie della R. Accademia di scienze, lettere ed arti in Padova (a. 370, n. s., vol. 27, 1910–11) appendix 1, 102–122. I have also consulted the original manuscript dossier in Biblioteca Marciana, Venice, Mss. lat., cl. XIV, 290 (=4261), fasc. III. The accounts were considered by *Léon Poliakov*, Les banchieri juifs et le Saint-Siège du XIIIe au XVIIe siècle (Paris 1965) 134n, 150–51.

These were used as evidence to prove both that he lent money illegally in Padua while being licensed to lend only in Piove di Sacco and Este where he had some of the pawns transferred, and that he sometimes charged compound interest on overdue loans (a charge made against the Jewish lenders of Padua as a whole). As a result, the entries translated for the court reflect occasional loans, made more or less secretively, to the wealthy rather than the daily operation of a normal bank, but they are nonetheless enlightening. The first entries concern a doctor in arts and medicine, *maistro Nicolò di maistro Galeazzo di Santa Sofia*, whose entries for the years 1433 to 1441 show that he continually renewed his loans and his pawns, obviously turning over valuables he did not need but did not wish to sell in exchange for liquidity, for sums ranging from as little as £30 *di piccoli* to as much as 110 ducats. Some pawns were kept for as long as three years for loans paying the legal rate of 20% interest per year, before being redeemed; they were entered on the books of the bank at Este, where the pawns themselves had probably been transferred. Nicolò was one of Joseph's accusers, even though he had been a client for 25 years, continually adjusting his balances and exchanging his pawns. Among the professors and medical doctors was the jurist Francesco Porcellino, who borrowed 90 ducats in 1444 on valuables, while his brother and another Porcellino, also jurists, borrowed 18 ducats each on books (*II letture cum tavola*, *uno Degesto vechio*); Joseph registered one loan in Este, the other in Piove di Sacco, but kept the books in his residence in Padua. Among the notable clients of Joseph were at least two Venetian noblemen (Alvise Storlato[53] and Piero Badoer), the marquis Taddeo d'Este, mercenary captain in the Venetian army for thirty years, beginning in 1416, his wife Margherita Pio, and Alberto Pio, lord of Carpi, who was represented by Taddeo d'Este's chancellor. Quite a few clients were Paduan noblemen. There were also artisans and shopkeepers, like the three *speziali* who borrowed sums of 79, 50 and 16 ducats; three dyers of the same family took loans of 70–90 ducats in 1438 and again in 1447, on the same pawns, perhaps as renewals; even a Paduan banker (*banchiero*, *cambiadore*), Giovanni Moreia, in 1428 borrowed £ 110 (21.6 ducats) and renewed the same loan ten years later, on different pawns. Some clients were students, like Giovanni *de Cicilia* who pawned a copy of Avicenna for 6 ducats. Several borrowers exchanged pawns at the time of renewal of their loan. In brief, this court case takes us outside the clauses of the usual *condotta*, which insisted on a fixed maximum term for a loan on collateral, generally one year plus 15 days. Joseph had well-to-do clients who stayed with him for many years, clients who formed part of the Paduan ruling group (Braunstein reports a request for an inter-

[53] Procurator of San Marco, twice rector in Padua (podestà in 1435, capitano in 1446), Storlato was married to Maria di Iacopo di Francesco il Vecchio da Carrara: *Medin* and *Tolomei*, Per la storia 120, n. 2. Storlato, who was very wealthy indeed, also pawned jewels in Mestre, as we know from the papers of his estate, administered by the Procurators of San Marco. On 13 July 1459 the latter repaid the Jew Zaccaria, factor of the Jew Cressono, *tenenti banchum usure in Mestre, pro capitali* [30 ducats] *et usure* [6 ducats], that is, at 20% for an undefined period, upon which a mounted ruby (*ballasium in tabula*) was re-consigned. See ASV, Procuratori di San Marco, commissarie, de ultra, b. 265, commissaria Alvise Storlato, reg. 1, fol. 7.

est-free loan for the friend of a client and an anomalous loan made to one of the negotiators for the commune of the then current *condotta*). Even though his lending activity in Padua was in the end ruled illegal and he was finally condemned after having to go from one court to another in both Padua and Venice, he seems not to have been considered an interloper by the licensed Jewish bankers of the city since after sentencing the authorities sequestered the pawns and liquid funds he had deposited at their banks, which the latter had in no way been obliged to accept[54].

If the accounts of the Paduan pawn banker Joseph were out of the ordinary, those produced during the prosecution of Jews in Brescia a generation later for the same crime – non-observance of the charter – seem more in line with daily practice, even if they cover only ten days. Upon the accusation of a citizen of Brescia in 1488 that Jews were running illegal lending operations there and keeping the pawns in their homes rather than transferring them to their licensed banks elsewhere, an investigation was initiated by the Venetian podestà. Accounting materials – a sheet of paper of Moysé, a small notebook of Lazzaro and two regular accountbooks of some 140 folios each of Vitale and Joseph – were sequestered and the accuser found a Jew who would translate entries for the last ten days of October, under oath but also under protection of anonymity. The entries reflect mostly small loans on relatively poor collateral made to a cross section of members of the populace. Only five loans exceeded 12 lire (the highest was £ 66 5s granted by Moysé to a tailor on pawns of cloth and clothing); quite a few were of £ 1 or less, one for as little as 2s; a bed-sheet or covering (*linzuolo*) brought each of three borrowers 34s, 10s and 8s respectively; nine borrowers were tailers (some of them masters) and one of them had recourse to two lenders; even persons called goldsmiths appear as borrowers of very small sums of money (11s to £ 5). The podestà Giovanni Donà threw out the case as baseless and unjust (*tamquam indebite, injuste et calumniose*), the accuser was forced to promise he would not bring similar charges in the future, and the accounts were returned to the Jewish lenders[55]. Thus, if the accusation against the Jews in Brescia was the same as that against Joseph in Padua, the outcome was just the opposite: rapid justice and a sentence of not guilty.

What is important to underscore here, despite the perfectly correct insistence in recent historiography that attention be given to a more complete social and economic history of the Jewish minority in Christian society, is that Christian society had need of moneylenders. If Jewish lenders closed their banks out of protest against demands made by local authorities, the populace might protest and force the council to come to terms[56]. Examples from the accounts of Joseph son of mas-

[54] See the dossier cited above, notes 47 and 52, fols. 95v–97r, accounts not published by *Medin* and *Tolomei* in Per la storia.

[55] *Fabio Glissenti*, Gli Ebrei nel Bresciano al tempo della dominazione veneta. Nuove ricerche e studi (Brescia 1891) 21–22, 56–61.

[56] See the examples in *Ciscato*, Gli ebrei in Padova 42–46, referring to negotiations held in the 1430s.

ter Abraham clearly reflect the extent to which Jews were necessary, not only to the poor or, in the case of Padua, to impecunious students, mentioned in the documents as prime clients, but also to members of the urban elite. The latter – as long as they dealt with that particular lender – did not have to observe those clauses of the charters that called for repayment of loans within a given time, after which the pawn or pawns were to be sold. Loans to members of the elite could be in the hundreds, even thousands of ducats. There are cases of recourse to Jews for sizeable loans by religious entities – bishops in Padua and Verona, the cathedral chapter of Padua, the major confraternity of Mestre (for the construction of a sacristy), the hospital of Treviso[57] – as well as by city governments[58]. The Jewish lenders, as long as they were accepted, were part and parcel of the whole urban economic system.

Closely connected to moneylending was the trade in second-hand goods, the *strazzaria* or *pezzaria*, that flourished among the Jews especially in certain urban centers. While Jews in Mestre had to bring unredeemed pawns to Venice for sale at public auction, supervised by the Venetian Sopraconsoli, in order to safeguard the collateral of Venetians and to guarantee that they did not lose any eventual residual balance (*soprabondanza*) above principal and interest, those in Padua and especially those in Vicenza were not so obliged and after a given time the lenders could claim complete ownership of the pawns. These they were then free to keep or to sell at the best price possible, to cover at least the principal and interest of the loans for which they had been collateral and perhaps something more. As a result, the *strazzaria* grew rapidly into a trade that dealt in selling unredeemed pawns, as well as other second-hand – and sometimes even new – goods. Of course that put them in direct competition with Christian second-hand dealers; those of Padua accepted the Jews as members of their guild, with a special "section" of their own and with

[57] For the loan of 500 ducats made to the bishop Albanio Michiel by four Jews in 1409–11, guaranteed on contributions by the faithful and by sureties who were among the principal citizens of Padua, repaid after two years by the "Paduan clergy", see ibid. 46–47, *Carpi*, L'individuo e la collettività 203, 206, and *Antonio Rigon*, Clero e città: "fratalea cappellanorum", parroci, cura d'anime in: Padova dal 12° al 15° secolo (Padua 1988) 145 (kindly brought to my attention by M. Melchiorre). Zen Benetti mentions as client also Francesco Capodilista, Paduan nobleman, doctor, and bishop of Foligno, as well as an anonymous *dominus episcopus* of Padua: Prestatori ebraici e cristiani 649, n. 90. Even Ermolao Barbaro, when named bishop of Verona, had dealings with a local Jew, authorized to make a payment on an episcopal *mandatum*: *Varanini*, Società cristiana e minoranza ebraica 159, n. 48. The Paduan cathedral chapter borrowed money from a Jew (probably Leone di Salomone da Costanza) at the bank of the *Volto dei Negri*, on pawns of the *sacrestia*; the loan was repaid with £ 216.6 (38 ducats) in 1449 by the canon Giacomo Condulmer, relative of the recently deceased Eugenius IV; since the pawns were ritual items, as was expressly forbidden by the terms of the *condotta*, the Venetian Senate and the local *podestà* intervened to order their restitution: *Matteo Melchiorre*, Conti in Cattedrale. Storia economica della Sacrestia del Duomo di Padova nella prima metà del Quattrocento, unpublished thesis of the "laurea specialistica", (University of Venice 2006) 201–203. The hospital of S. Maria dei Battuti in Treviso borrowed money from *Jacob Iudeus* in 1414 *ad usuram* in order to pay two outstanding debts: Archivio di stato di Treviso, Ospedale, b. 393 (under the year 1414). For Mestre, see above, note 43.

[58] Vicenza, to give only one example, took loans in 1438 for the purchase of arms and wheat "necessary for the marketplace and for the city": *Scuro*, La presenza ebraica a Vicenza 111.

special privileges, while those of Vicenza seem to have insisted on payment to the guild of the matriculation fee for the right to open shops, without thereby granting them full membership[59].

The case of Vicenza shows how the *pezzaria* was reinforced after the termination of the license to lend in the city in 1445, a termination caused both by Minorite preaching and by pressure from Christian moneylenders, especially local patricians, anxious to see their competition leave the city. When local notables took over lending in the city, largely via fictitious contracts, at least one Jewish banker resettled in Arzignano, the major town of the contado. The former employees of the bankers, however, remained in Vicenza without the need of a charter and managed shops offering for sale used clothing and goods, including, in all likelihood, the unredeemed pawns left with the very banks that had been forced to relocate. In social terms, it was the Ashkenazi pawn bankers who retired from the city, while the Italian Jews remained to ply the flourishing trade of the *pezzaria*[60].

Two special cases: Capodistria and Corfu

Two cases stand out as particularly interesting, the first in the Istrian peninsula, considered sometimes as part of the Terraferma, sometimes as part of the *Stato da Mar*, the other the city and island colony of Corfu[61].

Capodistria

The case of Capodistria is unique to the extent that what is for all practical purposes a charter for the presence of Jewish moneylenders in the city, but without specific names of Jews and without any temporal reference, was included as chapter 76 of Book II of the statutes of the city, dated 1423. In fact, the title of the chapter is *De pactis et conventionibus usurariorum* and it seems that the terms were put to the test in actual *condotte* contracted with Jewish lenders in 1391 and 1409 and only then included in the statutes. The wording is left generic so that it would apply to *quilibet Iudeus vel Iudea* wishing to lend money at usury "to the people, citizens and inhabitants of Capodistria". He or she would merely have to register at the communal chancery before opening for business. It is a quite flexible and permissive text, dating from the same year that Bernardino da Siena was preaching in the Veneto against those city governments which treated Jews as other than infidels, to be kept strictly apart from the Christian population[62].

59 *Ciscato*, Gli ebrei in Padova 253–260, doc. X (1448), and *Scuro*, La pezzaria ebraica a Vicenza nella seconda metà del Quattrocento, in: Zakhor 9 (2006) 13–43.

60 *Scuro*, La presenza ebraica a Vicenza 108–115.

61 In general, see *Benjamin Arbel*, Colonie d'oltremare, in: Storia di Venezia, vol. V, Il Rinascimento: società ed economia, ed. by *Alberto Tenenti* and *Ugo Tucci* (Rome 1996) 947–985.

62 The statutes, printed in Venice in 1668, were edited by *Lujo Margetić*, Lo statuto del comune di Capodistria del 1423 con le aggiunte fino al 1668 (Rovigno 1993) 92–94 for cap. 76. The most re-

Clauses regarding the status of the Jews are dispersed among those concerning rates of interest and other details of moneylending. No direct concession of citizenship was made, not even temporary, but the ambiguous formulation used in Trevisan charters appears here as well: the Jews were "to be treated and reputed as other citizens and inhabitants of Capodistria are treated, reputed and held"[63]. Similarly, the Jews were given the same right "to trade, to buy and to sell as other merchants of Capodistria, both movable goods and real estate and also customs farms"[64]. The exact date of the statute is not given, but it is clearly some months prior to the law of 26 September 1423 which forbade Jews in lands under Venetian domination to own real estate, which may have forced the authorities to amend the statute very soon after promulgation. At the same time, the Jewish moneylenders – for the statute regards only them and their extended families and employees – were exempted from paying local taxes, which obviously set them off from "other citizens" or other local "merchants".

The clauses regarding loans are scattered throughout chapter 76. First of all, the moneylenders were to operate *ad bancum publicum*; if they needed to leave the city on business, they had to find a replacement, who was bound by the same pact or charter. If they left definitively, they could cede their rights to other Jewish moneylenders, but they had to give four months' notice in order to permit borrowers to redeem their pawns. The total amount to be made available was 1 000 ducats. Loans made to citizens and residents on pawns could earn a maximum of 12.5% per year, loans on written notes 15%; the rate of interest on loans to "foreigners", on the other hand, was open to negotiation and had no ceiling. Unreclaimed pawns were to be sold at auction to the highest bidder on three successive Sundays.

Given the date of the statute, 1423, that is the same year that Bernardino da Siena was preaching in the Veneto, it is particularly interesting that the Venetian rector (*podestà*) was enjoined to see to it that no *ecclesiastica persona*, inquisitor or cleric, be allowed to molest the Jews, that is neither by legal prosecution nor in the course

cent analysis of chapter 76 in legal terms is by *Dea Moscarda*, L'area alto adriatica tra sovranità imperiale e autonomia locale, Deputazione di Storia Patria per la Venezia Giulia (Trieste 2002) 154–164, with bibliography referring also to the earlier *condotte*. This case and the pertinent bibliography were brought to my attention in a term paper written for my research seminar by Julie Florence Dournon, whom I thank for her assent to my using her material. For elsewhere in Istria, see the *capitoli* of 1484 in Piran, published by *Antonio Ive*, Dei banchi feneratizi e capitoli degli ebrei di Pirano e dei Monti di pietà in Istria, Italian translation (Rovigno 1881) appendix, and *Janez Peršič*, Židje in kreditno poslovanje v srednjeveškem Piranu (Jews and credit transactions in medieval Piran) (Lublijana 1999). *Rita Moretti*, La presenza ebrea a Rovigno in epoca veneta. Storie nascoste da non dimenticare, Centro di ricerche storiche, Rovigno, Atti 23 (1993) 471–80; the author cites the statutes of neighboring Muggia (1420), which refer to the *castighi che Dio diede alli falsi e perversi Giudei* (479). With the help of the librarians at the Rovigno Centro, I was able to check the statutes for the other urban centers of the Istrian peninsula, without finding anything even vaguely similar to chapter 76 in the statutes of Capodistria; it stands as an *unicum*.

[63] *Item quod debeant tractari et reputari sicut tractantur et reputantur et tenentur alii cives et habitatores Iustinopolis.*

[64] *Item quod dicti Iudei possint mercari, emere, vendere secundum quod alii mercatores Iustinopolis, tam bona mobilia quam stabilia et eciam datia possint emere.*

of sermons. Finally, the Jewish bankers were not required to wear the "O" or any other sign – in direct contradiction to what Bernardino was preaching at that very moment not far away[65].

Corfu

The condition of the Jews in the city and on the island of Corfu in the Middle Ages is rather unique, for the Jews, who were quite numerous, had rights tantamount to full citizenship and economic freedoms that were nearly complete. Cecil Roth went so far as to say that the treatment of the Jews in Venetian Corfu "was something absolutely unparalleled in the Middle Ages, anticipating to some extent, by many centuries, the emancipation which elsewhere came about only after the French Revolution"[66].

The mere size of the community is noteworthy to begin with. If Benjamin of Tudela mentions only one Jew, a dyer, in Corfu in the 1160s, the traveller Mešullam of Volterra reported that there were 300 families of Jews in 1481, when he visited the island city, and he noted that some of them were rich and honored. That figure would mean a community of at least 1500 members, a considerable part – easily 15% – of an urban population of some 9–10000 inhabitants. While a Venetian traveler in 1557 said merely that the Jews were "many", the Corfiote historian Antonio Marmora, who we will meet again shortly, wrote in 1662 that there were some 500 Jewish houses (*case*), constituting perhaps an even higher percentage of the total population of the city than was the case earlier[67].

[65] The existence of chapter 76 did not render charters unnecessary or avoid disputes. At various times we find the Jews reminded of their obligation to register ("se scribi") at the chancery to make a charter valid, and Venice often was called upon to recognize the dispensation of the Jews of Capodistria from the obligation to wear the "O", both clear reflections of the statute. On the other hand, notification of the law forbidding ownership of real estate was sent in a ducal letter dated 9 november and transcribed into the Liber Niger of the local chancery. Actual rates of interest were much higher than those indicated in the statute. Banks could be bought and sold at will, among Jews. See *Francesco Majer*, Gli ebrei feneratori a Capodistria, in Pagine istriane, a. 9 (1911) 235–246, 272–276; a. 10 (1912) 25–32, 182–185, 225–230, 275–279; a. 11 (1913) 31–42, 76–84, 129–130, 167–182. The fact that this kind of *condotta* was part of the communal statute probably made it easier for the city to continue to *habere Judeos*; representatives of Capodistria petitioned the Council of Ten to rescind the clause in a set of regulations concerning that city passed by the Senate in 1459 which would have made it impossible for it to keep Jewish lenders; the request seems to have been granted: ASV, Consiglio dei dieci, deliberazioni miste, reg. 15, fol. 186v (5 Sept. 1459).

[66] *Cecil Roth*, History of the Jews in Venice (London 1930, New York 1975) 310–331 (citation on 318).

[67] For Benjamin, see *Bowman*, Jews of Byzantium 75; *Mešullam da Volterra*, Viaggio in terra d'Israele, translated by *Alessandra Veronese* (Rimini 1989) 93. Alessandro Magno, the Venetian nobleman, noted in 1557 that the *borgo* of Corfu was inhabited also *da molti hebrei* and mentions that en route between Corfu and Valona the ship was met by Jews in several small boats from whom the travellers bought *diverse robbe*; see *Alessandro Magno*, Voyages (1557–1565), translation and notes by *Wilfred Naar* (Paris, Bari 2002) 589. *Antonio Marmora*, Historia

Corfu came under Venetian domination only in 1386, when the city and the island were convinced by the Venetian Captain general of the fleet, Giovanni Miani, to submit to Venice after the death of Charles III of Durazzo[68]. In order to negotiate the text of the so-called dedication, the council of Corfu in May 1386 sent a committee of six representatives or *sindici* to Venice, one of whom was David Sem (or de Semo), a Jew[69]. A Jew sent as formal representative of a subject city to the capital? Indeed, and the fact so disturbed the seventeenth century Corfiote historian Antonio Marmora that he simply suppressed it, giving the names of only five men[70]. When time came to give homage and swear fidelity in the name of the city and island of Corfù before doge Antonio Venier, all six, including David Sem the Jew, were there, *ad prestandum sacramentum*, in all solemnity[71]. Sem, a citizen of Corfu, was a plenipotentiary of his native city. But his presence in the delegation had a further significance, since the privileges of the Jewish community (or *universitas*) were to be discussed as part of the general negotiations, because it was obvious, states the preamble to the deliberation of the Venetian Senate that concluded the negotiations, *quod ipsi Iudei sunt utiles tam habitatoribus insule quam civitatis in casibus multis*...[72].

di Corfù (Venice 1672) 437: "Sono nella Città di Corfù da 500 Case di Giudei, comode e facoltose per gli traffichi e usure ch'esercitano col Levante e co' Ponentini ..." For the total population, see *George Plumidis*, I paesi greci sotto il dominio veneziano, 1503–1537, (in Greek) (Athens 1974) 41, with data extracted from the Diarii of Marino Sanuto for the years 1505–1534.

[68] See *Giorgio Ravegnani*, La conquista veneziana di Corfù, in: Venezia e le isole ionie, ed. by *Chryssa Maltezou* and *Gherardo Ortalli* (Venice 2005) 101–112.

[69] The fact itself is known; perhaps the most recent mention is in *Bowman*, Jews of Byzantium 290–291, doc. 98. To clarify the matter further, it is important to refer to the Venetian documentation. The six *veri, legittimi et generales sindici, yconomi certi et indubitati nunci speciales* sent by the council were three noblemen Petrus Capice, *miles*, Ricardus de Altavilla, Johannes Alexii Cavasule, then Antonius de Henrico, *notarius*, Nicolaus de Trachanioti, *comitus*, and David de Semo, *Iudeus*: ASV, Commemoriali, reg. 8, fols. 118 (28 May 1386) and 119 (8 January 1387 [modern style]). The first three of the above were among the five Corfiotes made citizens of Venice *de gratia* on the same occasion, on the basis of a promise made to them by the Captain General Miani. The other two Christian representatives and David Semo were not among them: ASV, Grazie, reg. 17, fol. 223 (21 January 1387, the day prior to the deliberation of the Senate marking the conclusion of the negotiations) and the databank www.civesveneciarum.net.

[70] *Marmora*, Historia di Corfù 231–251, as first revealed on the basis of documents once part of the archive of the Jewish community by *J. A. Romanos*, Histoire de la Communauté Israélite de Corfou, in: Revue des études juives 23 (1892) 3–14, then by *David Kaufmann*, Contributions a l'histoire des Juifs de Corfou, in: Revue des études juives vols. 32 (1896) 226–35, 33 (1896) 64–76, 219–32, and 34 (1897) 263–75. Among the documents published by Kaufmann are authorized translations, made by the chancery of Corfu in the eighteenth century at the request of the Jews, of those documents that named David Sem as member of the delegation and of the privileges registered in January 1387; his role was crucial to their history, as was continually recognized by them and by Venetian authorities in the following centuries. Finally, see also *Eugenio Bacchion*, Il dominio veneto su Corfù (1386–1797) (Venice 1956) 60.

[71] See the document of 8 January cited above in note 69.

[72] ASV, Senato misti, reg. 40, fol. 59v (22 January 1387).

Two unnamed representatives of the Jews of Corfu, who had clearly accompanied David Sem, asked confirmation of their privileges but also the correction of extorsions and gravamina to which Jews were subjected at home (*a multis extorsionibus et gravaminibus que eis illata fuerunt*). The first correction was to see to it that the hanging of criminals no longer be staged in the Jewish cemetery. But major emphasis was placed on rights of citizenship and what that entailed in terms of taxation, which was meant to be just the same as that asked of "other citizens of Corfu" (*ad conditionem aliorum civium civitatis et insule Corphoy*); the kinds of tax were registered as they came up in the discussion:

- the tax for arming the colony's galley and other ships necessary for defence;
- forced loans of such things as beds and beasts of burden, similarly necessary for defence;
- guard duties (*custodia*), which had been asked of Jews only four times per year, were from then on to be the same for Jews "as for other Christian citizens of Corfu".
- The right of *lapidatio*, the stoning of Jewish houses and of Jews during Holy Week, was considered in the same context, since in the past, it was said, this practice had been suspended only upon payment of a money fee – actually the extortion of ransom money from potential victims – "which is contrary to humanity (*qui est contra omnem humanitatem*)"; now it was reduced and circumscribed to what was called the minimum necessary for the ritual traditions of orthodox Christians (*iuxta morem et fidem grecorum*), namely the throwing of stones by public officials during recitation of the litany as the procession passed through the Jewish quarter. When the Orthodox asked in 1406 for reinstatement of the custom *de iudeis lapidandis*, the Senate confirmed the prohibition of the practice but as a partial concession, in contrast to the privileges confirmed in 1387, Jews would thenceforth be required to wear the yellow "O"[73].

The Jews were perfectly willing, if necessary, even to pay higher impositions – the essential was that they be the same as those asked of "other citizens", i.e. the orthodox and western Christians, the best way to define legal equality.

[73] In recounting the pluri-secular historical context of this Christian ritual in Europe, *Cecil Roth* recalled also this case of Venetian Corfu; see his The Eastertide Stoning of the Jews and its Liturgical Echoes, in: The Jewish Quarterly Review, n.s. 35 (1944–45) 361–70 (kindly brought to my attention by David Jacoby). Repeated accusations of ritual assassination lay behind these Christian rites, which in Corfu were strengthened to include, in the eighteenth century, the "old custom" of burning on Easter the effigy of a then living Jew, stuffed with fireworks, in the church of the Annunciation; an attempt by the authorities to sequester the effigy in 1760 gave the crowd occasion to sack the houses of the Jews. The situation was very similar in Zante. See *Ph. Carrer*, Ioudaismos kai Xristianismos (Zakinthos 1891) especially 111–119 (kindly brought to my attention by Marianna Kolyvà).

The question of lending money at usury by Jews in Corfu was set aside for further consideration[74]. When it came up four months later, it was on the basis of a proposal made by the three supervisors (*Provisores*) of Corfu in which there is actually no mention at all of Jews[75]. The proposal set maximum interest rates by type of contract:

- for a loan with personal property as collateral: 12%
- for a loan on real property or on written bond: 16%
- for loans on agricultural products and futures: 20%
- for current loans on old contracts and old pawns, 20% could be asked, but limits were set on how long existing contracts could still run.

The point to be made here is that moneylending was not considered a sector of the local economy restricted only to the Jews[76]. In fact, Corfiote Jews were heavily involved in all aspects of economic endeavour: in commercial ventures, in the export trade and in productive activity both as craftsmen and as manual laborers; only some lent money. In other words, their situation differed sharply from that of their coreligionists then residing in Venice itself and those who would be active later in the Terraferma. These communities were headed by moneylenders and their right to reside was based on temporally limited charters, while the Jews of Corfu were citizens whose standing privileges were recognized and defended by Venice. The Venetian Senate was continually forced to review blanket provisions regarding Jews, such as expulsions, special taxation, and prohibitions, for example to engage in the legal profession, and to exempt Corfiote Jews on the basis of their privileges[77].

Some of the doubts left open during the negotiations between Venice and the Jews in 1387 were addressed in an embassy of 1406 which produced a "golden bull" for the Jewish community, with such clauses as the following: a) Since the *lapidatio* was to remain illegal, substituted by the obligation of Jews to wear the yellow "O", the Venetian Collegio offered the Jews an alternative: for a fee of 300

[74] ASV, Senato misti, reg. 40, f. 59v. The decision to study further the regulation of loans on collateral was preceded by this statement: *Preterea cum in facto dandi ad usuram in civitate Corphoy inter Christianos et Iudeos Corphienses sint certa pacta et conventiones quibus ipsi Iudei valde gravant cives Corphoy in facto ipsarum usurarum, et utile sit super hoc providere de remedio oportuno*. The discussion does not touch the question of Jews being forced to act as executioners, a task bearing the mark of infamy; that Venetians forced Jews to do this in Crete and in Corfu is asserted by *Bowman*, The Jews of Byzantium 340–341; on the contrary, see the precedent, recognized by Venice, in the decree of Philip II of Taranto in 1370 which forbade making Jews in Corfu act as executioners, in: *Kaufmann*, Contributions vol. 33, 65.

[75] ASV, Senato misti, reg. 40, f. 59v, fol. 77 (29 May 1387).

[76] According to Cecil Roth, the above steps were taken to protect the inhabitants, including the Jews, from Christian usurers: *Roth*, History of the Jews in Venice 319. That there was formal moneylending by Jews later is reflected in a petition of 1680 favouring the 6% interest of the Monte di Pietà against the *strabochevoli e pesantissime usure di 17 per cento del giudaismo*: *E. Yotopoulou-Sicilianou* (ed.), Ambasciate of Venetian-Ruled Corfu (16th–18th centuries). Source for an outline reconstruction of the period [in Greek] (Athens 2002) 633.

[77] *Kaufmann*, Contributions vol. 32, 229–30, 233.

ducats per year, the obligation could be suspended. b) Landed property on the island connected with seignorial rights over peasants had to be sold within two years and real estate owned in the city was to be limited to that existing *intra Iudaycham*, although these clauses were probably a dead letter from the start and Roth considered them easily circumvented. c) A committee that exacted taxes was to have one Jewish member, as had been customary in the past. d) Jews were to be free to buy fruit, vegetables and bread on the local marketplace, and draw water from a well – to the construction of which they had contributed – just like Christians. The final petition of the representatives of the Jews regarded threats made on their lives and homes; the rectors were called upon to prosecute guilty parties for any "violence, injury or offence"[78]. Two years later the Jews, presumably taken as a whole, were permitted to own rural land up to a value of 4000 ducats, actually a very large sum[79].

In the early fifteenth century the Jews still lived on two streets in a *iudaica* – located between the old city and the fortress – known as the *mons Iudeorum*; in 1414 it was ordered that the *mons* be included inside a new defensive wall[80]. A final consideration about the habitat of the Jews underscores once again their unique condition. When the Venetian Senate in 1423 – as was mentioned above – forbade the ownership of real property to all Jews of the dominions of both Terraferma and Mar, the Jews of Corfu appealed the decision regarding their own situation and won. The Senate was forced in 1425 to amend the decision since the Jews of Corfu were "citizens and residents of our city of Corfu (*cives et habitatores civitatis nostre Corphoy*)" and as such could own their houses in the two *iudaiche* of the city. This final clause formally protected their right of ownership but was meant to limit their freedom of investment[81]. In the early sixteenth century the houses of the Jews in the two *iudaiche* were razed in order to make room for new defensive works and their residences were per force dispersed throughout the city, among the Christians. This brought a petition by the orthodox majority in 1516, asking that a quarter be set aside so that the Jews would live as before, *separatim*. Hardly four months after Venice's own decision to relegate Jews to the Ghetto (29 March–1 April), the Collegio granted the petition of the Corfiote Orthodox Christians and called for relocation of the Jews to a quarter of the city called Catto Cafero, where they

[78] *Constantinos N. Sathas* (ed.) Documents inédits relatifs à l'histoire de la Grèce au Moyen Age, vol. II (Paris 1881) 152–54 (the documents from this source were kindly brought to my attention by Nicholas Karapidakis).
[79] *Jacoby*, Venice and the Venetian Jews 53, note 26.
[80] *Sathas* (ed.), Documents, vol. III (Paris 1882) 45–46.
[81] The prohibition (see above note 19) was passed not long after Bernardino da Siena had been in Venice where he had perhaps preached during Advent (1422) and preached during Lent in Padova (1423): *Alfonso M. Berengo Morte, OFM*, San Bernardino da Siena nelle Venezie (Verona 1945) 32 and 231–233. The prohibition was reinforced the following year, eliminating loopholes and permitting only annual rent contracts for the house actually lived in: ASV, Senato misti, reg. 55, fol. 77 (30 December 1424). The exception for the Jews of Corfu is in ibid., fol. 111 (3 May 1425), printed in *Sathas*, Documents inédits vol. III, 286–87.

would be "united and safe" – a rather softer formulation than that used by the same organ regarding the Ghetto in Venice[82]. But many Jews successfully resisted this order and it was another century before a new attempt was made; even when there would be a Jewish quarter, it was not exclusively Jewish and there were no gates to be closed during the night, as in the rigorous Italian ghettos[83].

In brief, the social status of the Jews of Corfu constituted a notable exception in the panorama of the Venetian dominions: Jews were full citizens of their city in the Middle Ages; they were represented in the council and could represent the city, as did David Sem in Venice in 1386–87, despite the antagonism of many of their Christian fellow citizens[84].

If this is the social situation, we can learn something more about the economic activities of the Jews of Corfu by turning to the account book of a small Venetian commercial partnership which had a base in Corfu in the years 1440–1442[85]. The young Venetian nobleman, Zaccaria Giustinian, who ran the agency, had dealings with twelve different Jewish merchants over the two years. In businesses related to the trade of tanning hides, which however is not mentioned in the accounts, were two who dealt in sheepskins and a third was identified as as a furrier (*varoter*). One of them was a descendant of David Semo, the representative sent to Venice in 1386–87. The names of these men are listed in Table 2. Four are indicated as Corfiotes, three as from Ioannina on the Greek mainland[86].

[82] *Sathas*, Documents inédits vol. V, 261–62: ... *che 'l sii provisto de habitatione ad essi Hebrei in uno loco dicto Catto Cafero che è da la banda del Turrion del armiraglio ove starano bene uniti et securi.*

[83] *Roth*, History of the Jews in Venice 324–325. It is in the context of a discussion of attempts to prohibit Jews from owning real estate that Marmora, in 1672, gives vent to his ingrained anti-semitism: "A gran ragione si privano di stabili quei, che non han fermezza alcuna di fede; e troppo grande scorno sarebbe, se negli edificii, nelle ville e ne' campi si vedessero apertamente le loro usure. Non è convenevole che se perdettero le loro terre per havere ucciso Cristo, terre acquistino fra' Cristiani; ed essendo meritevoli di morte, loro non conviene di stabile che il sepolcro": *Marmora*, Della historia di Corfù 255–256.

[84] On the occasion of their successful appeal against the blanket expulsion order that followed the Venetian victory at Lepanto, the Jews of Corfu claimed that they had always been considered *per membro et una medesima cosa con essa* [città di Corfù], that before the existence of a *condotta* of Jews in Venice Corfiote Jews, *antichissimi suoi sudditi*, had traded with Venice, and that they would prefer to live in servitude under the protection of Venice than in freedom elsewhere (*essendone sotto le sue ale più gratiosa la servitù che altrove la libertà*). The Venetian rectors supported their claims and reminded the government that the Jews of Corfu *non vivono con altra industria che con la mercantia* and that they paid thousands of ducats in customs duties in Venice: *Kaufmann*, Considerations vol. 33, 20–23.

[85] *Reinhold C. Mueller*, A Venetian Commercial Enterprise in Corfu, 1440–1442, in: Money and Markets in the Palaeologan Era (13th–15th centuries) (acts of the congress, Chalkis, Greece, May 1998), ed. by *Nikos Moschonas*, Institute for Byzantine Research, National Hellenic Research Foundation (Byzantium Today 4, Athens 2003) 81–95.

[86] By comparison, in the very much larger account book kept by Giacomo Badoer in Constantinople, 1436–1440, only about thirty Jews are identifiable; cf. *Bowman*, Jews of Byzantium 175.

Table 2: Jewish merchants (iudii, zudii) and commercial partnerships active in Corfu, 1440–42.

Elia son of Salomon of Ioannina	
Elia son of Samuel of Ioannina	
Guarantors of Elia son of Samuel:	Samuel Cassan, "currently his rabbi" Salomon di Muli, his uncle (*barba*)
Grisom Seno, "currently living in Corfu"	
Moixè Chastoriano iudio, "who lives in Corfu"	
Mosco of Otranto and Abram son of Salomon Sazerdoto (Abram operated also on his own account)	
Salomon "the furrier" (*varoter*)	
Samaria de Natael, "who lives here in Corfu"	
Samuel of Ioannina	
Samuel Pizinin of Corfu	

They dealt in low-cost merchandise. The young Venetian merchant sold four German *panni di fontego*, or blanket-material, for 32 perperi to the Jew Elia of Ioannina, who, by barter, promised in return eight *schiavine* – an article of coarse wool used both as a kind of cape and as a blanket by seamen and pilgrims. When Elia paid, the Venetian charged a slight difference (less than 2 perperi) because he was dissatisfied with some of the merchandise (*algune sciavine el me de' in pagamento che le non me piexeva*). Since he did not pay on the spot, Elia had to provide sureties, once his rabbi, once his uncle Salomon di Muli.

Another Jew, Samuel of Ioannina, bought nearly a metric ton of iron from the Venetian, at only 85 perperi per thousandweight. In the same category, plowshares or *gomeri* produced in bulk in the smithies of Styria and Carinthia were sold largely via barter for *schiavine*, mostly to Jews: Elia son of Salomon of Ioannina bought five bales and Moixè Chastoriano four, while one bale each went to Mosco d'Otranto e Abram di Salomon Sazerdoto, partners, Grisom Semo, and Samaria di Natael. The bales, each containing 20–22 plowshares, were valued, for purposes of barter, at 21–22 perperi per bale; from the city they probably were forwarded to markets both on the island and on the Greek mainland.

Exchange commodities were wax, sheepskins and *schiavine*. Elia of Ioannina imported only a small quantity of 200 lbr. of wax, which he bartered for iron, and the partnership of Mosco of Otranto and Abram di Salomon delivered 13 lbr., which probably served to balance a small debt left over after a barter agreement. Sheepskins were brought to the market of Corfu especially by merchants from Kastoria, but the Jews Mosco of Otranto and Abram Sazerdoto, partners, and Elia of Ioannina provided a certain number valued at 14s each. The *schiavine*, finally, were much sought after in Venice. Of the 170 that Zaccaria purchased and loaded onto eight different voyages, half were from Elia di Samuel of Ioannina and a small number from Grisom Semo. Even if the accounts kept by this apprentice merchant involved Jews in low-cost merchandise, they reflect a kind of economic freedom and variety of activity that Jews in the Venetian Terraferma did not know.

Conclusion

It is in fact striking how different the position of Jews on the mainland was from that of Jews in the maritime provinces, even though both were excluded from rights of citizenship – with the notable exception of Corfu. The communities of the former revolved primarily around pawn banking, while commerce in used goods was secondary and other trades and professions were mostly those necessary to support relatively large communities, such as those of Padua and Treviso. The residence of Jews in a given subject city of the Terraferma was regulated by a temporary charter that could as well be terminated as renewed; their protected status as *subditi* lasted only the duration of their *condotta*. On the other hand, in Venice's *Stato da Mar* – especially in Crete and Corfu, where there were Jewish communities ten times larger than those found in Terraferma cities – Jews were considered *subditi* without limitations of the kind found in Italian charters. The Jews of Corfu, moreover, were recognized to be permanent citizens of their city. Despite the secular persistence of Orthodox rituals such as the *lapidatio*, which openly reflected Christian contempt of the Jewish minority, Byzantine traditions generally favored Jews by keeping open to them many branches of wholesale and retail commerce and the crafts. As a result, moneylending *tout court* and pawn banking in particular, often a source of friction in the Terraferma, were minor activities that did not characterize the large island community as a whole. The Jews of Corfu never tired of repeating in the ensuing centuries, when protecting their own historic rights against legal restrictions introduced elsewhere in the Venetian dominions, that their status was different from that of their coreligionists elsewhere; rather than being restricted by temporary charters, they were favored by enduring privileges[87].

[87] As late as the late eighteenth century the Inquisitori sopra l'università degli ebrei wrote that the Jews of Corfu were *non compresi nelle condote degl'Ebrei di questa Dominante, ma come privilegiati sudditi nostri, membro unito e congionto con quella città, cosicchè debbano essere mantenuti nel loro esser in cui sono stati fino di presente, nè molestati contro la forma di detti loro privileggi*: *Kaufmann*, Considerations vol. 34, 268.

Joseph Shatzmiller

Church Articles: Pawns in the Hands of Jewish Moneylenders

For the most part, the pawns that were to be found in moneylenders' "shops" in the central and late Middle Ages were cheap objects, almost worthless. Poor borrowers had nothing better to offer. However, some rich institutions and opulent individuals presented creditors with spectacular and precious objects of art. Moneylenders dealing with church institutions accepted as sureties cult-articles considered sacred by Christians. The following pages will confront jurisprudence – religious and secular – on this aspect of the commerce of money with the reality of economic life in which these sacred articles played an important role.

I.

Not all Jews were strangers to the interiors of churches and to the beautiful ecclesiastical ornaments they preserved when they entered cathedrals or monasteries of the time. In England of the twelfth and thirteenth centuries, some Jews, perhaps even the majority, would leave their money and valuables for safekeeping in these churches. This was the reason for their frequent visits to the institutions of the rival religion. Quite understandably, some clergymen complained about this lively Jewish traffic in the Christian holy buildings. At a church council at Oxford in 1222, Stephen Langton, the most prominent ecclesiastical figure of his time, promoted a decree forbidding Jews such entrance, *liberum ingressum et egressum*. The prohibition was repeated in the diocesan statutes of Worcester in 1240 and of London from 1245–1259. In 1253, King Henry III issued royal legislation in this spirit[1].

The late Professor Solomon Grayzel, master scholar of the relationship between the Church and the Jews in the Middle Ages, noticed the presence of Jews in these buildings of Christianity. He was of the opinion that the phenomenon was limited to England[2]. However, some of the Hebrew exempla, assembled around the year 1200 in the well-known "Sefer Hasidim", implied that things were not different in

[1] *Zephira Entin-Rokeah*, The Jewish Church-Robbers and Host Desecrators of Norwich (ca. 1285), in: Revue des études juives 141 (1982) 331–362, in particular 333–334.

[2] Cf. *Salomon Grayzel*, The Church and the Jews in the XIIIth Century, revised edition (New York 1966) 35, note 75.

the Rhineland of the time[3]. The pious authors of Germany hailed individuals who abstained from the practice. They gave the following illustration, "a Jew entered the court of a church. He heard a [Divine] voice (quoting 1Kings 14:9), 'And me, you cast away behind.'" To make up for the transgression, the Jew mortified himself for the rest of his life (Exemplum N° 1357). Another exemplum involves the case of a man who entered the church and then regretted it. He turned to a Sage for instruction of penance. The Sage suggested, "every year on the day [on which you committed the transgression], you should mortify yourself." And, so he did (N° 1358). The *Hasidim* considered as realistic a situation in which a shrewd cleric indebted to a Jew took refuge in the church knowing that the creditor would not follow him (N° 1362). They told also of a wonderful miracle that occurred during the funeral of a person who "made a point never to enter a church" (N° 1356).

In twelfth century England, the relationship between Jews and churches was not limited simply to visitations or to safekeeping. Prelates, under financial pressure, would offer holy ornaments as sureties to Jews against loans they wished to obtain. Bishop Nigel of Ely (East Anglia), in conflict with King Stephen, was forced to pawn relics to Jews of Cambridge. This must have occurred around the year 1140. A hagiographic source reported that among those relics was a golden crucifix belonging to King Edgar[4]. Some thirty years later, two Jews of Norwich, a father and son (Benedict and Deodatus, respectively), were sentenced to a considerable fine of twenty pounds for obtaining church vessels illegally as pawns[5]. Other English prelates involved in such transactions were Bishop Robert de Chesnay of Lincoln and Abbot William Waterville of Peterborough (active around 1155–1175). The abbot pledged, among other sacred relics, the arm of Saint Oswald[6].

Similar practices crossed the channel and took place in the heart of Europe as well. It is quite possible that sacred objects, belonging to none other than the monastery of Cluny, fell into the hands of Jews. Peter the Venerable (1156–1192), its most famous abbot, expressed rage over the very fact of having to deal with the Jews[7]. A much calmer mood is detected in a letter he wrote to Henry of Blois, who became Bishop of Winchester; the great ecclesiastic thanked Henry for the financial support that helped retrieve sacred objects in Jewish possession[8].

[3] *Jehuda Wistinetzki* (ed.), Das Buch der Frommen (Sefer Hasidim, Hebrew) (Frankfurt a.M. [2]1924). Each of the exempla has a number in this edition. These will be given in the text of this essay between brackets.

[4] Cf. *H. P. Stokes,* Studies in Anglo-Jewish History (Edinburgh 1913) 124.

[5] *Stokes*, Studies ibid.

[6] Cf. *Joe Hillaby,* The London Jewry: William I to John, in: Transactions of the Jewish Historical Society of England 33 (1992–1994) 1–44, in particular 9.

[7] *Jean Pierre Torrell,* Les juifs dans l'œuvre de Pierre le vénérable, in: Cahiers de civilisation médiévale 30 (1987) 331–346.

[8] *Giles Constable* (ed.), The Letters of Peter the Venerable, vol. I (Cambridge/Mass. 1967) 327–330, in particular 329.

II.

Christian sensitivity about sacred vessels goes back a long time. As early as the end of the sixth century (August 591), Pope Gregory the Great chastised two clerics of Venafro in Campania for having sold to a "certain Hebrew" sacred articles from the treasure of the local church. These included "two chalices of silver, two crowns with dolphins, the lilies of other crowns, as well as six palliums – great and small". The Jews, orders the Pope, should restore all they got; penance should be imposed on the clerics[9]. More than two hundred years later, in August 806, in a Carolingian capitulary, the clergy of the highest level were urged to prevent that "anything of the gems or the vessels or other ecclesiastical treasures should be sold to Jews". It further stated, "we have been told that Jewish merchants… boast that they are able to buy… whatever they like"[10]. Another capitulary, this time of suspected authenticity, menaced such Jews that "their right hands shall be cut off"[11].

In the twelfth and thirteenth centuries, when credit operations spread or intensified and became widespread, the attention moved from merchants and their acts of purchasing to moneylenders and the pawns and sureties they were holding. Pope Alexander IV (1254–1261) was one of many who expressed ire about it in these centuries. In a bull ("Bulla") issued on August 23, 1258, he urged the clergy to show reverence to "the vestment of their ministry, the sacred ornaments, the chalices and the ecclesiastical vessels". "We heard, and we speak of it not without bitterness of heart, that some clergy make no distinction between the sacred and the profane, and they dare leave such vestments, ornaments and vessels as loan pledges with the Jews." Here, the Pope's concern reached its highest point: "And these very Jews, like ingrate enemies of the cross and the Christian faith, treated these pledges with irreverence to the disgrace of the Christian religion. And [these Jews] acted so nefariously towards them as it is shameful to speak and horrible to hear."[12]

More than a hundred years earlier, Peter the Venerable had the following to say about the blasphemous treatment to which sacred objects were subjected: "Christ, through the otherwise insensible vessels consecrated to him, suffers directly the Jewish insults since, as I have often heard from truthful men… they direct such wickedness against celestial vessels as is horrifying to think and detestable to say." The venerable abbot goes on, "The sacred vessels held captive among them… as in olden times among Chaldeans, suffer shame even though they are inanimate. Indeed, Christ felt the Jewish abuse in these insensate vessels sacred to him."[13]

Rigord, the biographer of Philip Augustus of France, in his "Gesta", written and rewritten in the years 1196 and 1207–1208, was a bit more open writing about these

[9] Cf. *Amnon Linder*, The Jews in the Legal Sources of the Early Middle Ages (Detroit, Jerusalem 1997) 420–421.
[10] *Linder*, The Jews 344.
[11] *Linder*, The Jews 345 and note 324 there.
[12] Cf. *Grayzel*, The Church (as in note 21 infra) 62–64.
[13] Cf. *Robert Chazan*, Medieval Stereotypes and Modern Antisemitism (Berkeley 1997) 51.

"abuses": the biographer tells us that Phillip expelled the Jews in 1182 from his domain because of the "culmination of their wickedness". His explanation: "Certain ecclesiastical vessels consecrated to God, the chalices and crosses of gold and silver bearing the image of our Lord Jesus Christ crucified had been pledged to the Jews by the way of security... these they used so vilely in their impiety and scorn of the Christian religion that, from the cups in which the body and blood of our Lord Jesus Christ was consecrated, they gave their children cakes soaked in wine."[14]

With such allegations circulating in society, there was little wonder that, for some, the alleged nefarious behavior of the Jews amounted to what Professor Ivan Marcus labeled rightly "latrine blasphemy"[15]. The above-mentioned Rigord believed this was true. He knew of "a certain Jew" who held certain ecclesiastical objects as pledges. "He had a gold cross marked with gems, a book of the Gospels decorated with gold and precious stones in an extraordinary manner, silver cups and other vessels. He placed them all in a sack and vilely threw it into the deep pit which he used to relieve himself."[16] A hagiographic treatise, "The Miracles of Notre Dame", a collection of miracle stories, accompanied in some manuscripts by illuminations, relates the terrible story of the Jew of Constantinopolis who threw the icon of the virgin to the gutters. It had been saved, cleansed, and performed miracles. Christians could learn of it not only from books but also from observing church windows[17].

Ecclesiastical jurisprudence took seriously the account of such horror stories. In their assemblies, prelates made recourse to no uncertain prohibitive terminology when trying to change the course of events. Thus, the decree of a synod held by Odo of Sully, bishop of Paris (1197–1208), stated that "no cleric... shall... in any manner pledge to a Jew the books or the ornaments of a church"[18]. In Trier, in 1227, a somewhat more mitigated legislation was agreed upon: "The clergy shall never let out of their possession any of the church ornaments, nor shall they dare to give up to Jews any religious articles without special permission from us."[19] Two years later, in England, a regulation of the bishop of Worcester forbade Jews to receive ecclesiastical books, vestments or other ornaments as pledges or for any other reason. The bishop threatened to cut such Jews from any social intercourse with Christians[20]. Other thirteenth century assemblies employed similar rhetoric. In 1255, the diocesan synod of Valencia wanted things to be clear: "No cleric should

[14] Cf. *Jacob Rader Marcus*, The Jew in the Medieval World, A Source Book: 315–1791 (revised edition by *Marc Saperstein*, Cincinnati 1999) 27–30, in particular 29.
[15] *Ivan G. Marcus*, A Jewish-Christian Symbiosis: The Culture of Early Ashkenaz, in: *David Biale* (ed.), Cultures of the Jews: A New History (New York 2002) 449–516.
[16] *Ivan G. Marcus*, A Jewish-Christian Symbiosis 480.
[17] *Alexandre Laborde*, Les miracles de Notre Dame, compilés par *Jehan Miélot* (Paris 1929) 102 and plate N°xi. cf. also to *Ivan G. Marcus*, (as in note 16 above) 481.
[18] See *Grayzel*, (as in note 2 above) 300–301.
[19] *Grayzel*, The Church 318–319.
[20] *Grayzel*, The Church 320–321.

pledge [to a Jew] a chalice, vestments, covers of altars or books."[21] The commerce in "sacred objects" was a major concern of assemblies like that of Meaux in 1287 or that convened the same year by Jacob, Archbishop of Gniezno[22].

III.

For their part, Jews were aware of the rage these transactions aroused in society – they were also attentive to the danger which some of these moneylenders may have had to face. A rabbinic synod, convoked by Rabbi Jacob Tam (c. 1100–1175) around the mid twelfth century, tried to amend this state of affairs. In the decree issued by that synod, Jews were warned "not to accept church vessels as security for debt". "Not to buy the chalice or the cross or holy vestments or prayer books of a church or its vessels." And again, "Not to buy a stolen chalice or a cross or holy vestments or prayer books of a church or any of its vessels". The reason: "Because of the peril." The injunctions went further, warning the Jews "not to buy stolen things such as images or a chalice or priestly vestments and prayer books or vessels of worship" and again: "Because of the danger"[23]. A pupil of Rabbi Tam, Eliezer of Metz (c. 1115–1198), repeated his teacher's interdiction in his own "sefer yere'im" ("Book of the God fearing" Responsum N° 364)[24].

The moralists of "Sefer Hasidim" writing at the same time also contributed to this campaign of dissuasion[25]. Their exempla, to be sure, did not have the power of law, yet they hoped to influence – even to frighten – their audience by indicating practices one should avoid. A general observation is found in exemplum N° 1349 according to which "Most people who dealt with priests did not keep their wealth down to the end of their lives". The reason? "Because they provided them [the priests] with articles to [practice] their idolatry." An exemplary behavior was displayed on the other hand, in the case of a Jew, "who lent on pledges [like] crosses and other objects". Upon his demise, one of his coreligionists, who knew where the objects were stored, refused to divulge the whereabouts to the heirs, "If I shall tell it... they shall go ahead and sell them to priests and monks." Being closed-lipped, thus the Jew avoided committing a sin (N° 1349). The authors related in another story (N° 1359) an example of a Jew who did not refrain from selling orna-

[21] *Salomon Grayzel*, The Church and the Jews in the XIII Century, vol. II, ed. *Kenneth R. Stow* (New York, Detroit 1989) 276.
[22] *Grayzel*, The Church 280–281.
[23] For the three first quotations, cf. *Louis Finkelstein*, Jewish Self-Government in the Middle Ages (New York [2]1964). The first is to be found on page 201. Finkelstein's rendering of these paragraphs into English has the character of an interpretation rather than a close translation. The Hebrew original employs much more coarse language, cf. 178–195 and 211.
[24] I have not seen the original of "sefer yere'im" and count on information provided in: Jewish texts on the visual arts, edited with commentary by *Vivian B. Mann*; Rabbinic texts translated by *Eliezer Diamond* (Cambridge/U.K., New York 2000) 13 and 176 note 50.
[25] Cf. note 3 above.

ments to priests who embellished with them their places of worship. He was punished by Heaven on the day of his death.

These synodal decrees and moralistic warnings might have had some impact in the world of business. The following three examples may have lead to such a conclusion. In thirteenth century England, two church robbers, who were unable to dispose of their booty, claimed that "no Jew wants to receive them or to lend money against them".[26] A similar deadlock occurred in Zurich in 1272 or 1273: No Jew of the city would touch a chalice worth no less than seventy marks[27]. Abstention from such deals was mentioned in a short, yet precious, Hebrew document kept today in the Archives of Bern, Switzerland. There, an unknown Jew wrote a memorandum to himself noting the issues he may raise when negotiating a charter of privileges for himself. He should, among other benefits, be allowed to receive all sorts of pledges and pawns, with the exception of church vessels. He adds, "Because of the danger". Clearly, we have here an echo of the decrees and injunctions of the 1150 rabbinic assembly[28].

The bark of these decrees – Christian or Jewish – seemed, however, to have been more menacing than their bite. Jews and Christians found ways to circumvent – or ignore – them in the centuries that followed. As far as the Jews were concerned, they could count on the fact that not all rabbis followed the teaching of "Sefer Hasidim" or shared the fears of Rabbi Tam and his followers. The authority of the legendary founder of rabbinic studies in Western Europe, R. Gershom of Mainz, "The Light of the Diaspora" (ca. 960–1028), who saw nothing wrong in dealing with priestly vestments or any other church articles, would lend them a free hand. The great man's reasoning taught them "Gentiles [of our time] are not idolaters"[29]. This axiom was embraced by a plethora of followers.

R. Eliezer ben Nathan of Mainz (c. 1110–1190), known by the acronym "Ravan", a contemporary of Jacob Tam and a friend of his, advocated also a more permissive way of doing business. With the exception of incense ("levonah" in Hebrew) that serves in the church, almost any other articles should be exempted from interdiction. The Gentiles of his day – so goes his argument – were far from being inveterate idolaters. At times, they did not care about their holy days and went ahead with their work. Some did not attend church regularly. To the extent they did, it was simply due to the fact that they followed the ways of their ancestors, and because they enjoyed the surroundings. A Jew was allowed to sell priests' clerical vestments and coats ("Dossals"), as they served their personal use

[26] Cf. *Zefira Entin Rokéah*, Crime and Jews in the Late Thirteenth Century England: Some Cases and Comments, in: Hebrew Union College Annual 55 (1984) 135–136, note 132.

[27] Cf. *Gerd Mentgen*, Studien zur Geschichte der Juden im mittelalterlichen Elsaß (Hannover 1995) 441.

[28] This short and precious document was published by *Ben-Zion Dinur* in his multi-volume Israel in Diaspora (Hebrew). The original is preserved at the archives of the city of Bern (Switzerland). Cf. *Dinur*, op. cit., vol. B (1) (Tel Aviv 1965) 278–279.

[29] *Shlomo Eidelberg* (ed.), The Responsa of Rabbenu Gershom Meor Hagolah (Hebrew) (New York 1955) 75–77 Responsum N° 21.

only and did not cover any of their sacred objects. "The same way it is permitted to sell them [such objects], it is allowed to extend loans on the security of church vessels and of Dossals, for the reasons I have mentioned." The distinguished Sage continued, "Also, one can extend loans on the security of church vessels because they are there [only] for the priest to drink from them when praying." Apparently, Eliezer ben Nathan believed in these distortions of ecclesiastical practices. His tolerant attitude was not all encompassing. "It is forbidden to extend loans on security of their statues, icons and censer bearers", insisted the Mainz Rabbi[30].

The analysis, developed a generation later by Isaac b. Samuel of Dampierre followed essentially the same path. Isaac, known also as "The Ri", a nephew of Jacob Tam, replaced his uncle as head of the rabbinic academy of Champagne. He was considered the supreme authority of his time. A contemporary of the authors of "Sefer Hasidim" and a sympathizer of their mystical teaching, Isaac did not follow their lead in what concerned pawns and pledges. At the origin of his thinking was the distinction between what was essential for Christian worship and what was nothing more than paraphernalia for the personal use of the priests. Accordingly, to quote some of the examples he raised, Jews may do business with the rest of wax candles that were put away by priests and also with wax not intended to be used in the church. Loaves of bread were also legitimate objects of commerce as the Christian folk brought them to their holy places not as sacrifice to their deity but rather for the use of the church's personnel. Priestly vestments had nothing sacred inherent in them. They served just as ornament ("noy" in Hebrew, that is elegance) and should not be considered in the context of worshipping idolatry. The analysis applied also to vessels he called "chalice". It was his understanding that these vessels did not make up part of the Christian cult. Attention should be paid, nevertheless, regarding censer bearers of incense. R. Eliezer ben Nathan, too, maintained that they should be out of bounds for Jewish moneylenders[31].

IV.

Whether such lenient rulings encouraged Jews to lend against church objects or just condoned existing practices is not clear from the Hebrew sources. Archival documents, on the other hand, show that this kind of exchange was in full vigor in the high and late Middle Ages, and that Christians, no less than Jews, lent a deaf ear to restrictive legislation. In this respect, Italian data, revealed in recent years

[30] Cf. *Eliezer bar Nathan*, Sefer Ravan which is the book of Even ha-Ezer (Hebrew) (Jerusalem 1984) Responsa N°s 288–289.

[31] See *Isaac's* commentary to the tract "Idolatry" ("Aavodah Zarah") of the Babylonian Talmud, fol. 516. On him see *E. E. Urbach*, The Tosaphists: Their History, Writings, and Methods (Hebrew) (Jerusalem 1980) I:226–260, and *J. Fauer*, The Legal Thinking of the Tossafot, an Historical Approach, in: Dine Israel 6 (1975) XLIII–LXII, in particular LXVIII.

from the regions of Umbria by Professor Ariel Toaff, is very important. The following are just some of the findings[32]. The humble Umbrian canons of the Church of Santa Maria de la Pieve, some time in the year 1304, gave away an embossed silver chalice to Jews Cascia (Toaff N° 50 and N° 120). Almost one hundred years later, in November 1386, a gold frieze, embroidered with pictures of saints, formed a crucial part of a monetary transaction (N° 477). In March 1385, a long list of articles was recorded for a complicated transaction, with a significant amount of money was at stake. The borrower was the municipality of Assisi, the famous Umbrian town in central Italy. Its governing council approached the Jew, Anselmo, for a loan of one thousand two hundred gold Florins. The council persuaded the Church of St. Francis to lend them a collection of sacred articles that they handed over to Anselmo. The list included twenty-one items, most of them silver objects. The total weight of the objects was over sixty pounds. Included as well was a chalice made of gold that weighed close to four pounds and two statues of the virgin, one of which weighed more than five pounds. Also included were two censers ("Thuribules") one large and one small, a pedestal for a standing cross as well as four candelabras of silver. To the golden chalice mentioned above, six others made of silver were added. Embroidery was also present in the inventory: one piece that served as a cover to Mary's altar was decorated with pearls. Another two tapestries used golden thread, one in the form of a griffin. A priest's gown of red cloth was ornated on both sides with pearls in the form of the cross. Most astounding was an object that belonged to Pope Nicholas IV (1288–1292), a cape intended for wet weather that had been decorated with pearls[33]. Given the value of these treasures, the Church of St. Francis insisted that its loan be limited in time to two months and no more. A similar, yet even more complicated, arrangement was concluded in November 1435 in Bologna, the capital of the region of Emilia Romagna. The Jew, Habraam di Datilo, asked for securities for a loan of one thousand pounds, an enormous sum of money. The commune of the city appealed to no less than thirty-one religious institutions for help. Twenty-one of these were churches, five were monasteries, two were hospitals, and three may have been monasteries as well. Most institutions gave one article, although four churches and one monastery contributed two each. The list of the thirty-eight objects that were assembled this way included six chalices, fifteen chasubles, two copes, two covers of altars, four missals, seven antiphonaries and three priestly garments[34]. Other Umbrian communes that used the services of Jewish moneylenders were those of Todi and Spoleto. The first of the two appeared in the documentation in a different light than that of Assisi or Bologna: on

[32] *Ariel Toaff,* The Jews in Umbria, 3 vols. (Leyden 1993–1994). Professor Toaff calendared many of his documents and gave numbers to all of them. In what follows I shall refer to these numbers.
[33] *Ariel Toaff,* The Jews in Medieval Assisi 1305–1487: A Social and Economic History of a Small Jewish Community in Italy (Firenze 1979) 139–141.
[34] Cf. *Ludovico Frati,* La vita private di Bologna dal secolo XIII al XVII con appendice di documenti inediti (Bologna 1986) 240–241.

June 13, 1368 it purchased a chalice (probably redeemed) from the Jew, Guillelmo. The sum involved was just four florin and thirty-five shillings (Toaff, N° 232). In the midst of war in 1414, Spoleto was pressed for financial liquidity. In August, the rector of the city could see no other way but to hand part of his private silverware to a Jewish moneylender in order to secure a loan of one hundred and fifty Florins (N° 730).

Having sacred Christian objects in their possession was a phenomenon that, in all probability, was not limited to central Italy where systematic research has been carried out in recent years. Another region that benefited from scholarly attention was that of Campania, or more precisely the Aragonese court of Naples. Jews, among other creditors, had access to all kinds of luxurious items. One of them, Isach di Salam da Campobasso, was recorded in an inventory listed on January 1, 1470 as possessing a golden cross that had seven pearls, two diamonds and eight rubies attached to it[35]. In the city of Oberehnheim, in Alsace (another region thoroughly studied), a Jew had in his possession a gilded cross, while a coreligionist, from Rosheim, received a chalice as surety. Both were dealing with the Abbey of St. Leonard[36]. For the "transit region" of Savoy-Piemont, a document of the year 1404 stated that Josson Aaron, a Jew of Chambéry, had in his possession a gilded reliquary profusely adorned with small bells[37].

V.

It would be wrong to conclude from the Italian evidence that Christian sensitivity had been abolished altogether and that conciliar decrees were completely forsaken. While many, perhaps most, Christians did not follow these injunctions; their authority did not fade away without leaving any trace. A letter by Pope Urban V, sent in December 1370 to the Archbishop of Rossano in Calabria, can testify to that effect. It had to do with the misbehavior of a monastic superior ("archimandrite") by the name of Dorsiosus. The avalanche of accusations listed by the papal chancery of Avignon included the allegation that he pawned to "a certain Jew", against a usurious loan, chalices, silver crosses and other ecclesial ornaments that belonged to the Monastery of St. Maria in Patire[38]. Notice should be paid to the fact that these lines were written close in time to the exchange that took place in Assisi, as mentioned above. The Spoleto transaction of 1414 saved the uninitiated from another possible pitfall, namely from the illusion that Jews got access to luxurious

[35] Cf. *Filena Patroni Griffi*, Banchieri et gioielli alla corte aragonese di Napoli (Napoli 1992) 21.
[36] Cf. *Gerd Mentgen*, Elsaß (as in note 27 above) 39.
[37] Cf. *Thomas Bardelle*, Juden in einem Transit- und Brückenland. Studien zur Geschichte der Juden in Savoyen-Piemont bis zum Ende der Herrschaft Amadeus VIII. (Hannover 1992) 185–186.
[38] Cf. *Shlomo Simosohn*, The Apostolic See and the Jews; Addenda, Corrigenda, Bibliography and Indexes (Toronto 1991) 11–13, Appendix N° 13.

objects solely when dealing with ecclesiastics. The Rector of Spoleto was not the only secular figure who exposed Jewish moneylenders to the sumptuous and the elegant. Other individuals and institutions, not related to the church, made similar transactions. Their history, however, must be dealt with in a separate communication.

Annegret Holtmann

Medieval "Pigeonholes".

The Jewish Account Books from Vesoul and Medieval Bookkeeping Practices

Amongst the most exciting sources for Jewish medieval bookkeeping practices are the two business books of a Jewish merchants' company that had its headquarters in Vesoul in the County of Burgundy, also known as the Franche-Comté. The books were introduced to historical research for the first time in the late 19th century thanks to the efforts of Isidore Loeb[1]. Loeb provided a detailed description and much inspiration for further research, such as my doctoral thesis, in which I attempted to give a detailed analysis of the bookkeeping methods and the range of economic activities recorded in these books[2].

The two books are remarkable in several respects. First, they are among the earliest examples of private account books that have been preserved north of the Alps. Secondly, although both books are fragments today, the considerable number of 96 and 120 pages respectively have been preserved. In addition, both volumes offer entries on many different branches of business. The first account book, which covers the period from 1303 to about 1305, solely contains references to small loan transactions with village people in the immediate vicinity of Vesoul. Parts of the second book, which dates from 1300 to 1318, record the same kind of transactions. In addition, however, we also find loans on future wine harvests, entries on Jewish participation in the cloth trade of the local Lombard merchants, records of the Jews' money changing business and loans to the noblemen of the Franche-Comté.

[1] *Isidore Loeb*, Deux livres de commerce du commencement du XIVe siècle, in: Revue des études juives 8 (1884) 161–196, 9 (1884) 21–50, 187–213. I am grateful to Detlev Mares for the translation of this article.

[2] *Annegret Holtmann*, Juden in der Grafschaft Burgund im Mittelalter (Forschungen zur Geschichte der Juden A 12, Hannover 2003) esp. 153–289. See also *Meyer R. Malka*, Les pièces comptables hébraïques de la banque d'Héliot de Vesoul. Esquisse en vue d'une étude générale et de l'édition de ces pièces, Maîtrise de lettres et civilisations étrangères (hébreu), Université Lyon III (Lyon 1984); *Annegret Holtmann*, Jewish Moneylending as Reflected in Medieval Account Books: The Example of Vesoul, in: *Christoph Cluse* (ed.), The Jews of Europe in the Middle Ages (Tenth to Fifteenth Centuries). Proceedings of the International Symposium held at Speyer, 20–25 October 2002 (Tournhout 2004) 305–315.

The two books only represent a fraction of a much more comprehensive bookkeeping system of the Vesoul Jews. It is surprising that these fragments survived at all. Usually the business records of medieval merchants were destroyed when no longer needed. We do not know why the Jews (or somebody else?) chose to save these particular books. We also do not positively know how they ended up in the "Archives départementales de la Côte d'Or" in Dijon, where they are today[3]. We may assume that they were confiscated when the Jews of the County of Burgundy were expelled during the reign of the French King Philippe V le Long in 1321/22. The account books ended up in the ducal archives in Dijon when the duke of Burgundy took over the neighbouring county of the same name in 1330[4].

The two volumes offer fascinating insights for historical research. The recorded names of Jewish money-lenders, members of the company and of places of origin provide invaluable source material for the history of Jewish settlement and demography. The books also contain much information on the branches of business favoured by the Jewish traders. I have analysed these aspects elsewhere[5]. In the following pages, I would like to approach the account books from a different angle. I will try to use the results gained from the Vesoul documents for a comparison with similar material from other regions in Europe. First, I will give a survey of the major surviving records of medieval bookkeeping. This will underline the almost unique position of the Vesoul account books among the source material at our disposal. Then, I will describe the accounting practices of the Vesoul merchants and compare them to other examples from the same period. By placing the Vesoul accounts into the context of both Jewish and Christian business records, I hope to make a contribution to the growing body of research on Jewish economic activity and medieval bookkeeping in general.

Jewish and Christian Sources on Medieval bookkeeping

Any attempt at inter-regional comparison has to struggle with the rather sorry state and uneven preservation of source material. Only a small number of private business records from the middle ages have survived at all. They are mostly account books that were confiscated after a company went bankrupt[6]. In the case of

[3] Archives départementales de la Côte d'Or, B 10410 and B 10411.

[4] *Annegret Holtmann*, Jewish Settlement and Economic Activity in the Medieval Franche-Comté: The Account Books of Heliot of Vesoul, in: Jewish Studies 40 (2000) 69*–82*, 73*. On the expulsion of the Jews in 1321/22 see *Holtmann*, Juden 308–317.

[5] See *Holtmann*, Jewish Settlement 74*–81*; *Holtmann*, Juden, esp. 61–64, 119–120, 191–201, 206–226, 242–262, 278–285.

[6] *Basil S. Yamey*, Bookkeeping and Accounts, 1200–1800, in: *Simonetta Cavaciocchi* (ed.), L'impresa industria comercio banca, secc. XIII–XVIII. Atti della "Ventiduesima Settimana di Studi" 30 aprile – 4 maggio 1990 (Istituto internazionale di storia economica "F. Datini", Prato, Serie II – Atti delle "Settimane di Studi" e altri Convegni 22, Firenze 1991) 163–187, 164. See, for example, the surviving records of the Peruzzi and Bardi, which were confiscated at the financial collapse of the companies

Jewish records, confiscation might have occurred in times of persecution and expulsion, as in the Vesoul example. If we look for Jewish business records in particular, we find remarks in Christian title deeds or entries in loaned books. Apart from such instances, only few items have survived[7]. Comparisons are not made easier by the fact that most surviving items are fragments which originated in very different times and places. A short survey may show this.

To my knowledge, the oldest fragment stems from southern England. It consists of two pages of credit entries and repayments of loan, written by a Spanish Jew in about 1200 in the Arabic language and in Hebrew letters. The fragments survived because they were used in the bindings of a Jewish prayer book[8]. From the north of France, *zarfat*, only few records of Jewish moneylenders are known. Moïse Schwab discovered some pawnbrokers' entries in religious books which originated in 1213 and from the turn of the 13th and 14th centuries[9]. If we follow a chronological order, the next items to mention are the fragments from Vesoul, dating from the first two decades of the 14th century. Then there are 15 pages from a Hebrew business book from the Catalan town of Gerona from 1333. They were edited in 1990[10]. A sizeable but unpublished fragment of 96 pages has been preserved from Marseille in southern France. There, the business man Mardochée Joseph, who was active in the production of pine resin, recorded workers' wages, loans he offered on these wages and loan repayments in 1374[11]. Two single-sheet fragments have

in 1343 and 1346: *Armando Sapori*, I libri di commercio dei Peruzzi (Pubblicazioni della direzione degli "Studi Medievali" 1, Milano 1934); *Armando Sapori*, La crisi delle compagnie mercantili dei Bardi e dei Peruzzi (Biblioteca storica toscana 3, Firenze 1926); *Armando Sapori*, Storia interna della Compagnia mercantile dei Peruzzi, in: Archivio storico italiano 7e série, 22 (1934) 3–65.

7 There are indications for Hebrew business books from many places in Europe, such as the diocese of Trier, the Netherlands, Savoy, Moravia, Switzerland, Bavaria (Regensburg) and the Rhine (Ingelheim); see *Holtmann*, Juden 161, note 59 with literature.

8 *Malachi Beit-Arié*, The Hebrew-Arabic Document in Ms. Oxford, Corpus Christi College 133, in: *Malachi Beit-Arié*, The Only Dated Medieval Hebrew Manuscript Written in England (1189 CE) and the Problem of Pre-Expulsion Anglo-Hebrew Manuscripts (London 1985) 33–35. See also *Zefira Entin Rokéah*, A Jewish Payment-Memorandum, in: *Malachi Beit-Arié*, The Only Dated Medieval Hebrew Manuscript Written in England (1189 CE) and the Problem of Pre-Expulsion Anglo-Hebrew Manuscripts (London 1985) 36–56.

9 *Moïse Schwab*, Notes de comptabilité juive du XIIIe et du XIVe siècle, in: Revue des études juives 30 (1895) 289–294; *Moïse Schwab*, Notes hébraïques de comptabilité du XIIIe siècle, in: Revue des études juives 41 (1900) 149–153. Judith Olszowy-Schlanger, directeur d'études at the Ecole Pratique des Hautes Etudes in Paris, is currently preparing a collection of comparable material.

10 *Jordi Casanovas Miró* et al. (eds.), Libro de cuentas de un prestamista judío gerundense del siglo XIV (Judeolenguas marginales en Sefarad antes de 1492. Textos 1, Barcelona 1990). Attention was directed to this source by *José María Millàs I Vallicrosa*, Petita lista d'un prestamista jueu, in: Estudis Universitaris Catalans 12 (1927) 65–67.

11 *Moïse Schwab*, Le livre de comptes de Mardochée Joseph, banquier et négociant à Marseille en 1374, in: Académie des inscriptions et belles-lettres, comptes rendus des séances (1913) 105. *Moïse Schwab*, Livre de comptes de Mardochée Joseph (manuscrit hébréo-provençal), in: Notices et extraits des manuscrits de la Bibliothèque Nationale et autres bibliothèques 39 (1916) 469–502. Due to the very complex paleographic and structural problems, Schwab only analysed selected aspects, such as passages with linguistic characteristics from the Provençe region, currencies, weights and measures as well as paleographic particularities.

been preserved in southern Germany. In the years from 1329 to 1332, a Jewish money lender from the Bavarian town of Straubing registered 98 loans to clients in the surrounding countryside. The second is a single sheet of paper from the business book of a Constance pawnbroker that can be dated to 1372. Both fragments were published and analysed by Michael Toch and Wolfgang von Stromer[12]. The first preserved Jewish fragments from Italy, the cradle of bookkeeping, only date from the 15th century and already reflect rather modern accounting practices. Let me just name the pawnbroker's register of a Jew from Montepulciano dating from 1409 to 1410[13], and two books from Florence. The first is a pawnbroker's register from 1473 to 1475 which was ascribed to Isaac of San Miniato[14], the second a pawn register of the Florentine Banco alla Vacca from 1477[15].

In contrast to Jewish sources, there is no shortage of surviving Christian merchants' accounts that might invite comparison of bookkeeping methods. However, they originated in a wide variety of places and show considerable differences in terms of content. In this case, the oldest fragments originate from Italy and were produced in the first half of the 13th century[16]. When Italian trade expanded north

12 *Michael Toch*, Geld und Kredit in einer spätmittelalterlichen Landschaft. Zu einem unbeachteten hebräischen Schuldenregister aus Niederbayern (1329–1332), in: Deutsches Archiv für Erforschung des Mittelalters 38 (1982) 499–550; *Wolfgang von Stromer, Michael Toch*, Zur Buchführung der Juden im Spätmittelalter, in: *Jürgen Schneider* (ed.), Wirtschaftskräfte und Wirtschaftswege. Festschrift für Hermann Kellenbenz, vol. I: Mittelmeer und Kontinent (Bamberg 1978) 387–412. For the date see *Toch*, Geld und Kredit 504, note 18.

13 *Daniel Carpi*, The Account Book of a Jewish Moneylender in Montepulciano (1409–1410), in: Journal of European Economic History 14 (1985) 501–513; *Daniel Carpi*, On the history of the Jewish moneylenders in Montepulciano in the 14th and at the beginning of the 15th century, in: Jews in Italy. Studies Dedicated to the Memory of U. Cassuto on the 100th Anniversary of his Birth (Jerusalem 1988) 231–274 (Hebr.). Moïse Schwab also published a Hebrew fee sheet from the first half of the 16th century. It was discovered by accident and lists the outstanding fees an Italian teacher was due to receive from his pupils' fathers: *Moïse Schwab*, Une page de comptabilité de 1525–1528, in: Revue des études juives 12 (1886) 116–117.

14 *Umberto Cassuto*, Gli ebrei a Firenze nell'età del Rinascimento (Pubblicazioni del R. Istituto di studi superiori pratici e di perfezionamento in Firenze, Sezione di filosofia e filologia, Firenze 1918, reprint Firenze 1965) 160–167; *Flavia Careri*, Il banco di pegni di Isacco da San Miniato: Firenze 1473–1475, Tesi di laurea in storia medioevale, Università degli studi di Firenze (Firenze 1992).

15 *Umberto Cassuto*, Un registro ebraico di pegni del secolo XV, in: Zeitschrift für hebräische Bibliographie 15 (1911) 182–185, 16 (1913) 127–142; see also *Cassuto*, Ebrei a Firenze 168–171, and *Careri*, Banco di pegni 59–62. Joseph Shatzmiller alerted me to a further Hebrew account book from Italy, which is preserved in a monastery in (or around) Cava de' Tirreni.

16 See for example *Armando Sapori*, Libri di commercio LXVI; *Raymond de Roover*, The Development of Accounting Prior to Lucca Paciolo According to the Account Books of Medieval Merchants, in: *Raymond de Roover* (*Julius Kirshner*, ed.), Business, Banking and Economic Thought in Late Medieval and Early Modern Europe (Chicago, London 1974 [original edition 1956]) 119–180, 121–122. Also see *Raymond de Roover*, Aux origines d'une technique intellectuelle: la formation et l'expansion de la comptabilité à partie double, in: Annales d'histoire économique et sociale 9 (1937) 171–193, 270–298, 177; *Geoffrey Lee*, The Oldest European Account Book: A Florentine Bank Ledger of 1211, in: Nottingham Medieval Studies 16 (1972) 28–60; *Geoffrey Alan Lee*, The Development of Italian Bookkeeping 1211–1300, in: Abacus. A Journal of Accounting and Business Studies 9 (1973) 137–155.

of the Alps, accounting practices started to diversify[17]. The great Italian merchants' companies that were active at the Champagne trade fairs, in Flanders and in England, used several interconnected books and adapted their accounting practices to their specific needs. This applies to the books of the Ugolini company (Siena) from the mid-13th century[18], the documents from the London branch of the Gallerani-company (Siena) from 1305–1308[19] as well as the books of the Bardi and Peruzzi from the first half of the 14th century[20]. However, these items do not really offer themselves to comparison since in any case Italian bookkeeping practices were further advanced than the methods used in other countries[21].

More suited to comparison with the Vesoul books are accounting fragments from Germany and France. In the case of the earliest French item, a ledger of a Lyon cloth trader, three sheets of originally at least 227 have survived. They carry dates from the years 1320 to 1323[22]. The business book of the versatile merchant and money lender Johan Blasi from Marseille dates from 1329 to 1337[23]. The fragment of the account book of Ugo Teralh still consists of 20 folio pages. It dates from 1330 to 1332 and records his trading in cloth in his home town of Forcalquier (Provence)[24]. A further cloth trader, Jean Saval, lived in Carcassonne and left parts of an account book from 1340 to 1341[25]. Two books have been preserved from the banking family Bonis of Montauban: a ledger from 1345 to 1359 and an account book kept between 1347 and 1359[26]. From Avignon, we have the records from 1365 to 1371 of the wood trader Guilhem Vial[27]. In addition there is Jacme Olivier from Narbonne. He

[17] *De Roover*, Development of Accounting 121.

[18] *De Roover*, Development of Accounting 126–127.

[19] *Georges Bigwood, Armand Grunzweig* (eds.), Les livres des comptes des Gallerani, 2 vols. (Académie Royale de Belgique, Commission royale d'histoire, Koninklijke Belgische Academie, Koninklijke Commissie voor Geschiedenis, Bruxelles 1961, 1962); *Christopher W. Nobes*, The Gallerani Account Book of 1305–1308, in: The Accounting Review 57/2 (1982) 303–310.

[20] *Sapori*, Libri di commercio; *Sapori*, Crisi; *Sapori*, Storia interna.

[21] For more details, see for example *de Roover*, Development of Accounting 120–164.

[22] *Paul Meyer, Georges Guigue*, Fragments d'un grand livre d'un drapier de Lyon, in: Romania 35 (1906) 428–444.

[23] The account book still holds 37 sheets: *Dietrich Hauck*, Das Kaufmannsbuch des Johan Blasi (1329–1337). Ausgabe mit sprachlichem und wirtschaftsgeschichtlichem Kommentar, (Diss. phil. Saarbrücken 1965); *Pierre Paul*, Transcription et traduction du Livre de Raison de Jean Blaise. Un manuscrit en ancien Provençal des Archives Communales de Marseille, 2 vols., typescript (Aix 1980).

[24] *Paul Meyer*, Le livre-journal de Maître Ugo Teralh, notaire et drapier à Forcalquier (1330–1332), in: Notices et extraits des manuscrits de la Bibliothèque Nationale 36 (1899) 129–170.

[25] *Ch. Portal*, Le livre-journal de Jean Saval, marchand-drapier à Carcassonne (1340–1341), in: Bulletin philologique et historique du Comité des travaux historiques et scientifiques (1901) 418–449.

[26] *Edouard Forestié*, Les livres de comptes des frères Bonis, marchands montalbanais du XIVe siècle, 2 vols., Première partie (Archives historiques de la Gascogne, fascicule 20, Paris, Auch 1890), Deuxième partie (Archives historiques de la Gascogne, fascicule 23, Paris, Auch 1893). The main book contains data from 1338 to 1369.

[27] *P. Pansier*, Guilhem Vial, fustier, fournisseur du pape et de nos seigneurs les cardinaux (1351–1388), in: Mémoires de l'Académie de Vaucluse, 2e série, 7 (1907) 331–363.

was a cloth trader and money lender, but he also dealt in grain, honey and cattle. He left a sizeable account book that lists personal accounts from 1381 to 1391[28].

Finally, a brief glance at the German situation. The earliest surviving items originated in the Hanseatic area and in Upper Germany[29]. One of the major examples is the account book of the Nuremberg merchant family Holzschuher. It dates from 1304 to 1307 and lists cloth sales on credit and the subsequent repayments[30]. One might also mention the account book of two Lubeck merchants, Hermann Warendorp and Johann Clingenberg. Between 1330 and 1336, they kept accounts of their long-distance trading activities when one of the companions was absent[31]. Another example of trade in cloth is preserved in the account book of the Hamburg merchant Vicko von Geldersen and his son Johannes. It lists cloth sales on credit from 1367 to 1392[32]. Last but not least, the ledger of the Regensburg merchants' family Runtinger claims special mention. It dates from 1383 to 1407 and holds a prominent place due to its advanced bookkeeping methods and its sheer size[33]. These examples may suffice to show that there is a whole list of account books that allow comparisons with the Vesoul items although basically all of them are only preserved as fragments and originate from different times and places.

The Vesoul Account Books in the Context of European Bookkeeping Practices

From the late 13th century, the Jew Héliot and his family lived in Vesoul[34]. Héliot and his trading partners received incentives from the counts of Burgundy to settle

[28] *Alphonse Blanc* (ed.), Le livre de comptes de Jacme Olivier, marchand narbonnais du XIVe siècle, vol. 2, part 1 (Paris 1899). The results of Blanc's research, published in vol. 50 of the Bulletin de la commission archéologique de Narbonne in 1896, were not available to me.

[29] For a survey see *Franz Bastian*, Das Runtingerbuch 1383–1407 und verwandtes Material zum Regensburger-südostdeutschen Handel und Münzwesen, 3 vols. (Deutsche Handelsakten des Mittelalters und der Neuzeit VI, I–III, Regensburg 1944, 1935, 1943) vol. I, 201–254; *Wolfgang von Stromer*, Das Schriftwesen der Nürnberger Wirtschaft vom 14. bis zum 16. Jahrhundert, in: Beiträge zur Wirtschaftsgeschichte Nürnbergs, vol. 2 (Beiträge zur Geschichte und Kultur der Stadt Nürnberg 11/II, Nuremberg 1967) 751–799, esp. 753–757; *Wiltrud Eikenberg*, Das Handelshaus der Runtinger zu Regensburg. Ein Spiegel süddeutschen Rechts-, Handels- und Wirtschaftslebens im ausgehenden 14. Jahrhundert (Veröffentlichungen des Max-Planck-Instituts für Geschichte 43, Göttingen 1976) 11–18.

[30] *Anton Chroust, Hans Proesler* (eds.), Das Handlungsbuch der Holzschuher in Nürnberg von 1304–1307 (Veröffentlichungen der Gesellschaft für fränkische Geschichte X. Reihe: Quellen zur Wirtschaftsgeschichte Frankens I, Erlangen 1934).

[31] *Fritz Rörig*, Das älteste erhaltene deutsche Kaufmannsbüchlein, in: *idem*, Hansische Beiträge zur deutschen Wirtschaftsgeschichte (Veröffentlichungen der Schleswig-Holsteinischen Universitätsgesellschaft 12, Breslau 1928 [original edition 1925]) 174–216.

[32] *Hans Nirrnheim*, Das Handlungsbuch Vickos von Geldersen (Hamburg, Leipzig 1895).

[33] *Bastian*, Runtingerbuch. See also *Eikenberg*, Das Handelshaus der Runtinger (note 29).

[34] Héliot's first tax payment is recorded for 1296: *Jean-Pierre Redoutey*, Le comté de Bourgogne de 1295 à 1314: problèmes d'administration, in: Mémoires de la société pour l'histoire du droit et

in the territory. The counts tried to encourage the economic activities in their region by a variety of means, such as *chartes de franchises*, tariffs, road building, and settlement privileges for Jews and Lombards. These measures were supposed to enhance the importance of the County of Burgundy as a region of transit for the international trade between the North and South of Europe[35].

During the first two decades of the 14th century, the Jewish company in Vesoul established a wide variety of business activities. The above-named Héliot of Vesoul, apparently the head of the company, was probably assisted by his son Vivant. A great number of business partners, among them at least twelve members of Héliot's family, were involved in the many branches of the company's business. French sources report that these *compeignons* sometimes acted in Héliot's name (*en son nom*). So far, it has not been possible to establish the precise number of Jews involved in the company, but about 70 seems to be a good estimate. They lived in Vesoul and in some of the nearby smaller villages, in some cases also in more distant centres of economic importance[36]. The Jews in the County of Burgundy were spared the expulsion of the French Jews in 1306, even though the French king Philippe IV le Bel had been ruling the northern part of the Franche-Comté since 1295[37].

The Vesoul company was mainly active in the credit business. Small loans to the population of the neighbouring villages provided the staple of its activities, but we also find close business relationships with members of the aristocracy from all over the Franche-Comté. A good example for the scale of activities are the company's small loans to the population in the villages close to Vesoul. The number of loans granted to people from this area ran into hundreds in the first years of the 14th century. Clients came from all walks of life, farmers, craftsmen and small traders as well as officials, clerics and knights[38]. Almost 70% of the loans were much lower than one pound, only 30% ran higher. As securities, the Jews accepted the naming

des institutions des anciens pays bourguignons, comtois et romands 33 (1975–1976) 7–65, esp. 39; *Holtmann*, Juden 59.

[35] See for example *Alexandre Tuetey*, Etude sur le droit municipal au XIIIe et XIVe siècle en Franche-Comté et en particulier à Montbéliard, in: Mémoires de la société d'émulation de Montbéliard (1865–1867) 109–429 ; *Roland Fiétier*, Les chartes de franchises octroyées par la famille de Chalon, in: Mémoires de la société pour l'histoire du droit et des institutions des anciens pays bourguignons, comtois et romands 26 (1965) 257–260; *Gisèle David*, Les chartes de franchises dans le Comté de Bourgogne au Moyen Age, in: De l'autonomie des villes. Besançon 1290–1990. Actes du colloque organisé par l'Association du Septième Centenaire des Franchises de Besançon, Besançon, septembre 1990 (Annales littéraires de l'Université de Besançon 470 – Cahiers d'études comtoises 49, Paris, Besançon 1992) 47–53.

[36] See *Loeb*, Deux livres 167–170; *Holtmann*, Juden 179–182.

[37] For the 1306 expulsion see *Robert Chazan*, Medieval Jewry in Northern France. A Political and Social History (The Johns Hopkins University Studies in Historical and Political Science; Ninety-First Series, 1973; 2, Baltimore, London 1973) 191–201; *William Chester Jordan*, The French Monarchy and the Jews: From Philip Augustus to the Last Capetians (Middle Ages Series, Philadelphia 1989) 200–213. For possible reasons why the Jews were not expelled from the County of Burgundy see *Holtmann*, Juden 293–294.

[38] See the example of Villers-le-Sec in *Holtmann*, Juden 213–216.

of guarantors. The records show a close-knit community where guarantor and debtor were often related to each other. The loans had to be repaid within a couple of weeks or several months. Extensions or partial repayments meant that in practice many loans where only payed off after more than a year or even after a couple of years[39]. The credit activities mentioned so far are reflected in the so-called "Account Book I" that was exclusively reserved for small loan operations. The first entries were made at the beginning of the Jewish year 5064, that is, in the autumn of 1303, while the last entries probably date from the autumn of 1305[40]. When the book was put in use, open loans were transferred into it from a so-called "old book"[41].

How did a business transaction find its way into the book? When Héliot, a family member or his companions had granted a credit to debtors in Vesoul or other places, the bookkeeper was notified about the operation either orally or by written statement. He then entered the loan sum into the book, arranging the proceedings village by village. Initially, a certain number of pages had been reserved for each village[42]. All loans to the inhabitants of a particular place were entered into the respective village account in chronological order of the deals. The bookkeeper took care to leave a certain amount of free space between the different entries. At the same time, the bookkeeper tried to arrange for personal accounts. If a client needed a further loan in the future, the new deal was entered next to his prior loan. In this way, the gaps between the entries would be gradually filled, although as a result, the chronological order suffered[43].

What did a single entry look like? The entries all followed a standard pattern (see Appendix). Before the book had been put in use, the page had been divided into separate columns by incision with a knife. On the beginning of a line at the right side of the page, the amount of the loan was entered in Hebrew letters. In the left column, first the debtor's name was recorded, then his place of residence and sometimes family relationships. Next, the name and the place of residence of the guarantor were given, as well as the date when repayment was due. Occasionally, there were remarks on currencies or other issues connected with the deal[44]. If repayment came on time, the amount owed was crossed out. If there was only partial repayment or if the loan had to be extended or increased, the original sum was crossed out and the new amount was noted above or to the right of the original sum. Moreover, the original due date was crossed out and a new one added. If all the business transactions on a page were concluded or transferred to a new book, the whole

[39] See *Holtmann*, Juden 220–223.

[40] For the calculation of the dates see *Holtmann*, Juden 175–177.

[41] Examples for similar transfers can be found in other account books of the period, for example on the first 28 pages of the third main book („Livre C") kept by the Bonis brothers from Montauban or in the records by the Holzschuher from Nuremberg: *Forestié*, Livres de Comptes, Première partie VIII and Edition; *Chroust*, Einleitung I, in: *Chroust*, *Proesler* (eds.), Handlungsbuch IX–XXXV, XII, XVII–XVIII.

[42] See table 2 in the appendix in *Holtmann*, Juden 355–362.

[43] *Holtmann*, Juden 174–175.

[44] *Holtmann*, Juden 171–173.

page was crossed out. This is the case with most of the pages that are preserved from this account book[45].

A comparison of the bookkeeping practices in the first account book to other examples from the same period shows both similarities and some differences. Personal accounts can be found in the account book of the Nuremberg Holzschuher company, in the book of the Lyon cloth trader from 1320 to 1321 and in the so-called "Book C of the Bonis brothers" from Montauban[46]. Yet the arrangements of the single elements of an entry differed from each other. In terms of convenience, it was an ingenious idea of the Jews to enter the credit sum at the start of the line in a separate column. This made changes in the sum, which might be caused by belated repayments or extensions of the credit, very simple. In such cases, a new entry was unnecessary. The Jewish money lenders from Straubing and Constance entered in their lists of outstanding debts both the date of the original credit operation and the due date[47]. For the Vesoul Jews, the due date was sufficient. The same was the case in the records of the Nuremberg Holzschuher family whose account book dates from the same period as the Vesoul examples[48].

Like other Jewish bookkeepers, the Vesoul Jews used Christian feasts as due dates. This reflects the fact that their operations had to be adapted to the seasonal routines of their Christian environment. In one respect, however, the Vesoul account books differ not only from Christian, but also from other Jewish examples. The Vesoul Jews often characterised their due dates with the week day of the respective *parasha*, that is the weekly Torah lecture. Unlike the German Jewish money lenders from Straubing and Constance, they did not use the Jewish month system nor did they denote their entries according to the Julian calendar, as Jews in Italy, Marseille and Catalonia did. This peculiarity reflects the conventions known from other business records as well as from gravestones in *zarfat* (Northern France)[49] and can thus be explained by characteristic regional influences[50].

As mentioned above, the Vesoul Jews did not only trade locally in small loans but also dealt with noblemen from the northern part of the County. The clients were members of the small gentry as well as the high aristocracy. The Jews also maintained business contacts to family members of the former counts of Burgundy[51]. The political situation at the beginning of the 14th century was favourable to

45 *Holtmann*, Juden 173, 177.

46 *Hans Proesler*, Einleitung II, in: *Chroust*, *Proesler* (eds.), Handlungsbuch XXXV–LXXXIII, LX; *Meyer*, *Guigue*, Fragments 429; *Forestié*, Livres de comptes, Première partie. Jacme Olivier from Narbonne also kept personal accounts in his book in the 1380s: *Blanc* (ed.), Livre de comptes.

47 *von Stromer*, Buchführung 396–397; *Toch*, Geld und Kredit 513.

48 *Chroust*, Einleitung I, in: *Chroust*, *Proesler* (eds.), Handlungsbuch XVI, note 1; *Toch*, Geld und Kredit 513. Loeb erroneously assumed that the small loan book from Vesoul lists the date when the credit was granted: *Loeb*, Deux livres 162; see *Holtmann*, Juden 171.

49 *Schwab*, Notes de comptabilité 290–292. *Gérard Nahon*, Inscriptions hébraïques et juives en France médiévale (Franco-Judaïca 12, Paris 1986).

50 *Holtmann*, Juden 173–174.

51 In detail *Holtmann*, Juden 183–205.

money lending activities. Many noblemen were heavily in debt after a war against the French king, whose rule over parts of the province they resented[52]. The Jews took great care to cultivate their aristocratic clientele. The resulting business contacts often lasted for many years. Some deals with the aristocracy only involved small sums of money, for instance when a couple of pence were needed for the shoeing of a horse. In general, however, the business deals with noblemen were much more complex than the small loans operations with the local rural population. The noblemen often needed considerable sums of money. Such transactions were usually properly authenticated with the nobleman's seal or the Vesoul seigniorial seal. The Jews also accepted securities such as jewellery, costly tableware and expensive garments. Transactions with the aristocracy were challenging because they were often conducted in different places in the county and might involve large sums of money, complicated repayment schemes and repeated extensions of the credit. This meant that from time to time the bookkeepers had to summarise prior transactions and calculate an interim balance of individual accounts. Accordingly, one section of the second account book was arranged by personal accounts. Each transaction was recorded in a separate paragraph. These personal accounts might refer to an individual or a family. The account of the Rougemont family provides a good example (see Appendix). It takes up about two thirds of folio 45v[53]. This family account records credits to the *seigneur de Rougemont*, his wife and his son. Two entries show Humbert of Rougemont's seal when he was acting as a guarantor for other people[54].

The Rougemont entries cover a period from 1305 to 1314, but the business relationship may have been older still. The account, compiled by Héliot of Vesoul and the seigneur of Rougemont himself on 23rd April 1306 (Saint George's day), starts with a summary of all previous open loans[55]. Apparently, there were disagreements over the outstanding debt. While Héliot's calculation arrived at the sum of 431 pounds, the debtor only wanted to repay 411. Perhaps the conflict was solved by Héliot granting a favourable interest rate on a large part of the loan sum. Humbert had to pay 60 pounds in interest on 300 pounds of the sum he owed, which made for a rather low interest rate of 20%[56]. The Rougemont account also contains a loan from 1305 that had to be recorded again since it had been forgotten in the summary, and several transactions from 1307 to 1310[57]. On 23rd November 1311 Humbert de Rougemont made a partial repayment of 300 pounds and a year later, he made a repayment of all "what was written above". Both the company and the nobleman mutually granted receipts of the payments and the bookkeeper crossed out the whole entry. Interestingly, the Jews now explicitly noted that they had not

[52] For more detail see *Holtmann*, Juden 33-36.

[53] Archives Départementales de la Côte d'Or, B 10410, fol. 45v. See the picture and transcription of the account in the appendix to this paper. See also *Holtmann*, Juden 195–197.

[54] See appendix, fol. 45v (5) and (15).

[55] Appendix, fol. 45v (8).

[56] Appendix, fol. 45v (8).

[57] Appendix, fol. 45v (9).

charged any interest at all on Rougemont's loans[58]. A further credit of 400 pounds, which had to be repaid in two equal parts in May and in September 1312, was recorded below the crossed out section[59]. The bookkeeper finally squeezed in two further loans at the bottom of the page[60]. With these entries, the space reserved for the Rougemont account was definitely exhausted. When altogether seven further loans running to more than 400 pounds had to be registered in 1313 and 1314, the bookkeeper was forced to move towards the top of the account and make his entries above the original first entry[61]. This final group of entries is only partially crossed out and there are no signs of a summary or balance[62]. Perhaps the account was transferred to a new book and administered from there.

We can see from this example that personal accounts were structured equally simple as the village accounts even though they covered more complicated transactions. Apparently the Vesoul Jews did not reserve a full page in their account book for each of their noble clients. As a result, they had to be very pragmatic in arranging their entries. We find the Jews tentatively summarising or balancing the account. However, this was only done when there seemed to be an immediate need to do so. Stating regular balances was not yet the routine process it was to be in more advanced accounting systems. Striking similarities to the personal accounts of the Vesoul Jews can be found in the fragment of the cloth trader from Lyon. In his book, the accounts were ordered alphabetically. Loans and repayments were listed one below the other and summarised from time to time (introduced by the word *soma*)[63]. The Holzschuher company also proceeded in this way, as did Jacme Olivier in Narbonne and the Runtinger family in Regensburg[64].

Apart from personal accounts, the second account book also features another kind of entry, a register of goods received. These accounts had their origin in money lending activities. Many local farmers did not only till the soil, but also worked one or several vineyards. They frequently borrowed money by pawning their future wine harvests rather than by naming guarantors. The Jewish creditors received their repayments in the form of must or wine. Some customers also offered the vineyards themselves as security for the money they borrowed. In this case, half the returns went to the Jews, the other half remained with the debtor (*métayage*). Fifteen pages in the second account book were devoted to wine deliveries from 1315 to 1318[65]. Each harvest year had its own account that was subdivided according to the villages where the wine came from. Again, the entries followed a uniform pattern: first, the name of the supplier, occasionally also the name of the vineyard,

[58] Appendix, fol. 45v (17) and (18).
[59] Appendix, fol. 45v (18).
[60] Appendix, fol. 45v (19) and (20).
[61] Appendix, fol. 45v (1)–(7).
[62] See also *Holtmann*, Juden 196–197.
[63] *Meyer*, *Guigue*, Fragments.
[64] *Chroust*, Einleitung I, in: *Chroust*, *Proesler*, Handlungsbuch XVII–XIX; *Blanc* (ed.), Livre de comptes; *Bastian*, Runtingerbuch, vol. 2.
[65] Archives Départementales de la Côte d'Or, B 10410, fol. 21r–29r.

then the amount delivered and the type of wine, finally the sum by which the debt was lessened by the wine delivery. By the way, the Jews also owned their own vineyards which they cultivated for their own consumption. The yields from their own vineyards were also registered in this account[66]. The wine accounts clearly demonstrate the characteristics of single entry bookkeeping: incoming and outgoing payments were combined in a single account. This meant that expenses, for example for harvest helpers or for the tithe, are registered among the deliveries the Jews received. Let me just add briefly that further accounts recorded Jewish participation in the local Lombards' cloth trade. One account is a four-column register of outgoing and incoming payments and contains a summary of the transactions[67]. Another one takes the form of personal accounts that list payments of the Jews to the Lombard merchants as well as their profits from the trade deals in which they had invested[68].

I hope this survey is sufficient to give an impression of the varied and pragmatic bookkeeping methods of the Vesoul company. As mentioned above, the two surviving account books are fragments from a much larger bookkeeping system. We frequently find references to other account books[69], but too often all we know is the fact that there existed an "old book"[70], a "red book"[71], the "other book"[72], or the "other paper"[73]. There was also a special wine-paper[74] and a "paper of my father", perhaps the personal account book of Héliot[75]. However, these references are too vague to allow the reconstruction of the complete bookkeeping system.

Results and Questions

May we speak of fundamental differences between "Jewish" and "Christian" bookkeeping practices? The answer should be "no". The Vesoul accounts do show similarities to other Jewish account books, for example in the use of the vocabulary for "payment", "repayment" and so on[76]. Yet the outline above also found instances of marked differences between Jewish account books. Partly, these may be explained

[66] For more detail see *Holtmann*, Juden 242–262, 387–390.

[67] Archives Départementales de la Côte d'Or, B 10410, fol. 4r. See the transcription and translation in *Malka*, Pièces comptables 48–59.

[68] Archives Départementales de la Côte d'Or, B 10410, fol. 9v; *Holtmann*, Juden 281–283.

[69] See *Holtmann*, Juden 170–171.

[70] For example Archives Départementales de la Côte d'Or, B 10411, fol. 9r (4), 36r (1).

[71] For example Archives Départementales de la Côte d'Or, B 10411, fol. 9v (1), 10v (2) etc.

[72] For example Archives Départementales de la Côte d'Or, B 10411, fol. 9r (14), (15), 9v (10), (15) etc. For the second account book see *Loeb*, Deux livres, REJ 9 41.

[73] Archives Départementales de la Côte d'Or, B 10411, fol. 9v (2).

[74] Archives Départementales de la Côte d'Or, B 10410, fol. 41v, last entry; *Loeb*, Deux livres 41.

[75] *Loeb*, Deux livres 41.

[76] The list of Hebrew professional terms in *Casanovas Miró* et al. (eds.), Libro de cuentas 74–79, mostly agrees with the terms applied by the Jews from Vesoul.

by the differences of the source material itself. For example, while the fragments from Vesoul and Gerona may be termed "account books", the pages from Southern Germany are lists, which were produced during inheritance cases or confiscations[77]. While there are differences between Jewish account books, there are striking similarities to instances of Christian bookkeeping, especially with the Holzschuher accounts from Nuremberg.

These results may be primarily grounded in the practice of single entry bookkeeping itself. In contrast to double entry bookkeeping, "no simple description or definition [of single entry bookkeeping] is possible"[78]. As Yamey pointed out, "so-called single entry ... was used in a variety of forms"[79]. Each bookkeeper developed his own style according to the needs of his particular situation[80]. The Vesoul account books illustrate this perfectly. At first sight, the pages look confusing, the handwriting seems prohibitive, the arrangement of entries chaotic. However, a closer look reveals a well-ordered system. The small loan book in particular displays a uniform pattern where entries were made in the form of village accounts in combination with personal accounts. This system was perfectly adapted to the requirements of merchants moving around the villages of the Franche-Comté to do business there, for example on market days. The book also displays instances of a balancing of accounts which was done when the book was full and active accounts had to be transferred to a new book – a well-known feature of medieval bookkeeping[81].

The results are more complex in the case of the second account book. How can we classify this collection of accounts that served different purposes, from personal debt accounts to accounts listing goods received? Are these primary records or books of original entry that were collected into one book? Or do we have here a ledger that covered different branches of business? At the moment, there is no answer to this question. But we can say that the book seems to have been perfectly adequate to allow control over the business transactions. Perhaps it is our wish to classify the book that is inadequate, not the bookkeeping system the book displays. If we take a look at the account book of Johan Blasi of Marseille, we find a similar picture of seemingly incongruous bookkeeping. There are entries on grain purchases and grain sales, investments in a fishing company and trade in shipbuild-

[77] During the Munich conference, this opinion was also supported by Michael Toch, who analysed and edited both fragments.
[78] *Yamey*, Bookkeeping 170.
[79] *Yamey*, Bookkeeping 170.
[80] *Raymond de Roover*, Characteristics of Bookkeeping before Pacioli, in: Accounting Review 13 (1939) 144–149, esp. 149. Ugo Teralh from Forcalquier had his customers accept their debts by making them enter the sums into his account book (1330–1332) with their own hand. Jewish customers used Hebrew: *Meyer*, Livre-journal 132; in detail *Israël Lévi*, Le Livre-Journal de Maitre Ugo Teralh, in: Revue des études juives 37 (1898) 259–265. The same procedure was used by Jean Saval from Carcassonne (debtors and/or guarantors wrote into the book): *Portal*, Livre-journal 428.
[81] *De Roover*, Characteristics 148.

ing material, next to entries on the trade in oil, almonds, fur and leather, followed by entries on money lending transactions. And this is not even to mention the inventory of Blasi's mobile and immobile possessions or his last will[82].

In order to understand why single entry bookkeeping was sufficient for a long period of time, it is perhaps worthwhile to turn to the most basic question: Why did merchants such as the Vesoul Jews needed bookkeeping in the first place? Raymond de Roover noted a close connection between the expansion of trade and the progress in bookkeeping practices. If a company expands the geographical range and scale of its trading activities, its accounting has to become more precise and more differentiated. On the other hand, profitable trading is not possible without a certain routine in accounting practices that are suited to the specific needs of the company[83]. De Roover singles out three crucial factors for the further development of bookkeeping: the rising number of trade partnerships, the increasing sale of goods on credit, which necessitated a permanent control of debts, and the naming of agents in the administration of a company's capital[84]. If we apply this to the Jewish company in Vesoul, we are reminded of its widespread activities in a Christian environment, in a region that had seen recent political turmoil, in an area where the Jews had to deal with rural people as well as noblemen, but also with Lombard merchants. In order to keep these widespread activities under control, a system of bookkeeping was indispensable. The bookkeeping system had to be adapted to this particular situation, and the single entry system the Vesoul Jews developed seems to have been perfectly adequate for their needs. This applies to the village accounts of "Book One" as well as to the different accounts in "Book Two". If compared to other business records of their age, the Vesoul books display solutions which were fully up to date, occasionally even more advanced than other examples.

Single entry bookkeeping has had a bad press since the arrival and dominance of double entry bookkeeping. The latter one established a standard that was much more universally applicable than the single entry systems which always carried the marks of their particular situation of origin. But whatever the advantages of double entry bookkeeping – single entry bookkeeping was perfectly able to guarantee the function that was most important to a medieval merchant: control over a company's business transactions. Raymond de Roover once pointed out the basic idea behind both single and double entry bookkeeping: "Accounting is largely a means of classifying entries into their proper pigeonholes, which are called accounts."[85] The single entry variant provided adequate pigeonholes for many merchants for a considerable length of time.

[82] See *Hauck*, Kaufmannsbuch; *Paul*, Transcription.
[83] *De Roover*, Aux origines 171.
[84] *De Roover*, Development of Accounting 120–123.
[85] *De Roover*, Characteristics 146; also quoted in *Yamey*, Bookkeeping 166.

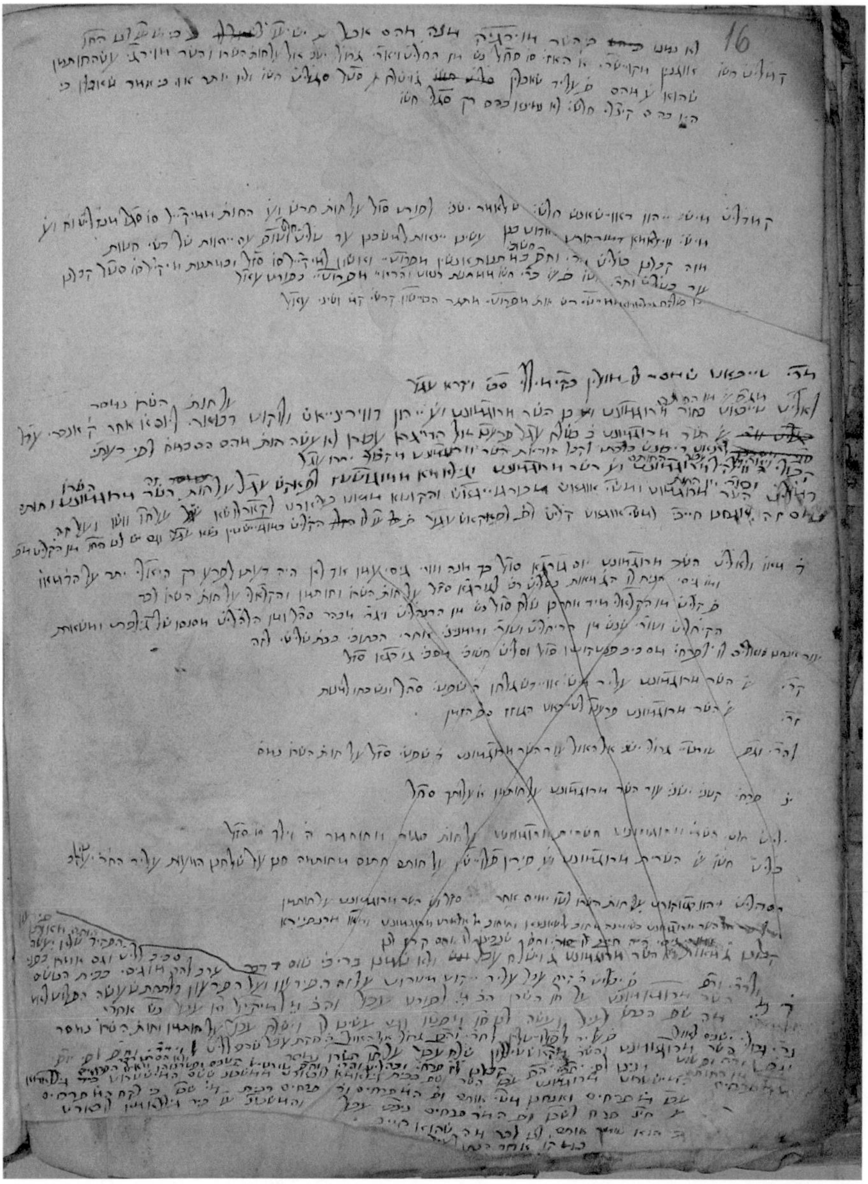

Appendix

The Rougemont-account[1]
The first entry of the transcript corresponds to the third entry of the page shown in the picture (fol. 45v.).

(1)	מ' די'	טייבאט שמסר לו מולין בק'ימיללי סבי' ויקרא עגל'
(2)	לא' ליט'	מג' פ' עו' מן החותם טייבאט בחור מרוג'מונט וע' בן השר מרוג'מונט וע' ייהון דווירצייאש ולוקוט דבוארי ליום א' אחר ק' אנדרי עדל'
(3)	~~כג' ליט'~~	~~וו' די'~~ עו' השר מרוג'מונט ב' בשלח עגל' פרענו אל הדויגרא עבורו לא עשה חות' מהם הם במח' לפי דעתי
(4)	~~פו'\סו' די'~~	~~מסרנו~~ לרנט דיב'ונש? בלכתו לקבל הוראת\הודאת השר מרוג'מונט מקכו' לי' יתרו עגל'
(5)	קכו' לי'	ויא' די' עבור החותם ~~נמסר~~ זה השרו' ב' ווילקיל מרוג'מונט וע' השר מרוג'מונט וגילאמא ממוג'ושטין לפאקש עגל' על חות' השר מרוג'מונט וחותם
(6)	רמ' ליט'	וכא' די' מן החות' השר מרוג'מוט ומשי' אוגאש מבורגויינ'אש והקוטא ממוט בליארט לק'אדלושא עגל' על חו' וושו ועל זה
(7)	נמס' זה	אנחנו חייבי' למשי' אוגאש ק' ליט' ל' פ' לפאקאש עגל' פ' ~~על~~ עו' ~~הקלו~~ הק' ליט' במוג'ויישטין נשא עגל' וגם יש לנו החו' מן הק' ליט' מ' פ'
(8)	ד' מאו' ולא' ליט'	השר מרוג'מונט יום ג'ורג'א סול' כך מנה מורי גיסי עמו אך לא היה דעתו לפרע רק היא' לי' יתר על הד' מאו' ומו' גיסי הניח לו הג' מאות בס' ליט' רבי' לגורג'א סזל' על חות' השרו' וחותמו והקלא' לי' על חות' השרו' לבד פ' ק' ליט' מן הקלא' לי' מיד' אחר כן שלח סול' נש' מן הרנה' ליט' ויג' די' מבהר סהל' ומן הלה' ליט' מסוסו של ג'ילברט ומשארת הקיח' ליט' וטו' די' שנש' מן הריח' ליט' וטו' די' וממנייני' אחרי הכתובי' בכת' שלישי לזה

[1] Archives Départementales de la Côte d'Or, B 10410, fol. 45v.

(9)		עוד אנחנו שואלים לו ל' פרחי' מסביב פנטקוטא סול' וס' ליט' חשובי' מסבי' ג'ורגא סדל'
(10)	ק' די'	עו' השר מרוג'מונט על יד מישי אויידש גלחו ה' שפטי' סהל' ונשכחו למ[illegible]ות
(11)	ז' די'	עו' השר מרוג'מונט פרענו לטייבאט הגוזז ס' פ' \ הפ' הזמן
(12)	לה' די' וג' פ'	טורנויי' גדולי' ישני' אל האול עוד השר מרוג'מונט ד' שפטי' סזל' על חות' השרו' נמס'
(13)	צ' פרחי'	קטני' ישני' עוד השר מרוג'מונט על חותמו א' עלותך סחל'
(14)	י' ליט' חלשי'	השר מרוגמונט השרית מרוג'מונט על סגור מחתמה ה' וילך סו' סזל'
(15)	ב'\כ' ליט' חשו'	עו' השרית מרוג'מונט וע' פירין פ'לוייש'ין על חותם חתום מחותמה חמן על' שלחנו המעות על יד החר יעקב כהן
(16)	רסה' ליט'	ייהון דג'אקורט על חות' השרו' לטו' ימים אחר ____[2] סזל' וע' השר מ־וג'מונט על חותמו
(17)	יט' ליט'	מן השר מרוג'מונט כשמנה\בשמנה? מחוב ליטאנצא וח' חוב של\אל אלארט מרוג'מונט ומאו' מדמפיירא
(18)		ומורי גיסי היה חייב לו סו' די' וח'\יח' פ' שנכינו לו והם קרן לנו קבלנו ג' מאות מן השר מרוג'מונט ג' וישלח עבל' ~~ונש'~~ ולא שמנו בריבי' שום ד דבר

[2] Word scratched out.

פירעון
חותם מאותו
הפקיד שלא יעשה
סביב ל' ליט' וגם אמרו בפני
ערב להם מו' גיסי בבית הנושים
ולד' די' וד' פ'   פ' יב' ליט' ה' קרח עבל' על יד ייקוט מיטרוט על זה הפירעון ועל הפירעון דלתחת שעשה הפרוטלאט

(19) ד' מ' השר מרוג'אמונט על חו' השרו' הב' מ' לפורט עבל' והב' מ' למיק'יל סו' עבל' נש' אחרי
מה שפ' ההכתו' לעיל ועשה לנו חו' ומפטו' וגם עשינו לו וישלח עבל' על חותמו וחות' השרו' נמסר

ישנין לאול   פ' על יד לפלוייטליין לח' די' וה' פ' גדולי' אל האול ה' חקת עבל' שהם ל' ליט'

(20) ב' די' וג' פ' גדולי' השר מרוג'אמנט והשר מק'אשאיללון שלח עבל' על חו' השרו' נמסר

ויד' די' וח' פ' לפי' יו' פ'
ולא הסרנו דבר
מן החות'   מנינו לפי יח' די' הפ'   קבלנו לז' פרחי' וכה' ליט' וה' די' וח' פ' טורנויש קטנים ופטרנוהו מאילו הפרחים

(21) מד' פרחים המישטרוט מרוג'מונט עבו' השר שפ' בבית גילאמא לובארט ממשכונ' ששם המישטרוט ביד גיללאמא
עבו' מ' פרחים ואנחנו מטי' אותם ופ' המ' פרחים וד' פרחים רבית מי' שבו' כי לקח המ' פרחים
ע' חצ' פרח לשבו' ופ' המד' פרחים נצבי' עבל'   והמשכונ' עו' ביד גיללאמא לובארט
כי הוא שומר אותם לנו לבד מה' שהוא חייב
במקו' אחר הכתו' לעיל

Markus J. Wenninger

Juden als Münzmeister, Zollpächter und fürstliche Finanzbeamte im mittelalterlichen Aschkenas

„Da es völlig widersinnig wäre, wenn ein Lästerer Christi über Christen Gewalt ausübt, erneuern wir wegen des Übermuts der Frevler auf diesem Generalkonzil, was darüber das Konzil von Toledo weise verordnet hat, und verbieten, daß Juden an die Spitze von öffentlichen Ämtern gestellt werden, weil sie sich dabei den Christen gegenüber höchst feindselig erweisen. Wer ihnen ein solches Amt anvertraut, soll auf einem Provinzialkonzil ... nach vorangegangener Mahnung gebührend bestraft werden. Ein [jüdischer] Amtsinhaber soll aber so lange von den Christen bei seinen Geschäftsangelegenheiten und sonst boykottiert werden, bis zugunsten armer Christen ... das restituiert wird, was er von den Christen anläßlich seiner Amtsführung erworben hat. Das Amt, das er respektloserweise angenommen hatte, soll er mit Schimpf und Schande wieder hergeben."[1]

So lautete eine jener Bestimmungen, mit welchen im Jahr 1215 das 4. Laterankonzil den Standort und die Bedingungen jüdischen Lebens in der christlichen Welt festsetzen wollte. Auch wenn als Vorlage nur ein Kanon des 3. Konzils von Toledo, das im Jahr 589 zusammengetreten war und dessen Bestimmungen keineswegs für die gesamte katholische Welt, sondern nur für das damalige Westgotenreich galten, genannt wird[2], steht hinter dieser Verordnung doch eine über ein gutes Jahrtausend reichende Tradition der kirchlicherseits behaupteten und geforderten

[1] 4. Laterankonzil, c. 69; Latein. Text bei *Antonio García y García*, Constitutiones Concilii quarti Lateranensis una cum commentariis glossatorum (Roma 1981) 108, c. 69; *Giovanni D. Mansi*, Sacrum conciliorum nova et amplissima collectio, Bd. 22 (Paris 1903, Ndr. 1961) Sp. 1054ff.; *Julius Aronius*, Regesten zur Geschichte der Juden im Fränkischen und Deutschen Reiche bis zum Jahre 1273 (Berlin 1887–1902, Ndr. Hildesheim, New York 1970) Nr. 395, S. 176; Übersetzungen bei *Aronius*, 175f., und *Raymond Foreville*, Lateran I–IV (Mainz 1970) 443f.

[2] Der Text des hier angesprochenen c. 14 des 3. Konzils von Toledo bei *Mansi*, conciliorum collectio, Bd. 9, 996, und *Amnon Linder*, The Jews in the legal sources of the early Middle Ages (Detroit 1997) 484f. Das 3. Konzil von Toledo fällt in die Phase des Übertritts der bisher arianischen Westgoten zum Katholizismus. In Übereinstimmung mit den Intentionen Kg. Reccareds wurde auf ihm das einheitliche katholische Bekenntnis aller Christen des Reichs offiziell festgelegt, und bezeichnenderweise erließ man gleichzeitig erstmals für das gesamte Westgotische Reich Judengesetze, die sich an bisher nur für Katholiken gültigen Bestimmungen sowie spätrömischen Gesetzen und Konzilsbestimmungen orientierten. Dazu *Alexander Pierre Bronisch*, Die Judengesetzgebung im katholischen Westgotenreich von Toledo (Forschungen zur Geschichte der Juden A 17, Hannover 2005) 23ff.

Unterordnung der Juden unter die Christen. Diese beginnt mit theologischen Schriften, in denen seit Tertullian (gest. 222) die Unterordnung der Juden unter die Christen vertreten wurde, und führt über die von diesen Schriften und Ansichten beeinflußte Gesetzgebung des christlich gewordenen spätrömischen Reichs[3] und frühmittelalterliche Konzilsbestimmungen[4] zu den hochmittelalterlichen Laterankonzilien und weiter bis ins ausgehende Mittelalter. Die zahlreichen Wiederholungen dieser Forderung durch kirchliche Personen und Institutionen – wenn auch in unterschiedlichen Formulierungen und unterschiedlicher Schärfe[5]; es ist aber bemerkenswert, daß gerade die Tätigkeit von Juden als Zöllner des öfteren ausdrücklich untersagt wird[6] – zeigen, daß sie über weite Strecken nur unzureichend beachtet, vielleicht sogar völlig negiert wurde. Für das hier behandelte Thema ist dies insofern von Bedeutung, als Juden in jeder der im Titel genannten Funktionen bestimmte Befugnisse über Christen ausüben konnten bzw. auszuüben hatten. Wie in vielen anderen Zusammenhängen zeigt sich auch hier, daß kirchenrechtliche Bestimmungen nur dann allgemein durchgesetzt werden konnten, wenn sie mit den gesellschaftlichen Gegebenheiten der jeweiligen Zeit und des jeweiligen Raumes einigermaßen übereinstimmten und auch die Unterstützung der weltlichen Machthaber fanden.

Genau das war aber im gegebenen Zusammenhang lange Zeit nicht der Fall. In Einzelfällen wurden zwar entsprechende Bestimmungen in weltliche Privilegien aufgenommen, aber das blieben Ausnahmen, deren konkreter Anlaß jeweils zu untersuchen ist. So war es im Deutschen Reich gerade der in anderem Zusammenhang wegen seiner Unvoreingenommenheit und Toleranz gegenüber den Juden bekannte Kaiser Friedrich II., der in einem 1237 für die Stadt Wien ausgestellten

[3] Dazu *Karl Leo Noethlichs*, Das Judentum und der römische Staat. Minderheitenpolitik im antiken Rom (Darmstadt 1996), und *ders.*, Die Juden im christlichen Imperium Romanum (4.–6. Jahrhundert) (Berlin 2001); zu den Vorläuferbestimmungen des Judenartikels von Toledo 589 s. *Bronisch*, (wie vorige Anm.) 25.

[4] Als Beispiele seien hier genannt: 535 verbot das Konzil zu Clermont, Juden zu Richtern über Christen zu setzen (*Aronius*, Nr. 24, S. 10), 581 jenes zu Mâcon, Juden zu Richtern oder Zöllnern zu bestellen, damit nicht die Christen ihnen untergeordnet erscheinen (*Aronius*, Nr. 40, S. 15), und 614 bestimmte das 5. Konzil von Paris, daß kein Jude militärische oder Verwaltungsämter vom König erbitten oder bekleiden solle. Eine Woche darauf verbot König Chlotar II. den Juden, öffentliche Ämter zu bekleiden (*Aronius*, Nr. 57f., S. 20f.); weitere Hinweise bei *J. E. Scherer*, Die Rechtsverhältnisse der Juden in den deutsch-österreichischen Ländern (Leipzig 1901) 33f., 40f. u. 328f., sowie bei *Heinz Schreckenberg*, Die christlichen Adversus-Judaeos-Texte und ihr literarisches und historisches Umfeld, Bd. 3: 13.–20. Jh. (Europ. Hochschulschriften XXIII, 497, Frankfurt 1994) 365, 375f. und 398f.

[5] Vgl. z. B. das Mainzer Provinzialkonzil von 1259 (*Aronius*, Nr. 646, S. 271f.). Auch ein Schreiben Papst Gregors IX. an die hohe deutsche Geistlichkeit von 1233 März 4 wegen diverser Mißstände, die in Deutschland hinsichtlich der Juden bestünden, zeigt, daß die Tätigkeit von Juden als fürstliche Amtleute offenbar weit verbreitet war (*Aronius*, Nr. 460, S. 202).

[6] So z. B. auf den Provinzialkonzilien von Breslau und Wien 1267. Deren Judenartikel bei *Aronius*, Nr. 724f., S. 301–305; zu ihrem zeitgenössischen Hintergrund s. *Klaus Lohrmann*, Judenrecht und Judenpolitik im mittelalterlichen Österreich (Handbuch zur Geschichte der Juden in Österreich B 1, Wien, Köln 1990) 94–102, u. *Markus J. Wenninger*, Grenzen in der Stadt? Zu Lage und Abgrenzung mittelalterlicher deutscher Judenviertel, in: Aschkenas 14 (2004) 9–29, hier 11–15.

Privileg dieser das Ämterverbot für Juden zugestand[7]. Auch König Andreas II. von Ungarn, der in seiner Goldenen Bulle vom Jahr 1222 den Großen seines Reichs ein ähnliches Zugeständnis machte[8], ist sonst keineswegs durch irgendwelche antijüdischen Maßnahmen aufgefallen. Das 1222 ausgesprochene Ämterverbot wurde denn auch in weiterer Folge in Ungarn offenbar kaum oder gar nicht beachtet[9]. Die mittelalterlichen deutschen Rechtsbücher kennen dagegen mit Ausnahme des gerade auch hinsichtlich seiner Judenartikel stark vom Kirchenrecht beeinflußten Schwabenspiegels keine Bestimmungen gegen jüdische Zöllner, Münzer oder sonstige Amtsträger[10].

Bei der Beschäftigung mit Urkunden über einschlägige Geschäfte ist dagegen zu beachten, daß nicht jede Nennung eines Juden im Zusammenhang mit einem der genannten Ämter bedeutet, daß er dieses Amt auch tatsächlich ausgeübt hat, denn in manchen Fällen wurden Juden anscheinend nicht die Ämter selbst mit der dazugehörenden Amtsgewalt übertragen, sondern sie erhielten nur die Nutzung der Einkünfte aus diesen Ämtern. Das scheint z.B. bei der Verpfändung des öster-

[7] Die Stadt Wien hatte sich in seinem Streit mit Herzog Friedrich II. von Österreich auf seine Seite gestellt; das Privileg, das Wien kurzfristig zur Reichsstadt machte, enthielt an prominenter Stelle (dritte Bestimmung von neun) in Anlehnung an die genannten kirchlichen Formulierungen den Ausschluß der Juden von Ämtern. Das gesamte Privileg gedr. bei *Peter Csendes*, Die Rechtsquellen der Stadt Wien (FRA III,9, Wien, Köln, Graz 1986) Nr. 5, S. 39–43 (deutsche Übersetzung der 1. H. 14. Jh. ebd., Nr. 6, S. 43–47). Weitere Drucke und einschlägige Literatur bei *Eveline Brugger, Birgit Wiedl*, Regesten zur Geschichte der Juden in Österreich im Mittelalter, Bd. 1: Von den Anfängen bis 1338 (Innsbruck, Wien, Bozen 2005) Nr. 17, S. 28f. Ein angeblich gleichzeitig für Wiener Neustadt ausgestelltes, weitgehend gleichlautendes Privileg (*Aronius*, Nr. 509f., S. 220f.) ist allerdings eine spätere Fälschung (dazu *Brugger, Wiedl*, Regesten, Nr. 18, S. 29f.), ebenso das etwa gleichzeitig gefälschte, angeblich auf Herzog Leopold VI., den Vater Herzog Friedrichs II., zurückgehende Stadtrecht für Wiener Neustadt, in das diese Bestimmung ebenfalls aufgenommen wurde (*Brugger, Wiedl*, Nr. 9, S. 22f.). Zwei Jahre später erließ Herzog Friedrich II. von Österreich, der die Gewalt über sein Herzogtum inzwischen wieder zurückerlangt hatte, ein Privileg für Wiener Neustadt, in dem er u. a. versprach, künftig den Juden dieser Stadt kein Amt zu geben, mittels dessen sie die Bürger bedrücken könnten (1239 Juni 5, *Aronius*, Nr. 522, S. 224; *Brugger, Wiedl*, Regesten, Nr. 21, S. 32f.).

[8] Die Ämter der *comites camerarii monetarum, salinarii et tributarii* sollten den *nobiles regni* vorbehalten bleiben; *Ismaelite* (Moslems) und Juden sollten diese Funktionen ausdrücklich nicht ausüben können (Monumenta Hungariae Judaica, Bd. 1 [Budapest 1903], S. 4, Nr. 8); s. a. *Nora Berend*, At the Gate of Christendom. Jews, Muslims and 'Pagans' in Medieval Hungary, c. 1000–c. 1300 (Cambridge 2001) 121 und 155.

[9] Schon drei Jahre später (1225 Aug. 23) forderte Papst Honorius III. den zuständigen Erzbischof Ugrinus von Kalocsa und seine Suffragane auf, von König Andreas zu verlangen, daß er künftighin Juden und Heiden bei der Vergabe öffentlicher Ämter nicht mehr bevorzuge: *Shlomo Simonsohn* (ed.), The Apostolic See and the Jews, 1: Documents 492–1404 (Toronto 1988) Nr. 117, S. 120f.; dazu ebd., 7: History (Toronto 1991) 150; zu weiteren Übertretungen s. weiter unten.

[10] S. dazu *Christine Magin*, „Wie es umb der iuden recht stet". Der Status der Juden in spätmittelalterlichen deutschen Rechtsbüchern (Göttingen 1999) (da einschlägige Bestimmungen in keinem der von Magin behandelten Rechtsbücher vorkommen, äußert sie sich nicht zu diesem Problem). Nach dem Schwabenspiegel, den Magin aus bestimmten Gründen nicht in ihre Untersuchung mit einbezogen hat, dürfen Juden dagegen kein Richteramt bekleiden, s. *Heinz Schreckenberg*, Die christlichen Adversus-Judaeos-Texte und ihr literarisches und historisches Umfeld, 3 (13.–20. Jh.) (Europ. Hochschulschriften, R. 23, 497, Frankfurt a. M. 1994) 274–279.

reichischen Kammeramts an den Juden Lebmann von Wien im Jahr 1305 der Fall gewesen zu sein[11].

Auf den ersten Blick scheinen die im Titel genannten Tätigkeiten eines Münzmeisters, eines Zollpächters und eines Finanzbeamten (letztere Bezeichnung meint nicht – wie heute – den Angestellten einer Steuerbehörde, sondern eine Person in leitender Funktion in der fürstlichen Finanzverwaltung!) wenig miteinander zu tun zu haben. Im Mittelalter stellt sich die Situation jedoch grundlegend anders dar. Einerseits war die Verwaltung der Einnahmen nicht von jener der Ausgaben getrennt, so daß jene Personen, die Gelder für einen Fürsten einnahmen, regelmäßig oder über konkrete Anweisung auch viele seiner Ausgaben zu tätigen hatten[12] und nur die Differenz – die auch negativ sein konnte – bar ausgeglichen wurde; andererseits gehörten die aus der Münzproduktion, dem damit verbundenen Geldwechsel und den Zöllen fließenden Abgaben zu den wichtigsten Einnahmen eines Fürsten, so daß die in diesen Bereichen tätigen Personen oft eine wichtige Stellung in der fürstlichen Finanzverwaltung einnahmen. Hinsichtlich der Zölle ist außerdem zu bemerken, daß die Einsetzung eines fürstlichen Bediensteten als angestellter Zöllner und eine detaillierte Abrechnung erst gegen Ende des Mittelalters zur Regel wurde. Noch im 14. Jahrhundert war es dagegen über weite Strecken üblich, daß ein Zoll an eine einzelne Person oder – vor allem bei ertragreichen und daher in der Pacht teuren Zöllen – an ein Konsortium von Geldgebern verpachtet wurde[13]. Der Fürst erhielt dafür jährlich eine vereinbarte Summe im Voraus, die der bzw. die Pächter aus den Erträgen des Zolls mit Gewinn wieder einzubringen suchten. Als Zöllner fungierte in diesem Fall der Pächter selbst oder eine von ihm bestellte Person. In ähnlicher Weise waren Personen, die eine Münzstätte gepachtet hatten, selbst oder über einen von ihnen beauftragten *monetarius* (Münzmeister) für den Betrieb dieser Münzstätte verantwortlich. Für den Fürsten hatte das den Vorteil, mit gesicherten regelmäßigen Einnahmen rechnen zu können, ohne sich um Details kümmern zu müssen, für die es ohnedies noch kein geschultes Personal gab. Wesentliche Voraussetzung, ein solches Amt in der Finanzverwaltung wahrnehmen zu können, war natürlich, über beträchtliches Kapital zu verfügen.

Gut sichtbar werden diese Verhältnisse bei den in den Jahrzehnten um 1300 in den Territorien Graf Meinhards IV. (II.) von Görz-Tirol und seiner Nachfolger, die vom heutigen Tirol über Kärnten und Friaul bis Krain und Istrien reichten, tätigen Juden. Meinhard intensivierte und rationalisierte die Verwaltung seiner Länder wie kaum ein anderer zeitgenössischer Fürst, und zur Durchführung dieser Maßnahmen holte er gezielt Finanzfachleute ins Land: Angehörige italienischer, vor allem

[11] *Brugger*, *Wiedl*, Regesten (wie Anm. 7) Nr. 134, S. 143f., dazu *Eveline Brugger*, Adel und Juden im mittelalterlichen Niederösterreich. Die Beziehungen niederösterreichischer Adelsfamilien zur jüdischen Führungsschicht von den Anfängen bis zur Pulkauer Verfolgung 1338 (Studien und Forschungen aus dem niederösterreichischen Institut für Landeskunde 38, St. Pölten 2004) 78–81.

[12] Vgl. dazu etwa das unten ad Anm. 58f. zu Moses Nürnberger Gesagte.

[13] In der Literatur wie auch in edierten Regesten wird, ausgehend von der Art der betreffenden Urkunden, die in der Art von Pfandurkunden gestaltet sind, im allgemeinen von einer Verpfändung dieser Zölle gesprochen. Der Sache nach handelt es sich jedoch um eine Pacht.

toskanischer Bankhäuser ebenso wie Juden, die nach Ausweis ihrer Namen ebenfalls überwiegend aus dem italienischen Raum gekommen sein dürften, und einzelne Kaufleute aus oberdeutschen Städten. Hier sollen uns jedoch nur die Juden interessieren[14].

Über fast zwei Jahrzehnte sind zu Beginn des 14. Jahrhunderts die Geschäfte Isaks von Lienz, der zu dieser Zeit nicht nur der „Hausbankier" der Grafen von Görz war, sondern auch der bedeutendste jüdische Bankier des Ostalpenraums gewesen zu sein scheint, zu verfolgen. Als Geldleiher, Münz-, Zoll- und Geleitspächter wird er in zahlreichen Urkunden genannt[15]. Seine Geschäftstätigkeit spielte sich dabei zwischen Meran, Innsbruck, Villach, dem görzischen Besitz in Krain und Latisana, dem Hafen der Grafen von Görz oberhalb der Mündung des Tagliamento in die Adria, ab, wo Isak zugleich mit den wichtigsten krainischen Mauten im Juli 1308 die Hafenmaut pachtete[16]. Sie umfaßte damit den gesamten Görzer Besitz mit Ausnahme Istriens. Die Geschäfte selbst sind nicht nur hinsichtlich ihrer räumlichen Ausdehnung und ihrer Größenordnung bemerkenswert, sondern vor allem wegen der Gesellschaften, die für etliche von ihnen gegründet wurden. Denn im Gegensatz zur allgemeinen Annahme, daß die berufsmäßigen jüdischen und christlichen Geldleiher – letztere, die auch in Mitteleuropa überwiegend aus Italien und Südfrankreich stammten, sind aufgrund ihrer Herkunft unter den Bezeichnungen Lombarden und Kawerschen bekannt – in einem scharfen Konkurrenzverhältnis gestanden seien, können wir aus diesen Gesellschaften eine intensive Zusammenarbeit der jüdischen und lombardischen, teilweise auch einheimischen, Finanzfachleute erschließen[17]. Und auch wenn sich die anderen Görzer Juden zur Abwicklung größerer Finanzgeschäfte im allgemeinen untereinander zu Gesellschaften zusammenschlossen, war es doch keineswegs nur Isak, der gemeinsam mit Lombarden Geschäfte tätigte[18].

Denn im ausgehenden 13. und der ersten Hälfte des 14. Jahrhunderts lebten in den Territorien der Grafen von Görz mehrere sehr bedeutende jüdische Familien, die umfangreiche Geldgeschäfte durchführten und eng in die Finanzverwaltung der Grafen eingebunden waren. Die Grafen verpachteten diesen Juden nicht nur

[14] Ausführlich dazu *Markus J. Wenninger*, Juden im Herrschaftsbereich der Grafen von Görz und Görz-Tirol, in: *Franz Nikolasch* (Hrsg.), Symposium zur Geschichte von Millstatt und Kärnten 2000 (Salzburg, Millstatt 2000) 108–133.

[15] *S. Wenninger*, ebd., ad Anm. 57, sowie *Wilhelm Wadl*, Geschichte der Juden in Kärnten im Mittelalter (Das Kärntner Landesarchiv 9, Klagenfurt [2]1992) 229ff., u. *Lohrmann*, Judenrecht (wie Anm. 6) 245. Die Regesten der einschlägigen Urkunden jetzt bei *Brugger*, *Wiedl*, Regesten (wie Anm. 7).

[16] Die Maut *in Portu Latisane*. Dazu und zu den gleichzeitig gepachteten unterkrainischen Mauten an der Hülben und der Rupp (*in Rup et Hulba*) s. *Christoph Haidacher*, Die älteren Tiroler Rechnungsbücher. Analyse und Edition, Bd. 1 (Tiroler Geschichtsquellen 33, Innsbruck 1993) 74, und *Josef Riedmann*, Die Beziehungen der Grafen und Landesfürsten von Tirol zu Italien bis zum Jahre 1335 (SB Wien 307, Wien 1977) 229.

[17] Die Gesellschaftsgeschäfte Isaks sind näher ausgeführt bei *Wenninger*, Görz, ad Anm. 60–69.

[18] Weitere Gesellschaften oder zumindest eine Zusammenarbeit von Juden und Lombarden genannt ebd., ad Anm. 22 u. 112.

viele ihrer Zollstätten, darunter gerade die wichtigsten[19], sondern auch Münzstätten[20] und Geleitsrechte[21] und wickelten bedeutende Geldtransaktionen über sie ab. Es wirft ein bezeichnendes Licht auf die gesellschaftliche Stellung und die Bedeutung dieser Juden, daß Heinrich, Herzog von Kärnten und Graf von Tirol, von einem von ihnen, einem gewissen *Bonaventura*, der in der Generation nach Isak von Lienz der wichtigste Görzer Finanzverwalter gewesen war[22], anläßlich der Erwähnung eines mit ihm früher getätigten großen Geschäfts als „unserem getreuen Juden" (*Judaeo fideli nostro*) sprach[23]. Als „Getreuer" bzw. „fidelis" wurden im allgemeinen nur adelige Gefolgsleute bezeichnet. Von wem in dieser Art gesprochen wurde – mir ist bisher nur ein weiteres Beispiel bekannt[24]; ähnlich zu werten ist aber auch die Bezeichnung als „Herr"[25] –, der gehörte sicherlich nicht nur zur

[19] Abgesehen von den schon erwähnten Verpachtungen s. ebd., ad Anm. 45, 53, 56 u. 97.

[20] Alle inneralpinen Münzstätten der Grafen von Görz (Meran, Lienz, St. Veit, Völkermarkt und Obervellach) waren zeitweise an Juden verpachtet oder es waren jüdische Münzmeister in ihnen tätig, vgl. ebd. ad Anm. 60f., 64, 66, 86f.

[21] Vgl. ebd., ad Anm. 74 u. 101.

[22] Ausführlicher zu ihm ebd., ad Anm. 89–104.

[23] Urkunde ausgestellt am 9. Feb. 1335 auf Schloß Tirol. Regesten in: Monumenta Historica Ducatus Carinthiae, Bd. 9 (Klagenfurt 1965) Nr. 710, S. 215, sowie in Brugger, Wiedl, Regesten (wie Anm. 7) Nr. 387.

[24] 1364 beauftragte Pfalzgraf Ruprecht bis auf Widerruf seinen *getruwen Mose Nurnberger juden ze Heidelberg* mit wesentlichen Aufgaben seiner Finanzverwaltung (s. dazu weiter unten in diesem Aufsatz). Die betr. Urkunde auszugsweise gedr. bei *Franz-Josef Ziwes*, Studien zur Geschichte der Juden im mittleren Rheingebiet während des hohen und späten Mittelalters (Forschungen zur Geschichte der Juden A 1, Hannover 1995) 167, Anm. 334. In eine ähnliche Richtung geht auch jene Urkunde, mit der Kaiser Friedrich I. 1182 den Regensburger Juden ihre Rechte bestätigte. In der Arenga begründete er dies nämlich mit der Pflicht des Kaisers, Recht und Frieden aller *fidelium nostrorum* zu wahren, nicht nur der christlichen, sondern auch jener, die sich von diesem Glauben unterscheiden und nach den Überlieferungen ihrer Väter leben (*verum etiam a fide nostra discolis ritu paternae traditionis suae viventibus*), s. Die Urkunden Friedrichs I. 1181–1190, bearb. v. *Heinrich Appelt* (MGH DD X,4, Hannover 1990) S. 43f., Nr. 833; dazu *Alfred Haverkamp*, Judenvertreibungen in Mittelalter und Frühneuzeit – Erscheinungsformen und Zusammenhänge, Betrachtungsweisen und Erkenntnischancen. Zur Orientierung, in: Judenvertreibungen in Mittelalter und früher Neuzeit, hrsg. v. *Friedhelm Burgard, Alfred Haverkamp, Gerd Mentgen* (Forschungen zur Geschichte der Juden A 9, Hannover 1999) 1–21, hier 7; wenn *Aronius* (Regesten, Nr. 314a) den Begriff *fidelium nostrorum* einfach mit „Untertanen" übersetzt, geht das an seiner tatsächlichen Bedeutung weit vorbei. Allerdings vermied es Barbarossa, die Juden ausdrücklich als *fideles* zu bezeichnen, denn sie wurden zwar in diesen Begriff in umschreibender Form miteinbezogen (vgl. den oben angeführten Textauszug), aber im folgenden ist bei ihrer konkreten Nennung eben trotzdem nur von *Iudaeis nostris* bzw. *Iudeorum in imperio nostro degentium* – ohne entsprechenden Zusatz – die Rede. Insofern gehen die Formulierungen Herzog Heinrichs und Pfalzgraf Ruprechts mit ihrem konkreten Herausgreifen jeweils eines einzelnen „getreuen Juden" über die allgemeine Formulierung des Barbarossa-Privilegs noch deutlich hinaus. Jene des Pfalzgrafen ist dabei noch bemerkenswerter, denn im Gegensatz zu den Görzer Verhältnissen, wo man entsprechend der Herkunft der Mehrzahl der Görzer Juden aus dem oberitalienischen Raum mit dem Einfluß dortiger Gepflogenheiten rechnen muß, wo diese Bezeichnung nicht ungewöhnlich war (vgl. dazu den Beitrag von *Reinhold Mueller* in diesem Band), kommt das für die Pfalz wohl nicht in Frage.

[25] Dazu *Markus J. Wenninger*, Von jüdischen Rittern und anderen waffentragenden Juden im mittelalterlichen Deutschland, in: Aschkenas 13 (2003) 35–82, hier 45f.

jüdischen Oberschicht, sondern der durfte sich auch zur deutschen Hochfinanz seiner Zeit zählen.

Wie wohl kaum eine andere Fürstenfamilie im mittelalterlichen Deutschen Reich haben sich die Grafen von Görz zur Verwaltung ihrer Finanzen der Dienste jüdischer Bankiers bedient. Ähnliche Ämter und Funktionen, wenn auch in geringerem Umfang, hatten Juden aber auch in vielen anderen Territorien inne. In Savoyen z. B., das hinsichtlich Lage – beide Territorien waren den Alpenhauptkamm übergreifende, hinsichtlich ihrer Bevölkerung mehrsprachige „Paßstaaten" –, wirtschaftlichen Gegebenheiten und Territorialentwicklung (inklusive des Aufbaus einer „modernen", von italienischen Verhältnissen beeinflußten und weitgehend schriftlich unterstützten Verwaltung in der zweiten Hälfte des 13. Jahrhunderts, wodurch die Tätigkeit der Juden erst quellenmäßig nachvollziehbar wird![26]) zahlreiche Parallelen zur Grafschaft Görz(-Tirol) aufweist[27], sind Juden ebenfalls ungewöhnlich häufig als Zollpächter nachgewiesen[28], allerdings nicht in anderen Verwaltungsfunktionen. Ein weiterer wesentlicher Unterschied zwischen den beiden Ländern besteht darin, daß im Ostalpenraum Zölle fast ausschließlich im Rahmen hoher Geschäftsabschlüsse an Gesellschaften, an denen die bedeutendsten Financiers des Landes beteiligt waren, verpachtet wurden. Dagegen scheinen die in Savoyen auftretenden Pächter weit überwiegend Einzelpersonen gewesen zu sein[29].

In beiden Ländern übten jedoch Juden die Funktion eines Zollpächters anscheinend wesentlich häufiger aus, als das in anderen Territorien üblich war, in Savoyen – wo der erste jüdische Zollpächter bereits 1274 erwähnt wird[30] – vielleicht noch etwas früher als in Tirol und Görz, doch liegt das eventuell auch nur an den hier schon etwas früher einsetzenden einschlägigen Quellen. Allerdings stellt sich in diesem Zusammenhang grundsätzlich die Frage, ob die im Vergleich zu anderen Territorien in den genannten Alpenländern größere Intensität der Tätigkeit von Juden in der Zoll- und Finanzverwaltung so der Realität entspricht, oder ob uns das nur durch die hier bessere Quellenlage so erscheint. Mit anderen Worten: für viele andere Länder gehen uns wahrscheinlich nur die Quellen ab, die eine ähnlich intensive Tätigkeit von Juden belegen würden.

Denn die Tätigkeit der jüdischen Zollpächter, Münzmeister und Finanzbeauftragten in Savoyen-Piemont und Görz-Tirol ist zwar vergleichsweise gut bezeugt, aber sie waren weder die ersten, noch zu ihrer Zeit die einzigen Juden, die in diesen Sparten tätig waren. Die eingangs erwähnten kirchenrechtlichen Bestimmungen

[26] Zu Savoyen vgl. diesbezüglich *Thomas Bardelle*, Juden in einem Transit- und Brückenland. Studien zur Geschichte der Juden in Savoyen-Piemont bis zum Ende der Herrschaft Amadeus VIII. (Forschungen zur Geschichte der Juden A 5, Hannover 1998) 9f., zu Görz-Tirol *Haidacher*, Rechnungsbücher (wie Anm. 16) 11–17, u. *Josef Riedmann*, Mittelalter, in: *Josef Fontana* u. a., Geschichte des Landes Tirol, Bd. 1 (Bozen, Innsbruck, Wien 1985) 405.

[27] Zur Geschichte der Juden in Savoyen s. insbesondere *Bardelle*, (wie vorige Anm.).

[28] Bei *Bardelle* bes. 197–200.

[29] Jedenfalls gehen aus den von *Bardelle* genannten Angaben nur sehr selten auf Zölle bezogene Gesellschaftsgeschäfte hervor, so z. B. 177.

[30] S. ebd. 197.

zeigen vielmehr, daß sie schon in der Zeit um 1200 und wahrscheinlich noch früher eine nennenswerte Zahl von Vorläufern gehabt haben müssen. So war bezeichnenderweise der erste in Österreich nachgewiesene Jude, ein gewisser Schlom, ein Münzmeister, den Herzog Leopold V. 1194 offenbar zu dem Zweck ins Land holte, daß er die Ausprägung seines Anteils am Lösegeld für den englischen König Richard Löwenherz, einer Summe von vermutlich mehreren zehntausend Mark Silber, in Münzen in der dafür neu gegründeten Münzstätte Wien in die Wege leite[31].

Einige Jahre später (zwischen 1207 und 1223) wird auf einer Münze Bischof Ottos von Würzburg der Jude Jechiel als Münzmeister erwähnt[32]. Wesentlich umfangreicher war die gleichzeitige Tätigkeit jüdischer Münzmeister in Polen, wo aus dem Hochmittelalter zahlreiche Münzen mit hebräischen Inschriften und Münzbildern mit jüdischen Inhalten (Judenhut, am Judenhut kenntlicher Kopf eines Juden – man geht davon aus, daß es sich um ein Porträt des [vermuteten] jüdischen Münzmeisters handelt – usw.) erhalten sind[33]. Offenbar von solchen Vorbildern in der östlichen Nachbarschaft beeinflußt ist eine Münze Herzog Bernhards von Sachsen (1180–1212), die verschiedene eine Umschrift andeutende Zeichen enthält, die teilweise Ähnlichkeit mit hebräischen Buchstaben haben, als solche aber keinen Sinn ergeben. Unklar bleibt, ob diese Münze von einem jüdischen Münzmeister mit mangelhaften Kenntnissen, oder von einem christlichen, der das Bild einer von einem jüdischen Meister angefertigten Münze nachzuahmen versuchte, hergestellt wurde[34].

Daß hebräische Buchstaben auf Münzen zwar auf eine Mitwirkung von Juden an deren Herstellung hindeuten, aber noch nicht eo ipso Belege für einen jüdischen Münzmeister sind, zeigt sich auch an zahlreichen erhaltenen ungarischen Stücken des 13. Jahrhunderts, die sich abgesehen von einzelnen darauf abgebildeten hebräischen Buchstaben nicht von den sonstigen Erzeugnissen der königlich-ungarischen Münzstätten dieser Zeit unterscheiden. Denn diese Buchstaben sind wahrscheinlich nicht als Zeichen eines Münzmeisters (als der für den unmittelbaren Betrieb der Münzstätte und die dortige Münzproduktion verantwortlichen Person; auf die Existenz solcher jüdischer Münzmeister gibt es in Ungarn im 13. Jahrhundert keinen über die Münzen hinausgehenden Hinweis) zu sehen, sondern eher als Zeichen des diesem übergeordneten zuständigen „Kammergrafen“ (*comes camere*)[35]. Allerdings ist die Funktion dieser Kammergrafen im wesentlichen ein ungarisches Spezifikum, das nur gelegentlich auch in benachbarten Ländern übernommen wurde.

In anderen Ländern waren, wie sich das besonders gut an den oben genannten Görzer Beispielen zeigen läßt, die Funktionen der fürstlichen Finanzbeamten und der Münzmeister häufig miteinander verschmolzen. Und neben den eingangs ge-

[31] Zu ihm s. *Lohrmann*, Judenrecht (wie Anm. 6) 47f., dort auch die weiterführende Literatur.

[32] *Aronius*, Nr. 425, S. 188f.

[33] Dazu ausführlich *Marian Gumowski*, Hebräische Münzen im mittelalterlichen Polen (Graz 1975).

[34] Vgl. *Aronius*, Nr. 389, S. 173.

[35] So jedenfalls die Interpretation von *Berend*, At the Gate (wie Anm. 8) 124ff.; zu den Kammergrafen s.o. Anm. 8 und weiter unten.

nannten indirekten Hinweisen aus dem Kirchenrecht gibt es zahlreiche Quellen, welche gerade im Hochmittelalter die Tätigkeit von Juden an bedeutenden Positionen vor allem der Finanzverwaltung, aber teilweise auch in weit darüber hinaus gehenden Funktionen, in einer Reihe von Ländern klar belegen.

Schon für das Jahr 1124 schildert Cosmas von Prag den Fall des Juden Jakob Apella, der bei Herzog Wladislaw I. von Böhmen das Amt eines Vicedominus bekleidete, was – zumindest in den Augen des geistlichen Chronisten – *erat magnum cahos christiano populo*. Cosmas, ein Zeitgenosse der Ereignisse und als Domdechant in Prag gut über sie informiert, berichtet darüber allerdings nur, weil Jakob, den er deshalb auch als „Sohn Satans" bezeichnet, nachdem er getauft worden war[36] wieder vom Christentum abfiel[37]. In vergleichbarer Weise scheint er den einige Generationen älteren Juden Podiva, der um die Mitte des 11. Jahrhunderts gelebt haben dürfte, als Gründer der Burg Podivin in Mähren nur wegen seiner späteren Konversion für der Erwähnung wert befunden zu haben. Da sich in Podivin eine der bedeutendsten Zollstationen Mährens und die wahrscheinlich älteste Münzstätte des Landes befand, liegt die Vermutung nahe, daß Podiva auch Zoll- und Münzpächter gewesen war[38]. Insgesamt müssen wir daher davon ausgehen, daß es in Böhmen und Mähren vom 11. zumindest bis zum 13. Jahrhundert noch eine Reihe weiterer Juden in ähnlicher Stellung gab, die aber – da sie weder durch einen Religionswechsel noch in anderer Weise, jedenfalls nicht durch ihre offenbar keineswegs ungewöhnliche Position oder Tätigkeit, auffielen – den Chronisten nicht als erwähnenswert erschienen.

Urkundliche Nachrichten haben wir jedoch über einige Juden aus dem 13. Jahrhundert, die als sogenannte Kammergrafen, also in hohen Positionen der Finanzverwaltung, teilweise grenzübergreifend im ungarisch-österreichisch-böhmischen Raum tätig waren und in dasselbe Umfeld einzureihen sind[39]. An den eben ge-

[36] Die Darstellung bei *Gottlieb Bondy*, *Franz Dworský* (Hrsg.), Zur Geschichte der Juden in Böhmen, Mähren und Schlesien von 906–1620, Bd. 1: 906–1576; Bd. 2: 1577–1620 und Nachträge (Prag 1906) Bd. 1, Nr. 13, S. 7, daß sich Jakob taufen ließ, um dieses Amt zu erlangen (*Aronius* vermutet S. 102 dasselbe), läßt sich aus der Chronik des Cosmas, die den Zeitpunkt der Taufe völlig offen läßt, nicht herauslesen, und die sonst hier genannten Beispiele zeigen, daß es keineswegs nötig war zu konvertieren, um ein hohes Amt zu erlangen. Die Bemerkung, daß seine Installation als Vicedom „dem christlichen Volk" – realiter wahrscheinlich vor allem einem Teil des Klerus – ein großes Ärgernis war, belegt vielmehr, daß er damals noch Jude war.

[37] *Cosmas von Prag*, Chronica Boemorum III 57, gedr. MGH SS 9, 128f., und MGH SS NS 2, 231f.; *Aronius* Nr. 220, S. 101f., mit Diskussion unterschiedlicher Interpretationen über das Geschehen. Bei *Bondy*, *Dworský* (wie vorige Anm.) vermischen sich Regest und Interpretation. Zu Cosmas von Prag s. LexMA III, Sp. 300f. Zur Funktion des Vizedoms (Vicedominus) – ein meist vor allem mit wirtschaftlichen Angelegenheiten betrauter Vertreter geistlicher oder weltlicher Herren in unterschiedlich hoher Position – s. LexMA VIII, Sp. 1621f.

[38] S. dazu Germania Judaica, Bd. 1 (Tübingen 1964) [weiterhin: GJ I] 147f. (Artikel Kostl).

[39] In Ungarn waren die Kammergrafen für die dem König zustehenden Gebiete des Münzwesens, Salzhandels und Zollwesens zuständig, *Berend*, At the Gate (wie Anm. 8) 121ff., in Österreich wohl in einem allgemeineren Sinn – Details sind nicht faßbar – für verschiedene Bereiche der herzoglichen Finanzverwaltung (dazu vor allem *Lohrmann*, Judenrecht [wie Anm. 6] passim [s. im Register unter Teka, Lublin und Nekelo]; dort auch die weitere Literatur).

nannten Podiva erinnern diese Juden auch insofern, als sie offenbar in jeder Hinsicht ein rittermäßiges Leben führten[40]. Zu diesen Nachrichten paßt gut der Bericht des Bischofs Bruno von Olmütz aus dem Jahr 1273 an Papst Gregor X. über den Zustand der Kirche in Böhmen, Mähren und Österreich unter dem bezeichnenden Titel *Quoniam dies mali sunt*, in dem er unter anderem die mangelnde Einhaltung der Konzilsbestimmungen[41] bezüglich der Juden beklagt: Denn diese hätten christliche Ammen, würden offen Zinsen nehmen und damit die Bedürftigen über das Maß hinaus belasten, indem sie innerhalb eines Jahres daraus die Höhe des entliehenen Kapitals einziehen würden. Sie würden öffentliche Ämter bekleiden und als Zolleinnehmer und Münzmeister eingesetzt werden[42].

Ähnliche Positionen haben Juden noch einige Jahrzehnte später auch in Schlesien eingenommen, wie eine aus unbekanntem Anlaß gestartete Initiative des Bischofs Heinrich von Breslau (1302–1319) zeigt. Dieser bemühte sich um 1315, den Hof- und Küchenmeister Herzog Heinrichs VI., einen Juden namens Salmon, zum Rücktritt von diesen seinen Funktionen zu veranlassen. Tatsächlich gab Salmon zunächst sein Amt auf, kehrte aber nach kurzer Zeit – jedenfalls auf Wunsch des Herzogs – wieder in dessen Dienst zurück, worauf der Bischof unter Androhung der Exkommunikation allen Christen verbot, Salmon gehorsam zu sein. Ob er damit Erfolg hatte, ist unbekannt[43]. Als Hofmeister war Salmon für die Gesamtorganisation der herzoglichen Hofhaltung verantwortlich, und auch die Funktion des Küchenmeisters beschränkte sich keineswegs auf die herzogliche Küche und Tafel, sondern hatte vor allem mit seiner Finanzverwaltung zu tun, so daß sich auch hier wieder das nun schon bekannte Bild zeigt.

Diverse weitere Beispiele aus anderen Regionen des Deutschen Reichs zeigen, daß Juden – auch wenn ihre konkrete Position und ihr Aufgabenbereich häufig nicht eindeutig zu definieren sind; von einem Zusammenhang mit Zöllen, Münzen und/oder Finanzen ist jedoch in jedem Fall auszugehen – im 13. Jahrhundert als fürstliche Amtleute in der Finanz- und Domänenverwaltung weit verbreitet, vielleicht sogar annähernd flächendeckend tätig waren[44]. An dieser Situation änderte

[40] Dazu *Wenninger*, Von jüdischen Rittern (wie Anm. 25) 39ff.

[41] Gemeint ist das Wiener Konzil von 1267 (dazu s.o. Anm. 6).

[42] *Publica exercent officia, telonearii, monetarii fiunt*, gedr. bei *Bondy*, *Dworský*, (wie Anm. 36) 37, Nr. 30; in den Abhandlungen der baier. Akad. d. Wiss., Hist. Kl. (1846) 28; sowie in *Boczek*, Codex diplomaticus Moraviae, Bd. 6, 369. Die beiden letzteren zit. n. *Hermann Baerwald*, Die Beschlüsse des Wiener Conciliums über die Juden aus dem Jahre 1267, in: Jahrbuch für Israeliten 6 (1859/60) 181–208, hier 202f. Weitere Vorwürfe beziehen sich auf den Handel mit gestohlenen Kelchen, Meßgewändern und -büchern.

[43] S. Germania Judaica, Bd. 2: Von 1238 bis zur Mitte des 14. Jahrhunderts, 2 Teile, hrsg. v. *Zvi Avneri* (Tübingen 1968) [weiterhin: GJ II] 129.

[44] 1266 April 14 verlieh Fürst Heinrich von Mecklenburg der Stadt Wismar ein Privileg, das u. a. die Bestimmung enthält, daß, wenn sich fürstliche Amtsträger wie Vögte, Münzmeister, Zöllner, Müller, auch Juden und Hofbeamte, in Ausübung ihrer Ämter etwas zu Schulden kommen lassen, sie nicht von den städtischen Richtern, sondern vom Fürsten bestraft werden sollen (*Aronius*, Nr. 713, S. 296). 1267 Juli 24 verliehen die Grafen Gunzelin und Helmold von Schwerin der Stadt Boitzenburg das lübische Recht mit dem Zusatz, daß sich keiner ihrer Amtleute in der Stadt, er sei Münzer, Zöllner oder Jude, vor dem Richter des lübischen Rechts verantworten solle, sondern nur

sich auch im 14. Jahrhundert vorerst wenig. Höchst bemerkenswert ist z.B. die Rolle, welche bedeutende jüdische Finanzleute, von denen sich einer mehrfach als *receptor et distributor domini mei Treverensis* (also als Einnehmer und Ausgeber [der Gelder] meines Herrn von Trier) bezeichnete, zur Zeit Erzbischof Balduins von Luxemburg (1307–1354) im Erzstift Trier einnahmen, auch wenn die ältere Einschätzung einiger von ihnen als „Finanzminister“ des Erzbischofs nicht haltbar ist[45]. Eher könnte man von einer Vorform des Hofjudentums sprechen, doch letztlich handelt es sich um den üblichen Aufgabenbereich mittelalterlicher fürstlicher Finanzverwalter, wie wir ihn schon bei den Görzer Juden kennengelernt haben: Vorstreckung größerer Summen gegen Verpachtung bzw. Verpfändung von Zöllen – vor allem mehrere der überaus ertragreichen Rhein- und Moselzölle – und anderen herrschaftlichen Einnahmerechten, Abwicklung größerer finanzieller Transaktionen und verschiedentlich Empfang und Ausgabe weiterer Gelder. Für diesen Zweck führten diese Juden ein – nicht erhaltenes – hebräisches Rechnungsbuch, das für die abschließende Entlastung ins Lateinische übertragen wurde[46]. Als Balduin 1328 auch Provisor des Erzstiftes Mainz geworden war (er übte diese Funktion bis 1337 aus), dehnten seine Juden ihre Geschäfte auch auf dieses Gebiet aus, indem sie Balduins Unternehmungen finanzierten und dafür die Mainzer Rheinzölle von Lahnstein und Ehrenfels erhielten[47]. Die herausragende Stellung von Juden in der trierischen Finanzverwaltung endet jedoch mit dem Jahr 1347. Offenbar waren sie nicht in der Lage, den durch die Thronkandidatur seines Großneffen Karl stark gestiegenen Geldbedarf Erzbischof Balduins ausreichend zu befriedigen, zumal dieser gleichzeitig seinen Druck auf die Juden kräftig erhöhte, so daß er von nun an mehr mit christlichen Bankiers, vor allem aus Köln und Metz, zusammenarbeitete[48].

vor den Grafen (*Aronius*, Nr. 729, S. 308). Relativ umfangreich war auch die Tätigkeit von Juden in der Finanzverwaltung der Grafen von Burgund in der zweiten Hälfte des 13. und der ersten des 14. Jahrhunderts, s. *Annegret Holtmann*, Juden in der Grafschaft Burgund im Mittelalter (Forschungen zur Geschichte der Juden A 12, Hannover 2004) 262f. und öfter.

45 Dazu ausführlich *Alfred Haverkamp*, Erzbischof Balduin und die Juden, in: *Franz-Josef Heyen* (Hrsg.), Balduin von Luxemburg. Erzbischof von Trier – Kurfürst des Reiches 1285–1354 (Quellen und Abhandlungen zur mittelrheinischen Kirchengeschichte 53, Mainz 1985) 437–483, hier vor allem 469–475; dort auch die weitere einschlägige Literatur. Vgl. dazu auch die Einschätzung in GJ II, 828. Zu erzstiftisch-trierischen Juden in der Finanzverwaltung s. a. *Friedhelm Burgard*, Die Wittlicher Juden im Mittelalter, in: „Das Wichtigste ist der Mensch“. FS für Klaus Gerteis zum 60. Geburtstag, hrsg. v. *Angela Giebmeyer* u. *Helga Schnabel-Schüle* (Trierer Historische Forschungen 41, Mainz 2000) 309-331, hier 314f.

46 Näheres bei *Karl Lamprecht*, Deutsches Wirtschaftsleben im Mittelalter. Untersuchungen über die Entwicklung der materiellen Kultur des Plattenlandes aufgrund der Quellen zunächst des Mosellandes, Bd. I, 2 (Leipzig 1886; Ndr. Aalen 1969) 1472ff., u. Bd. III, Nr. 291 (Rechnung für die Periode 1. Okt. 1336 bis 1. Okt. 1341) S. 419–435; auf S. 423 Hinweis auf die hebräischen Rechnungsbücher; auf 429 zu *Mussem Iudeus* als Inhaber des Moselzolls zu Koblenz 1339/40; s. a. ebd. Nr. 292, S. 437.

47 *Ziwes*, Studien (wie Anm. 24) 119ff.; *Haverkamp*, Balduin (wie Anm. 45) 473.

48 *Haverkamp,* ebd., 467ff.; s. a. *ders.*, Die Juden im Erzstift Trier während des Mittelalters, in: Die Juden in ihrer mittelalterlichen Umwelt, hrsg. v. *Alfred Ebenbauer* u. *Klaus Zatloukal* (Wien, Köln, Weimar 1991) 67–89, hier 75f.

Im Erzstift Mainz hatten jedoch auch schon vor Balduins Einflußnahme einige Juden wichtige Positionen in der erzbischöflichen Finanzverwaltung eingenommen, und auch unter Erzbischof Heinrich III. von Virneburg (1328/37-1346/53)[49] war dies der Fall. Insbesondere in den vierziger Jahren des 14. Jahrhunderts erlangten einige dieser Juden eine ähnliche Stellung wie wir sie eben von jenen im Erzstift Trier kennengelernt haben. Heinrich verpachtete ihnen nicht nur mehrere wichtige Rheinzölle, sondern 1343 wurden Abraham von Kreuznach, der zu dieser Zeit auch bedeutende Zölle innehatte, nachdem ihm der Erzbischof bei einer Abrechnung 458 Pfund Heller schuldig geblieben war, sogar die erzbischöflichen Einnahmen von den Juden zu Bingen und an anderen Orten in Art einer Pacht oder Verpfändung übertragen[50].

Aber auch in der Finanzverwaltung der anderen deutschen Erzbistümer (mit Ausnahme Hamburg-Bremens) und auch einiger Bistümer spielten Juden zumindest zeitweise wichtige Rollen. So geht aus Notizen, welche vom päpstlichen Kollektor 1283 anläßlich einer Revision des neun Jahre zuvor vom Zweiten Konzil von Lyon beschlossenen Kreuzzugszehents in Salzburg angefertigt wurden, hervor, daß bei der Aufbringung dieses Geldes und wohl auch bei seiner Transferierung aus entfernteren Teilen des Erzstifts in die Stadt Salzburg wie bei der erzbischöflichen Finanzverwaltung in Kärnten der Friesacher Jude Isak eine wesentliche Rolle spielte[51]. Einige Jahre früher hatte der Villacher Jude Troyanus zusammen mit mehreren Dienstleuten des Bischofs Berthold von Bamberg die Bürgschaft für die Bezahlung einer anläßlich der Beilegung einer Fehde vereinbarten Entschädigungssumme übernommen[52]; Voraussetzung dafür war wohl, daß er in die Finanzverwaltung der bambergischen Gebiete in Kärnten, zu denen Villach gehörte, eingebunden war. Daß solche Tätigkeiten von Juden in den bambergisch-Kärntner Gebieten üblich waren, zeigt sich trotz der hier spärlichen Quellenlage daran, daß in Villach noch 1363 ein Jude namens Friedel als *mauter* genannt wird[53].

Ein früher Hofjude – der aber offensichtlich nicht nur an die Person eines einzelnen Fürsten gebunden, sondern in breiteren Kreisen anerkannt war – war Samuel (laut dem folgend erwähnten Schreiben des Papstes genannt *Smol*) von Derenburg, der von 1347 bis zu seinem Tod kurz vor 1383 mehreren Magdeburger

[49] Aufgrund seiner Parteinahmen im Streit Kaiser Ludwigs des Bayern mit den Päpsten konnte er die Herrschaft im Erzstift nur in den Jahren 1337–1346 ohne Gegenkandidaten ausüben (s. LexMA, Bd. 3, Sp. 2084).

[50] S. GJ II, 82f. (Art. Bingen), u. *Hermann Kellenbenz*, Die Juden in der Wirtschaftsgeschichte des rheinischen Raumes. Von der Spätantike bis zum Jahre 1648, in: Monumenta Judaica. 2000 Jahre Geschichte und Kultur der Juden am Rhein. Handbuch, hrsg. v. *Konrad Schilling* (Köln 1963) 199–241, hier 215, sowie *Ziwes*, Studien (wie Anm. 24) 120ff.

[51] Vgl. die Belege bei *Wadl*, Kärnten (wie Anm. 15) 182f.

[52] S. ebd., 164f.

[53] Zu ihm und anderen Juden an der Villacher Maut s. ebd. 45f., 110, 215 u. 222, sowie Germania Judaica, Bd. 3: 1350–1519, hrsg. v. *Arye Maimon, Mordechai Breuer* u. *Yacov Guggenheim*, T. 1-3 (Tübingen 1987–2003) [weiterhin: GJ III] 1534. Im Sinn des oben in Anm. 13 Gesagten wird man auch in diesem Fall nicht von einer Verpfändung (so an den genannten Stellen), sondern von einer Verpachtung der Maut ausgehen müssen.

Erzbischöfen in führender Stellung diente, und das nicht nur in der Finanzverwaltung, sondern auch als Ratgeber und Diplomat. Zusammen mit anderen Juden pachtete er verschiedene Zölle und Geleitsrechte. Schon von Erzbischof Dietrich v. Portitz (1361–67) hatte er Einkünfte in Groß-Salze erworben, wo er auch mit nicht näher genannten Verwaltungsaufgaben betraut wurde und anscheinend auch seinen Hauptwohnsitz hatte oder in der Folge hinverlegte. Denn Erzbischof Peter (1371–81) erlaubte ihm in einer dort gelegenen, vermutlich nicht mehr in Gebrauch stehenden Kapelle die Einrichtung einer Synagoge, womit er sich den Tadel des Papstes zuzog[54]. Auch der folgende Erzbischof Albrecht IV. von Querfurt verpfändete (wohl besser: verpachtete) 1388 Geleit und Zoll in Groß-Salze an einen Magdeburger Juden, um an Bargeld zu kommen, das er u. a. für die Bezahlung von Schulden bei verschiedenen christlichen Gläubigern benötigte[55].

Etwa gleichzeitig hatte ein Jude namens Marquard, vielleicht ein Bruder des genannten Samuel/Smol, eine bedeutende Stellung am Hof des Naumburger Bischofs Gerhard von Schwarzburg (1359–72) inne. Nach einem Schreiben Papst Gregors XI. vom selben Tag wie das eben genannte hätte Gerhard diesen Marquard in sein Hofgesinde aufgenommen (*in tuum familiarem teneas*); dieser würde oft christlichen Gerichten vorstehen und für den Bischof von Christen Gelder einziehen (*qui sepius Christianorum preest iudiciis, et pecunias nomine tuo immaniter extorquet ab eis*). Der Bischof möge, falls dies wahr sei, diesen Zustand schleunigst korrigieren[56]. Und in derselben Zeit (1375/76) engagierte mit Friedrich III. v. Saarwerden auch ein Kölner Erzbischof einen jüdischen *scheffener* (Finanzmanager), zu dem er auch vorher schon intensive Beziehungen gehabt haben dürfte. Noch im Jahr vorher ist dieser, Isaak von Monschau, als Kölner „Judenbischof" (Gemeindevorsteher) bezeugt, war also einer der bedeutendsten Juden der Stadt Köln, die er aber gerade in einer kritischen Situation (während des zwischen der Stadt und dem Erzbischof ausgebrochenen „Schöffenkrieges") verließ, worauf die Stadt ein ihr früher von Isaak gewährtes Darlehen nun als „Feindesgut" einbehielt[57].

In weltlichen Territorien sind Juden in der Finanzverwaltung in der zweiten Hälfte des 14. Jahrhunderts zwar seltener nachgewiesen, kommen aber auch noch vor. Eine bedeutende Position nahm hier vor allem Moses Nürnberger in Heidel-

[54] S. GJ III/2, 777, mit den dortigen Literaturangaben. Die Verwaltungsaufgaben (*regimen*) und die Errichtung der Synagoge gehen aus einem Schreiben Papst Gregors XI. vom 15. Juni 1372 (*Simonsohn*, Documents, wie Anm. 9, Nr. 425, S. 451) hervor, mit welchem er den Erzbischof deshalb tadelte und, falls die Sache wahr sei, rascheste Änderung befahl. Dafür, daß die Kapelle als solche nicht mehr in Gebrauch war, spricht die Aussage des Papstes, daß der Jude die Synagoge in einer Kapelle errichtet hätte, *ubi erat altare consecratum*. Der Altar scheint also zum Zeitpunkt der Errichtung der Synagoge nicht mehr bestanden zu haben; trotzdem sah der Papst diesen Tatbestand als ein *fidelium scandalum et Catholice fidei detrimentum*.

[55] GJ III/3, 1953f.

[56] *Simonsohn*, Documents (wie Anm. 9), Nr. 426, S. 451f. Offensichtlich hatte damals jemand aus der Umgebung der sächsischen Bischöfe beim Papst wegen der Juden interveniert. Zu Marquard s. a. GJ III, 931f., 1964, mit der dort angegebenen Literatur.

[57] GJ III, 1903, und *Matthias Schmandt*, *Judei, cives et incole*. Studien zur jüdischen Geschichte Kölns im Mittelalter (Forschungen zur Geschichte der Juden A 11, Hannover 2002) bes. 118f.

berg ein[58], der 1364 von Pfalzgraf Ruprecht I. bis auf Widerruf beauftragt wurde, das Ungeld in der Stadt Heidelberg, die zu Martini (11. Nov.) fällige Judensteuer (*juden bede*), alle zu diesem Termin zu Heidelberg *und in der marke daselbist* fälligen Zinse sowie die Jahreszinse von den Krambuden zu Heidelberg einzunehmen[59]. Von diesen Einnahmen sollte er die Weingärten des Pfalzgrafen zu Heidelberg *buwen* (also für ihre Instandhaltung und Pflege sorgen) und die Wächter auf den beiden Burgen und in der Stadt zu Heidelberg bezahlen. Mit dem dann jährlich noch übrigen Betrag sollte Moses die jeweiligen Baumaßnahmen des Pfalzgrafen in Heidelberg – zu denken ist wohl vor allem an den Ausbau des Schlosses – unterstützen (*an unsern buwe zu Heidelberg ... legin, wa wir buwen*). Moses hatte damit über wesentliche Teile des pfalzgräflichen Einkommens zu verfügen. Die damit verbundene Vertrauensstellung drückt sich auch in seiner Verantwortung für die Entlohnung der Wächter gerade in der Residenz des Pfalzgrafen aus.

Als letztes Beispiel – sowohl in der Auflistung hier wie auch vom Zeitpunkt seiner Erwähnung her – sei Joselin von Mühlhausen genannt, der 1398 von Markgraf Balthasar von Meißen, Landgraf v. Thüringen, mit der Abwicklung des Wechsels in seiner Münzstätte zu Sangerhausen beauftragt wurde[60]. Dieser Wechsel erfolgte zu Zwangskursen und kam einer Art Kapitalbesteuerung gleich; damit verbundene Aufgaben berührten also ebenfalls die hoheitliche Finanzverwaltung.

Wenn ich nichts übersehen habe, habe ich damit alle im dritten Band der „Germania Judaica", der die Zeit des ausgehenden Mittelalters ab der Mitte des 14. Jahrhunderts behandelt, enthaltenen einschlägig tätigen Juden erfaßt, denn mit dem Ende des 14. Jahrhunderts reißen entsprechende Nachrichten völlig ab[61].

[58] Zu ihm s. a. oben Anm. 24.

[59] S. GJ III, 523f., und vor allem *Ziwes*, Studien (wie Anm. 24) 167; formal wurde Moses nicht einfach mit der Einhebung dieser Gelder beauftragt, sondern es wurden ihm die betreffenden Steuern und Abgaben *verschaft*. Darin drückt sich noch das alte System der Pacht dieser oder anderer Einnahmerechte (Münze, Zölle) aus, was aber bei Moses offenbar nicht mehr so der Fall war, da er ja Gelder, die nicht anderweitig verbraucht wurden, in die Bauten des Pfalzgrafen investieren sollte. Es versteht sich aber von selbst, daß Moses – auch wenn das in der Urkunde nicht gesagt wird – mit den Einnahmen auch seine Unkosten decken und auf irgend einem Weg Gewinn machen konnte.

[60] Er hatte *dem wechsil vorczustende an silber, groschin und an andere were* (GJ III, 458). Daß Joselin den Wechsel (also den Tausch von ungemünztem Silber und fremder Währung in Sangerhausener Münze) organisieren sollte, bedeutet nicht, daß er der Münze des Landgrafen vorstehen sollte (so *Michael Toch*, Die wirtschaftliche Tätigkeit, in: GJ III, 2146), also Münzmeister gewesen wäre.

[61] Nicht berücksichtigt habe ich hier aus mehreren Gründen die in GJ III, 1119 mit Anm. 120, und dem folgend in GJ III, 2146 in denselben Zusammenhang gestellten, für das frühe 16. Jh. in Prag angeblich noch belegten jüdischen „Münzarbeiter": 1. bezieht sich die in der angegebenen Literatur als Beleg angeführte Quelle („Ramschacksche Chronik") tatsächlich auf das frühe 15. Jh.; 2. scheint diese Quelle – die mir im Original nicht zugänglich war – insgesamt fragwürdig zu sein. Nach dem nur inhaltlich wiedergegebenen Text bei *Bondy, Dworský*, wie Anm. 36, Bd. 2, Nr. 1147, S. 911, wurden in der königlichen Münze zu Prag „die jüdischen Arbeiter erst aus Anlass des allgemeinen Judenausweisungs-Ediktes entlassen (zwischen 1419–1430)"; ein solches Edikt ist aber sonst nicht bekannt und es gibt auch durch keine anderen Hinweise darauf (vgl. GJ III, 1134f.); 3. ist hier ausdrücklich von Münzarbeitern die Rede, also von untergeordnetem Personal, nicht von Münzmeistern (die allein für die vorliegende Untersuchung von Bedeutung wären). Die Quellenstelle wird deshalb auch von *Bondy, Dworský* zusammen mit anderen als Argument „gegen den Vorwurf der Arbeitsscheu der Juden" angeführt.

Versuchen wir damit zu einer Gesamteinschätzung der Entwicklung zu kommen. Auch wenn die Beraubungen und Plünderungen während der Pestpogrome einen beträchtlichen Aderlaß für das jüdische Kapital bedeutet hatten, der in Einzelfällen auch zum Ausscheiden von Juden aus der fürstlichen Finanzverwaltung geführt haben mag, so wurden doch auch nach der Mitte des 14. Jahrhunderts noch Juden in vielen über das ganze Reich verstreuten Territorien mit bedeutenden einschlägigen Aufgaben betraut[62]. Voraussetzung dafür war, daß sie auch zu dieser Zeit noch im Besitz von Kapitalien waren, die ihnen die Wahrnehmung solcher Funktionen ermöglichten[63].

Mit dem Ende des 14. Jahrhunderts war jedoch auch das Ende von in der fürstlichen Finanzverwaltung tätigen Juden gekommen. Diese Entwicklung, die trotz der nur vereinzelten Beispiele im gesamten Reich klar gegeben ist, läßt sich durch die dichtere Quellenlage in den Görzer Ländern sowie in Savoyen und in der Dauphiné detaillierter nachvollziehen. Nach Ausweis der Quellen war hier das Engagement von Juden in Zollpachten in den Jahrzehnten um 1300 am stärksten und nahm während des 14. Jahrhunderts, in dessen zweiter Hälfte hier wie dort nur mehr wenige Zollverpachtungen an Juden erwähnt werden (zumindest in Tirol allerdings bei schlechter werdender Quellenlage), mehr oder weniger kontinuierlich ab, d.h. die Entwicklung in den beiden Ländern zeigt deutliche Parallelen sowohl untereinander wie auch zur allgemeinen Entwicklung. Auf eine dieser Regionen allein bezogene Erklärungsversuche, die hinter der geschilderten Entwicklung „eine bestimmte Absicht" einzelner Fürsten oder ein geschwundenes Interesse der Juden, für die die Pacht nicht mehr lukrativ gewesen sei, da die Verlagerung von Handelswegen die Einnahmen habe zurückgehen lassen, vermuten[64], greifen daher nicht. Auch eventuelle Langzeitwirkungen der Pestpogrome sind als Ursache auszuschließen, weil es solche Pogrome in den görzischen Ländern, aber auch in Böhmen und anderswo, nicht gab, und weil außerdem die genannte Entwicklung schon vor der Pest einsetzt[65]. Allenfalls mögen sie an einzelnen Orten den Anlaß gegeben haben, eine schon vorher begonnene Entwicklung zu beschleunigen.

Vielmehr müssen zwei andere Ursachen ausschlaggebend gewesen sein, die sich wahrscheinlich ergänzt haben, von denen aber auch jede für sich genommen genügend Potential gehabt haben dürfte, die Juden aus der fürstlichen Finanzverwaltung zu drängen. Zum einen ist dies die zunehmende Erschöpfung der jüdischen

[62] Die von *Georg Caro*, Sozial- und Wirtschaftsgeschichte der Juden im Mittelalter und der Neuzeit, Bd. 1: Das frühere und hohe Mittelalter (Leipzig 1908) 443, nicht nur für diese Spätzeit, sondern auch für die vorangegangenen Jahrhunderte getroffene Feststellung, daß sich im Deutschen Reich außer in Österreich nirgends eine unmittelbare Beteiligung von Juden an der fürstlichen Finanzverwaltung nachweisen lasse, ist daher heute nicht mehr haltbar.

[63] Vgl. dazu oben ad Anm. 12f.

[64] So die Erklärungsansätze von *Bardelle*, Juden (wie Anm. 26) 200.

[65] Zumindest im rheinischen Raum machen sich erste Kapitaleinbußen bei den Juden schon vor 1350 bemerkbar, vgl. *Alfred Haverkamp*, Die Juden im mittelalterlichen Trier, in: Kurtrierisches Jahrbuch 19 (1979) 5–57, hier 26f.; vgl. a. oben zu Trier.

Kapitalien durch weitgreifende Schuldentilgungen, die in den habsburgischen Ländern bereits 1370, im Reich 1385 einsetzten und in mehreren Wellen den Großteil der deutschen Juden betrafen, von denen daraufhin viele abwanderten, vor allem nach Italien. Daß den jüdischen Bankiers seit dieser Zeit wesentlich weniger Kapital zur Verfügung stand, zeigt sich auch am Wandel der Schuldnerkreise und der sinkenden Durchschnittshöhe der entliehenen Kapitalien[66]. Überhöhte Steuerforderungen – Stichwort: Dritter Pfennig – verhinderten in der Folge nicht nur eine sonst eventuell mögliche Erholung des jüdischen Kapitals, sondern trugen im Gegenteil zu seinem weiteren Niedergang bei[67].

Von mindestens eben so großer Bedeutung scheint aber ein anderer Umstand gewesen zu sein: Offenbar wurden seit der Mitte des 14. Jahrhunderts die am Beginn dieses Aufsatzes besprochenen kirchlichen Forderungen nach Ausschluß der Juden von allen Ämtern, in denen sie Gewalt über Christen ausüben konnten, allmählich stärker beachtet. Jedenfalls fällt auf, daß dieses Problem in den kirchenrechtlichen Bestimmungen und Konzilsbeschlüssen des 15. Jahrhunderts kaum mehr thematisiert wurde. Das Konzil von Basel etwa gab 1434 die meisten auf die Juden bezogenen älteren Konzilsbestimmungen, so auch das Ämterverbot, nur ganz kurz wieder, während es sich den zu seiner Zeit noch nicht allgemein durchgesetzten Fragen der Kennzeichnung und der Einrichtung gesonderter Wohnbezirke für Juden erheblich ausführlicher widmete[68], so daß man davon ausgehen kann, daß die Besetzung von Ämtern mit Juden in dieser Zeit keine Frage von Bedeutung mehr war. In jenem Judendekret, mit welchem Kardinal Nikolaus von Kues auf seiner Legationsreise im gesamten Reich 1450/51 den kirchlichen Judenbestimmungen Geltung verschaffen wollte, wurde die Ämterfrage nicht einmal mehr erwähnt, und auch vom bekannt judenfeindlichen Johannes von Capestrano, der 1453 predigend durch Deutschland zog, ist keine Äußerung in dieser Richtung überliefert[69].

Daneben könnten auch noch einige andere Aspekte eine gewisse Rolle gespielt haben, wenn auch keine entscheidende. So wurde gegen Ende des Mittelalters eine zunehmende Zahl von Mauten und Münzstätten überhaupt nicht mehr verpachtet, sondern von Beauftragten des betreffenden Fürsten unmittelbar verwaltet; diese Frage ist aber meines Wissens noch nicht näher untersucht[70]. Nicht zu vernachläs-

[66] Dazu ausführlich *Michael Toch*, Die wirtschaftliche Tätigkeit, in: GJ III, 2139–2164, hier 2150–2163.

[67] Vgl. *Markus J. Wenninger*, Man bedarf keiner Juden mehr. Ursachen und Hintergründe ihrer Vertreibung aus den deutschen Reichsstädten im 15. Jahrhundert (Beih. zum Archiv für Kulturgeschichte 14, Wien, Köln, Graz 1981) 240ff.

[68] Lat. Text und dt. Übersetzung bei *Josef Wohlmuth* (Hrsg.), Dekrete der ökumenischen Konzilien, Bd. 2: Konzilien des Mittelalters vom ersten Laterankonzil (1123) bis zum fünften Laterankonzil (1512–1517) (Paderborn u. a. 2000) 483f.; s. a. Kirche und Synagoge, Handbuch zur Geschichte von Christen und Juden. Darstellung mit Quellen, hrsg. v. *Karl Heinrich Rengstorf* u. *Siegfried von Kortzfleisch*, Bd. 1 (Stuttgart 1968; München ²1988) 248f.

[69] Vgl. Kirche und Synagoge (wie vorige Anm.) 224f.

[70] Für dieses Argument spricht möglicherweise auch, daß etwa gleichzeitig mit dem Ausscheiden der Juden aus den Münzstätten Deutschlands auch die lombardischen Münzmeister aus diesen verschwanden (Hinweis von Reinhold Mueller in der Diskussion).

sigen war vielleicht auch der allmählich sinkende soziale Status der Juden, der es möglicherweise weniger als früher geraten sein ließ, sie mit solchen Ämtern zu betrauen. Denn gerade im Zusammenhang mit Zöllen und Mauten fällt dieser Statuswandel insofern besonders ins Auge, als die Juden, die in der ersten Hälfte des 14. Jahrhunderts noch einen erheblichen Teil der Zolleinnehmer gestellt hatten, im 15. Jahrhundert an einer zunehmenden Zahl von Mautstellen Leibzoll entrichten mußten und damit vom Subjekt zum Objekt der Mauteinhebung geworden waren[71]. Es ist nur naheliegend, daß an einer Mautstelle, an der von Juden Leibzoll verlangt wurde, nicht gleichzeitig ein Jude als Zöllner agieren konnte.

Für einen Zusammenhang der jüdischen Zöllner und Münzmeister des Mittelalters zu jenen jüdischen Zoll- und Münzpächtern, die in Litauen seit dem späteren 15. Jahrhundert[72], in Polen, den habsburgischen und anderen Ländern im 16. und 17. Jahrhundert wieder verstärkt auftreten, gibt es keinerlei Hinweis[73], weshalb ich an dieser Stelle auch nicht näher auf sie eingehe. Vielmehr sind diese neuen jüdi-

[71] Erste konkrete Belege für im Rahmen des Transports jüdischer Leichen eingehobene Zölle stammen aus dem 14. Jahrhundert: 1332 in Prag (*Bondy, Dworský*, wie Anm. 36, 48f., Nr. 67), 1366 in Rosheim im Elsaß (GJ III, 1249). Doch zeigt die im berühmten Privileg Herzog Friedrichs II. von Österreich von 1244 für Leichname garantierte Zollfreiheit (*Brugger, Wiedl*, Regesten, wie Anm. 7, Nr. 25, S. 34f., § 13), daß schon in der ersten Hälfte des 13. Jahrhunderts für Leichen von Juden verschiedentlich Zoll verlangt wurde. Die ältesten konkreten Belege für von lebenden Juden eingehobenen Leibzoll stammen aus dem beginnenden 15. Jahrhundert, decken in dieser Zeit aber schon den gesamten süddeutschen Raum ab: 1400 in Kaisten (einer Vorstadt von Rheinfelden in der Schweiz, s. GJ III, 1241), 1406 in Erlangen (GJ III, 343f. [Art. Forchheim, Anm. 38]), 1416 in Weiden in der Oberpfalz (GJ III, 1559), 1417 in Fribourg (Freiburg im Üechtland, GJ III, 400), vor 1425 an der Mautstelle von Werfen südlich von Salzburg, und um die Mitte des 15. Jahrhunderts (vor 1453) an jener von Arnoldstein am Weg von Villach nach Italien , s. *Herbert Hassinger*, Geschichte des Zollwesens, Handels und Verkehrs in den östlichen Alpenländern vom Spätmittelalter bis in die zweite Hälfte des 18. Jahrhunderts. Bd. 1: Westkärnten – Salzburg (Stuttgart 1987) 509ff. bzw. 254f. Ältere Befreiungen vom Leibzoll, teilweise gegen Entrichtung einer Pauschalsumme (Thüringen 1368, Bayern 1380, Bistum Würzburg 1403, s. GJ III, 2266), zeigen jedoch, daß er auch im 14. Jahrhundert schon eingehoben wurde. Kurz nach der Mitte des 15. Jahrhunderts werden die Belege wesentlich zahlreicher und erstrecken sich nun auch über norddeutsche Gebiete; aufgelistet bei *Peter Rauscher*, Den Christen gleich sein. Diskriminierung und Verdienstmöglichkeiten von Juden an österreichischen Mautstellen in der Frühen Neuzeit (16./17. Jahrhundert), in: *Sabine Hödl, Peter Rauscher, Barbara Staudinger* (Hrsg.), Hofjuden und Landjuden. Jüdisches Leben in der Frühen Neuzeit (Berlin, Wien 2004) 283–332, hier 289ff. u. Anm. 33ff. (S. 315f.); dort auch weiterführende Literatur.

[72] *Jacek Wijaczka*, Die Einwanderung der Juden und antijüdische Exzesse in Polen im späten Mittelalter, in: Judenvertreibungen in Mittelalter und früher Neuzeit, hrsg. von *Friedhelm Burgard, Alfred Haverkamp* u. *Gerd Mentgen*, 214–256, hier 245f.

[73] Für den österreichischen Raum s. insbesondere *Rauscher*, Den Christen gleich sein (wie Anm. 71), für Polen-Litauen *Jürgen Heyde*, Jüdische Eliten in Polen und Litauen zu Beginn der Frühen Neuzeit, in: Aschkenas 13 (2003) 117–165, nach dem dort erst unter König Alexander (1501–1506) „die jüdischen Wirtschaftseliten erstmals auch in den westlichen Landesteilen verstärkt Zugang zur Pacht königlicher Einkünfte" erhielten (ebd., 118). Für Niedersachsen vermerkt *Rotraud Ries* in ihrer umfangreichen Untersuchung Jüdisches Leben in Niedersachsen im 15. und 16. Jahrhundert (Veröff. d. Hist. Komm. f. Niedersachsen u. Bremen XXXV, 13, Hannover 1994) 382f. gerade einmal einen einzigen jüdischen Münzpächter, der 1565 die Münze von Wunstorf pachtete, damit aber schon nach wenigen Jahren Schiffbruch erlitt.

schen Zollpächter im Zusammenhang mit dem neuen Element des Hofjudentums zu sehen, in dem Juden ja auch in der Finanzverwaltung mancher Fürsten wieder eine große Rolle spielten – wobei es aber ebenfalls keinerlei direkte Traditionslinie zu während des Mittelalters in der fürstlichen Finanzverwaltung tätigen Juden zu geben scheint. Das reichsrechtliche Schriftgut, das sich aufgrund dieser neuerlichen Aktualität seit dem 17. Jahrhundert gelegentlich der Funktion von Juden als Zöllnern widmete[74], blieb inhaltlich den einschlägigen kirchenrechtlichen Bestimmungen des Mittelalters verhaftet, hatte damit aber genau so wenig Erfolg wie diese im Hochmittelalter.

[74] Dazu *Rauscher*, ebd. 301.

Rainer Barzen

„Was der Arme benötigt, bist Du verpflichtet zu geben"[1].

Forschungsansätze zur Armenfürsorge in Aschkenas im hohen und späten Mittelalter

Die „Zedaka" als jüdische Form der „Caritas" gehört seit der Antike zu den wichtigsten Säulen des jüdischen Gemeindelebens. Dennoch ist die Geschichte der jüdischen Armenfürsorge nach wie vor schlecht erforscht. Dies gilt insbesondere für das Judentum in Aschkenas während des hohen und späten Mittelalters. Keine monographische oder ähnlich umfangreiche Studie ist bisher zur jüdischen Armenfürsorge in Aschkenas im Mittelalter verfaßt worden. Die wenigen vorhandenen Untersuchungen waren in der Vergangenheit zunächst Teil von Gesamtdarstellungen, die die jüdische Armenfürsorge durch die Jahrhunderte behandelten[2]. Das Hauptaugenmerk war dabei mehrheitlich auf die Entwicklungen der Neuzeit gerichtet, so daß Armenfürsorge der Juden während des Mittelalters nur in verkürzter Form ihre Darstellung fand. Symptomatisch hierfür ist ein Satz von Rudolf Glanz in seinem in den dreißiger Jahren begonnenen, aber erst 1968 erschienenen Werk „Geschichte des niederen jüdischen Volkes in Deutschland"[3]. Dort heißt es nach allgemeinen Bemerkungen zur Armenkasse: „Im Rahmen dieser Arbeit über das jüdische Bettlertum muß leider auf umfassende Behandlung der jüdischen Armenordnungen, wie sie sich von 1200–1500 herauskristallisiert haben, verzichtet werden."[4]

[1] Hilchot Matanot Aniim, Kap. 1–10, in: Mishneh Torah by *Moses Maimonides*, Bd. VI, Book of Zeraim (hebr.), edited by *Shabtai Frankel* (Jerusalem, Benei Brak 1990) 74–134, hier Kap. 7.3; im folgenden zitiert: *Frankel*, Mishneh Torah, Zeraim, Hilchot Matanot Aniim.

[2] *Jehudah Bergman*, Poor Relief (HaZedakah) in Israel (hebr.) (Jerusalem 1943); im folgenden zitiert: *Bergman*, HaZedakah; *Jacob R. Marcus*, Communal Sick-Care in the German Ghetto (Cincinnati 1947); im folgenden zitiert: *Marcus*, Communal Sick-Care; *Salo W. Baron*, The Jewish Community I–III, hier II (Philadelphia 1942) 319–350; im folgenden zitiert: *Baron*, Jewish Community; *Yom Tov Assis*, Les Institutions sociales: les logiques de la charité collective et de l'association, in: La société juive à travers l'histoire I–IV, hier II (Les liens de l'alliance), hrsg. von *Shmuel Trigano* (Paris 1992) 181–217.

[3] *Rudolf Glanz*, Geschichte des niederen jüdischen Volkes in Deutschland. Eine Studie über historisches Gaunertum, Bettelwesen und Vagantentum (New York 1968), im folgenden zitiert: *Glanz*, Geschichte.

[4] Ebd. 9.

An dieser Situation hat sich bis heute wenig geändert. Neben Versuchen, den theologisch-halachischen Hintergrund jüdischer Armenfürsorge zu analysieren[5], entstanden lediglich aktuellere Darstellungen in Enzyklopädien[6] oder theologischen Lexika[7]. Diese versuchten, sich erneut der historischen jüdischen Armenfürsorge anzunähern, wobei auch mittelalterliche Gepflogenheiten am Rande gestreift wurden. Größere, in Form von Aufsätzen erschienene Studien konzentrierten sich dabei vor allem auf das späte Mittelalter[8]. Hier wären zunächst die beiden Abhandlungen Israel Yuvals zu den Anfängen des jüdischen Hospitals[9] und den Almosen der Gemeinde Nürnberg zur Finanzierung sowohl der Juden im Lande Israel wie auch eigener Gemeindeeinrichtungen zu nennen[10]. Andere kleinere Abhandlungen nehmen für das 15. Jahrhundert lokale Verhältnisse der Armenfürsorge in den Blick[11] oder widmen sich den umherziehenden jüdischen Bettlern zwischen Spätmittelalter und Früher Neuzeit[12]. Ebenso an der Schwelle zur Frühen Neuzeit bewegt sich Elliot Horowitz[13] mit seinen Untersuchungen zur „Zedaka" unter den

[5] *Birgit Klein*, Idealisieren, neutralisieren, bekämpfen? Ansichten zur Armut im rabbinischen Judentum, in: Juden und Armut in Mittel- und Osteuropa, hrsg. von *Stefi Jersch-Wenzel* (Köln, Weimar, Wien 2000) 15–30.

[6] *Raphael Posner, Haim Hillel Ben Sasson, Isaac Levitats*, Charity, in: Encyclopaedia Judaica V (1996) 338–353; *Louis Isaac Rabinowitz, Isaac Levitats*, Gemilut Hassadim, in: Encyclopaedia Judaica VII (1996) 374–377; *Menachem Elon, Isaac Levitats*, Hekdesh, in: Encyclopaedia Judaica VIII (1996) 279–287.

[7] *Michael Brocke*, Armenfürsorge I. Judentum, in: Theologische Realenzyklopädie IV (1979) 10–14; *Johann Maier*, Armut. IV. Judentum, in: Theologische Realenzyklopädie IV (1979) 80–85.

[8] Zur Armenfürsorge im späten Mittelalter siehe: Germania Judaica III (1350–1519) 3. Teilband: Gebietsartikel, Einleitungsartikel und Indices, hrsg. von *Arye Maimon* s.A., *Mordechai Breuer* und *Yacov Guggenheim* (Tübingen 2003) 2093–2094, im folgenden zitiert: GJ III.3.

[9] *Israel Jacob Yuval*, Hospices and their Guests in Jewish Medieval Germany (hebr.), in: Proceedings of the Tenth World Congress of Jewish Studies (Jerusalem, August 16–24, 1989), hrsg. von *David Assaf*, Bd. I: The History of the Jewish People (Jerusalem 1990) 125–129; im folgenden zitiert: *Yuval*, Hospices.

[10] *Israel Jacob Yuval*, Alms from Nuremberg to Jerusalem (1375–1392) (hebr.), in: Zion 46 (1981) 182–197; im folgenden zitiert: *Yuval*, Alms.

[11] *Fritz Backhaus*, „Im Heckhuß die Lahmen, Blinden und Hungerleider ...". Die sozialen Institutionen in der Frankfurter Judengasse, in: Juden und Armut in Mittel- und Osteuropa, hrsg. von *Stefi Jersch-Wenzel* (Köln, Weimar, Wien 2000) 31–54.

[12] *Yacov Guggenheim*, Meeting on the Road. Encounters between German Jews and Christians on the Margins of Society, in: In and Out of the Ghetto. Jewish-Gentile Relations in Late Medieval and Early Modern Germany, hrsg. von *Ronnie Po-chia Hsia* und *Hartmut Lehmann* (New York 1995) 125–136; *ders.*, Von den Schalantjuden zu den Betteljuden. Jüdische Armut in Mitteleuropa in der Frühen Neuzeit, in: Juden und Armut in Mittel- und Osteuropa, hrsg. von *Stefi Jersch-Wenzel* (Köln, Weimar, Wien 2000) 55–69; im folgenden zitert: *Guggenheim*, Schalantjuden.

[13] *Elliot Horowitz*, Processions, Piety, and Jewish Confraternities, in: The Jews of Early Modern Venice, hrsg. von *Robert Charles Davis* und *Benjamin Ravid* (Baltimore, London 2001) 231–301; *ders.*: „(Deserving) Poor Shall Be Members of Your Household": Charity, the Poor and Social Control in the Jewish Communities of Europe between the Middle Ages and the Beginning of Modern Times (hebr.), in: Religion and Economy. Connections and Interactions, edited by *Menahem Ben-Sasson* (Jerusalem 1995) 209–231.

Juden der aschkenasischen Gemeinden in Norditalien für den Zeitraum vom 15. bis zum 17. Jahrhundert[14].

Besonders defizitär ist die Forschung zur Armenfürsorge in den aschkenasischen Gemeinden der Jahrhunderte des Hochmittelalters bis zur Zäsur der Pestverfolgungen um die Mitte des 14. Jahrhunderts. Hierzu haben sich verschiedene Autoren des frühen 20. Jahrhunderts im Kontext umfassenderer Fragestellungen zum Thema „Zedaka"/Armenfürsorge geäußert[15]. Die Rolle der Zedaka hinsichtlich der Gemeindebildung und der weiteren Gemeindestruktur fand dabei keine Berücksichtigung. Wenig mehr Aufmerksamkeit sollten die theologischen Voraussetzungen und ihre innerjüdischen Diskussionen erfahren, wobei dann auch mittelalterliche gemeindliche Formen der Armenfürsorge am Rande Erwähnung fanden[16]. Schließlich wurde von anderer Seite versucht, die Motivation zur jüdischen Armenfürsorge vor dem Hintergrund einer vermeintlich völligen Ausgrenzung der Juden gegenüber der christlichen Mehrheitsgesellschaft zu erklären[17], ohne dabei allerdings die jüdische Tradition einer organisierten Armenfürsorge aus vorchristlicher Zeit wie auch deren jüdische Praxis in nichtchristlichen (z. B. islamischen Kontexten) zu diskutieren.

Erst in letzter Zeit widmeten sich wenige junge Forscher erneut dem weiten Themenbereich von Krankheit[18], Armut und Armenfürsorge[19] und gelangten dabei zu neuen Einsichten zur Rollen des „Hospitals" im innerjüdischen Kontext[20], sowie hinsichtlich des Vergleichs mit der Armenfürsorge innerhalb der lateinischen Christenheit[21].

14 Dieser Forschungsbereich konnte vor kurzem durch Ergebnisse einer Trierer Dissertation bereichert werden: *Angela Möschter*, Juden im venezianischen Treviso 1389–1509 (Dissertation, Typoskript, Universität Trier 2004) Kap. IV.3, 119–120, Anm. 71 und 72. Siehe hierzu auch Responsa Juda Minz (Krakau 1887) Nr. 7.

15 *H[irsch] J[akob] Zimmels*, Beiträge zur Geschichte der Juden in Deutschland im 13. Jahrhundert insbesondere aufgrund der Gutachten des R. Meir von Rothenburg (Wien 1926) 28–30, 91; im folgenden zitiert: *Zimmels*, Beiträge; *Baron*, Jewish Community (wie Anm. 2) II 319, 327–329.

16 *Mayer A. Halévy*, Die Idee der Caritas in der jüdischen Religion, in: Historia Hospitalium. Mitteilungen der deutschen Gesellschaft für Krankenhausgeschichte (Sonderheft 1970) 10–19; *Tzvi Marx*, Priorities in Zedakah and their Implications, in: Judaism 29.1 (1979) 80–89.

17 *Aryeh Grabois*, Der Jude als ‚der Fremde' der mittelalterlichen Gesellschaft und die Wohltätigkeitspraxis, in: Zedaka. Jüdische Sozialarbeit im Wandel der Zeit. 75 Jahre Zentralwohlfahrtsstelle der Juden in Deutschland 1917–1992, hrsg. von *Georg Heuberger* (Frankfurt a. M. 1992) 30–39, hier 38–39.

18 *Ephraim N. Shoham-Steiner*, European Jewish Madmen in the High Middle Ages (hebr.), in: Zion 69 (2004) 299–327.

19 *Judah D. Galinsky*, „For the greater glory that his name shall be remembered". On the Custom to Establish a „Heqdesh" in Christian Spain and on the Commemoration of the Deceased's Memory (hebr.), in: Masechet 2 (2004) 113–131.

20 *Judah D. Galinsky*, Commemoration and Heqdesh in the Jewish Communities of Germany and Spain during the 13th Century, in: Stiftungen in Christentum, Judentum und Islam vor der Moderne. Auf der Suche nach ihren Gemeinsamkeiten und Unterschieden in religiösen Grundlagen, praktischen Zwecken und historischen Transformationen, hrsg. von *Michael Borgolte* (Stiftungsgeschichten 4, Berlin 2005) 191–204; im folgenden zitiert: *Galinsky*, Commemoration.

21 *Rainer Barzen, Monika Escher-Apsner, Dirk Multrus*, Religiös motivierte Barmherzigkeit und karitatives Handeln von Gemeinschaften im hohen und späten Mittelalter, in: Inklusion/Exklu-

Jüdische Armenfürsorge in Aschkenas im Spiegel der Quellen

Man könnte vermuten, daß die Vernachlässigung selbst einer nur oberflächlichen Betrachtung des Armenwesens im 11., 12. und 13. Jahrhundert in Aschkenas auf eine überaus schlechte, wenn nicht sogar völlig disparate Quellensituation hindeutet. Dies ist jedoch so nicht richtig. Formen der Armenfürsorge sind bereits anhand des „Kassenwarts" („Gabai") der Gemeinden in Mainz und Trier zur Zeit des Ersten Kreuzzuges nachgewiesen[22]. Zwar ist ein ausführlicher, programmatischer Text, der dem des Maimonides[23] zum Themenfeld „Zedaka" für den sephardischen Kulturkreis vergleichbar wäre und einen Entwurf für ein „aschkenasisches Fürsorgewesen" liefern würde, noch nicht bekannt. Doch hat es offensichtlich solche grundsätzlichen Überlegungen zu einer theologisch-halachischen Begründung, wie auch zur Praxis einer für alle verpflichtenden Fürsorge auch im aschkenasischen Bereich gegeben, wie die „Hilchot Zedaka", die „Rechtsbestimmungen zum Fürsorgewesen" des Isaak Or Sarua aus der ersten Hälfte des 13. Jahrhunderts nahelegen[24]. Die in 30 Abschnitte gegliederte Sammlung leitet das halachische Kompendium „Sefer Or Sarua" dieses Gelehrten ein, was die Bedeutung des Textes noch hervorhebt. Es bleibt darum höchst verwunderlich, daß dieser Text bis heute, obwohl er in der Forschung zur Kenntnis genommen wurde[25], keine nähere Untersuchung erfahren hat.

Auch Takkanot, also Rechtssatzungen von Gemeinden, aus dem 12. und 13. Jahrhundert harren noch einer systematischen Auswertung. Diejenigen der rheinischen Gemeinden von Mainz, Worms und Speyer („Takkanot Schum") bieten dabei eine Reihe von Quellen zum gemeindlichen Fürsorgewesen[26]. Damit böten sich auch Vergleichsmöglichkeiten zu ähnlichen Regelungen in christlichem Kontext.

sion. Studien zu Fremdheit und Armut von der Antike bis zur Gegenwart, hrsg. von *Andreas Gestrich* und *Lutz Raphael* (Frankfurt a. M., Berlin u. a. 2004) 397–422.

[22] *Eva Haverkamp*, Hebräische Berichte über die Judenverfolgungen während des Ersten Kreuzzugs (MGH, Hebräische Texte aus dem mittelalterlichen Deutschland I, München 2005) 368, Anm. 1 (Mainz); 476, Anm. 47 (Trier).

[23] *Frankel*, Mishneh Torah, Zeraim, Hilchot Matanot Aniim (wie Anm. 1) Kap. 1–10. Siehe auch: *Moses Maimonides*, Mishneh Torah (Yad Hazakah) (hebr./engl.), edited from rare manuscripts and early texts, vocalized, annotated and provided with an introduction by *Philip Birnbaum* (New York 1944/1967) 153–160.

[24] Sefer Or Sarua des Isaak von Wien (hebr.), Teil I, hrsg. von *Akiba Lehren* (Zhitomir 1862) 12–18, Nr. 1–30 (Hilchot Zedakah).

[25] *I. Kahan*, Or Sarua als Geschichtsquelle, in: Jahrbuch der Gesellschaft für Geschichte der Juden in der Čechoslovakischen Republik 9 (1938) 43–99, hier 80; *J. Wellesz*, Isaak b. Mose Or Sarua, in: Monatsschrift für die Geschichte und Wissenschaft des Judenthums 48 (1904) 129–144, 209–213, 361–371, 440–456, 710–712, hier 363–364; *ders.*, Über R. Isaak b. Mose's „Or Sarua", in: Jahrbuch der Jüdisch-Literarischen Gesellschaft IV (1906) 75–124, hier 88; *Uziel Fuks*, Studies on Sefer Or Sarua of R. Isaak ben Mose of Vienna (hebr.) (Master Thesis, Hebrew University, Jerusalem 1993) 37; *Galinsky*, Commemoration (wie Anm. 20) 197.

[26] *Louis Finkelstein*, Jewish Self-Government in the Middle Ages (New York 1924, Neudruck Greenwood 1972) 230, Nr. 24/25; im folgenden zitiert: *Finkelstein*, Jewish Self-Government.

Innerhalb der Überlieferung des Sefer Chassidim hat sich des weiteren eine nicht unerhebliche Anzahl von Exempla erhalten, die im alltäglichen Blick – selbstverständlich aus der Perspektive der „Frommen von Aschkenas" – Fragen von Armut und Not thematisieren. In ihnen werden u. a. die Folgen einer falschen Almosenpraxis als Ursache persönlicher Not angesprochen[27]. Auch gelten karitative Handlungen als Sühne für zurückliegende Vergehen[28]. Angesichts von Hunger und Not treten auch die Vorbehalte gegenüber Apostaten in den Hintergrund: Ihre Almosen dürfen angenommen werden[29].

Die Mehrzahl an Überlieferungen zum Fragenkomplex von Vorsorge und Fürsorge für die Armen hat sich, wie zu erwarten war, in der Responsenliteratur (juristischen Anfragen, die von Gemeinden und Einzelpersonen an die Rechtsgelehrten ihrer Zeit gerichtet wurden) erhalten[30]. Hier erfahren wir anhand des täglichen Rechtsstreits viel von der Norm und Praxis der Fürsorge, wie sie in der örtlichen Gemeinde, aber auch im Rahmen der Familie wie auch in unterschiedlichen Bereichen der jüdischen Gesellschaft üblich und rechtens war. Dabei zeigen die verschiedenen Streitfälle, daß ein an die Quellen herangetragenes Verständnis von Fürsorge als einer Versorgung von wirtschaftlich Gescheiterten nur einen Teil des zeitgenössischen Verständnisses zu erfassen vermag. Es ist vielmehr ebenso im Spannungsfeld von „potens et pauper" nach weiteren Formen von „Armut" und Bedürftigkeit zu fragen, gesellschaftlicher Machtlosigkeit, einer Verletzlichkeit wegen des Fehlens eines Beziehungsnetzes, was die Zeitgenossen wie selbstverständlich im Blick hatten. Diese erweiterte Perspektive schließt letztlich auch das Verhältnis zu den nichtjüdischen Armen ein. Hier wäre nach den Motiven und Motivationen von Handlungsweisen zu fragen, die – wenn auch nur in wenigen Beispielen nachgewiesen – auch dem nichtjüdischen Armen Almosen zukommen ließen[31].

Der Aktionsrahmen jüdischer Armenfürsorge

Innerhalb der jüdischen Gesellschaft des Hochmittelalters verfestigten sich in verschiedensten Bereichen bereits „Solidaritätsphänomene" bzw. „Solidaritätsstrategien", die in ihren unterschiedlichen Ausformungen vorgestellt werden sollen.

[27] Sefer Chassidim (hebr.), hrsg. von *Jehuda Wistinetzky* (Frankfurt a. M. 1924, Jerusalem 1969) Nr. 1232, 1681; im folgenden zitiert: *Wistinetzky*, Sefer Chassidim; Sefer Chassidim (hebr.), hrsg. von *Reuven Margaliot* (Jerusalem 1993) Nr. 1030, 1074; im folgenden zitiert: *Margaliot*, Sefer Chassidim.

[28] *Wistinetzky*, Sefer Chassidim (wie Anm. 27) Nr. 35, 273; *Margaliot*, Sefer Chassidim (wie Anm. 27) Nr. 32.

[29] *Wistinetzky*, Sefer Chassidim (wie Anm. 27) Nr. 1701f.

[30] Wobei neue Textfunde in unveröffentlichten Handschriften unsere Kenntnisse gerade für das 12. und 13. Jahrhundert erweitern: *Simcha Emmanuel*, Responsa of the Sages of Ashkenaz concerning Poor Relief (Zedakah), in: Maayan 41.2 (2001) 15–21 (hebr.), im folgenden zitiert: *Emmanuel*, Zedakah.

[31] *Frankel*, Mishneh Torah, Zeraim, Hilchot Matanot Aniim (wie Anm. 1) 7.7.

Vorsorge und Fürsorge für sich und die engsten Angehörigen lassen sich vor allem anhand von Stiftungen im Rahmen von Erbschaften nachweisen. Dabei steht zunächst die eigene Vorsorge, d.h. die nach dem eigenen Tod zu sichernde Memoria im Vordergrund[32]. Als wichtigstes Element einer familiären Zedaka auch über die Kernfamilie hinaus wären die privaten Armenkassen zu nennen[33]. Solche privaten Kassen konnten freilich nur von besonders wohlhabenden Einzelpersonen bzw. deren Familien eingerichtet werden, wobei es oft umstritten blieb, welche Personen, auch innerhalb der Familie bzw. des Hauses, als Nutznießer solcher Kassen zugelassen wurden. Die Untersuchungen solcher Rechtsstreitigkeiten in den Responsen lassen Aufschlüsse über verschiedene Formen innerfamiliärer Absicherung erwarten.

Vorsorge- und Fürsorgeeinrichtungen in Form von Bruderschaften, wie sie unter den Christen weit verbreitet waren, konnten bei den Juden des lateinischen Europa für das hohe und späte Mittelalter bisher lediglich in den Ländern der iberischen Halbinsel[34] und im Süden Frankreichs[35] nachgewiesen werden. Hatten solche „Gesellschaften" („Chevrot") innerhalb der jüdischen Gemeinschaft schon während der Antike bestanden[36], so begegnet uns in Aschkenas, genauer in Prag, erst an der Schwelle zur Frühen Neuzeit eine solche Vereinigung[37]. Vor diesem Datum konnte in der aschkenasischen Überlieferung kein eindeutiger Beleg für eine „Chevra", eine „Bruderschaft", gefunden werden[38]. Waren also bruderschaftliche Vereinigungen bei den aschkenasischen Juden des hohen und späten Mittelalters nicht gebräuchlich? Zumindest im Kontext von Zedaka, von Vorsorge und Fürsorge lassen sich durchaus Organisationsformen von Gruppen erkennen, die an bruderschaftliche Organisationsformen erinnern. Hierzu gehören nach Haverkamp am Beispiel des christlichen Kontextes „alle auf Dauer zielenden Vereinigungen von prinzipiell

[32] *Galinsky*, Commemoration (wie Anm. 20) 197; *Emmanuel*, Zedakah (wie Anm. 30) 6.

[33] *Meir von Rothenburg*, Rechtsgutachten (hebr.), hrsg. von *Moshe Arie Bloch* (Berlin 1891/1892) 5, Nr. 13, im folgenden zitiert: MRB; *Zimmels*, Beiträge (wie Anm. 15) 28, Anm. 88. Für das Spätmittelalter siehe *Jacob Weil*, Responsa I. (hebr.), hrsg. von *Yonathan Shraga Domb* (Jerusalem 2001) Nr. 133; GJ III.3 2094, Anm. 94.

[34] *Fritz Baer*, Der Ursprung der Chewra, in: Zeitschrift für jüdische Wohlfahrtspflege 1 (1929) 241–247, hier 243–244; *ders.*, Die Juden im christlichen Spanien, Bd. 1 (Berlin 1929–1936) 229, Nr. 179; *Marcus*, Communal Sick-Care (wie Anm. 2) 61; Responsa Ascher ben Jechiel (hebr.), hrsg. von *Itzchak Shlomo Yudlow* (Jerusalem 1994) Kap. 13. 12.

[35] Für das Jahr 1380 sind in Perpignan fünf jüdische Bruderschaften bekannt, darunter eine Begräbnisbruderschaft und eine Bruderschaft zum Besuch von Kranken: *Marcus*, Communal Sick-Care (wie Anm. 2) 62f.

[36] *Bergman*, HaZedakah (wie Anm. 2) 151, Anm. 36; *Marcus*, Communal Sick-Care (wie Anm. 2) 57–60.

[37] Erstmals für das Jahr 1564 in der Gemeinde Prag nachgewiesen: *Heinrich Flesch*, Zur Geschichte der mährischen „heiligen Vereine" (Chewra Kadischa), in: Jahrbuch der Jüdisch-Literarischen Gesellschaft 21 (1930) 217–258, hier 217. Zu jüdischen Bruderschaften auch für andere Aufgabenbereiche im aschkenasischen Raum der Frühen Neuzeit siehe *Baer*, Ursprung (wie Anm. 34), und *Marcus*, Communal Sick-Care (wie Anm. 2) passim.

[38] *Marcus*, Communal Sick-Care (wie Anm. 2) 64, Anm. 92, nach *Wistinetzky*, Sefer Chassidim (wie Anm. 27) 131, Nr. 453.

gleichberechtigt partizipierenden Männern und/oder Frauen, die sich selbst Satzungen gaben ..." Dabei „verpflichteten [sie] sich zu gemeinsamen religiös-kultischen Handlungen in Versammlungen, die in der Regel mit Messen [dh. Gottesdiensten] und Mahlen verknüpft waren ... Sie intendierten auf diese Weise, aber auch ... die Förderung des irdischen Wohlergehens und des Seelenheils ihrer lebenden und verstorbenen Mitglieder."[39]

Bereits in den Takkanot Schum erfahren wir vor der Mitte des 13. Jahrhunderts von der expliziten Zugehörigkeit des Einzelnen zur „Synagoge, wo er zu beten pflegt"[40], wenn mehrere Synagogen am Ort anzutreffen sind. Diese eindeutige Zuordnung wird dann wichtig, wenn, wie ebenfalls in den Takkanot gefordert, Strafzahlungen des Einzelnen der Synagoge zugute kommen sollen, wo der Delinquent betet[41]. Hierbei muß bemerkt werden, daß Geldstrafen in der Regel der Armenkasse zuflossen. Diese Vorgehensweise wird dann völlig einsichtig, wenn wir davon ausgehen, wie uns Meir von Rothenburg mitteilt, daß den einzelnen Synagogen Spenden zur Armenversorgung nach der Anzahl der Armen zugeteilt wurden, die zur jeweiligen Synagoge gerechnet wurden[42]. Die Armen wurden in diesem Fall offenkundig von einer Armenkasse der einzelnen Synagoge und nicht von einer zentralen Armenkasse der Gemeinde versorgt.

Weitere aus Nordfrankreich stammende bruderschaftliche Rituale, im Kontext christlicher gemeinschaftlicher Memoria, finden dort im 12. Jahrhundert zunächst Eingang ins jüdische Brauchtum, um schließlich, wie überliefert in den Takkanot Schum, auch in den Gemeinden am Rhein Verbreitung zu erlangen. Die Rede ist von der Pflicht der einzelnen Juden aus kleineren Niederlassungen im Umkreis einer größeren Gemeinde, bei ihren Besuchen an den Hochfesten wie Neujahr und Versöhnungstag eine Wachskerze mitzubringen, die dann vor Ort, also in der Synagoge in der Stadt, bleiben muß. Kann sich der Einzelne zwei Kerzen leisten, so muß die eine in der Synagoge der großen Gemeinde verbleiben, die zweite soll zurück ins Dorf an den Ort genommen werden, wo gemeinsam gebetet wird[43].

Wie schon von christlichen Bruderschaften (z.B. der Matthias-Bruderschaft in Trier) bekannt[44], drückt auch im jüdischen Kontext die Kerze die Verbundenheit

[39] *Alfred Haverkamp*, Bruderschaften und Gemeinde im 12. und 13. Jahrhundert, in: Ordnungskonfigurationen im hohen Mittelalter, hrsg. von *Bernd Schneidmüller* und *Stefan Weinfurther* (Vorträge und Forschungen 64, Stuttgart 2006) 153–192, hier 163–164.

[40] *Meir ben Baruch von Rothenburg*, Rechtsgutachten (hebr.) (Edit. Princ., Prag 1610), neu hrsg. von *Moshe Arie Bloch* (Budapest 1895) Nr. 1022, fol. 159a; im folgenden zitiert: MRP.

[41] Ebd. Nr. 1002, fol. 159b.

[42] MRB (wie Anm. 33) 237. Nr. 231; *Zimmels*, Beiträge (wie Anm. 15) 29, Anm. 100.

[43] *Rainer Barzen*, Benei haKefarim – die Leute aus den Dörfern. Zur jüdischen Siedlung auf dem Lande in Aschkenas und Zarfat im hohen und späteren Mittelalter, in: Campana pulsante convocati. Festschrift anläßlich der Emeritierung von Prof. Dr. Alfred Haverkamp, hrsg. von *Frank G. Hirschmann* und *Gerd Mentgen* (Trier 2005) 21–37, hier 34–35; *Finkelstein*, Jewish Self-Government (wie Anm. 26) 123.

[44] Zu Kerzen bei Bruderschaften, auch als Eigenbezeichnung, siehe *Benjamin Laqua*, Zusammenhänge zwischen Bruderschaften und Hospitälern in Köln während des 12. und 13. Jahrhunderts (Examensarbeit FB III, Universität Trier 2005) 79. Als Teil des Totenkults siehe *Peter Löffler*,

der außerhalb der Stadt lebenden Mitglieder mit der dortigen Gemeinde aus. Gleichzeitig wird das Anzünden dieser Kerze an Neujahr wie auch am Versöhnungstag zum Momentum der gemeinsamen Memoria der Verstorbenen der Gemeinschaft.

Noch zur Jahrtausendwende befand sich das jüdische Leben in den deutschen Landen in einer ausgeprägten Pioniersituation. Doch läßt sich beobachten, daß Fragen zur Armenfürsorge schon von Anfang an die Siedlungsgeschichte im späteren aschkenasischen Raum begleiteten. Durch die Definition der Almosenabgabe als göttliches Gebot und ihre Bindung an die einzelne Person kommt ihr im Rahmen der jüdischen Selbstorganisation eine entscheidende Bedeutung zu. Sie ist nicht eine Gemeindeinstitution, die aus der konstituierten Gemeinschaft hervorgeht. Vielmehr schafft sie Gemeinschaft und Selbstorganisation durch die Armenkasse, die zum gemeinsamen Erfüllungsort eines für jeden Einzelnen geltenden Gebotes wird. Die Armenkasse steht somit am Anfang aller jüdischen Gemeinschaft in jeder neu entstehenden und sich entfaltenden Niederlassung. Am Ende des 11. Jahrhunderts war in den großen jüdischen Zentren des Rheinlandes eine organisierte Form der Armenfürsorge bereits selbstverständlich[45]. Mit der Armenkasse für die ganze Gemeinde entstanden bald verschiedene Aufgabenbereiche, die von der Gemeinde beaufsichtigt wurden. Die hebräischen Titel der Aufgabenträger wie auch die Organisation ihrer Aufgabenbereiche wurden in der Regel aus der vorhandenen Terminologie des rabbinischen Schrifttums entlehnt.

Weitere Einzelheiten der Armenfürsorge jüdischer Gemeinden, vor allem des 13. Jahrhunderts, begegnen uns in den Responsen. Aus den überlieferten Auseinandersetzungen geht hervor, daß neben einer verbreiteten allgemeinen Almosenwesenpraxis jede Gemeinde ihre besonderen Eigenheiten als lokalen Brauch entwickeln konnte, der in jedem Falle jeder Regelung von außen vorzuziehen war.

Die Abgabe des Zehnten stellte in den jüdischen Gemeinden die finanzielle Grundlage für die verschiedenen Bereiche der Armenfürsorge dar. Diese Regelung hatte sich bereits in den Gemeinden des Nahen Ostens als praktikabel erwiesen. Dabei war in Gegensatz zu Entwicklungen im christlichen Kontext, wo der Zehnte als Abgabe an die Kirche sich spätestes ab 1200 mehrheitlich von der Pfarrkirche und damit von der Kirchengemeinde gelöst hatte[46], die Verbindung des jüdischen Zehnten zur jüdischen Gemeinde erhalten geblieben. Die Gelder waren dabei den Armen vorbehalten. So schrieb Meir von Rothenburg (gest. 1293), der wichtigste und angesehenste jüdische Rechtsgelehrte des 13. Jahrhunderts: „Aber auf die Gelder der Zehnten haben die Armen einen Anspruch auf Grund des Brauches, der in der ganzen Diaspora üblich ist. Man darf daher nicht dieselben für andere wohltätige Zwecke verwenden."[47] Dennoch setzten sich auch andere Bräuche durch. In

Studien zum Totenbrauchtum in den Gilden, Bruderschaften und Nachbarschaften Westfalens vom Ende des 15. Jahrhunderts bis zum Ende des 19. Jahrhunderts (Forschungen zur Volkskunde 47, Münster/Westfalen 1975) 187, 223.

[45] *Eva Haverkamp*, Hebräische Berichte 368, Anm. 1 (Mainz); 476, Anm. 47 (Trier).

[46] *R. Puza*, Zehnt, in: Lexikon des Mittelalters IX (1998) 499–501.

[47] MRP (wie Anm. 40) Nr. 74; *Zimmels*, Beiträge (wie Anm. 15) 28, Anm. 84.

einigen Gemeinden war es üblich, nur die Hälfte des Zehnten in die gemeinsame Armenkasse abzuliefern. Die andere Hälfte stand dem Einzelnen zur freien Verfügung, um sie für weitere Projekte im Sinne der Zedaka einzusetzen[48]. Allerdings waren solche Regelungen an die von den „Tovei haIr", den „Viri Boni" der Gemeinde im Mehrheitsbeschluß geschaffenen Rechtssatzungen gebunden[49]. Niemand durfte sich solchen Takkanot entziehen oder ihre Aufhebung durch ein Gericht fordern[50]. Diese von der Gemeinde geschaffene Organisation einer Armenversorgung war zunächst den Bedürftigen der Gemeinde verpflichtet. Dies wurde in Situationen deutlich, in denen eine Gemeinde zu Hilfszahlungen für die Armenfürsorge einer anderen Gemeinde aufgefordert wurde, dieser Aufforderung aber nur dann nachkam, wenn es nicht zum Nachteil der „eigenen Armen" gereichte. Die Privilegierung der Gemeindearmen trat aber in den Hintergrund, wenn auswärtige Arme persönlich in einer anderen Gemeinde vorstellig wurden. Dort wurden sie aus der Armenkasse der Gemeinde nach Möglichkeit versorgt, wobei die einheimischen Armen ihnen nicht per se vorgezogen werden durften[51].

Die beschriebene Armenkasse der Gemeinde finanzierte sich nicht ausschließlich aus den regelmäßigen Abgaben der Gemeindemitglieder. Neben einmaligen Spenden[52], den Erträgen aus Gelübden[53] oder Hinterlassenschaften für das eigene Totengedächtnis[54], waren es – wie schon erwähnt – vor allem Geldstrafen, mittels derer die Armenkasse auf eine breitere finanzielle Basis gestellt wurde. Hierzu gehörten solche aufgrund einer Übertretung der gültigen Rechtssatzungen (Takka-

[48] MRB (wie Anm. 33) 5, Nr. 13; *Zimmels*, Beiträge (wie Anm. 15) 28, Anm. 88. Dabei konnte die Frage nach der Würde des einzelnen Armen bei der Verteilung der Almosen eine Rolle spielen.

[49] Auch gab es für den Rabbiner der Gemeinde die Möglichkeit, Takkanot im Rahmen der Armenfürsorge einzusetzen, wenn er genügend Autorität besaß. Mose Minz regelte 1469 in Bamberg die Modalitäten der Abgabe für die Armenkasse neu. *Mose Minz*, Responsa I/II (hebr.), hrsg. von *Yonathan Shraga Domb* (Jerusalem 1991) I 244–245, Nr. 60; GJ III.3 2094.

[50] MRB (wie Anm. 33) 209, Nr. 140; *Zimmels*, Beiträge (wie Anm. 15) 22, Anm. 6.

[51] MRB (wie Anm. 33) 66, Nr. 512; *Zimmels*, Beiträge (wie Anm. 15) 29, Anm. 102f.

[52] Hierzu gehörten auch Summen, die ohne einen genannten Zweck für die Wohltätigkeit gelobt wurden: MRB (wie Anm. 33) 50, Nr. 316; *Zimmels*, Beiträge (wie Anm. 15) 28, Anm. 91; MRP (wie Anm. 40) Nr. 884, *Zimmels*, Beiträge (wie Anm. 15) 28, Anm. 89. Auch war es möglich, bei finanziellen Engpässen der Gemeinde, bei Hochzeiten und am Purimfest Spenden einzusammeln, um die Gemeinde zu entlasten: *Meir von Rothenburg*, Rechtsgutachten (hebr.), hrsg. von *M. Rabinowitz* (Lemberg 1860) Nr 112; im folgenden zitiert: MRL; *Zimmels*, Beiträge (wie Anm. 15) 21, Anm. 86.

[53] Hierzu zählen auch Gelübde zur Selbstdisziplinierung, wie etwa das Versprechen, eine bestimmte Summe der Armenkasse zu überlassen, wenn man sich erneut einer bestimmten Verhaltensweise schuldig macht. Auch in diesem Fall bleibt der Gelobende an seine Gemeinde gebunden. Sein Bußgeld wird nicht der Gemeinde zufallen, wo sich der Delinquent gerade zufällig aufhält, sondern dessen Heimatgemeinde zugute kommen: MRP (wie Anm. 40) Nr. 500; *Zimmels*, Beiträge (wie Anm. 15) 29, Anm. 98.

[54] Im Falle einer schweren Krankheit wurden häufig Vorkehrungen getroffen, den im Falle des Todes zurückbleibenden Besitz den Armen zugute kommen zu lassen: MRB (wie Anm. 33) 157, Nr. 33; *Zimmels*, Beiträge (wie Anm. 15) 28, 91, Anm. 92. Wurde in diesem Zusammenhang schon vor dem Eintritt des Todes mit der Verteilung der Güter unter die Armen begonnen, konnte dies erfolgreich von den Erben angefochten werden: MRB (wie Anm. 33) 158, Nr. 34; *Zimmels*, Beiträge (wie Anm. 15) 28, Anm. 92.

not) der Gemeinden[55], aber auch Bußgelder, die bei Übertretungen verschiedenster Art verhängt wurden[56].

Das große finanzielle Aufkommen so mancher Armenkasse führte in vielen Fällen dazu, daß Teile des Kapitals an Privatpersonen verliehen wurde. Meir von Rothenburg berichtete von Krediten, die einzelne Personen aus der Armenkasse erhielten, wenn sie derselben Kasse in regelmäßigen Abständen feste Summen zugunsten der Armenfürsorge zukommen ließen[57]. Dies wiederum führte zu einer Vergrößerung der regelmäßigen Zuwendungen der jeweiligen Armenkasse, was ihren breiten Aufgabenfeldern zugute kam.

Die Versorgung der Armen der Gemeinde schloß auch die armen Toten mit ein, die auf Kosten dieser Kasse bestattet wurden[58]. Hierbei konnte es sich um Verstorbene handeln, die nach der Auszahlung der im Ehevertrag festgesetzten Summe an die Witwe und nach der Begleichung aller Forderungen eventueller Gläubiger über keine weiteren Mittel mehr verfügten[59].

Das jüdische Hospital seit dem 13. Jahrhundert

Im Laufe des 13. Jahrhunderts zeichnete sich in Aschkenas eine Veränderung der Versorgung der jüdischen Armen ab, die sich auch auf eine wandelnde Lebensweise der Bedürftigen zurückführen ließ. Bezeichnend dabei ist, daß sich die aschkenasische Literatur zeitgleich eines neuen Begriffes, nämlich dem des „Gastes", bediente[60]. Noch zu Beginn des 13. Jahrhunderts wurden im Sefer Chassidim (Buch der Frommen) unter diesem Begriff Arme, Händler und Reisende subsumiert[61]. Allerdings stand weiterhin den Armen unter den Gästen die Solidarität der jüdischen Gemeinschaft zu. Es scheint sogar für die jüdischen Armen dieser Zeit charakteristisch geworden zu sein, zumindest für eine begrenzte Periode von Gemeinde zu Gemeinde zu ziehen, um durch die vor Ort gewährte Armenfürsorge den Lebensunterhalt der eigenen Familie zu sichern, die in der Heimatgemeinde wohnhaft geblieben war[62].

[55] MRB (wie Anm. 33) 237, Nr. 231; *Zimmels*, Beiträge (wie Anm. 15) 29, Anm. 95.

[56] MRP (wie Anm. 40) Nr. 132; *Meir von Rothenburg*, Rechtsgutachten (hebr.) (Cremona 1557) Nr. 242, 285; im folgenden zitiert: MRC; MRL (wie Anm. 52) Nr. 492; *Zimmels*, Beiträge (wie Anm. 15) 29, Anm. 96, 97.

[57] MRB (wie Anm. 33) 58, Nr. 477; MRL (wie Anm. 52) Nr. 426; *Zimmels*, Beiträge (wie Anm. 15) 29, 30, Anm. 108; MRC (wie Anm. 56) Nr. 253; *Zimmels*, Beiträge (wie Anm. 15) 30, Anm. 110. Meir von Rothenburg lehnte diese Praxis ab, war sich aber auch bewußt, daß er gegen sie nichts ausrichten konnte: MRP (wie Anm. 40) Nr. 73; MRL (wie Anm. 52) Nr. 478; *Zimmels*, Beiträge (wie Anm. 15) 29, Anm. 105.

[58] MRP (wie Anm. 40) Nr. 149, 176; MRC (wie Anm. 56) Nr. 184, 243; *Zimmels*, Beiträge (wie Anm. 15) 26, Anm. 64.

[59] MRP (wie Anm. 40) Nr. 176; *Zimmels*, Beiträge (wie Anm. 15) 71, Anm 539.

[60] *Yuval*, Hospices (wie Anm. 9) 125.

[61] *Wistinetzky*, Sefer Chassidim (wie Anm. 27) Nr. 845; *Yuval*, Hospices (wie Anm. 9) 125.

[62] *Wistinetzky*, Sefer Chassidim (wie Anm. 27) Nr. 903; 1248; *Yuval*, Hospices (wie Anm. 9) 125–126.

Die Versorgung dieser umherziehenden Armen als „Gäste" blieb zunächst individuell und nicht institutionell. Dennoch scheint die ständige Zunahme an umherziehenden jüdischen Armen die Entstehung von durch die Gemeinde getragenen Häusern, ähnlich den christlichen Hospitälern, beschleunigt zu haben[63]. Unter den Bezeichnungen „Bait leAniim"[64] (Armenhäuser) bzw. „Beit Ospisanchiah"[65] sind solche Einrichtungen zum ersten Mal in einer hebräischen Quelle, dem Sefer Chassidim, erwähnt[66]. Die begriffliche Nähe zum christlichen Hospital muß dabei keineswegs überraschen, wobei die Multifunktionalität der jüdischen Einrichtungen denen der christlichen Xenodochien und Hospitäler entsprach.

Etwa zeitgleich zur Erwähnung im Sefer Chassidim ist innerhalb eines städtischen Kontextes als frühestes Beispiel im Jahre 1210 in Regensburg das Gebäude eines jüdischen Hospitals erwähnt[67]. Weitere Einrichtungen dieser Art begegnen uns 1247 bzw. 1253 in der jüdischen Gemeinde zu Köln[68], 1290 in Augsburg[69] und 1322 in Würzburg[70]. Auch die jüdischen Gemeinden von Koblenz[71] und Nürnberg[72] besaßen bereits in der ersten Hälfte des 14. Jahrhunderts ein Hospital. Die Überlieferung solcher Einrichtungen ist jedoch weitgehend zufällig und mitunter von Nachrichten über Gebäude abhängig, die unter der Bezeichnung „Hospital der Juden" nach der Pestverfolgung zunächst leer standen und dann veräußert wurden. Es muß darum vielmehr davon ausgegangen werden, daß schon im 13. Jahrhundert jede größere städtische jüdische Gemeinde, die auch als Mittelpunkt eines Friedhofsbezirkes fungierte, eine solche Einrichtung unterhielt.

63 So *Yuval*, Hospices (wie Anm. 9) 125.
64 *Wistinetzky*, Sefer Chassidim (wie Anm. 27) Nr. 1529; *Yuval*, Alms (wie Anm. 10) 187, Anm. 26.
65 *Yuval*, Hospices (wie Anm. 9) 125. Derselbe Terminus findet sich auch bei *Jacob Weil*, Responsa I 66, Nr. 41.
66 *Yuval*, Hospices (wie Anm. 9) 125.
67 *Julius Aronius*, Regesten zur Geschichte der Juden im fränkischen und deutschen Reiche bis zum Jahre 1273 (Berlin 1902, Neudruck Hildesheim, New York 1970) 168–170, Nr. 381: „hospitale Judeorum".
68 Geschichte der Juden im Mittelalter von der Nordsee bis zu den Südalpen, hrsg. von *Alfred Haverkamp*, Teil 1: Kommentarband (Forschungen zur Geschichte der Juden A 14, 1–3, Hannover 2002) 183; im folgenden zitiert: *Haverkamp*, Nordsee I; *Robert Hoeniger*, *Moritz Stern*, Das Judenschreinsbuch der Laurenzpfarre zu Köln (Quellen zur Geschichte der Juden in Deutschland 1, Berlin 1888) 6, Nr. 35–37; Germania Judaica, hrsg. von *Zvi Avneri* (Tübingen 1968) Bd. II.1, 426, im folgenden zitiert: GJ II.
69 *Haverkamp*, Nordsee II 27; GJ II.1 33.
70 „Hospitium Judaicum", *Haverkamp*, Nordsee II 394; GJ II.2 931.
71 Das Gebäude ist 1355 (*Haverkamp*, Nordsee II 182) vor der erneuten Ansiedlung von Juden nach der Pestverfolung – freilich als ungenutzt – nachgewiesen, was auf eine Nutzung durch die jüdische Gemeinde vor ihrer Auslöschung schließen läßt.
72 *Haverkamp*, Nordsee II 260; GJ II.2 602. Siehe auch *Moritz Stern*, Die israelitische Bevölkerung der deutschen Städte. Teil III: Nürnberg im Mittelalter (Kiel 1894–1896) 131; im folgenden zitiert: *Stern*, Nürnberg; *Siegmund Salfeld*, Das Martyrologium des Nürnberger Memorbuches (Quellen zur Geschichte der Juden in Deutschland 3, Berlin 1898) 91, 300; im folgenden zitiert: *Salfeld*, Martyrologium; *K. Baas*, Jüdische Hospitäler im Mittelalter, in: Monatsschrift für die Geschichte und Wissenschaft des Judenthums 57 (1913) 455.

Die disparate Überlieferung mag auch erklären, warum sich gerade für die jüdischen Zentren des mittleren Rheingebietes in Mainz, Worms und Speyer, die in vielen Schlüsselbereichen zu den führenden Gemeinden des Reiches zählten, für die Zeit vor den großen Pestverfolgungen keine jüdischen Hospitäler nachweisen lassen. Zumindest aber ist in einem Gedicht des Israel ben Joel Susslin aus der Zeit der Pestverfolgung für die Gemeinde Speyer ein Gemeindebeauftragter erwähnt, der sich um die Kranken zu kümmern hatte[73]. Erst für das Spätmittelalter verdichten sich zumindest für Mainz und Speyer die Hinweise[74] auf die Existenz von jüdischen Hospitälern. Diese waren Teil eines größeren Netzes solcher jüdischen Einrichtungen, die sich nun ab dem späten 14. Jahrhundert in einigen Gemeinden des Reiches – wie Worms, Trier, Frankfurt am Main, Nürnberg, Ulm, Rothenburg ob der Tauber, Wien, Wiener Neustadt, Eger, Znaim und Marchegg sowie Rappoltsweiler – nachweisen lassen[75].

Neben den in den städtischen Gemeinden lokalisierten jüdischen Hospitälern sind auch einige jüdische Leprosorien bekannt. Auch in ihrem Falle ist, vergleichbar mit den christlichen Leprosenhäusern[76], von einem wenn auch „großmaschigen" Netz von Einrichtungen auszugehen, die vor allem außerhalb der urbanen Zentren zu suchen sind. Bislang kennt die Forschung nur wenige Beispiele: Aus dem französischen Raum ist für das 13. Jahrhundert für die Stadt Provins, wohl außerhalb der Mauern gelegen, ein jüdisches Refugium für Leprakranke bezeugt[77]. Im frühen 14. Jahrhundert ist eine solche Institution auch für die deutschen Lande, genauer für die Stadt Germersheim, nachgewiesen[78]. Daß in dieser Einrichtung mit

[73] *Haverkamp*, Nordsee II 332; *Simon Bernfeld*, Sefer haDemaot II: Von der Rintfleischverfolgung bis zur Verbrennung der Marranen in Ancona (hebr.) (Berlin 1924) 126.

[74] Mainz 1473 (*Haverkamp*, Nordsee II 215; Germania Judaica III 786); Worms 1500 (*Haverkamp*, Nordsee II 392; GJ III 1671); Speyer 15. Jahrhundert, belegt durch archäologische Funde: *Haverkamp*, Nordsee II 332; *Günther Stein*, Der mittelalterliche Judenhof und seine Bauten, in: Geschichte der Juden in Speyer (Beiträge zur Speyerer Stadtgeschichte 6, Speyer 1981) 48–64, hier 63.

[75] Trier 1422: „hospitale Iudeorum" (*Haverkamp*, Nordsee II 350; GJ III 1470); Worms um 1430 (*Haverkamp*, Nordsee II 392; GJ III 1671, Anm. 23); Frankfurt a. M. 1474 (*Haverkamp*, Nordsee II 121, GJ III 346); Nürnberg nach 1373 (*Haverkamp*, Nordsee II 260; GJ II.2 602) 1499 (GJ III 1001, Anm. 19, 1002, 1006, Anm. 91); Ulm 1499/1500 (*Haverkamp*, Nordsee II 356; GJ III 1498, Anm. 17/26, 1507); Rothenburg 1509 „selhaus" baufällig (*Haverkamp*, Nordsee II 297; GJ III 1253, Anm. 15); Wien vor 1387/1424 (GJ III.2 1606, Anm. 212; 1596, Anm. 9; 1597, Anm. 21); Wiener Neustadt 1453 (GJ III 1619, Anm. 13); Eger 1430/1469 (GJ III 267, Anm. 8/9, berichtigt GJ III 1264, Anm. 15); Znaim 1401 (GJ II 1721, Anm. 9); Marchegg 1489/99 (GJ III 848, Anm. 6); Rappoltsweiler 1425 (*Haverkamp*, Nordsee II 284; *Gerd Mentgen*, Studien zur Geschichte der Juden im mittelalterlichen Elsaß (Forschungen zur Geschichte der Juden A2, Hannover 1995) 56.

[76] *Martin Uhrmacher*, Leprosorien in Mittelalter und früher Neuzeit (Geschichtlicher Atlas der Rheinlande, Beiheft VIII/5, Köln 2000).

[77] *François-Olivier Touti*, Domus judeorum leprosorum: une léproserie pour les Juifs à Provins au XIIIe siècle, in: Fondations et œuvres charitables au Moyen Ages, sous la direction de *Jean Dufour* et *Henri Platelle* (Paris 1999) 97–106.

[78] *Haverkamp*, Nordsee II 131; GJ II.1 277; *Franz-Josef Ziwes*, Studien zur Geschichte der Juden im mittleren Rheingebiet während des hohen und späten Mittelalters (Forschungen zur Geschichte der Juden A 1, Hannover 1995) 91–93.

den Kranken auch Gesunde zusammenlebten, legt eine Äußerung aus dem Nürnberger Memorbuch nahe[79]. Die innere Organisation solcher Einrichtungen bleibt beim jetzigen Stand der Forschung noch im Dunkeln.

Die Finanzierung solcher öffentlichen Stätten der Fürsorge war auf unterschiedlichste Weise gesichert. Zunächst waren es die privaten, freiwilligen Gaben Einzelner, die beispielsweise dem Hospital von Lebenden wie auch testamentarisch von bereits Verstorbenen zugedacht waren. Letztere spendeten zum Wohle des eigenen Seelengedächtnisses. Zu diesem Zwecke wurden die Namen der Spender und die Summe der Spende im Memorbuch der Gemeinde verzeichnet und zu festen Zeiten des liturgischen Jahres während des Gottesdienstes vorgetragen[80]. Seit dem Ende des 13. und während des 14. Jahrhunderts scheint die allgemeine Abgabe der Gemeindemitglieder zur Zedaka ausschließlich den jüdischen Hospitälern zugeflossen zu sein. Die Konzentration der gemeindlichen Armenfürsorge allein auf die Stiftung des Hospitals scheint eng mit der Veränderung des Rechtsstatus der jüdischen Gemeinden zusammenzuhängen, wie sie sich im Laufe des 14. Jahrhunderts innerhalb der jüdischen Gemeinden in Aschkenas vollzog. Bei den weiterhin als „Gäste" bezeichneten Bewohnern des örtlichen jüdischen Hospitals handelte es sich nicht mehr vordergründig um Personen, die aus verschiedenen Gründen umherzogen, sondern fast ausschließlich um Arme, die wegen ihres Aufenthalts im Hospital als Fremde angesehen wurden[81]. Diese Betrachtungsweise hing eng mit dem Wandel des jüdischen Rechtsstatus der Juden in Bezug auf die sie beherbergenden Städte zusammen. Spätestens seit der Wiederansiedlung von Juden innerhalb der Städte des Reiches, unmittelbar nach den Pestverfolgungen, wurde klar, daß Aufnahmeprivilegien zukünftig nur noch Einzelpersonen verliehen wurden, und nicht mehr ganzen Gemeinden. Dies führte dazu, daß deren Aufnahme von der Fähigkeit der betreffenden Juden abhing, Geldgeschäfte zu betreiben. Es bedeutete aber auch, daß die Stadt armen Juden kein Bürgerrecht verlieh[82]. In dieser Situation konnte die jüdische Gemeinde armen Juden nur den Status von „Gästen" zubilligen, für deren Unterhalt die Gemeinde durch die Stiftung des „Hekdesch", eines Hospitals, aufkam. Gleichzeitig konnte ein wohlhabendes Gemeindemitglied die Steuerzahlungen armer Juden gegenüber der Stadt übernehmen und so das Aufenthaltsrecht der Armen gegenüber dem Stadtherrn sichern helfen[83]. Meir von Rothenburg formulierte hierzu treffend: „Wenn dem Fürst bekannt würde, daß die Armen keine Steuern zahlten, dann wären sie vertrieben worden."[84] Die Armen der Stadt wurden

[79] *Salfeld*, Martyrologium (wie Anm. 72) 60.
[80] *Stern*, Nürnberg (wie Anm. 72) 191–205; MRP (wie Anm. 40) Nr. 998; *Zimmels*, Beiträge (wie Anm. 15) 26, Anm. 59.
[81] *Yuval*, Hospices (wie Anm. 9) 126.
[82] Ebd. 127.
[83] So geschehen in Breslau im Jahre 1354, als Isaak Smoglin die Steuer für acht arme Juden mit übernahm: *Ludwig Oelsner*, Schlesische Urkunden zur Geschichte der Juden im Mittelalter, in: Archiv für Kunde österreichischer Geschichts-Quellen 31 (1864) 59–144, hier 112, Nr. 12; GJ III 164, Anm. 64; *Yuval*, Hospices (wie Anm. 9) 128.
[84] MRL (wie Anm. 52) Nr. 130. *Yuval*, Hospices (wie Anm. 9) 128.

im selben Moment, in dem sie von der Gemeinde in die Verantwortung des Hospitals übergeben wurden, von regulären Gemeindemitgliedern zu „Fremden“. In diesem Sinne muß auch der Begriff „Gäste“ verstanden werden, der uns in den Opferlisten der Rintfleischverfolgung von 1298 begegnet. Es handelte sich dabei eben nicht in ihrer Mehrheit um durchziehende Fremde, sondern um ortsansässige Arme[85].

Die hier aufgeführten unterschiedlichen Formen von Vorsorge und Fürsorge stellen selbstverständlich nur einen Teil der Ausdrucksformen von Zedaka dar, wie sie bei einer Vertiefung der hier aufgezeigten Ansätze erwartet werden könnten. Fast völlig unberücksichtigt mußte in dieser Phase die Untersuchung der realen Armut unter den Juden bleiben, die zweifelsohne vorhanden war und deren Verbreitung sich an der Wandlung der Funktion des Hekdesch, des jüdischen Hospitals, zumindest ansatzweise ablesen läßt. Auch konnte bereits eine große Affinität zwischen jüdischen und christlichen Fürsorgeformen aufgezeigt werden. Diese wahrgenommene „Nähe“ muß jedoch mit gebotener Vorsicht betrachtet und darf keinesfalls als eine wie auch immer geartete „Assimilation“ verstanden werden. Vielmehr ist sie als analoge Entwicklung innerhalb der jüdischen wie der christlichen Gesellschaft anzusehen, wo ähnliche (oder gleiche) Probleme zu ähnlichen (oder gleichen) Lösungsansätzen geführt haben.

Wie durch die beschriebene Situation der jüdischen Hospitäler in Aschkenas deutlich wurde, konnte die Etablierung von Anstalten der Armenversorgung auch zu Ausgrenzungen innerhalb der jüdischen Gesellschaft führen. Die Übertragung der Verantwortung des einzelnen Juden auf die Stiftung des jüdischen Hospitals nahm als soziale Trennung die räumlich-geographische Separierung von wohlhabenden und armen Juden vorweg, wie sie dann durch das Umherziehen der armen Juden seit dem 15. Jahrhundert in vielen Fällen nachvollzogen und gelebt wurde[86]. Trotz dieser Trennung blieben arme und reiche Juden durch die gebotene Barmherzigkeit des Einzelnen wie auch durch die gemeindliche institutionalisierte Armenfürsorge aufeinander bezogen. Die Existenz der armen, weiterhin in die jüdische Gemeinschaft eingeschlossenen Juden wurde durch die Einrichtungen der jüdischen Gemeinde garantiert. So blieben die jüdischen Armen Teil der fortbestehenden jüdischen Gemeinschaft. Erst als die großen Gemeinden am Ende des Mittelalters durch Vertreibungen zu existieren aufhörten, hatten auch die jüdischen Armen ihren Zufluchtsort verloren.

85 *Yuval*, Hospices (wie Anm. 9) 129.
86 *Guggenheim*, Schalantjuden (wie Anm. 12).

Martha Keil

Mobilität und Sittsamkeit: Jüdische Frauen im Wirtschaftsleben des spätmittelalterlichen Aschkenas

Dieser Beitrag widmet sich einem Aspekt der jüdischen Wirtschaftsgeschichte des spätmittelalterlichen Aschkenas, der in den bisherigen Forschungen noch kaum Erwähnung fand: der Mobilität von jüdischen Frauen allgemein und im speziellen der Geschäftsfrauen und ihrem tatsächlichen oder scheinbaren Widerspruch zur von Frauen geforderten Häuslichkeit und Sittsamkeit. „Mobilität" meint hier nicht die freiwillige oder erzwungene Migration oder das Umherziehen der nicht seßhaften Unterschichten, welche selbstverständlich beide, so gut wie nie explizit erwähnt, auch die Frauen betrafen[1], sondern das wörtlich zu nehmende „sich von einem Ort zum anderen Bewegen" aus beruflichen, privaten und religiös-kultischen Gründen. Knut Schulz wählte für eine Sektion der 35. Versammlung deutscher Historiker im Jahr 1984 zum Thema „Mobilität im Spätmittelalter" den Begriff „Unterwegssein", welcher „im Unterschied zu den vieldeutigen anderen Bezeichnungen im stärkeren Maß die Bewegung selbst" erfaßt[2].

Zwei wesentliche Beweggründe für das „Unterwegssein", nämlich das Studium an einer Jeschiwa außerhalb des Wohnortes und die Abenteuer- oder Bildungsreise

[1] Siehe dazu *Michael Toch*, Jewish Migrations to, within and from Medieval Germany, in: *ders.*, Peasants and Jews in Medieval Germany. Studies in Cultural, Social, and Economic History (London 2003) X, 639–652; Karten zu jüdischen Siedlungsorten und den Wanderungen des Menchin von Trier 649–652, und *ders.*, Die Verfolgungen des Spätmittelalters (1350–1550), in: Germania Judaica III/3, hrsg. von *Arye Maimon*, *Mordechai Breuer*, *Yacov Guggenheim* (Tübingen 2003) 2298–2327; im folgenden zitiert: GJ III/3. Zum Westen des Reiches mit einer Migrationsanalyse zu Menchin von Trier siehe *Friedhelm Burgard*, Zur Migration der Juden im westlichen Reichsgebiet im Spätmittelalter, in: Juden in der christlichen Umwelt während des späten Mittelalter, hrsg. v. *Alfred Haverkamp* und *Franz-Josef Ziwes*, Zeitschrift für Historische Forschung, Beiheft 13 (1992) 41–57, bes. 47–49, mit Karten 56f.; im folgenden zitiert: *Burgard*, Zur Migration. Zu den fahrenden und seßhaften Armen siehe *Yacov Guggenheim*, Social Stratification of Central European Jewry at the End of the Middle Ages: The Poor (hebr.), in: Tenth World Congress of Jewish Studies, Div. B, Vol. 1 (Jerusalem 1990) 130–136 und *ders.*, Von den Schalantjuden zu den Betteljuden. Jüdische Armut in Mitteleuropa in der Frühen Neuzeit, in: Juden und Armut in Mittel- und Osteuropa, hrsg. von *Stefi Jersch-Wenzel* (Köln, Weimar, Wien 2000) 55–69.

[2] *Knut Schulz*, Unterwegssein im Spätmittelalter. Einleitende Bemerkungen, in: *Peter Moraw* (Hrsg.), Unterwegssein im Spätmittelalter (ZHF Beiheft 1, Berlin 1998) 9–15, hier 10; im folgenden zitiert: *Schulz*, Unterwegssein. Auch *Burgard*, Zur Migration 42f. griff diese Bezeichnung auf.

kamen für jüdische Frauen im Mittelalter nicht in Frage[3]. Über die anzunehmende häufige Motivation der Berufsmigration, nämlich den Antritt als Dienstbote im Haus eines Verwandten oder anderen Arbeitgebers, unterrichten uns die Quellen kaum[4]. Neben kurzen Erwähnungen von Reisen aus privaten Gründen wie Besuchen, Hochzeiten oder Pilgerreisen soll hier also in erster Linie von Geschäftsreisen die Rede sein, denn aus dem maßgeblichen Anteil der Frauen am Darlehensgeschäft ist, wie ich annehme, auch auf ihre erhöhte Reisetätigkeit zu schließen.

In seinem für die jüdische Frauengeschichte des Spätmittelalters bahnbrechenden Artikel „Die jüdische Frau im Erwerbsleben des Spätmittelalters"[5] berechnete Michael Toch den Anteil von Frauen am jüdischen Darlehensgeschäft in Deutschland mit einem Viertel. Dieser hohe Prozentsatz zeigt sich sowohl aus dem gesamten für das Projekt Germania Judaica III gesammelten Quellenmaterial als auch in Mikrostudien einzelner jüdischer Wohnorte. Toch begründete diese überraschend intensive Geschäftstätigkeit außer mit der erzwungenen Monopolstellung der Geldleihe auch mit „weiteren Grundtatsachen jüdischen Lebens im Spätmittelalter. Die Geldleihe spielte sich (hauptsächlich) im heimischen Bereich ab; sie ließ sich mit der Führung des Haushalts kombinieren; es bestand kaum Bedrohung der weiblichen Ehre durch die Bewegung in der Fremde; …"[6]

Der genaueren Untersuchung dieser Aspekte ist dieser Beitrag gewidmet: Wenn Geldleihe im Spätmittelalter im Gegensatz zur Fernhandelstätigkeit im Frühmittelalter und den häufigen Messebesuchen in Handelsmetropolen in der Frühen Neuzeit kaum Mobilität verlangte, müßte diese Tatsache in gleichem Maße für Männer gelten[7]. In der Forschungsliteratur zur jüdischen Geldleihe wurde der praktischen

[3] Zur Mobilität der Bachurim siehe allgemein *Mordechai Breuer, Yacov Guggenheim,* Die jüdische Gemeinde, Gesellschaft und Kultur, in: GJ III/3, 2079–2138, hier 2110f. und Anm. 190; sowie *Israel J. Yuval*, A German-Jewish Autobiography of the Fourteenth Century, in: Jewish Intellectual History in the Middle Ages, hrsg. von *Joseph Dan*, Binah 3 (Westport Conn., London 1994) 79–99, bes. 86–90. Zu den Reisen zur „Horizonterweiterung" siehe *Michael Harbsmeier*, Reisen in der Diaspora. Eigenes in der Fremde in der jüdischen Reiseliteratur des Mittelalters, in: Fernreisen im Mittelalter, hrsg. von *Folker Reichert*, Das Mittelalter. Perspektiven mediävistischer Forschung, Zeitschrift des Mediävistenverbandes 3/2 (1998) 63–80 mit älterer Literatur S. 66, Anm. 4; im folgenden zitiert: *Harbsmeier*, Reisen.

[4] Zur großen Anzahl der Dienstboten in der jüdischen Bevölkerung siehe *Michael Toch*, Die jüdische Frau im Erwerbsleben des Spätmittelalters, in: *Julius Carlebach* (Hrsg.), Zur Geschichte der jüdischen Frau in Deutschland (Berlin 1993) 37–48, hier 40; im folgenden zitiert: *Toch*, Die jüdische Frau. Einige Einblicke in das Alltagsleben von Dienstboten gibt *Elliott Horowitz*, Jüdische Jugend in Europa: 1300–1800, in: Geschichte der Jugend, Bd. 1: Von der Antike bis zum Absolutismus, hrsg. von *Giovanni Levi, Jean-Claude Schmitt* (Frankfurt a. M. 1996) 113–165, bes. 143–150.

[5] *Toch*, Die jüdische Frau 40. Zu den Verhältnissen in Österreich siehe *Martha Keil*, Geschäftserfolg und Steuerschulden. Jüdische Frauen in österreichischen Städten des Spätmittelalters, in: Frauen in der Stadt, hrsg. von *Günther Hödl, Fritz Mayrhofer, Ferdinand Opll* (Linz 2003) 37–62, hier 38–42; im folgenden zitiert: *Keil*, Geschäftserfolg.

[6] *Toch*, Die jüdische Frau 44.

[7] Siehe dazu künftig *Wolfgang Treue*, In die *Jeschiwe* und auf den Jahrmarkt: Jüdische Mobilität in Aschkenas in der Frühen Neuzeit, in: Räume und Wege. Jüdische Geschichte im Alten Reich 1300–1800, hrsg. von *Rolf Kießling, Peter Rauscher, Stefan Rohrbacher, Barbara Staudinger* (Augsburg 2007) 191–205.

Durchführung von Geschäftsreisen bislang keine Aufmerksamkeit geschenkt, und in den allgemeinen Untersuchungen zum Reisen im Mittelalter stellten Motivation, Transportmittel, Zustand der Straßen und die Gefahren die Hauptthemen dar[8]. Daher kann eine Untersuchung des „Unterwegsseins" von Geldleiherinnen auch Erkenntnisse zum Berufsalltag von Männern bieten.

Die Anwendung des kulturell zugeschriebenen Geschlechts, Gender, als methodische Kategorie bringt im christlichen wie im jüdischen Bereich die Zuordnung von Mobilität zum Mann und von Stabilität zur Frau ins Wanken. Bei der Darstellung der Migration ganzer Familien ist der einseitige Fokus auf die meist männlichen Haushaltsvorstände für die Unsichtbarkeit der Frauen – und Kinder! – verantwortlich. Für die offensichtlichen Migrationsbewegungen alleinstehender Frauen, vor allem Witwen, in größere Städte, die höhere Chancen für berufliche Betätigung boten, bestanden vor der Entwicklung der Gender-Methode kein Interesse und keine Erklärungswerkzeuge, da die historische Forschung bis in die 1980er Jahre Frauenarbeit, so offensichtlich sie in den Quellen auch aufschien, kaum wahrnahm[9]. Die Verbindung von weiblicher Erwerbstätigkeit und damit verbundener Mobilität ist also auch in der Erforschung der christlichen Mehrheitsgesellschaft ein relativ neues Thema[10]. Katalin Szende untersuchte beispielsweise die Handelsaktivitäten in Sopron/Ödenburg (Westungarn), das nur eine Tagesreise von Wiener Neustadt entfernt – mit der zweitgrößten jüdischen Gemeinde Österreichs vor und der größten nach 1420 – an einem wichtigen Verkehrsknotenpunkt liegt. Die Soproner Kaufleute gehörten zur oberen Bürgerschicht, waren in der „Kramerzech" organisiert und hatten signifikanten Einfluß auf die Verwaltung der Stadt. Ihre Ehefrauen führten eigene Geschäfte durch und übernahmen als Witwen den Betrieb. Auch die weniger wohlhabenden Fragnerinnen und Hökerinnen genossen Eigenständigkeit und reisten zu Handelszwecken häufig alleine nach Wiener Neustadt[11].

Über die Tatsache, daß wie für andere Kaufmannsberufe auch für den Geldhandel ein gewisses Maß an Mobilität erforderlich war, scheint Konsens zu herrschen. Da sich, wie die zahlreichen erhaltenen Geschäftsurkunden und Einträge eindeutig zeigen, weibliche Geldleihe in keinem Merkmal von der männlichen unterschied, haben wir auch bei Frauen von einer erhöhten Reisetätigkeit auszugehen, welche

[8] Siehe zum Beispiel *Norbert Ohler*, Reisen im Mittelalter (München ^{4}2004); *Holger Th. Gräf, Ralf Pröve*, Wege ins Ungewisse. Reisen in der Frühen Neuzeit. 1500–1800 (Frankfurt a. M. 1997) und *Rainer Babel, Werner Paravicini* (Hrsg.), Grand Tour. Adeliges Reisen und europäische Kultur vom 14. bis zum 18. Jahrhundert (Beihefte der Francia 60, Stuttgart 2005).

[9] *Dorothee Rippmann, Katharina Simon-Muscheid*, Weibliche Lebensformen und Arbeitszusammenhänge im Spätmittelalter und in der frühen Neuzeit. Methoden, Ansätze und Postulate, in: *Mireille Othenin-Girard, Anna Gossenreiter, Sabine Trautweiler* (Hrsg.), Frauen und Öffentlichkeit (Beiträge der 6. Schweizer Historikerinnentagung, Zürich 1991) 63–98.

[10] *Grethe Jacobsen*, Female Migration and the Late Medieval Town, in: *Gerhard Jaritz, Albert Müller* (Hrsg.), Migration in der Feudalgesellschaft (Studien zur Historischen Sozialwissenschaft 8, Frankfurt a. M. 1988) 43–55; im folgenden zitiert: *Jacobsen*, Female Migration.

[11] *Katalin G. Szende*, Sopron (Ödenburg): A West-Hungarian Merchant Town on the Crossroad between East and West, in: Scripta Mercaturae 31/2 (1997) 29–49, hier 43.

sie über kürzere oder längere Zeit von ihren Pflichten im Haushalt fernhielt. Hier verstellt eventuell ein spätromantisch-bürgerlicher Blick die Beurteilung mittelalterlicher Lebensformen: Ob Frauen im Mittelalter zur Führung ihres Haushalts tatsächlich unabkömmlich waren, läßt sich schwer einschätzen, denn über ihren Arbeitsalltag ist, abgesehen von halachischen Problemen bezüglich Kaschrut und Pessach, nicht allzu viel in den Quellen zu finden. Vermutlich erleichterte in Mittel- und Oberschichthaushalten die Aufnahme von – nicht nur – weiblichen Verwandten und vor allem von Dienstpersonal, welches auch in Privilegien für Jüdinnen eingeschlossen war, die Haushaltsführung wesentlich[12]. Weitere Hinweise auf die Abwesenheit von Frauen geben die Warnungen von Raschi und anderen Autoritäten, Säuglinge nicht im Haus der Amme, sondern diese im eigenen Wohnhaus schlafen zu lassen oder zumindest bei Abwesenheit der Eltern das Haus der Amme regelmäßig durch andere Juden zu kontrollieren. Die Tosafisten zu Avoda Sara 26a sagen explizit, daß im Fall einer Jüdin, die „aus der Stadt hinausgeht" und ihr Kind bei einer nichtjüdischen Amme läßt, andere jüdische Frauen im Haus „ein- und ausgehen" sollten, um das Kind zu beaufsichtigen. Auch in der Nacht sollte es nicht mit der Amme alleine gelassen werden. Die in diesem Zusammenhang von Elisheva Carlebach zitierten Quellen behandeln die Sicherheit des Säuglings vor der Bedrohung durch eine christliche Amme und seine Bewahrung vor einer späteren Neigung zur Abtrünnigkeit. Es interessierte dabei nicht, daß hier eine jüdische Frau ihre „Mutterpflichten" versäumte und auch nicht der Grund für ihre sogar nächtliche Abwesenheit[13].

Informationen über mobile Frauen sind wie die obige oft in einem völlig anderen Kontext überliefert, und daher um so verläßlicher. Daß Frauen nicht nur zu Fuß unterwegs waren, sondern sehr wohl auch reiten konnten, belegt ein *Din* (Rechtsspruch) des Rabbiners Menachem Merseburg (letztes Drittel des 14. Jahrhunderts), welches die zur Steuerzahlung verpflichtende Mindestaufenthaltsdauer von 30 Tagen an einem Wohnort behandelt. Die *Parnassim* (Vorsteher) konnten einen fremden Juden, dessen Anwesenheit die Gemeinde vergrößerte und dadurch eventuell ihre Steuersumme erhöhte, zwingen, „... in dreißig Tagen wenigstens einmal mit allen seinen Hausgenossen für eine Übernachtung die Stadt zu verlassen, und auch wenn er nur für sich allein ist, soll er nicht dreißig aufeinanderfolgende Tage dort sein, sondern auch er soll manchmal weggehen und zu seinem Wohnsitz an den Ort seiner Hausgenossen kommen. Und wenn er behauptet, daß die Schwangerschaft seiner Frau ihn zwingt, ist das kein Argument, denn einige Frauen reiten noch im siebenten und achten Monat, und noch dazu nur für eine Übernachtung außerhalb der Stadtgrenzen, aber wenn die Vorsteher ihm erlauben,

[12] Zum Beispiel das Privileg für Scharlat von Görz, siehe *Martha Keil*, „Maistrin" und Geschäftsfrau. Jüdische Oberschichtfrauen im spätmittelalterlichen Österreich, in: Die jüdische Familie in Geschichte und Gegenwart, hrsg. von *Sabine Hödl, Martha Keil* (Berlin, Bodenheim bei Mainz 1999) 27–50, hier 33f.; im folgenden zitiert: *Keil*, Maistrin.

[13] *Elisheva Baumgarten*, Mothers and Children. Jewish Family Life in Medieval Europe (Princeton, Oxford 2004) 139–144, hier 140; im folgenden zitiert: *Baumgarten*, Mothers and Children.

seine Frau dort zu lassen, bis sie gebiert, dann wiegt kein Wille schwerer als dieser, denn wenn sie mit ihrer (der Vorsteher) Erlaubnis dort bleibt, ist das, als wäre sie hinausgegangen ...“[14]

Frauen benützten natürlich auch Reisewagen, unterlagen allerdings den Vorschriften der *Nida* (Separation) während der Zeiten kultischer Unreinheit: „Ein Mann darf mit seiner Frau auf einem Wagen fahren. Und so sagte mir ein Schüler in seinem (Israel Isserleins, Anm.) Namen, daß der Fürst Jakob Molin, das Andenken des Gerechten zum Segen, so gesagt hatte. Und umso mehr auf einem Boot mit ihr, aber sie dürfen einander nicht berühren. ... Und er (Israel Isserlein) schrieb in seinem Buch: Nur wenn ein Mann mit seiner Frau, die *Nida* ist, gemeinsam auf einem Wagen sitzt, der von Stadt zu Stadt fährt, ist es erlaubt, aber als „Liebesreise“ (oder: als Art des Vergnügens) auf einem Wagen, der sie zum Beispiel zu einem Garten bringt, um darin zu spazieren, nicht.“[15] Die Fahrt „von Stadt zu Stadt“ geschah also nicht zu Vergnügungszwecken, sondern aus geschäftlichen oder anderen Gründen.

Weibliche Geschäftstätigkeit

Im Laufe des Mittelalters erweiterten die rabbinischen Gelehrten das jüdische Recht in für Frauen günstige Ehe- und Erbrechtsbestimmungen. Sie konnten über Mitgift, Geschenke während der Ehe, Erbe und im Fall von unschuldiger Scheidung und Verwitwung in noch größerem Maße über die Eheverschreibungssumme (*Ketubba*) und das Geschäftskapital verfügen[16]. Dieses Maßnahmenbündel sicherte das Vermögen für die Kernfamilie und ermöglichte den Weiterbestand des Familienbetriebs, auch wenn die halbverwaisten Kinder noch minderjährig waren.

Die in den Quellen oft zu beobachtende bruchlose Geschäftsübernahme durch die Ehefrau nach dem Tod des Mannes läßt auf ihre intensive Mitarbeit im Betrieb

[14] Nimukei Morenu ha-Raw Menachem, in: *Jakob Weil*, Sche'elot u-Teschuwot, hrsg. von *Izchak Sela* (Venedig 1549, Nachdruck Jerusalem 1988) 167–176, hier 170, äußere Spalte, 3. Din (eigene Zählung); im folgenden zitiert: *Jakob Weil*, Sche'elot u-Teschuwot. Die nur bruchstückhaft erhaltenen Rechtssprüche dienten als Grundlage für die ausführlichen Steuergutachten Rabbi Israel Isserleins: *Israel Isserlein bar Petachja*, Sefer Terumat ha-Deschen ha-schalem. 1. Teil: Sche'elot u-Teschuwot, 2. Teil: Pesakim u-Khetawim, 3. Teil: Teschuwot Chadaschot, hrsg. von *Schmuel Abitan* (Jerusalem 1991), Terumat ha-Deschen 342–346; im folgenden zitiert: *Israel Isserlein bar Petachja*, Terumat ha-Deschen. Zu Menachem siehe GJ III/2, 867 und *Eric Zimmer*, R. Menachem Merseburg we-Nimukav (hebr.), Sinai 78 (1976) 75–88.

[15] *Josef Jossel bar Mosche*, Leket Joscher, hrsg. von *Jakob Freimann* (Berlin 1903, Nachdruck Jerusalem 1964) II, 23; im folgenden zitiert: Leket Joscher. *Israel Isserlein bar Petachja*, Terumat ha-Deschen Nr. 251.

[16] *Michael Toch*, Die Juden im mittelalterlichen Reich (Enzyklopädie deutscher Geschichte 44, München ^{2}2003) 14–16; *Keil*, Maistrin 28–30; *Birgit Klein*, „Der Mann – ein Fehlkauf“. Entwicklungen im Ehegüterrecht und die Folgen für das Geschlechterverhältnis im spätmittelalterlichen Aschkenas, in: Der Differenz auf der Spur. Frauen und Gender in Aschkenas, hrsg. von *Christiane E. Müller*, *Andrea Schatz* (Berlin 2004) 73–76.

schon zu seinen Lebzeiten schließen, obwohl sich diese selten in den Geschäftsurkunden niederschlägt. Ein seltenes Zeugnis für eine solche „unsichtbare" Mitarbeit ist die hebräische Quittung von Röslein, Frau des Häslein von Friesach. Sie bestätigte formelhaft, daß ihr Schwager „Schemarja, Sohn des geehrten Mordechai" – sein Rufname war Freudmann – ihr zwei Urkunden zur Aufbewahrung übergeben hatte:

„Ich, die unten Unterzeichnende, tue kund, daß Herr Schemarja, Sohn des geehrten Herrn Mordechai mir aus eigener Vollmacht zwei nichtjüdische (wörtlich: kultisch untaugliche) Schriftstücke vom Grafen von Ortenburg gegeben hat. Ein Schriftstück sagt 600 Gulden und ein Schriftstück sagt 100 Mark Agleier. Und das war am Sonntag, am 12. des Monats Tewet 128 nach der kleinen Zeitrechnung (5.12.1367). Rosa, Tochter des geehrten Herrn Izchak, seine Seele lebe im Paradies. Schalom, Sohn des Märtyrers Rabbi Jehuda, das Andenken des gerechten Märtyrers sei zum Segen."[17]

Rosa, sie war die Frau des prominenten Geldleihers Häslein von Friesach, trat, soweit bis jetzt bekannt, nicht mit eigenen Darlehensgeschäften hervor. Die Bitte ihres Schwagers, für ihn zwei Schuldurkunden aufzubewahren, läßt auf die Buchhaltung und Verwaltung des Geschäftsarchivs vielleicht der gesamten großen Bankiersfamilie – zwei weitere Brüder Häsleins gehörten zum Konsortium – schließen. Sichtlich konnte sie die deutsche Urkunde lesen und verstehen, und ihre vermutlich eigenhändig ausgestellte Bestätigung[18] zeigt ausreichende Kenntnisse der hebräischen Sprache und Schrift. Wie auch andere Frauen beherrschte sie also eine Art „Geschäftshebräisch", welches vermutlich zu ihrer Grundausbildung durch Vater, Brüder, Ehemann oder vielleicht sogar Mutter gehörte[19].

Die meisten Frauen traten erst nach dem Tod ihres Mannes wahrnehmbar in das Geschäftsleben ein. Manche gehörten sogar zu den Spitzenbankiers ihrer Zeit und verliehen an Stadträte, Adelige und Herrscher Summen zwischen tausend und

[17] Diese Bestätigung hängt laut Shelomo Spitzer an einer Urkunde von Schemarja Freudmann im Haus-, Hof- und Staatsarchiv Wien (künftig: HHStA) Allgemeine Urkundenreihe (künftig: AUR) 1368 Juli 15. Die richtige Datierung ist 16. Juli 1368, und leider ist der Zettel laut Dir. Leopold Auer vom HHStA nicht auffindbar. Maschinenschriftlich transkribiert und übersetzt in *Shelomo Spitzer*, Hebräische Urkunden des 14. Jahrhunderts aus Kärnten, in: Carinthia I, 174. Jg. (1984) 141–154, hier 146ff., Nr. 3, Transkription 153, sowie *ders.*, Hebrew Documents from Austria from the 14th Century (hebr.), in: Yearbook of the Bar Ilan University. Jewish Studies and Humanities 20–21 (1983) 192–213 mit denselben Angaben wie in der Carinthia. Schemarja, genannt Freudmann, ließ sich kurz darauf auf den Namen Paul taufen, siehe *Martha Keil*, „Petachja, genannt Zecherl": Namen und Beinamen von Juden im deutschen Sprachraum des Spätmittelalters, in: Personennamen und Identität, hrsg. von *Reinhard Härtel* (Grazer grundwissenschaftliche Forschungen 3, Schriftenreihe der Akademie Friesach 2, Graz 1997) 119–146, hier 144f.; im folgenden zitiert: *Keil*, Petachja, genannt Zecherl. Sein Vater Mordechai war wahrscheinlich der ab 1329 nachweisbare Merchel von Murau. Siehe *Wilhelm Wadl*, Geschichte der Juden in Kärnten im Mittelalter. Mit einem Ausblick bis zum Jahre 1867 (Das Kärntner Landesarchiv 9, Klagenfurt 1981) 193–209, dort die Urkunde mit richtiger Datierung, ohne Erwähnung des hebräischen Zettels; im folgenden zitiert: *Wadl*, Juden in Kärnten.

[18] Ein Handschriftenvergleich ist derzeit wegen der Unauffindbarkeit des Zettels nicht möglich.

[19] Siehe auch *Keil*, Geschäftserfolg 43–47.

zwölftausend Gulden. Aschkenasische Frauen eroberten sich im Laufe der Jahrhunderte ihrer Geschäftstätigkeit einen festen Platz in der Wirtschaft ihrer Lebensorte und Gesellschaften und nahmen diese Position auch an neue Wohnorte mit. Miriam Davide beobachtete für die jüdischen Gemeinden von Padua, Treviso, Triest und Friaul, daß die zugewanderten aschkenasischen Frauen weitaus aktiver und mobiler im Geschäftsleben waren als ihre italienischen Glaubensgenossinnen[20].

Um die Bedeutung dieser Frauen für ihre Gemeinden ein wenig zu veranschaulichen, seien die wichtigsten aschkenasischen Geldleiherinnen des 13. bis 15. Jahrhunderts kurz vorgestellt.

Mit wenigen Ausnahmen – die erste urkundlich erwähnte Jüdin in Österreich, Dreslina, lieh 1257 100 Pfund an den Propst von Klosterneuburg[21] – treten im 13. Jahrhundert im deutschen und österreichischen Raum noch kaum Geldleiherinnen namentlich in Erscheinung, was auch an der Überlieferungsgeschichte der Quellen liegt. In England war unter den 38 namentlich bekannten Geldleiherinnen neben Chera und Belia vor allem Licoricia von Winchester die herausragende Persönlichkeit. Für den Wiederaufbau der Westminster Abbey trug sie alleine 4000 Mark (2791 englische Pfund) bei, während die gesamte Judenschaft von England 170300 Pfund leistete[22]. Aktenkundig wurde sie nicht nur durch ihre hohen Darlehens- und Steuersummen und ihr geschäftliches Naheverhältnis zu König Heinrich III., sondern auch durch ihre Prozesse mit der Obrigkeit und ihr tragisches Ende durch Raubmord in ihrem Haus[23].

Im 14. Jahrhundert mehren sich die Urkunden von weiblichen Geldleiherinnen signifikant: Plume von Klosterneuburg kam um 1320 vermutlich aus Regensburg nach Klosterneuburg. Bereits ein Jahr später gewährte sie Otto, Abt von Zwettl, ein Darlehen von 100 Pfund[24]. In den folgenden Jahren versorgte sie die Wiener

[20] *Miriam Davide*, Il ruolo delle donne nelle comunità ebraiche dell'Italia nord orientale (Padova, Treviso, Trieste e Friuli), in: Ebrei nella Terraferma veneta del Quattrocento, hrsg. von *Gian Maria Varanini, Reinhold C. Mueller* (Quaderni di Reti Medievali 2, Florenz 2005) 31–43, hier 32 und *dies.*, Il ruolo economico delle donne nelle comunità ebraiche di Trieste e di Treviso nei secoli XIV e XV, in: Zakhor. Rivista di storia degli ebrei d'Italia VII (2004) Ebrei: demografia e storia 193–212.

[21] *Keil*, Maistrin 27.

[22] *Suzanne Bartlet*, Three Jewish Businesswomen in Thirteenth-Century Winchester, in: Jewish Culture and History 3/2 (2000) 31–54, hier 46; im folgenden zitiert: *Bartlet*, Three Jewish Businesswomen. Zu Licoricia siehe auch *Cheryl Tallan*, The Economic Productivity of Medieval Jewish Widows, in: Proceedings of the Eleventh World Congress of Jewish Studies, Div. B, Vol. 1 (Jerusalem 1993) 151–158, hier 154. Zu den bedeutenden Geldleiherinnen von York siehe kurz *Barrie Dobson*, The Medieval York Jewry Reconsidered, in: Jewish Culture and History 3,2 (2000) 7–20, hier 15f. und 20, Anm. 39 und 40; im folgenden zitiert: *Dobson*, The Medieval York Jewry.

[23] *Cheryl Tallan,* Structures of Power Available to Two Jewish Women in 13th Century England, in: Proceedings of the 12th World Congress of Jewish Studies, Div. B, History of the Jewish People (Jerusalem 1997) 85–90, hier 87f. Siehe auch *Bartlet*, Three Jewish Businesswomen 41f., 45–50, und *dies.*, Women in the Medieval Anglo-Jewish Community, in: The Jews in Medieval Britain: Historical, Literary, and Archaeological Perspectives, hrsg. von *Patricia Skinner* (Woodbridge 2003) 113–127, Literatur S. 114, Anm. 5.

[24] Stiftsarchiv Zwettl, Codex 7 (14. Jh.), fol. 6r. Zu Plume und ihrer berühmten Familie siehe *Klaus Lohrmann*, Gemeinde – Haushalt – Familie. Die Bedeutung der Familie in der jüdischen Gemeinde des Mittelalters, in: *Sabine Hödl, Martha Keil* (Hrsg.), Die jüdische Familie in Geschichte und

und Klosterneuburger Bürgerschaft mit Krediten und erarbeitete sich einen adeligen Kundenkreis. Im August 1335 versprachen die österreichischen Herzöge Albrecht II. und Otto dem Jans Turs von Rauheneck, statt der Bezahlung von 300 Pfund für Kriegsdienste seine Schulden bei Plume zu übernehmen[25]. Von hohen Darlehen an Eberhard und Heinrich von Walsee-Drosendorf erfahren wir indirekt aus einer Schuldentilgung durch Albrecht II. Plume mußte sich mit einer – sicher nur teilweisen – Rückzahlung von 800 Pfund zufrieden geben[26]. Ihr Sohn Abraham, genannt Hendlein, war Rabbiner und ging Geschäften mit nur geringen Summen nach. Plume baute ihr Unternehmen weiter aus und übergab es in den 1340er Jahren ihrem Enkel David Steuss, der zum bedeutendsten Finanzier des Hauses Habsburg werden sollte[27].

Reynette von Koblenz war nach dem Tod ihres ersten Mannes Leo von Münstermaifeld beinahe 30 Jahre, zwischen 1365 und 1394, die führende Geldleiherin zwischen Bonn und Bingen am Rhein. 1373 schuldete ihr die Stadt Andernach 8000 Gulden, ein Teil der Rückzahlung erfolgte in Wein[28]. Auch Erzbischof Adolf I. von Nassau, dem Reynette mit ihren Krediten seine Machtkämpfe finanzierte, war bei ihr hoch verschuldet. Für einen Kredit von mehreren tausend Gulden erhielt sie Einkünfte aus dem Zoll von Oberlahnstein als Pfand. Ihre zweite Ehe mit dem Gelehrten Moses ben Jakob Bonenfant minderte ihre Geschäftstätigkeit keineswegs, er nannte sich sogar bisweilen „Ich Moisse, Reynetten man". Zwar übernahm er den Koblenzer Moselzoll für jährlich 2200 Gulden, doch vermutlich nur *pro forma*, weil die Verpfändung derartiger Hoheitsrechte an eine Frau doch die Möglichkeiten der Zeit überstieg[29]. Reynette benützte, eher selten bei Juden und noch mehr bei Jüdinnen, ein Siegel, jedoch kein eigenes, sondern das ihrer beiden Ehemänner[30].

Gegenwart (Berlin u.a.1999) 9–26, hier 15ff. und *ders.*, Die Juden im mittelalterlichen Klosterneuburg, in: *Floridus Röhrig* (Hrsg.), Klosterneuburg. Geschichte und Kultur Bd. 1: Die Stadt (Klosterneuburg, Wien 1992) 209–223, hier 216. Zu Plumes Hauptschuldnern, den Grafen von Walsee-Drosendorf, siehe auch *ders.*, Judenrecht und Judenpolitik im mittelalterlichen Österreich (Wien, Köln 1990) 275f.; im folgenden zitiert: *Lohrmann*, Judenrecht.

[25] HHStA AUR 1335 August 24. Regest: *Meir Wiener* (Bearb.), Regesten zur Geschichte der Juden in Deutschland während des Mittelalters Bd. 1 (Hannover 1862) 221, Nr. 28; im folgenden zitiert: *Wiener*, Regesten.

[26] HHStA AUR 1339 Dezember 24. Regest: *Wiener*, Regesten 1, 222, Nr. 36; *Lohrmann*, Judenrecht 136 und 275.

[27] Siehe zu ihm GJ III/3, 1985; *Lohrmann*, Judenrecht 211–216, und *ders.*, Die Wiener Juden im Mittelalter (Berlin, Wien 2000) 186 (Register).

[28] *Franz-Josef Ziwes*, Reynette – eine jüdische Geldhändlerin im spätmittelalterlichen Koblenz, in: Koblenzer Beiträge zur Geschichte und Kultur 4 (1994) 25–40, hier 32.

[29] Ebd. 36. GJ III/1, 627, Nr. 6. Siehe auch *Toch*, Die jüdische Frau 41. Zu ihrer Tochter aus erster Ehe, Mede, siehe *Franz-Josef Ziwes*, Die jüdische Gemeinde im mittelalterlichen Koblenz – „Yre gude ingesessen burgere", in: Geschichte der Stadt Koblenz. Von den Anfängen bis zum Ende der kurfürstlichen Zeit (Stuttgart 1992) 247–257 und 508, hier 256. Zum Zoll s. den Beitrag von *Wenninger* in diesem Band.

[30] *Daniel Friedenberg*, Medieval Jewish Seals from Europe (Detroit 1987) 224; im folgenden zitiert: *Friedenberg*, Jewish Seals.

Jentlin oder Gentlin von Konstanz, Tochter des Lazarus, war 1413 gemeinsam mit anderen Juden von König Sigmund privilegiert worden und besaß ein Haus in Konstanz. Ihre Hauptgeschäftstätigkeit fiel zwischen ca. 1420–1430. Als sie 1428 in zweiter Ehe den ebenfalls bedeutenden Geldleiher und Rabbiner Seligmann ehelichte, zog dieser an ihren Wohnort, und nicht etwa umgekehrt. Von den im Konstanzer Amman-Gerichtsbuch verzeichneten 31 jüdischen Geldleihenden waren immerhin neun Frauen, also beinahe ein Drittel, unter denen Gentlin – hier „Jentli" geschrieben – die führende war. 1425 leistete sie von der Gesamtsumme der Judensteuer von 253 Gulden alleine 60 Gulden[31].

Die große und bedeutende *Kehilla* von Frankfurt bot mehreren Frauen die Chance zu einer überdurchschnittlichen Geschäftstätigkeit. Zorline von Frankfurt, etwa zwischen 1380 und 1395 aktiv, war auch als Ehefrau von Fifelin von Dieburg und danach Süßkind von Weinburg die reichste und aktivste Geldleiherin der Stadt. Auch zu ihren Schuldnern gehörte Erzbischof Adolf I. von Nassau, 1388 mit einer Summe von 1000 Gulden. 1391 betrugen ihre ausständigen Darlehen sechzig Prozent aller Außenstände von 31 Frankfurter Geldleihern[32].

Eva (Hebe oder Hefe), nach ihrem Hauszeichen „zum Buchsbaum" genannt, lebte mit kurzer Unterbrechung von 1401 bis zu ihrem Tod 1452 in der Stadt. Als Mutter der Rabbiner Natan ha-Lewi und Semel war sie Stammutter der Gelehrtendynastie „von Eppstein"[33]. Obwohl verheiratet, agierte sie als selbständige Geschäftsfrau und trug 1430 zur Hussitensteuer der Frankfurter Juden in der Höhe von 300 Gulden zusätzliche 150 bei[34]. Wie andere jüdische Geschäftsfrauen, denen ihre hohe Steuerleistung Ansehen und Macht in der Gemeinde verschaffte, vertrat sie, bereits Witwe, gemeinsam mit dem Schwiegervater ihres Sohnes Natan, Smohel von Augsburg (auch: von Emmerich), ihre Gemeinde in Verhandlungen mit König Albrecht II. über den Dritten Pfennig anläßlich seiner Krönung. Während die Juden wegen der über sie verhängten Reichsacht die Stadt verlassen mußten und sich in der Grafschaft Hanau niederließen, konnten sich Eva und Smohel zwischen 1. Mai und 3. Dezember 1439 als Unterhändler in Frankfurt aufhalten und die Verhandlungen unter Vorauszahlung der geforderten Summe zu Ende führen[35]. An-

[31] GJ III/1, 668 mit Anm. 95–98. Privileg König Sigmunds in *Heymann Chone*, Zur Geschichte der Juden in Konstanz, in: Zeitschrift für die Geschichte der Juden in Deutschland (ZGJD) 6 (1936) Nr. 1, 3–16, hier 13; zu den Geldleihern und Steuern siehe 3 und 7, Anm. 13. Allerdings rechnet er die Darlehen des Ehepaares bereits ab 1423 zusammen, obwohl Seligmann erst ab 1428 im Amtmann-Gerichtsbuch erscheint (GJ III/1, 672, Anm. 98). Die Geschäfte der Jahre davor bestritt Gentil also alleine; siehe ebd. 4.

[32] GJ III/1, 349 mit Anm. 160 und 367, Nr. 60; *Toch*, Die jüdische Frau 40.

[33] GJ III/1, 360, Nr. 10 und 363f., Nr. 39.

[34] *Dietrich Andernacht*, Regesten zur Geschichte der Juden in der Reichsstadt Frankfurt am Main von 1401–1519 (Forschungen zur Geschichte der Juden, Abt. B: Quellen, Band 1, 1. Teil, Hannover 1996) 103, Nr. 359 (1430 August 26); im folgenden zitiert: *Andernacht*, Regesten.

[35] GJ III/1, 367. *Andernacht*, Regesten I/1, 152, Nr. 544; 155f., Nr. 558; 157f., Nr. 565; 158f., Nr. 570 (Unterhändlerin); 159f., Nr. 573–575. In ebda. 238f., Nr. 915 (1450 Juli 14) wird Susse, die Witwe des Smohel Emmerich als Schwiegermutter Natans von Eppstein bezeichnet; siehe auch 239, Nr. 916 und GJ III/1, 366, Nr. 55.

läßlich der von den Juden geforderten Ablösung verschiedener Dienste beim Empfang von König Friedrich IV. im Sommer 1442 führten wiederum Eva zum Buchsbaum und Smohel von Augsburg die Verhandlungen mit dem Rat und dem königlichen Gesandten[36].

Ricke, die kurz nach Evas Ableben in Erscheinung trat, ist von 1457 bis zu ihrem Tod zwischen 1471 und 1473 mit einer zweijährigen Unterbrechung in Frankfurt nachweisbar. In der ersten Erwähnung besiegelte sie gemeinsam mit einem Juden namens Saul ihren Verzicht auf alle Ansprüche an Erzbischof Dietrich von Mainz, nachdem sie wegen Zollvergehens in Haft gesessen hatte. Daß der Bürgermeister von Frankfurt, Heinrich Katzmann, für sie bürgte, weist auf eine bereits früher bestehende Ansiedlung in Frankfurt mit entsprechenden Leistungen hin[37]. Im Jahr 1464, bereits Witwe, bezahlte sie den höchsten Einzelzins einer Stättigkeit, nämlich 75 Gulden, knapp gefolgt von Evas zum Buchsbaum Enkel Jakob Eppstein, genannt „der fette Jakob", mit 72 Gulden[38]. Von ihr ist ein für Juden allgemein und vor allem für Frauen überaus seltenes Dokument erhalten, nämlich ein deutschsprachiges Testament, verfaßt am 9. November 1470. Es wurde, da nur von drei Ratsherren mit dem „kleinen" Stadtsiegel beglaubigt, in den sogenannten „Minor-Währschaftsbüchern" aufbewahrt, die auch Testamente von Christen und alle Arten von Besitzverfügungen enthalten. Daß Rickes Testament als einziges jüdisches aufgenommen wurde, spricht für ihre starke Stellung auch innerhalb der christlichen Gemeinde. Leider enthält es kein Inventar, doch sind Gold, Silber, Kleinode und auch Bücher in ihrem Besitz erwähnt. Zweck der Verfügung war die Versorgung ihres Enkels Isak, welcher als Vollwaise vermutlich bei ihr im Haus gelebt hatte. Sie bestellte außer dessen zweiter Großmutter Fromet auch den Gelehrten Simon Katz von Mainz zum Vormund, welcher zunächst Assistent an der Jeschiwa des Mosche Minz war und Ende der 1450er Jahre eine eigene Jeschiwa unterhielt. Für ihre Pflichten erhielten die *truwenhendere* freie Kost und Logis und zehn bzw. fünfzig Gulden jährliche Unterstützung[39].

Im Herzogtum Steiermark übernahm Sara, genannt Gutlein, Isserleins Witwe von Wiener Neustadt, die hochkarätigen Darlehensgeschäfte von ihrem Mann –

[36] *Andernacht*, Regesten I/1, 188, Nr. 685 und 686; 189, Nr. 690; 190, Nr. 693–695. Reichstagsakten (RTA) Bd. 16: Unter Friedrich III. 2. Abt., 1. Hälfte 1441–1442, hrsg. von *Hermann Herre* (Gotha 1921) 367f., Nr. 194, Anm. 1 (1442 Juni 21): Der Rat von Frankfurt schrieb an Walter von Schwarzenberg dem Älteren, daß bei ihnen „Smohel und Heffe, unsere Judenburgere", wegen der Zahlung von 800 Gulden gewesen seien. Siehe auch ebda. 665, Nr. 289 (1442 Juli 21).

[37] *Andernacht*, Regesten I/1, 285, Nr. 1120 (1457 Juli 3); die Urkunde ist nur in Abschrift im Mainzer Ingrossaturbuch vorhanden.

[38] GJ III/1, 364, Nr. 41; *Andernacht*, Regesten I/1, 262, Nr. 1422 (1464 Juli 28).

[39] *Isidor Kracauer*, Ein jüdisches Testament aus dem Jahre 1470, in: Monatsschrift für Geschichte und Wissenschaft des Judentums (MGWJ) 60, Heft 4 (1916) 295–301, die Abschrift des Testaments 298–301. Zu Schimon von Mainz siehe GJ III/2, 804f., Nr. 50 und GJ III/1, 365f., Nr. 51. Einen Beleg der dort erwähnten Angabe, Schimon sei Rickes Schwiegersohn gewesen, habe ich nicht gefunden. Zu seiner Gelehrtentätigkeit siehe auch Leket Joscher, Einleitung LI, Nr. 132. Ricke ernannte allerdings Isak, Sohn des Lazarus von Gehingen, zum Vermögensverwalter, *Kracauer*, ebd. 299.

nicht mit dem gleichnamigen Rabbiner verwandt – , der aus der weitverzweigten Dynastie des Werach von Wiener Neustadt stammte[40]. Im Februar 1479 kämpfte sie an der Spitze ihrer Schwiegersöhne mit Graf Jörg von Pottendorf um die Rückzahlung von insgesamt 6812 Gulden. Pfand für diese gewaltige Summe war Herrschaft und Markt Kirchschlag im südlichen Niederösterreich (ca. 30 km von Wiener Neustadt entfernt), welche bereits eineinhalb Jahre zuvor, im September 1477, für 1100 Gulden an ihren Mann versetzt worden war. Vermutlich waren zu diesen alten Ausständen neue hinzugekommen. Ob und auf welche Weise Sara tatsächlich Herrschaftsrechte in Kirchschlag ausübte, ist nicht bekannt und aufgrund des Judenrechts auch kaum wahrscheinlich[41].

Maßgebliche Wirtschaftstätigkeit führte zwangsläufig zu einem signifikanten Steuerbeitrag, der auch Frauen, die ansonsten von den Machtpositionen in der jüdischen Gemeindeverwaltung ausgeschlossen waren, Positionen von einigem politischen Einfluß verschaffte. Selbstverständlich waren solche Erscheinungen die Ausnahme, und sie änderten das grundsätzliche Machtgefälle zwischen den Geschlechtern nicht, doch diese Beispiele zeigen, daß die ökonomische Tätigkeit die herkömmlichen Gender-Zuschreibungen aufheben konnte. Auf dem Gebiet des heutigen Österreich läßt sich nur ein solcher Beleg finden, nämlich Seld von Radkersburg, welche 1338 für die inneren Steuern ihrer Gemeinde verantwortlich war[42]. Ab 1336 war Nenneke von Dortmund gemeinsam mit ihrem Gatten Johel für die Anordnung der Gräber auf dem dortigen jüdischen Friedhof zuständig, im Falle des Ablebens eines Ehepartners sollte der bzw. die andere diese Aufgabe alleine weiterführen[43].

Wie schon bei Eva zum Buchsbaum in Frankfurt am Main festgestellt, prädestinierte eine führende wirtschaftliche Stellung Frauen zur Vertretung ihrer Gemeinden bei finanziellen Verhandlungen: 1480 führte Gutrat, die Schwester von Mayr Schalmann und nach ihm auch die „Schalmannin" genannt, dem reichsten Geldhändler von Regensburg, mit einer weiteren Frau namens Bela und einem gewissen Wolffel die Verhandlungen mit Kaiser Friedrich III. zur Freilassung der 17 von der

[40] Zum Stammbaum der Familie siehe *Martha Keil*, Der Liber Judeorum von Wr. Neustadt (1453–1500) – Edition, in: Studien zur Geschichte der Juden in Österreich, hrsg. von *Martha Keil*, *Klaus Lohrmann* (Wien, Köln, Weimar 1994) 41–99, hier 97.

[41] HHStA AUR 1477 September 15 und 1479 Februar 12.

[42] *Eveline Brugger*, *Birgit Wiedl*, Regesten zur Geschichte der Juden in Österreich im Mittelalter. Bd.1: Von den Anfängen bis 1338 (Innsbruck, Wien, Bozen 2005) hier 342f., Nr.446; *Keil*, Geschäftserfolg 61f.; *dies.*, Namhaft im Geschäft – unsichtbar in der Synagoge: die jüdische Frau im spätmittelalterlichen Aschkenas, in: Europas Juden im Mittelalter. Beiträge des internationalen Symposiums in Speyer, 20.–25. Oktober 2002, hrsg. v. *Christoph Cluse* (Trier 2004) 344–354, hier 347; im folgenden zitiert: *Keil*, Namhaft im Geschäft. Erwähnt, aber den Kontext nicht erkannt bei *Hermann Kurahs*, Zur Geschichte der Juden in Radkersburg, in: Jüdisches Leben in der Steiermark. Marginalisierung, Auslöschung, Annäherung, hrsg. von *Gerald Lamprecht* (Innsbruck, Wien, München, Bozen 2004) 59–91, hier 59; Germania Judaica II: Von 1238 bis zur Mitte des 14. Jahrhunderts, hrsg. von *Zvi Avneri* (Tübingen 1968) 672.

[43] *Bernhard Brilling*, *Helmut Richtering* (Hrsg.), Westfalia Judaica 1 (Stuttgart ^{2}1992) 109, Nr.102–103 (beide 1336 Januar 26). *Keil*, Namhaft im Geschäft 347.

Stadt Regensburg im Zuge des Ritualmordprozesses 1476–1480 in Gefangenschaft genommenen Juden; darunter befand sich auch ihr Bruder. Zu diesem Zweck reiste sie mit kaiserlichem Geleit mehrmals nach Wien, ein prominenter Anlaß für die Mobilität von jüdischen Frauen[44]. Regensburg ist die einzige Stadt, in der, sogar zweimal, eine Frau im Kreis der Vorsteher genannt ist: 1354 wurde Kaendlein, Witwe des Mosche aus Grez (südlich von Regensburg) vom Stadtrat beauftragt, den Steueranteil der hinzugezogenen fremden Juden festzusetzen. Sie war selbst erst drei Jahre in der Stadt und hatte sich sehr rasch eine führende Position verschafft, was sich in ihrer Steuerleistung von 60 Pfund jährlich gegenüber 23 Pfund Durchschnittsleistung der anderen Juden niederschlug. Ein Jahr später nahm Kaendlein im Namen der Gemeinde von Regensburg als Erstgenannte mit fünf weiteren Judenvorstehern eine Anzahl von neuen Mitgliedern auf. Kaendlein fiel spätestens 1365 im eigenen Haus einem Mordanschlag zum Opfer[45].

Zwanzig Jahre nach Kaendleins erster Nennung als Steuerverwalterin versprachen am 3. März 1374 die zwölf Vorsteher der Judengemeinde, von ihren Auswanderungsplänen Abstand zu nehmen und die Stadt in den nächsten zwölf Jahren nicht zu verlassen. Alle hatten darüber einen schweren Eid auf die Tora geschworen und mit ungewöhnlichen Selbstverfluchungen, wie nicht mehr Juden sein, Schweinefleisch essen und Christenwein trinken zu wollen, bekräftigt. An vorletzter Stelle der zwölf ist „ich Joseppine" gereiht, in eindeutiger Funktion einer *Parnesset* (Vorsteherin) – in weiblicher Form existiert das Wort allerdings nicht[46]. Die Frage, warum ausgerechnet in Regensburg Frauen derart gehäuft in Machtpositionen anzutreffen sind und ob dabei der auf mehrere christliche Obrigkeiten verteilte Judenschutz eine Rolle spielt, ist noch nicht geklärt und wurde in der Forschungsliteratur auch noch nicht gestellt. Nach bisheriger Durchsicht der Urkundenbücher sind unter den Mitgliedern des christlichen Rates, der Genannten und den städtischen Zeugen jedenfalls keine Frauen zu finden.

[44] Ihr Geleitbrief vom 26. Juni 1480 „für ein ganzes Jahr" in *Wiener*, Regesten 173, Nr. 511 (1480 Juni 26). Zu ihren Konflikten mit der Gemeinde siehe *Keil*, Namhaft im Geschäft 348. Zum Ritualmordprozess siehe GJ III/ 2, 1200.

[45] *Franz Bastian, Josef Widemann* (Bearb.), Regensburger Urkundenbuch Bd. 2: Urkunden der Stadt 1351–1378 (Monumenta Boica 54, München 1956) 45, Nr. 117 (1354 September 6: Festsetzung der Steuern); 63, Nr. 160 (1355 August 15–24: Zuständigkeit Kaendleins bei der Steuereinnahme); 66, Nr. 166 (1355 September 16: Aufnahme von David von Herzogenburg und anderen); 83, Nr. 196 (1356 Juni 8: Aufnahme von Aron von Prag); 134, Nr. 310 (1358 Oktober 8: Steuerleistungen); 275, Nr. 628 (1365 August 18: Erwähnung von Kaendleins Ermordung); im folgenden zitiert: Regensburger Urkundenbuch. GJ III/2, 1191, Nr. 13 (Hanna) erwähnt nur ihre Funktion bei der Steuereinnahme.

[46] Regensburger Urkundenbuch 2, 411, Nr. 1038: Die Selbstverfluchung lautet: „Und sol auch dann unser dheiner nymmer ein jud sein noch heizzen, wir noch alle unser erben noch geslachtt. Und was wir dann fleyschs ymmer verzirn, wir, unsere chint und nachkommen, daz daz sweynein fleischs sey, und allen den wein, den wir trinchen, dieweil wir leben, unserew chind und nachkomen, daz daz sey christenwein, gezogen auz einem zapfen uns und christenmenschen." In GJ III/2, 1171, ist Joseppine nicht erwähnt.

Als Beispiel für die Tatsache, daß manche jüdische Geschäftsfrauen wie weibliche Angehörige des christlichen Adels und Patrizierstandes Siegel führten, wurde bereits Reynette von Koblenz genannt, welche allerdings dasjenige ihrer beiden Ehemänner benutzte. Dislub oder Dislaba bat Mosche – ihr Name läßt auf eine böhmisch-mährische Herkunft schließen – besaß zwei hebräische Siegel, die sie 1391 alleine und 1398 gemeinsam mit ihrem Mann Saadja bar Morenu ha-Raw Elieser benutzte[47]. Wie Andrea Stieldorf feststellte, führten auch in der christlichen Gesellschaft weitaus weniger Frauen als Männer ein Siegel, und es bestanden lokale Unterschiede und Rechtsbräuche[48]. Der Anteil von Juden war ohnehin gering, und der entsprechende weibliche Prozentsatz noch marginaler. Im jüdischen Urkundenwesen diente allerdings ein Siegel mehr der Repräsentation als der rechtlichen Absicherung, diese geschah durch die eigenhändige hebräische Unterschrift, deren Bezeichnung *Chatima* den Rechtsvorgang des Siegelns, *Chatam*, beinhaltet. Allerdings schien auch dies vom örtlichen *Minhag* abzuhängen: Aus Territorien, wo hebräische Beglaubigungen an deutschen Urkunden relativ häufig anzutreffen sind, wie zum Beispiel im Herzogtum Steiermark, sind einige von Frauen unterschriebene Urkunden erhalten. Auch Henna, Witwe des Aron von York (um 1270) unterschrieb Hebräisch, ihre Zeit- und Ortsgenossin Belassez besaß sogar die Kenntnisse, Urkunden und Siegel zu fälschen, oder sie wurden ihr zumindest zugetraut[49].

Wie ihre männlichen Berufskollegen blieben auch die Geldleiherinnen nicht von Gewalttaten verschont, waren sie nun obrigkeitlich „gerechtfertigt" oder ungesetzliche Verbrechen. Wie erwähnt preßten die „Schutzherren" Licoricia von Winchester und Ricke von Frankfurt für deren Freilassung aus dem Gefängnis hohe Summen ab. Letztere saß wegen angeblichen Zollvergehens in Höchst in Haft und verzichtete als Gegenleistung auf alle Ansprüche an Erzbischof Dietrich von Mainz[50]. Auch Plume von Klosterneuburg mußte sich eine Schuldentilgung in nicht überlieferter Höhe gefallen lassen – ihr blieben 800 Pfund, die ursprüngliche Summe war also garantiert um ein Vielfaches höher –, und Eva zum Buchsbaum zahlte im Februar 1439 für die Freilassung ihrer Söhne aus der Haft – angeblich hatten sie Hehlerei mit Kirchengut begangen – die enorme Summe von 1100 Pfund. Ihre Schwiegersöhne wurden des Geschlechtsverkehrs mit „Christen-

[47] *Friedenberg*, Jewish Seals 198f., Nrn. 95 und 96, mit Abb. Siegelbild sind Blume und Rosette bzw. Mond und Stern, siehe auch *Martha Keil*, Ein Regensburger Judensiegel des 13. Jahrhunderts. Zur Interpretation des Siegels des Peter bar Mosche haLevi, in: Aschkenas, Zeitschrift für Geschichte und Kultur der Juden 1 (1991) 135–150, hier 143, Anm. 41. Auch Dislubs Mann Saadja besaß neben einem deutschen zwei hebräische Siegel, siehe *Friedenberg*, ebda. 196f., Nrn. 92–94. Zum Namen Dislub siehe *Alexander Beider*, A Dictionary of Ashkenazic Given Names. Their Origins, Structure, Pronunciation, and Migrations (Bergenfield, New Jersey 2001) 581 (Tislave).

[48] *Andrea Stieldorf*, Rheinische Frauensiegel. Zur rechtlichen und sozialen Stellung weltlicher Frauen im 13. und 14. Jahrhundert (Rheinisches Archiv 142, Wien, Köln 1999) 67, 140f.

[49] Siehe *Keil*, Petachja, genannt Zecherl 138–141 und *dies.*, Geschäftserfolg 43–47. Zu York siehe *Dobson*, The Medieval York Jewry 16.

[50] *Andernacht*, Regesten I/1, 285, Nr. 1120, 1457 Juli 3. Nicht erwähnt in GJ III/1, 364, Nr. 41.

weibern“ bezichtigt[51]. Licoricia von Winchester und Kaendlein von Regensburg fielen, wie bereits erwähnt, einem Raubmord im eigenen Haus zum Opfer. Auch in Friedberg wurde eine nicht genannte Jüdin in ihrem Haus ermordet aufgefunden. Der Rat von Friedberg fahndete nach einer Frau, die bei dem Opfer Pfänder stehen und bei ihr übernachtet hatte[52].

Reisen und Gefahren

Reisen zu Geschäftspartnern, seien sie zu Vorverhandlungen, zum Geschäftsabschluß, zur Schuldeintreibung oder Neuverhandlung bei Nichtzahlung, wurden von Männern wie von Frauen ebenso unternommen wie zum Aufsuchen des Gerichtsstandortes oder des Hoftags. Studienreisen lagen, wie erwähnt, nicht in der Möglichkeit von Frauen, doch ist nicht auszuschließen, daß auch Mädchen zum Zweck der Ausbildung etwa als Ärztin, Hebamme oder Geschäftsfrau zu Verwandten oder Bekannten reisten. Die Flucht vor einem unerträglichen Ehemann und die Rückkehr in das Elternhaus nach Verstoßung oder Scheidung konnte zuweilen ebenfalls ein Motiv weiblicher Mobilität sein[53].

Die größte Motivation zu reisen stellten für Christinnen die regionalen und überregionalen Wallfahrten, hauptsächlich zur Einlösung von Gelübden nach Krisensituationen, dar. Die relativ kurzen Wege, vor allem zu nahe der Städte gelegenen Marienheiligtümern, waren in einem Tag zu bewältigen und brachten eine willkommene Abwechslung und anregende Gesellschaft in den Alltag von Städterinnen. Dorfbewohnerinnen blieb die Möglichkeit dieser akzeptierten Vergnügungen jedoch verwehrt[54]. Auch Jüdinnen leisteten in Krisenzeiten Gelübde und pilgerten zu den Gräbern von Vorfahren und „Heiligen“ oder „Gerechten“, also Märtyrern oder berühmten Rabbinern. Das folgende Responsum Maharils an Elchanan Katz erwähnt zwei Anlässe für das Unterwegssein einer jüdischen Frau, eine Wallfahrt nach Gelübde und eine Geschäftsreise: „Es geschah einer Frau, die gelobt hatte, zu den Gräbern der Gerechten (*Zadikim*) nach Regensburg zu reisen, und sie war viele Tage verhindert, und dann geschah es, daß sie ohnehin dorthin

[51] Zu Plume siehe Anm. 24; zu Eva siehe *Andernacht*, Regesten I/1, 138, Nr. 488; 145, Nr. 514 und Nr. 534; 168, Nr. 607.

[52] *Andernacht*, Regesten I/1, 119, Nr. 415 (1433 Mai 25).

[53] *Jacobsen*, Female Migration 48; *Avraham Grossman*, Medieval Rabbinic Views on Wife Beating, 800–1300, in: Jewish History 5 (1991) 53–62.

[54] *Gabriela Signori*, Ländliche Zwänge – Städtische Freiheiten? Weibliche Mobilität und Geselligkeit im Spiegel spätmittelalterlicher Marienwallfahrten, in: *Mireille Othenin-Girard, Anna Gossenreiter, Sabine Trautweiler* (Hrsg.), Frauen und Öffentlichkeit (Beiträge der 6. Schweizer Historikerinnentagung, Zürich 1991) 29–45. Die Wallfahrten standen in engem Zusammenhang mit dem weiblichen Lebenszyklus, vor allem mit Schwangerschaft und Geburt, hier 33, 37, 43f. Zur weiblichen „Wallfahrtsgeselligkeit“ siehe 42f. Tagesreisen umfaßten eine Entfernung von etwa 30 km, siehe *Christian Krötzl*, Wallfahrt und „Ferne“, in: Wallfahrt und Alltag in Mittelalter und Früher Neuzeit. Internationales Round-Table-Gespräch Krems an der Donau 8. 10. 1990 (Wien 1992) 221–235, hier 232. Seine Quellen stammen hauptsächlich aus dem Norden Europas.

reisen mußte, und Maharil wurde gefragt, ob ihr Gelübde durch diese Reise erfüllt sei."[55] Israel Isserlein gelobte ebenfalls, zu den „Gräbern der Väter" nach Regensburg zu reisen. Man schloß daraus die Herkunft seiner Familie aus Regensburg, was auch der dort belegte, ansonsten seltene Name Petachja nahelegt, doch ist es auch gut möglich, daß er, wie Elchanans Frau, die Gräber der von ihm verehrten und rezipierten „Chasside Aschkenas" besuchen wollte. Aufgrund einer zweiten Erkrankung mußte er sich von seinem Gelübde lösen lassen und zahlte dafür die hohe Summe von 100 Pfund Wiener für die Armen[56].

Wie die männlichen Pilger unternahmen auch die Frauen beider Religionen die strapaziöse Reise nach Jerusalem. Die Motivation lag im Glauben an die Heiligkeit des Landes und seine besondere Kraft zur Erfüllung von Bitten sowie im vergangenen oder zukünftigen Erscheinen des Messias. Die Präsenz der Stadt Jerusalem in Architektur, Literatur, Frömmigkeitsriten, Andachtsorten wie dem Kalvarienberg und Symbolik war vor allem seit den Kreuzzügen in einer mittelalterlichen Stadt allgegenwärtig, in Kirchen wie in Synagogen. Auch Frauen trugen zu dieser Vergegenwärtigung tatkräftig bei, wie die Görlitzer Witwe George Fingerlin, welche im Gefolge des Herzogs von Sachsen eine Pilgerreise unternahm und die Heiligen Stätten vermessen ließ[57]. Jerusalem war der Sehnsuchtsort männlicher und weiblicher Spiritualität und die Pilgerfahrt dorthin höchster Ausdruck von Frömmigkeit. Berühmte Mystikerinnen wie Birgitta von Schweden (1302–1373) und Margaret Kempe (1373–1438) waren unter den Wallfahrerinnen und nahmen ihre Eindrücke in ihren Büchern auf. Sie verstießen damit allerdings gegen das Ideal der *castitas*, das Pendant zur jüdischen *Zniut*, welches für fromme Frauen und vor allem Nonnen ein Leben in häuslicher Abgeschiedenheit bzw. hinter Klostermauern vorsah. Tatsächlich gingen, soweit bekannt, keine Nonnen auf Jerusalemfahrt, doch die Anzahl der Asketinnen und auch Ehefrauen, die ihre Männer auf den Kreuzzug begleiteten, nahm im Laufe des Mittelalters zu. 1353 wurde am Zionsberg sogar ein Hospiz mit Raum für 200 Frauen gegründet[58].

[55] *Jakob Molin (Maharil)*, Sche'elot u-Teschuwot, hrsg. von *Izchak Satz* (Jerusalem 1979) Nr. 118 (alte Nr. 126); im folgenden zitiert: *Maharil*, Sche'elot u-Teschuwot. Erwähnt bei *Israel J. Yuval*, Scholars in their Time. The Religious Leadership of German Jewry in the Late Middle Ages (hebr.) (Jerusalem 1988) 317f., Anm. 18. Maharil erkannte die Geschäftsreise nicht als Erfüllung des Gelübdes an. Der Wohnort von Elchanan Katz und seiner Frau ist leider nicht bekannt.

[56] Leket Joscher II, 24.

[57] *Wilfried Ehbrecht*, Überall ist Jerusalem, in: Die Stadt als Kommunikationsraum. Beiträge zur Stadtgeschichte vom Mittelalter bis ins 20. Jahrhundert. Festschrift für Karl Czok zum 75. Geburtstag, hrsg. von *Helmut Bräuer, Elke Schlenkrich* (Leipzig 2001) 129–185, hier 168; im folgenden zitiert: *Ehbrecht*, Überall ist Jerusalem. Zu Sophie von Bentheim, die 1176 auf ihrer dritten Jerusalemreise verstarb, siehe 150f. Zu jüdischen Jerusalemfahrern siehe *Harbsmeier*, Reisen 69f.

[58] *Sylvia Schein*, Bridget of Sweden, Margery Kempe and Women's Jerusalem Pilgrimages in the Middle Ages, in: Mediterranean Historical Review 14/1 (1999) 44–58, hier 46–49; zu Brigitta und Margery siehe 50–52. Der Aufsatz von *Kristine Utterback*, The Vision Becomes Reality; Medieval Women Pilgrims to the Holy Land, in: *Bryan F. Le Beau, Menachem Mor* (Hrsg.), Pilgrims & Travelers to the Holy Land (Jewish Civilization Studies 7, Omaha 1996) 159–168, stand mir leider nicht zur Verfügung.

Konkreter Anlaß konnte auch hier ein Gelübde sein, das in Notzeiten geleistet wurde, um bei Erfüllung der an Gott gerichteten Bitte eingelöst zu werden, wie im Fall des italienischen Pilgers Meschullam ben Menachem, der sich aus diesem Grund im Jahr 1481 auf seinen, wie er selbst errechnete, insgesamt 8748 Meilen langen Weg machte. Er lag wie alle seine Reisegefährten in Jerusalem mehrere Wochen schwer krank danieder und bezeichnete es als Wunder, daß es trotz allem Pilger gab, die diese Strapazen überlebten. Einige Jahre nach seiner Rückkehr nach Volterra verfaßte er einen hebräischen, mit italienischen Ausdrücken durchsetzten Reisebericht[59]. Von Frauen stehen, soweit bekannt, Berichte dieser Art nicht zur Verfügung, Meschullam erwähnt allerdings, daß auch Frauen von aggressiven Zolleinhebern, welche vor Alexandria die Reisenden auf versteckte Bargeld untersuchten, nicht verschont blieben[60]. Auch die Gelübde von Frauen wurden normalerweise nur in von Männern verfaßten Texten quellenkundig, nämlich wenn sie nicht eingehalten werden konnten und die Gebundene, wie die erwähnte Frau von Elchanan Katz, eine Lösung durch ein rabbinisches Gericht benötigte[61]. Dadurch erfahren wir indirekt von der Pilgerfahrt einer jüdischen Frau:

Josman Katz, um die Mitte des 15. Jahrhunderts der Gemeinderabbiner von Wiener Neustadt, teilte seinem Kollegen Juda – möglicherweise der Sohn von Rabbi Schalom von Neustadt – mit, daß er in Angelegenheit des Gelübdes einer Frau seinen Lehrer – vermutlich Israel Isserlein – um seine Rechtsmeinung gefragt habe: „… In der Angelegenheit einer Frau, die gelobt hatte, in die Heilige Stadt zu reisen, und nun wurde sie beraubt und vergewaltigt und sie strebt nicht mehr danach, dorthin zu gehen und kam, um wegen (der Lösung) ihres Gelübdes zu fragen. Und so tat ich und fragte meinen Lehrer, sein Eingang und Ausgang sei behütet, und er antwortete mir, daß es eine klare Sache ist, ihr das Gelübde zu lösen …“[62]

Wie in diesem zitierten Fall einer auf ihrer Reise überfallenen und vergewaltigten Frau anklingt, bestand in den Gefahren, die auf den Straßen außerhalb der befestigten und mehr oder weniger gesicherten Stadt lauern konnten, ein guter Grund, von Fahrten über Land tunlich Abstand zu nehmen. Auch wenn es die Quellenlage zum Spätmittelalter nicht erlaubt, eine Kriminalstatistik zu den auf der Straße verübten Raubüberfällen und anderen Verbrechen zu erstellen und, worauf Timothy Reuter hinwies, die Unsicherheit auf den Straßen durch die „bösen Räuber“ in den

[59] *Harbsmeier*, Reisen 77–80. Der hebräische Text ist ediert von *A. M. Luncz*, Jerusalem. Jahrbuch zur Beförderung einer wissenschaftlich genauen Kenntniss des jetzigen und des alten Palästina (Wien 1882). In englischer Übersetzung bei *Elkan Nathan Adler* (Hrsg.), Jewish Travellers. A Treasury of Travelogues from Nine Centuries. With a Preface by *Cecil Roth* (New York, NY ²1966, Nachdruck New Delhi 1995) 156–208; im folgenden zitiert: *Adler*, Jewish Travellers. Zum Gelübde siehe 174, zur Weglänge 208, zur Strapaze 195.

[60] *Adler*, Jewish Travellers 158.

[61] Zu unbedachten und nicht einhaltbaren Gelübden aus Zorn oder Verzweiflung siehe *Martha Keil*, Rituals of Repentance and Testimonies at Rabbinical Courts in the 15th Century, in: *Gerhard Jaritz, Michael Richter* (Hrsg.), Oral History of the Middle Ages. The Spoken Word in Context (Medium Aevum Quotidianum XII, CEU Medievalia 3, Krems, Budapest 2001) 164–176, hier 175f.; im folgenden zitiert: *Keil*, Rituals.

[62] Leket Joscher II, 24f. Zu Josman Katz siehe GJ III/2, 1627.

„wilden Wäldern" als Topos und Gegenbild zur Friedenswahrung des guten Herrschers auf den sicheren Königsstraßen herhalten mußte, ist doch die Gefährlichkeit einer Reise, bei der wertvolle Güter und Geld mitgeführt wurden, gut nachvollziehbar. Der Übergang zwischen der Gewalttat eines Kriminellen und dem gewalttätigen Konflikt zwischen Adeligen war allerdings fließend: Räuberei konnte auch eine Fehdeansage an einen Gegner sein, die auf dem Rücken von Reisenden ausgetragen wurde[63]. Der Begriff vom „Raubritter" stammt zwar erst aus der ersten Hälfte des 19. Jahrhunderts und diente dem Bildungsbürgertum zur kontrastvollen Selbstdarstellung. Doch finden sich in den zeitgenössischen Quellen des Spätmittelalters zahlreiche Berichte von Raub und Brand durch Adelige, seien sie nun aus Armut oder Machtpolitik begangen worden. Die Kontroverse über die Grenzen zwischen rechtmäßiger Fehde und Willkür beschäftigt die Fachwelt bis heute, und „die Chronik des Fehdewesens wäre bestimmt noch anklagender ausgefallen, wenn sie von den Bauern, den Hauptleidtragenden der Fehde, geschrieben worden wäre"[64]. Zu letzteren wären auch die Reisenden zu zählen, welche zusätzlich von verarmten Adeligen bedroht wurden, welche sich als Soldritter verdingten und nach ihrer Entlassung aus dem Kriegsdienst als Wegelagerer ihr Unwesen trieben[65].

Ein ständiges Bedrohungspotential bildeten selbstverständlich auch die fahrenden Unterschichten, die die wirtschaftliche Not zum Stehlen zwang. Aus dem Spätmittelalter sind nur relativ wenige Verhörprotokolle und Geständnisse erhalten, welche näheren Einblick in ihre Lebensumstände geben; die meist zum Thema „Kriminalität" herangezogenen Gerichts- und Stadtbücher, Achtbücher, Gerichtsrechnungen und Urfehden enthalten diese Informationen nicht[66]. Um einen Eindruck zu gewinnen, welches Ungemach Juden und Jüdinnen während ihres Unterwegsseins erwarten konnte, interessieren uns aus den von Arnold Esch bearbeiteten Dokumenten aus dem Berner Umland zwischen 1499 und 1510 eher die Beschaffenheit der Tatorte, der Tathergang und die Auswahl der Opfer als die Täterpersönlichkeiten. Oft lagen die Männer zu zweit oder in Banden von mindestens fünf, in diesem Fall verarmte Handwerker, wochenlang im Wald auf der Lauer, ehe sich ein Beraubungsobjekt zeigte. Zwar bestand die Beute meist nur aus Eßwaren, Klei-

[63] *Timothy Reuter*, Die Unsicherheit auf den Straßen im europäischen Früh- und Hochmittelalter: Täter, Opfer und ihre mittelalterlichen und modernen Betrachter, in: Träger und Instrumentarien des Friedens im hohen und späten Mittelalter, hrsg. von *Johannes Fried* (Vorträge und Forschungen 43, Sigmaringen 1993) 169–201, bes. 172–177, 186–189; im folgenden zitiert: *Reuter*, Unsicherheit. Zum „literarischen Unsicherheitstopos" siehe auch *Herta Mandl-Neumann*, Überlegungen zu Kriminalität und Mobilität im späten Mittelalter, in: *Gerhard Jaritz, Albert Müller* (Hrsg.), Migration in der Feudalgesellschaft (Studien zur Historischen Sozialwissenschaft 8, Frankfurt a. M. 1988) 57–63, hier 58; im folgenden zitiert: *Mandl-Neumann*, Überlegungen.

[64] *Werner Rösener*, Zur Problematik des spätmittelalterlichen Raubrittertums, in: Festschrift für Berent Schwineköper. Zu seinem siebzigsten Geburtstag, hrsg. von *Helmut Maurer* und *Hans Patze* (Sigmaringen 1982) 469–488, hier 488, siehe auch 469f., 472f. und 481f.; im folgenden zitiert: *Rösener*, Raubritter; dazu *Reuter*, Unsicherheit 187, Anm. 72.

[65] *Rösener*, Raubritter 486f., *Schulz*, Unterwegssein 12f. mit Literatur in Anm. 6. Siehe auch *Frantisek Graus*, Die Randständigen, in: *Moraw* (Hrsg.), Unterwegssein 93–104, hier 102.

[66] *Mandl-Neumann*, Überlegungen 58–60 sowie 63, Anm. 9.

dung und einem kleinen Geldbetrag, doch kostete der Überfall die Opfer trotzdem das Leben. Straßenverengungen und Furten waren besonders günstige, weil für die Auflauernden gut einsehbare Orte für Angriffe. In diesen Protokollen scheinen keine jüdischen Opfer auf, doch waren Wirte ein bevorzugtes Raubobjekt, denn bei ihnen war, wie die Verhafteten angaben, Bargeld zu vermuten, was sich auch von reisenden Geldleihern erwarten ließ. Auch Gemeindebeamte, Pfarrer und reiche Bauern gehörten in dieser ländlichen Gegend zum lukrativen Opferkreis[67]. Eine deutsche Bande, deren Steckbrief an den Rat von Bern gelangt war, hatte im Thüringer Wald 16 Kaufleute ermordet und beraubt, auch eine süddeutsche *rott* von 12 Männern trieb bei Basel ihr Unwesen. Eine Räuberbande hatte zwischen Freiburg und Bern fünf Morde begangen, zwei ihrer Opfer hatte sie, bei kläglicher Beute, „gebunden und in das wasser geworffen, ein weiteres ermuerdt unnd nebent sich in die studen gezogen". Eine ermordete Frau trug vier Gulden bei sich[68].

In Niederösterreich, dem mittelalterlichen Herzogtum unter der Enns, unternahm der 1462 in Spitz an der Donau hingerichtete Dieb Hans Swarzenperger seine Beutezüge. Er gestand 48 Diebstähle in einem regional begrenzten Raum rund um die oberösterreichische Stadt Wels. Die vor allem von Bauern und Handwerkern erbeuteten Güter, meist Vieh, Kleidung und Gegenstände aller Art, verkaufte er an vom Tatort entfernteren Orten[69]. 1516, in einer Zeit als in der Steiermark keine Juden mehr geduldet waren, wurde in Aussee der Räuber Hois Gryl hingerichtet, dessen Bande auch 31 Morde begangen hatte. Unter der Folter – diese begleitete und relativierte meist die Geständnisse – gab er die Namen von 34 weiteren Mitgliedern an[70]. Auch Übernachtungen in Herbergen und Tavernen waren nicht ungefährlich, wie beispielsweise Londoner Gerichtsakten aus dem späten 13. und frühen 14. Jahrhundert bezeugen: Mindestens 30 Kaufleute wurden von ihren Wirten oder Mitgästen nachts in ihren Quartieren ausgeraubt und ermordet. Wie die offene Straße boten auch Hospize und Wirtshäuser gute Möglichkeiten für unkontrolliertes Auftauchen und unerkanntes Verschwinden[71].

Die selten überlieferten Details von Mord und Tathergang werden von einer Quellengattung ganz anderer Art bestätigt, nämlich von rabbinischen Rechtsgut-

[67] *Arnold Esch*, Räuber, Diebe, Wegelagerer. Reviere, Beute, Schicksale in Berner Verhörprotokollen des frühen 16. Jahrhunderts, in: Hochfinanz, Wirtschaftsräume, Innovationen. Festschrift für Wolfgang von Stromer, hrsg. von *Uwe Bestmann, Franz Irsigler, Jürgen Schneider*, Bd. 2 (Trier 1987) 741–764, Literatur 756, Anm. 3 und 4. Die von ihm herangezogenen Stücke sind im Berner Staatsarchiv bezeichnenderweise unter dem Titel „Unnütze Papiere" registriert, ebd. 742, Edition 744–747.

[68] *Esch*, ebd. 751f. mit Beschreibung der Bandenmitglieder. Die Reviere dieser „lokalen" Diebe waren klein, hier 26 Tatorte eines einzelnen auf einem Gebiet von 20 mal 25 Kilometern; ebd. 752 und 754.

[69] *Gerhard Jaritz*, Probleme um ein Diebsgeständnis des 15. Jahrhunderts, in: Jahrbuch des Musealvereines Wels 21 (1977/78) 77–86. Die Edition des Protokolls hier 81–83 und 86, Karten der Tat- räume 84f.

[70] *Mandl-Neumann*, Überlegungen 62. Sie erwähnt auch das Geständnis eines Diebes im steirischen Aussee von 1519, dessen „Einzugsgebiet" von der Steiermark bis in den süddeutschen Raum reichte.

[71] *Reuter*, Unsicherheit 171, Anm. 5, und 194.

achten zu einem für Frauen besonders einschneidenden Problem: der *Aguna*, der „gebundenen" und verlassenen Frau. Hier geht es nicht um Männer, die ihre Frauen im Stich ließen, um an einem fernen Ort ein neues Leben zu beginnen – auch das mag vorgekommen sein –, sondern um Opfer von Raubüberfällen, die für eine Todeserklärung durch das *Bet Din* eindeutig und ohne die Absicht, im Interesse der Frau auszusagen, identifiziert werden mußten: „Wir liegen allhie in einem Geleit, die haben ein Judn der mort, nun hot men in drei schock gelobt, daß sie soln weisen, wo er is dermort worden." Dies ist die protokollierte und Rabbi Israel Isserlein übersandte Aussage einer Christin, welche die zwei jüdischen Informanten Jona und Jechiel mit eigenen Ohren gehört hatten[72]. Die unglückliche *Aguna* hieß Gelein, Tochter der Peslan und Gattin des Susslein von Tachau. Ein weiterer Christ kannte zwar nähere Einzelheiten über den Täter, wollte ihn aber nicht bei den Behörden anzeigen. Die am Rechtsentscheid beteiligten Nürnberger Rabbiner David Sprinz, David Frank und Salman Segal sowie Israel Isserlein diskutierten alle Erkennungszeichen des Susslein wie Kleidung, Gepäck und Aussehen sowie die Tauglichkeit der – in *Aguna*-Prozessen zugelassenen – christlichen Zeugenaussagen und kamen zu dem Schluß, Gelein die Wiederverheiratung zu erlauben und den für den Gerichtsbezirk zuständigen Rabbiner Elia von Prag zu informieren.

Ein weiterer ausführlich diskutierter Fall betraf Ester bat Abraham, deren Ehemann David bar Jakob, genannt Kuntel, unter ungeklärten Umständen ums Leben kam. Es bestand der Verdacht, daß er von seinen jüdischen Reisegenossen – nicht nur von christlichen Gaunern drohte Gefahr –, einem gewissen Sanwil Schranz sowie dessen Frau, ermordet worden war. Mit dem Fall waren die führenden zeitgenössischen Rabbiner befaßt: Elia von Prag, Jakob Weil, Israel Bruna, Mosche von Tarvis, Jakob von Padua, Simlin von Triest und ein bisher nicht identifizierter Josef bar Izchak[73].

Der ältere Sohn Michael Schranz gab unter Eid die Aussage seiner Mutter wieder, welche das Unterwegssein einer ganzen Familie beschreibt: „David ritt auf dem Pferd, sie und ihr Mann Sanwil Schranz und ihr kleiner Sohn und ihre kleine Tochter gingen mit ihm von der Stadt Neuhausen nach Prag. Und der kleine Sohn führte das Pferd, auf dem dieser David ritt, am Zaum. Sie und ihr Mann gingen in kurzem Abstand hinterher. Und da fiel David vom Pferd auf den Boden und sie und ihr Mann eilten herbei, um ihm zu helfen und ihn auf das Pferd zu heben, und sie dachten, daß er ohnmächtig geworden war. Und sie sprachen ihn an und sahen, daß er tot war."[74] Da die Zeugenaussagen in Verteidigungsabsicht erfolgt waren,

[72] *Israel Isserlein bar Petachja*, Pesakim u-Khetawim Nr. 161. Die in hebräischen Buchstaben wiedergegebenen deutschen bzw. jiddischen Zeugenaussagen sind gesammelt bei *Schneur Salman Schasar*, Ore Dorot. Mechakrim we-Ha'arot le-Toldot Israel be-Dorot ha-achronim (Jerusalem 1971) 239–31, hier 253, Nr. 16.

[73] *Israel Isserlein bar Petachja*, Pesakim u-Khetawim Nr. 218–221; *Israel me-Bruna*, Sefer Sche'elot u-Teschuwot, hrsg. von *M. Herschler* (Jerusalem 1959/60) Nr. 28 und 29; *Jakob Weil*, Sche'elot u-Teschuwot Nr. 164.

[74] *Israel Isserlein bar Petachja*, Pesakim u-Khetawim Nr. 218.

waren die gutachtenden Rabbiner kontroverser Meinung, bis Ester schließlich zur Witwe erklärt und ihr eine Wiederverheiratung erlaubt wurde[75].

Abgesehen vom halachischen Inhalt und von den realienkundlichen Einblicken in Reisebedingungen, Kleidung, Aussehen und Gepäckstücken, welche solche Responsen geben können, sind die darin bewahrten protokollierten Aussagen seltene Überlieferungen von gesprochener Sprache, an deren korrekter Wiedergabe aufgrund des Charakters der Quelle kaum zu zweifeln ist[76].

Eine andere Kategorie von Gefahren auf Reisen bestand im Abpressen von Zöllen, gleichsam einem „Lösegeld für Güter", deren Grenze zwischen „legaler" Abgabe und Straßenraub fließend war. Zwar wurde im Mainzer Landfrieden 1235 verfügt, daß der Einheber unrechtmäßiger Zölle „wie ein gemeiner Räuber und Wegelagerer" bestraft werden sollte, ob die Bestimmung jedoch praktische Anwendung fand, darf in Frage gestellt werden[77]. Eine Parallele bestand in der Unterscheidung zwischen ordentlichen und außerordentlichen Steuern, die in den jüdischen Quellen in polemischer Paraphrase des talmudischen Grundsatzes „Dina de-Malkhuta Dina" (bBaba Kama 13a) – Das Gesetz des Königreiches ist gültiges Gesetz – „Gesela de Malkhuta", Beutegut des Königreichs, genannt wurden. Die Wahrnehmung als „unrechtmäßig" bewahrte jedoch keineswegs vor der Zahlungsverpflichtung, außerdem konnten die Gemeinden durch die Einordnung als Zölle oder Sondersteuern auf einen geregelten Vorgang zur Aufbringung zurückgreifen[78].

Diese erpreßten Zahlungen betrafen selbstverständlich auch Pilger und aus anderen Gründen Reisende sämtlicher Religionen. Ein anonymisiertes Responsum von Israel Isserlein überliefert folgenden Fall: „Gruppen von Männern und Frauen, viele Menschen, reisten von Stadt zu Stadt zu einer Hochzeitsfeier, und sie zogen durch eine Stadt eines bösen Herrschers, und alle seine Diener waren böse. Und sie erhoben über die Juden eine Blutbeschuldigung und töteten sie und setzten alle gefangen und teilten sie auf die Häuser der Bürger in der ganzen Stadt auf, jeden Mann und jede Frau für sich. Und sie folterten sie und setzten sie ständig unter Druck, ihren Glauben zu wechseln. ... Ein Großteil der Gruppe, Männer und Frauen, widerstand der Versuchung und wurde zur Heiligung des Namens getötet ..."[79]

[75] Die halachische Diskussion um die Glaubwürdigkeit von Zeugen in ebda. Nr. 220.

[76] Siehe dazu *Keil*, Rituals 172–175.

[77] *Reuter*, Unsicherheit 177–180, Quelle Anm. 39, und 188.

[78] Für „Gesela de-Malkhuta" siehe z. B. bereits *Meir bar Baruch von Rothenburg*, Sche'elot u-Teschuwot I/1 (Druck Cremona, Nachdruck Jerusalem 1986) Nr. 222 und *Maharil*, Sche'elot u-Teschuwot Nr. 71 (alte Nummer 75), wo es um die Separierung eines Einzelnen von einer außerordentlichen Steuer geht. Er mußte sich beteiligen, auch wenn sie als „Gesela de-Malkhuta" eingestuft wurde. Zu den außerordentlichen Steuern siehe *Eberhard Isenmann*, Steuern und Abgaben, in: GJ III/3, 2208–2281, hier 2214–2216; *Eric Zimmer*, Harmony and Discord: An Analysis of the Decline of Jewish Self Government in 15th Century Europe (New York 1970) bes. 37–39, 139–141, 149–153.

[79] *Israel Isserlein bar Petachja*, Terumat ha-Deschen Nr. 241. Das halachische Problem ist hier die Rückkehr der gefangenen Frauen zu ihren Ehemännern, obwohl sie längere Zeit unter Nichtjuden inhaftiert waren und die Wahrscheinlichkeit einer Vergewaltigung bestand.

Eine Hochzeitsfeier war vermutlich der häufigste private Anlaß, sich auf die Straße zu begeben. Die Wahrscheinlichkeit, das Ziel sicher zu erreichen, hing auch von der aktuellen politischen Situation im Territorium ab. Am 20. April 1450 teilte Susse, die Witwe des bedeutenden Geldhändlers Smohel von Augsburg, dem Rat der Stadt Frankfurt am Main mit, daß sie sich mit ihren Kindern in den Schutz des Pfalzgrafen bei Rhein begeben habe. Als Begründung führte sie an, daß einer ihrer Söhne „in fremden landen" Hochzeit halte und sie auch für die Eintreibung von Außenständen auf Reisen gehen müsse. Sie und ihre Söhne bedürften des besonderen Schutzes, da sie durch Länder von Herren reisen müßten, die zu dieser Zeit mit der Stadt Frankfurt in Fehde lägen[80].

Schutzmaßnahmen

Schutzmaßnahmen vor den Gefahren auf den Reiserouten bestanden auf territorialer Basis in den verschiedenen Landfrieden, in die auch Juden aufgenommen wurden, und auf individueller Ebene in Geleitbriefen, welche zwar keinen Präventivschutz darstellten, doch die Sicherheit einer „Versicherungspolizze" boten, sich im Falle eines Übergriffs an das Gericht des Schutzherrn wenden und ihn für Schäden haftbar machen zu können[81].

Auch jüdische Frauen erhielten Geleitbriefe für einen kürzeren oder weiteren Bewegungsradius, häufig, um Außenstände in einem früheren Wohnort einzutreiben, wie im Februar 1414 Mergard (Miriam) von Fritzlar. Nach sechzehnjährigem Wohnsitz in Frankfurt am Main war sie Bürgerin in Oppenheim geworden, und der dortige Rat suchte für sie um Geleit an, um ihre finanziellen Angelegenheiten zu ordnen, das allerdings wegen der unklaren Rechtsverhältnisse erst im Oktober erteilt wurde[82]. Oppenheim liegt 20 km südlich von Mainz, also 45 km von Frankfurt entfernt, etwa eineinhalb Tagesreisen. Auch Sara von Eppstein, Eva zum Buchsbaum und Susse, Witwe des Smohel, erhielten städtisches Geleit für ihre Geschäftsbesuche. Andererseits bot die Ablehnung eines Geleitgesuchs ein probates Druckmittel, um Forderungen durchzusetzen[83].

Aktive Geldleiherinnen ließen sich in ihrem Privileg ihre Bewegungsfreiheit mit dem nötigen Geleitbrief garantieren, wie Scharlat von Görz, Witwe des Schalom, von Graf Meinhard VII. von Görz. Das Original und die Datierung sind nicht überliefert, ein ähnlich lautendes Privileg für Pascul von Triest vom Februar 1364 legt jedoch ein Datum kurz vor diesem Zeitraum nahe. Falls Scharlat die Herr-

[80] *Andernacht*, Regesten I/1, 235, Nr. 896. Siehe auch die Bitte um Geleit für ihren Sohn, ebda. 234f., Nr. 895.

[81] Zu den Landfrieden siehe *Rösener*, Raubrittertum 476–481 und zum Geleit: Lexikon des Mittelalters 4 (München 2002) 1204f.; auch *Reuter*, Unsicherheit 195f.

[82] *Andernacht*, Regesten I/1, 34f., Nr. 114–117; 44, Nr. 150 (1414 Oktober 3).

[83] *Andernacht*, Regesten I/1, 45, Nr. 154 (1414 November 14), 138, Nr. 488 (1438 März 13), 237, Nr. 910 (1450 Juli 9); Beispiele von Ablehnungen: 236, Nr. 901 (1450 Mai 26, Eva zum Buchsbaum), 238, Nr. 915 (1450 Juli 14, Susse, Witwe des Smohel).

schaft der Görzer verlassen wollte, erhielt sie für die Städte Laibach/Ljubjana, Triest und Cividale freies Geleit, und der Graf übernahm für zwei Monate den Schutz für ihren Besitz – für Pascul übernahm er ihn über ein Jahr. Im Fall einer Nichtverlängerung des Privilegs, was einer Vertreibung gleichkam, sicherte Meinhard Scharlat und ihrer Mutter Minz Geleit bis zu den drei Städten zu. Für diese und andere Rechte zahlten die Frauen jährlich 4 Mark Schillinge[84].

Beliebte Schutzmaßnahmen bei Juden wie bei Christen waren neben dem Zusammenschluß zu größeren Gruppen mit bewaffneter Begleitung vor allem Verkleidungen. Gewöhnliche Reisende verkleideten sich als Pilger, Frauen als Männer und Juden als Christen, doch „... nicht nur mangelnde Sprachkenntnisse konnten eine erfolgreiche Durchführung vereiteln, sondern auch oft genug die Unfähigkeit, die eigene standesspezifische Körperhaltung und Gestik zu unterdrücken“[85]. Zu ergänzen wäre die Beachtung der Gender-determinierten Haltungen, Gesten und Stimmfärbungen. Der Jerusalempilger Meschullam ben Menachem beschrieb sehr eindrücklich die Angst, als mit weißem Turban als muslimischer Türke verkleideter Jude von Räuberbanden erkannt zu werden. Die kleinste verräterische Geste konnte den Tod bedeuten[86].

Israel Isserlein erlaubte die Verkleidung als Christ, jedoch nur in Lebensgefahr und aus Angst vor Zwangstaufe, nicht jedoch, um etwa einer Zollzahlung zu entgehen[87]. Daß Juden sichtlich als Christen „durchgehen“ konnten, läßt auf relative Nicht-Unterscheidbarkeit in Aussehen, Sprache und Habitus schließen. Die von Isserlein angeführten Merkmale christlicher Kleidung bestanden in bunten Farben und modischen Zipfeln, eine Mode, an der auch konservative Christen Kritik übten. Die Verfasser des Sefer Chassidim führten an, daß sich jüdische Frauen zum Schutz vor Gefahren auf Reisen entgegen des biblischen Verbots als Männer und sogar als Nonnen verkleiden durften: „Obwohl die Tora sagt: Männertracht sei nicht an einer Frau, und ein Mann soll nicht ein Frauenkleid anziehen (Deut. 22, 5), gilt: Wenn Feinde die Stadt belagern oder wenn man unterwegs ist und wenn sie [die Nichtjuden] wissen, daß es Frauen sind, werden sie mit ihnen liegen. Die Frauen sollen daher in Männerkleidung gehen und auch mit

[84] „Wann auch oder zu welher zeit die egenanten juden under uns nicht peleiben wollten, so sullen wir ir leib und ir gut gelaiten haizzen gen Laubach (Laibach), gen Triest oder gen Sibdat (Cividale), an welher stat der dreyer sie das vordernt; und do wir ez hin getun mugen an geverde. Und was sie hab under uns liezzen, das sol in unserm scherm und sicherung sein von dem tag und sie sich von uns gezogen haben zway gancz manod, die darnach nachst nocheinander choment an geverd.“ HHStA Wien, Handschrift „weiß“ 594, fol. 62v–63r. Das Privileg ist nur in Abschrift vorhanden. Siehe dazu *Keil*, Maistrin 33f. Zur Judenpolitik der Grafen von Görz siehe *Lohrmann*, Judenrecht 239f. und *Markus J. Wenninger*, Juden im Herrschaftsbereich der Grafen von Görz und Görz-Tirol, in: Symposium zur Geschichte von Millstatt und Kärnten, hrsg. von *Franz Nikolasch* (Millstatt 2000) 108–133. Beide Privilegien ohne Namensnennung oder Erwähnung, daß eines davon für eine Frau bestimmt war, bei *Wadl*, Juden in Kärnten 118.

[85] *Reuter*, Unsicherheit 196 mit Beispielen in Anm. 133. Eine Botin aus Trier verkleidete sich als Mann.

[86] *Adler*, Jewish Travellers 182f.

[87] *Israel Isserlein bar Petachja*, Terumat ha-Deschen Nr. 197.

Schwert, sodass die Feinde meinen, sie seien Männer."[88] Es war also sogar erlaubt, sich als Nonne zu verkleiden, wie auch Rabbi Isserlein von Wiener Neustadt 150 Jahre später gestattete: „Die Frau, die unterwegs war und gehört hat, daß Nichtjuden ihr begegnen werden, und fürchtet, daß sie mit ihr liegen werden, kann sich als Nonne verkleiden, damit sie meinen, sie sei eine Nonne, und nicht mit ihr liegen."[89]

Mobilität und Sittsamkeit

Aus den Urkunden, Einträgen in Stadtbüchern und anderen Geschäftsquellen läßt sich nicht eindeutig schließen, ob und in welchem Ausmaß jüdische Frauen zur Erfüllung ihrer Geschäftspflichten unterwegs sein mußten. Doch daß eine Notwendigkeit bestand, sich über Gefahren auf Reisen, die Übernachtung in christlichen Herbergen oder gar in christlichen Privathäusern Gedanken zu machen, geht aus einigen Quellen sehr wohl hervor. Es stellt sich nun die Frage, in welcher Weise sich die Mobilität von Jüdinnen auf ihr religiöses, kulturelles oder gesellschaftliches Leben auswirkte. Hatte sie halachische Implikationen und waren die für die Männerehre bedeutsame Zucht und Sittsamkeit wichtiger als der Beitrag ihrer Frauen zum Familien- und Gemeindewohl?

Ein Pendant zur halachischen Situation der *Aguna*, welche sich nicht wieder verheiraten kann, solange ihr Ehemann nicht für tot erklärt wurde, existiert zwar auf der männlichen Seite nicht, doch befindet sich ein Mann, vor allem ein Kohen, dessen Frau eventuell vergewaltigt wurde, ebenfalls in einer Zwangslage: Wenn die Vergewaltigung eindeutig erwiesen ist, ist er gezwungen, ihr den Scheidebrief *Get* zu geben, auch wenn dies seinen Gefühlen von Zuneigung und Verantwortung zuwider laufen sollte[90]. So lautet die strenge Halacha, die zwar Ermessensspielraum in den Gerichtsurteilen läßt, aber doch unveränderbar in biblischen und talmudischen Gesetzen wurzelt. „Weich" waren die Konstruktionen von Ehre, Zucht und Sittsamkeit in Zusammenhang mit relativ großer geschäftlicher Freizügigkeit der Frauen[91].

[88] Sefer Chassidim, Ed. Parma Nr. 206 und Ed. Bologna Nr. 200. Zitiert in: *Susanne Borchers*, Jüdisches Frauenleben im Mittelalter. Die Texte des Sefer Chasidim, hrsg. von *Johann Maier* (Judentum und Umwelt 68, Frankfurt a. M., Berlin u. a. 1998) 156. Zu waffentragenden Juden siehe *Markus J. Wenninger*, Von jüdischen Rittern und anderen waffentragenden Juden im mittelalterlichen Deutschland, in: Aschkenas. Zeitschrift für Geschichte und Kultur der Juden 13/1 (2003) 35–82 und die weiteren Beiträge in dieser Nummer.

[89] Sefer Chassidim, Ed. Parma Nr. 261 und Ed. Bologna Nr. 702. Zitiert in *Borchers*, ebd. 159. *Israel Isserlein bar Petachja*, Terumat ha-Deschen Nr. 196. Siehe dazu *Keil*, Geschäftserfolg 53f.

[90] Siehe den Artikel „Aguna" in der Encyclopaedia Judaica 1 (Jerusalem 1970) col. 430–433.

[91] *Martin Dinges*, Die Ehre als Thema der historischen Anthropologie. Bemerkungen zur Wissenschaftsgeschichte und zur Konzeptualisierung, in: Verletzte Ehre. Ehrkonflikte in Gesellschaften des Mittelalters und der Frühen Neuzeit, hrsg. von *Klaus Schreiner* und *Gerd Schwerhoff* (Köln, Weimar, Wien 1995) 29–62, bes. 30 und 48. Siehe auch *Robert Jütte*, Ehre und Ehrverlust im spätmittelalterlichen und frühneuzeitlichen Judentum, in: *Schreiner, Schwerhoff*, ebd. 144–165.

In seinem Standardwerk zur jüdischen Frauengeschichte des 10. bis 12. Jahrhunderts „Pious and Rebellious. Jewish Women in the Middle Ages“ konstatierte Avraham Grossman die im Vergleich zur muslimisch-sefardischen Gesellschaft ungehinderte Mobilität von aschkenasischen Frauen, die vor allem aus ihren Geschäftsaktivitäten resultierte und keinerlei Anstoß bei Ehemännern und Rabbinern erregte: „There is not the slightest hint in any of these sources that these things (Geschäftsreisen, Verhandlungen mit Christen etc., Anm.) were seen as entailing any immodesty.“[92] Die von ihm herangezogenen rabbinischen Quellen stammen allerdings aus einer Zeit, als die weibliche Geldleihe ein ziemlich neues und sich rasch ausbreitendes Phänomen in der aschkenasischen Geschichte war. Sie behandeln auch nicht die *Zniut*, was wortwörtlich die sittsame Zurückgezogenheit im Haus bezeichnet[93], sondern das halachisch verbotene Alleinsein *Jichud* mit einem Mann außerhalb der Familie, und, erschwerend, mit einem Nichtjuden. Die Tosafot zu Avoda Sara 23a konstatieren jedoch in überraschender Deutlichkeit, daß es „unmöglich für eine jüdische Frau ist, nicht von Zeit zu Zeit mit einem Nichtjuden alleine zu sein“. Die Tosafot argumentierten, daß eine jüdische Frau bei einem alltäglichen Zusammentreffen mit einem Christen bei Bedrohung um Hilfe rufen und gerettet werden würde, und daß der Christ dies auch wüßte. Nur bei einer Einkerkerung durch einen Machthaber bestünde die Gefahr einer Vergewaltigung mit halachischen Folgen. Sicher spielte in diesen Argumenten die Tatsache eine Rolle, daß die Geschäftsfrauen im Hochmittelalter großteils Angehörige von Familien der jüdischen Oberschichten waren[94].

Für das Spätmittelalter sprechen einige Rabbiner eine schärfere Sprache, wenn auch die Aussagen zu diesem Thema, verglichen mit dem hohen Prozentsatz von Frauen im Darlehensgeschäft, erstaunlich selten sind. Deutlich zeigt sich diese Entwicklung zur größeren Strenge an zwei rabbinischen Statements zum selben Problem, zwischen denen etwa 250 Jahre liegen. Elieser ben Joel ha-Levi (1140–1225) und sein Kollege Simcha ben Schmuel von Speyer waren mit dem Fall einer verheirateten Frau konfrontiert, welche sich, nachdem keine Reisegruppe verfügbar war, mit einem einzelnen Juden auf den Weg machte. Ein Zweiter kam hinzu und die beiden Männer vergewaltigten sie während der Rast in einem Wald. Im Responsum wird ausdrücklich angemerkt, daß die Frau „weinte und schrie“. Entgegen der Halacha, wie Grossman betont, wurde sie ihrem Ehemann erlaubt, denn „täglich gehen die Frauen mit zwei oder drei Männern und sie sehen, daß die Gelehrten das nicht verhindern und kein Verbot aussprechen.“[95] Mosche Minz (gestorben vor

[92] *Avraham Grossman*, Pious and Rebellious. Jewish Women in Medieval Europe (Hanover, London 2004) 117; im folgenden zitiert: *Grossman*, Pious (engl.). Zur Benutzung der Quellen empfiehlt sich die hebräische Originalausgabe gleichen Titels (Jerusalem 2001); im folgenden zitiert: *Grossman*, Pious (hebr.).

[93] *Judith R. Baskin*, Midrashic Women. Formations of the Feminine in Rabbinic Literature (Hanover, London 2002) 113 zu bGittin 90a–b.

[94] *Grossman*, Pious (engl.) 117–121 und *ders.*, Pious (hebr.) 201.

[95] Sefer Ra'via §920, zitiert in *Grossman*, Pious (hebr.) 202. Die Vergewaltiger wurden verhaftet, flohen aber nach einer Bestechung. Den Fall bespricht auch der Schüler dieser beiden Rabbiner,

1469)[96] äußerte sich zum selben Problem in einer Mischung aus Schärfe und Resignation. Ob von einem aktuellen Fall die Rede ist, wird nicht klar, denn es handelt sich um einen Nachsatz zu einem langen Rechtsgutachten mit anderem Thema an seinen Verwandten Seligman Bing: „Und was du über die Angelegenheit des *Jichud* geschrieben hast, daß Frauen mit einem einzelnen Mann von Stadt zu Stadt gehen und ähnliches, so ist das die Wahrheit. Und weil sie es heutzutage wegen unserer vielen Sünden so tun, geschehen daraus weitere Verderben, denn diese Generation ist völlig verkommen. Und es ist nicht in meiner Macht, das oder was daraus hervorgeht zu verhindern. Der Ewige erbarme sich über uns in der Güte Seiner grundlosen Liebe."[97] Die Grundbedeutung des von ihm verwendeten Adjektivs *paruz* ist „durchbrechen, schrankenlos sein", im Talmud wird der Ausdruck für Männer, Frauen und Handlungen verwendet, die die Rabbiner als triebhaft und obszön verurteilten[98]. Somit konnotiert das Wort mit Prostitution, und eine „ehrbare" Frau als *Pruza*, Hure, zu bezeichnen zog einen Ehrenbeleidigungsprozeß mit Versöhnungsritual *Mechila* und einer Geldstrafe nach sich[99].

Eine Verschärfung ihrer Brisanz erfuhren die mit der Mobilität verbundenen Fragen durch die Tatsache, daß Frauen im Zuge ihrer Geschäftstätigkeit bei Christen übernachteten. Aus heutiger Sicht der mittelalterlichen *castitas* wäre zu erwarten, daß dies eine Grenze des Tolerierbaren bedeutete und daher nicht vorkam. Eines der wenigen Rechtsgutachten, die sich mit diesem Problem beschäftigen, stellt jedoch nicht in erster Linie das Übernachten bei Christen zur halachischen Diskussion, sondern die nachfolgende Gefangenschaft der betreffenden Frau:

„Frage: Eine mit einem gewöhnlichen Juden (*Israel*) verheiratete Frau ist regelmäßig in den Häusern von Christen allein, manchmal in der Nacht wie am Tag, aufgrund von Pfandleihe (oder: Immobiliengeschäfte) und Handel. Und sie geht üblicher Weise in die Dörfer und sehr oft übernachtet sie auch unter den Christen, etwa acht Tage oder mehr. Und sie verkaufte üblicher Weise auf Kredit von den Christen, was sie nicht einlösen durfte, und deshalb wurde sie viele Male verhaftet und für Tage und Wochen allein unter den Christen gefangen gehalten. Ist sie ihrem

Izchak bar Mosche Or Sarua: Sefer Or Sarua Bd. 1 (Schitomir 1862, Nachdruck Tel Aviv 1976) Hilchot Jabam we-Kidduschin 166, Nr. 615; im folgenden zitiert: Sefer Or Sarua.

96 Zu ihm siehe GJ III/2, 1197 und 1628.

97 *Mosche Minz*, Sche'elot u-Teschuwot, hrsg. von *Jonathan Schraga Dumaw*, 2 Bände (Jerusalem 1991) Bd. 2, Nr. 87, § 8; im folgenden zitiert: *Mosche Minz*, Sche'elot u-Teschuwot.

98 Maharil bezeichnete es als *Prizut*, wenn „eine Frau unter die Männer geht" und das Kind, wie es noch Ende des 13. Jahrhunderts verbreiteter Minhag war, als Patin (*Sandakit* oder *Ba'alat Berit*) während der Beschneidung auf ihrem Schoß hielt. Sefer Maharil: Minhagim, hrsg. von *Shelomo Spitzer* (Jerusalem 1989) Berit Mila 487, Nr. 22. Siehe dazu *Keil*, Namhaft im Geschäft 351 und *Lawrence A. Hoffman*, The Role of Women at Rituals of Their Infant Children, in: Judaism in Practice. From the Middle Ages through the Early Modern Period, hrsg. von *Lawrence Fine* (Princeton 2001) 99–114, sowie *Grossman*, Pious (hebr.) 321–324.

99 *Menachem Merseburg*, Dine Boschet, in: *Jakob Weil*, Sche'elot u-Teschuwot 176–178, hier 177, äußere Spalte, 3. Din. Das zweite Wort für Hure ist *Sona*, siehe ebd., innere Spalte, 5. Din (eigene Zählung).

Mann erlaubt oder verboten, oder wird sie wenigstens ‚Übertreterin des Gesetzes' genannt oder nicht?"[100]

Welches konkrete Vergehen dieser Frau vorgeworfen wurde, läßt sich aus den knappen Andeutungen schwer rekonstruieren. Entweder sie verkaufte verfallene Pfänder vor der vereinbarten Frist oder ohne sie vorher entsprechend dem Fridericianum dem Judenrichter zu zeigen, oder sie verkaufte unerlaubte Pfänder wie Kirchen- oder Diebesgut oder, wie in manchen Privilegien verboten, Grund und Boden, wie das hebräische Wort *Sarsarut* nahelegen könnte[101]. Möglicherweise erging es ihr wie der Frankfurter Geldleiherin Selkeit, von der das Gerichtsbuch vermerkt, „daz Selkeit die jydinne eyne missetad verbuszen musze von dez frabels wegin, daz sie die phande gewert hat"[102]. Das ihr zur Last gelegte Vergehen ist für unsere Fragestellung allerdings nicht relevant. Wichtig ist, daß sie die Frau eines *Israel* und nicht eines *Kohen* war, also die priesterlichen Reinheitsgesetze für sie nicht zur Anwendung kamen. Des weiteren schien nicht die simple Tatsache ihrer Übernachtung bei Christen das Problem darzustellen, sondern deren lange Dauer von einer Woche und mehr. Außerdem ist nicht klar, ob ihre oftmalige Gefangenschaft im *Jichud* mit Christen ein halachisches Verbot für ihren Ehemann ergab oder sie in einen Status als Gesetzesübertreterin (*Overet al Dat*) versetzte, demzufolge sie eine Scheidung mit Verlust ihrer *Ketubba* zu erwarten hatte. In jedem Fall hatte ihr guter Ruf Schaden gelitten, denn eine *Overet al Dat* wird im Talmud (bKet. 72b) mit sittenwidrigem Verhalten in Verbindung gebracht[103].

Israel Isserleins Antwort ist ausführlich und stützt sich vor allem auf eine *Teschuwa* des Ascher ben Jechiel vom Beginn des 14. Jahrhunderts. Nach ihm ist eine solche Frau ihrem Ehemann, sogar einem *Kohen*, erlaubt, gleichgültig, ob ihr Aufenthalt bei den Christen wegen Pfandleihe (oder Immobiliengeschäften) oder we-

[100] *Israel Isserlein bar Petachja*, Terumat ha-Deschen Nr. 242.

[101] Zu den Pfandbestimmungen im Fridericianum siehe *Lohrmann*, Judenrecht 57, 62; zum Verbot, Immobilien als Pfand zu nehmen, siehe ebd. 78f., 161f., 242.

[102] *Isidor Kracauer* (Hrsg.), Urkundenbuch zur Geschichte der Juden in Frankfurt am Main von 1150–1400, Bd. 1: Urkunden, Rechenbücher, Bedenbücher (Frankfurt a. M. 1914) 835, Gerichtsbücher 1396, fol. 69a. Selkeit ist häufig erwähnt, siehe ebd. Register 1037. Einen ähnlichen Fall überliefert *Israel Bruna*, Sche'elot u-Teschuwot Nr. 57: Die Bürger von Brünn nahmen eine Frau namens Schafra gefangen, der sie mobile Pfänder zum Verkauf gegeben hatten und die diese an einen gewissen Abraham Jekel und andere Juden weiterverliehen hatte, worauf „nach ihren Gesetzen die Todesstrafe steht". Das Problem war hier aber die Bürgschaft für Anteile des Lösegelds.

[103] Zur „Gesetzesübertreterin" siehe Mischna Ketubbot VII, 6: „Folgende sind ohne Morgengabe zu entlassen: Die das Gesetz des Moses (*Dat Mosche*; die Halacha, Anm.) und die jüdische (Sitte) (*Dat jehudit*) übertritt". Das Gesetz des Moses übertreten heißt: dem Ehemann etwas nicht Verzehntes zum Essen geben, als Menstruierende Verkehr erlauben, auf der Straße spinnen, keine Teighebe absondern, Gelübde nicht halten. Die jüdische Sitte übertreten heißt: barhäuptig auf der Straße gehen, sich mit jedem Menschen unterhalten, den Erzeuger in Gegenwart seiner Nachkommen zu schmähen und ungebührlich laut zu sprechen. Die Diskussion dazu in bKetubbot 72b, worin das Spinnen auf der Straße mit obszönen Gesten und das Unterhalten mit „Scherzen mit jungen Leuten" assoziiert wird.

gen Heilkunde (oder: Handel mit Arzneiwaren) erfolgt ist[104]. Auch nahm Isserlein das zitierte Argument der Tosafisten auf, daß es für eine jüdische Frau unmöglich ist, nicht hin und wieder mit Nichtjuden alleine zu sein. Die Kontroverse zwischen Raschi, den Tosafisten und anderen Autoritäten die „Gesetzesübertreterin" betreffend entschied Isserlein folgendermaßen: Ein freiwilliger *Jichud*, noch dazu mit Christen, die als *schitufe sima*, überaus obszön, bekannt sind (bSchabb. 152a), macht die Frau zur *Overet al Dat*, und wenn sich ihr Ehemann nicht scheiden läßt, wird er *Rescha*, Bösewicht, genannt[105]. Zum Absprechen der *Ketubba* ist allerdings eine offizielle Verwarnung vor zwei Zeugen (*Hatra'a*) nötig, welche in diesem Fall aufgrund der Umstände nicht erfolgen konnte[106]. Halachisch bestand also keine eindeutige Handhabe, eine solche Frau von ihren Geschäftsgewohnheiten oder -erfordernissen abzuhalten. Wenn der Ehemann damit einverstanden war, hatte sie außer dem mißbilligenden Blick mancher Rabbiner nichts zu befürchten. Anders lag der Fall bei einer Gefangennahme mit Drohung von Ermordung und Zwangstaufe. Die grausamen Ereignisse der Wiener Gesera von 1420/21 und anderer Verfolgungen gaben zur Diskussion der halachischen Konsequenzen reichlich Anlaß, sind aber in diesem Zusammenhang nicht von Bedeutung[107].

Zusammenfassung

Die zitierten Entscheide und resignierten Kommentare zeigen, daß Rabbiner, welche weibliche Geschäftstätigkeit oder zumindest deren konsequente Durchführung mit beruflich bedingten Übernachtungen bei Christen als in höchstem Maße sittenwidrig und ehrenrührig empfanden, keine Handhabe gegen die Frauen hatten. Die wirtschaftliche Pragmatik überwog sichtlich die moralischen Bedenken, anders wäre der hohe Prozentsatz von Frauen in der Geldleihe nicht erklärbar. Doch ob nun der in Terumat ha-Deschen 241 behandelte Fall einen, wie ich annehme, konkreten Anlaß hatte oder nur halachische Diskussion ist, er zeigt, daß die längere Aufenthaltsdauer bei Christen in Dörfern, wo keine jüdische Familie eine Übernachtungsmöglichkeit bot, eine verheiratete Frau in Verruf und in die Nähe von *Prizut*, Hurerei, bringen konnte. Auch die Gefahr der Vergewaltigung und

[104] Zu jüdischen Ärztinnen siehe *Wolfgang Treue*, Verehrt und angespien: Zur Geschichte jüdischer Ärzte in Aschkenas von den Anfängen bis zur Akademisierung. Würzburger medizinhistorische Mitteilungen 21 (2002) 139–204, hier 173 und 184–187; *Joseph Shatzmiller*, Jews, Medicine and Medieval Society (Berkeley, Los Angeles 1994) 108–112, *Toch*, Die jüdische Frau 38.

[105] Ebenfalls ein die Ehre beleidigender Ausdruck, siehe *Merseburg*, Dine Boschet (Schandprozesse), in: *Weil*, Sche'elot u-Teschuwot 179, äußere Spalte, 3. Din (eigene Zählung).

[106] Zum leichtfertigen Aussprechen einer *Hatra'a* vor zwei Zeugen siehe Sefer Or Sarua 1, Hilchot Jabam we-Kidduschin Nr. 616.

[107] Das Thema der bei der Gesera gefangenen Frauen bei *Israel Isserlein bar Petachja*, Terumat ha-Deschen Nr. 241, *Maharil*, Sche'elot u-Teschuwot Nr. 72, *Mosche Minz*, Sche'elot u-Teschuwot Nr. 103. Siehe *Mordechai Breuer*, Women in Jewish Martyrology (hebr.), in: Facing the Cross. The Persecutions of 1096 in History and Historiography, hrsg. von *Yom Tov Assis*, *Jeremy Cohen* u. a. (Jerusalem 2000).

Gefangennahme auf Reisen mit ihren halachischen Implikationen der Zwangsscheidung mochte Ehefrauen von berufsbedingtem längerem Unterwegssein abgehalten haben. Dies ist nicht der einzige Grund, warum sich vor allem unter den führenden Geschäftsfrauen größtenteils Witwen befanden, denn das jüdische Ehe- und Vermögensrecht begünstigt diesen Faktor ebenfalls in hohem Maße[108]. Doch die geforderte *Zniut* einer Tochter Israels, deren „Herrlichkeit im Inneren" liegt[109], mag zum Ausschluß der Frauen von bedeutenden Geschäften, die höhere Mobilität erforderten, maßgeblich beigetragen haben.

[108] Siehe Anm. 16.

[109] *Susan Grossman, Rivka Haut* (Hrsg.), Daughters of the King. Women and the Synagogue (Philadelphia, Jerusalem 1992) Einleitung XXII-XXIV, zu Psalm 45, 14: „Die Königstochter ist herrlich im Inneren".

Michael Toch

Economic Activities of German Jews in the Middle Ages*

I. Jewish Trade in the 10th–11th Centuries

The Jews first attracted to German lands were primarily merchants, as succinctly stated by Gershom ben Jehudah "Light of the Exile" of Mainz, the foremost religious authority of his time (ca. 960–1028): *Because their* (the Jews') *livelihood*

* This essay is the fruit of long years of research in the history of German Jews as well as in the economic history of European Jews, both topics for which a book each is in preparation. See also my collection of articles: *Michael Toch*, Peasants and Jews in Medieval Germany: Studies in Cultural, Social and Economic History (Aldershot 2003). All translations from the Hebrew sources, except where otherwise noted, are mine. The following abbreviations are used for works quoted a number of times: *Agus* = *Irving Agus* (ed.), Urban Civilization in Pre-Crusade Europe, 2 vols. (Leiden 1965); *Andernacht* = *Dietrich Andernacht* (ed.), Regesten zur Geschichte der Juden in der Reichsstadt Frankfurt am Main von 1401–1519, 3 vols. (Hannover 1996); *Aronius* = *Julius Aronius* (ed.), Regesten zur Geschichte der Juden im Fränkischen und Deutschen Reich bis zum Jahre 1273 (Berlin 1902, Hildesheim 1970); *Caro* = *Georg Caro*, Sozial- und Wirtschaftsgeschichte der Juden im Mittelalter und der Neuzeit, 2 vols. (Leipzig 1908–20, Hildesheim 1964); *Dinur* = *Ben-Zion Dinur* (ed.), Israel in the Diaspora, vol. II (Tel Aviv ^{2}1959, Hebrew); Germania Judaica I–III = Germania Judaica, vol. I: Von den ältesten Zeiten bis 1238, ed. by *M. Brann, I. Elbogen, A. Freimann, H. Tykocinski* (Breslau 1917–34, Tübingen ^{2}1963); vol. II: Von 1238 bis zur Mitte des 14. Jahrhunderts, ed. by *Z. Avneri*, 2 parts (Tübingen 1968); vol. III: 1350–1519, 3 parts, ed. by *A. Maimon, M. Breuer, Y. Guggenheim* (Tübingen 1987–2003); *Gershom* = The Responsa of Rabbenu Gershom Meor ha-Golah, ed. by *Shlomo Eidelberg* (New York 1955, Hebrew); *Hoffmann* = *Moses Hoffmann* (ed.), Der Geldhandel der deutschen Juden während des Mittelalters bis zum Jahre 1350 (Leipzig 1910); *Kisch* = *Guido Kisch*, The Jews in Medieval Germany. A Study of Their Legal and Social Status (Chicago 1949, New York 1970); *Linder* = *Amnon Linder* (ed.), The Jews in the Legal Sources of the Early Middle Ages (Detroit, Jerusalem 1998); *Maharam* = Responsa Meir ben Barukh of Rothenburg, ed. *M.-A. Bloch*, part 4, print Prague (Budapest 1891); *Mentgen* = *Gerd Mentgen*, Studien zur Geschichte der Juden im mittelalterlichen Elsaß (Hannover 1995); *Mutius* = *Hans-Georg von Mutius* (ed.), Rechtsentscheide rheinischer Rabbinen vor dem ersten Kreuzzug, 2 vols. (Frankfurt a. M. 1984–85); *Neubauer, Stern* = *Adolf Neubauer, Moritz Stern* (eds.), Hebräische Berichte über die Judenverfolgungen während der Kreuzzüge (Berlin 1892); *Schmandt* = *Matthias Schmandt*, Judei, cives et incole: Studien zur jüdischen Geschichte Kölns im Mittelalter (Hannover 2002); *Shatzmiller* = *Joseph Shatzmiller*, Shylock Reconsidered. Jews, Moneylending and Medieval Society (Berkeley, Los Angeles, Oxford 1990); *Soloveitchik*, Pawnbroking = *Haim Soloveitchik*, Pawnbroking. A Study in the Inter-Relationship between Halakhah, Economic Activity and Communal Self-Image (Jerusalem 1985, Hebrew); *Soloveitchik*, Principles = *Haim Soloveitchik*, Principles and Pressures: Jewish Trade in Gentile Wine in the Middle Ages (Tel

depends on their commerce[1]. What was its nature, which were its customers, what functions and needs did it fulfill in the economy of the period? The few extant Latin sources cannot answer such questions, even though scholars have used them for a long time to construct sweeping theories (see below). We are better served by the Hebrew texts, the earliest of which were penned by the before-mentioned Gershom in the late 10th and early 11th century. For the first part of the 11th century there are also the legal decisions collected in the *Sefer ha-Dinim* of Jehudah ha-Cohen (Mainz, to ca. 1055). For the second part of the century we have *Responsa* and legal decisions by a number of scholars active in Mainz and Worms[2].

What was the merchandise bought and sold? One commodity regularly mentioned – slaves – should be struck from the list. In all probability, German and other European Jews of the Early Middle Ages most did not practice the slave trade to any significant degree. They certainly did not dominate this trade[3]. Of other glittering treasures of inter-continental commerce too very little is found in the sources. Rather, this was a blend of staple goods such as wine, grains, salted fish, horses and cattle, dyed hides, raw wool, cloth, ready-made garments, metal vessels. In addition, there were more valuable goods such as spices, medicines, precious textiles and metals, and gilded vessels. Most of the merchandise was purchased on inland markets from Jewish and non-Jewish business partners, with the fair of Cologne the major venue and the Rhine River between Cologne, Mainz, and Worms the main artery of transport. Secondary routes were opened in the early 12th century towards the Netherlands to the west and central Germany to the east. Along these conduits over time schedules of shipping and hauling, lodging, partnerships, and accounting were established. Business trips to foreign parts were undertaken too – to Poland via Prague and Krakow, to Hungary and southern

Aviv 2003, Hebrew); *Toch*, Geld und Kredit = *Michael Toch*, Geld und Kredit in einer spätmittelalterlichen Landschaft. Zu einem unbeachteten hebräischen Schuldenregister aus Niederbayern 1329–1332), in: Deutsches Archiv 38 (1982) 499–550; *Toch*, Geldhandel = *Michael Toch*, Der jüdische Geldhandel in der Wirtschaft des deutschen Spätmittelalters: Nürnberg 1350–1499, in: Blätter für deutsche Landesgeschichte 117 (1981) 283–310; *Toch*, Tätigkeit = *Michael Toch*, Die wirtschaftliche Tätigkeit, in: Germania Judaica III/3 (Tübingen 2003) 2139–2164; *Toch*, Wirtschaft = *Michael Toch*, Wirtschaft und Geldwesen der Juden Frankfurts in Spätmittelalter und Frühneuzeit, in: *K. Grözinger* (ed.), Jüdische Kultur in Frankfurt am Main von den Anfängen bis zur Gegenwart (Frankfurt a.M. 1997) 25–46.

[1] *Gershom*, no. 21. The last word – *Sehorah* – means both commerce and merchandise.

[2] The greater part of the texts of the 10th and 11th centuries is available in English and German translation: *Hoffmann*, *Agus*, *Mutius*.

[3] For detailed arguments and source quotations on this hotly debated question see *Michael Toch*, Jews and Commerce: Modern Fancies and Medieval Realities, in: *S. Cavaciocchi* (ed.), Il ruolo economico delle minoranze in Europa. Secc. XIII-XVIII (Atti della XXXI Settimana di Studi, Istituto Francesco Datini, Prato) (Firenze 2000) 43–58. Michael McCormick has recently reaffirmed, also *contra* my arguments, the involvement of Jews in the slave trade. However, "Contrary to the common assertion that Jews dominated the slave trade, systematic scrutiny of the sources shows that early medieval... Christians, as well as Slavs and Muslims, all traded in slaves": *Michael McCormick*, New Light on the 'Dark Ages': How the Slave Trade Fuelled the Carolingian Economy, in: Past & Present 177 (2002) 52–53, note 88.

Russia via Regensburg and the Danube River, possibly also towards Venice along the mountain routes of southeastern Austria. However, compared to the frequency of visits to inland markets, travel in foreign lands was clearly not the rule[4]. Merchandise was packed in sachets, bags, and boxes and transported in saddlebags, carts, and boats. Sometimes it was considered so valuable as to warrant months of delay in order to regain lost or stolen goods. To be on the move was the normal condition for these merchants, one of whom explained in a legal argument: *I wished to take to the road, like all other men.*[5]

Early medieval Jews were thus deeply involved in commerce. Does this mean that they were *the guardians and tutors of the Germans in trade*, the *cornerstone of German urban culture*[6]? Did they indeed wield a mercantile hegemony, even a monopoly, as has been claimed by most historians for a long time now[7]? Leaving aside the general tendency to overstate the significance of the Jewish presence in Europe and especially in economics, for a number of concrete considerations the answer must be no. Scholars have frequently been led astray by the Latin phrase *Iudei et ceteri mercatores* (*Jews and other merchants*), which turns up with minor variations in five sources from 10th century Germany as well as in a further one of the 11th century[8]. They understood this to mean that Jews were perceived as the proverbial merchants, non-Jews but as an insignificant afterthought. This idea should be dropped as it stems from a mistaken reading. The texts designate Jewish and non-Jewish merchants by their most remarkable characteristic: Christian merchants differed from the rest of the population by their trade activities, their Jewish colleagues by religious identity. The only thing these texts do say is that there were both Jewish and non-Jewish merchants. This obvious conclusion is fully borne out by Hebrew sources that frequently mention not only Christian customers but also business associates. The existence of non-Jewish merchants is of course independently documented in a large number of Latin documents and has long been known to economic historians. Repeated misunderstanding has also been the lot of the Hebrew phrase *medinot ha-yam* and *medinat ha-yam*, literally *the lands/land of*

[4] On travelers to Russia, the enthusiastic reading of *J. Brutzkus*, Der Handel der westeuropäischen Juden mit dem alten Kiev, in: Zeitschrift für die Geschichte der Juden in Deutschland n. S. 3 (1931) 97–110, as well as of other scholars too numerous to be quoted needs to be balanced by the sober appreciation of *Shmuel Ettinger*, Kievan Russia, in: *Cecil Roth* (ed.), The World History of the Jewish People, 2nd series, vol. II: The Dark Ages (Tel Aviv 1966) 319–324.

[5] *Jehudah ha-Cohen*, Sefer ha-Dinim, in: *Maharam*, no. 880; transl. *Agus*, 112.

[6] *Raphael Straus*, Die Juden in Wirtschaft und Gesellschaft (Frankfurt a. M. 1964) 29, my translation. For an almost identical phrasing some years earlier see *Kisch*, 318.

[7] For the currents of historiography see *Toch*, Jews and Commerce (above, note 3). Lonely voices of dissent were *Caro*, I, 198, *Adriaan Verhulst*, Der Handel im Merowingerreich: Gesamtdarstellung nach schriftlichen Quellen (Gent 1970) 17–18, and lately *J.-P. Devroey*, La participation des Juifs au commerce dans le monde franc (VIe–Xe siècles), in: *A. Dierkens*, *J.-M. Sansterre* (eds.), Voyages et voyageurs à Byzance et en Occident du VIe au XIe siècle (Geneva 2001) 339–374. For the sources and detailed arguments for the following see my "Economic History of Medieval European Jews", vol. I, in preparation.

[8] *Linder*, 349, 378, 380, 382, 389; *Aronius*, no. 132.

the sea, which appears in a significant number of *Responsa* in the context of Jews going about their business[9]. Bringing to mind the medieval *outremer*, this has been taken to suggest Jewish merchant adventurers sailing the seven seas. However, *medinot ha-yam* is nothing more than a Talmudic expression meaning initially any place outside the Land of Israel, and later simply abroad, outside one's country of residence. Romantic as it might sound, this phrase tells nothing about overseas travel or sea-faring ventures.

Hebrew sources do mention frequent exchanges between scholars, sages and students in different parts of Europe, but almost no commercial contacts between Jews of *Ashkenaz* and *Sepharad*, let alone between those of Europe and of the Muslim world in the east. The decisive test is provided by the Cairo *Genizah*, the huge repository for trade information of Oriental Jews, written from the late 10th century onwards by merchants intimately informed of the affairs of their business partners[10]. Their commercial contacts were extremely intricate and frequent. They were conducted with fellow Oriental Jews ranging from Muslim Spain all along the North-African coast to Egypt and the eastern Mediterranean seaboard; with local Muslim merchants; as well as with Christian traders coming to Egypt and Muslim Sicily from Italy and Byzantium. European Jews as trade partners of Oriental Jews do not appear in the record[11]. Consequently, if an inter-continental Jewish trade system existed, Jews of Europe and of the Muslim world did not operate it *in tandem*. Considering all these factors, the supposed lead of Jews is reduced to much humbler proportions. Such proportions agree with population numbers, which were yet slight. When numbers began to grow in the later 11th century, a force much more significant than the Jews came to dominate the long-distance trade of Europe, namely the Italians.

Yet another and slightly conflicting notion was eagerly embraced by 19th century historians and remains current today: that money lending as a major occupation of Jews dates back if not to times immemorial, then at least to the Early Middle Ages. Most advocates of this view adduce no evidence besides an inborn Jewish inclination for such vocation, and there is no need to take issue with them. They were probably just following the stereotype of the eternal Jewish moneylender, on which Giacomo Todeschini expands in this volume. More conscientious ones went to some trouble to base their verdict on sources. Sadly, here too misunderstandings abound. The editors of *Germania Judaica* I, and others following them, quoted a *Responsum*, attributed by Rashi to Gershom's "Light of Exile", as proof for wide-

9 Source references in: The Responsa Project, Version 12+, Bar-Ilan University (Ramat Gan 2004, CD-Rom, Hebrew), under the terms *medinot ha-yam*, *medinat ha-yam*, and the abbreviation *mdhy*.

10 Cf. *Shlomo Dov Goitein*, A Mediterranean Society: The Jewish Communities of the Arab World as Portrayed in the Documents of the Cairo Geniza, 6 vols. (Berkeley, Los Angeles, London 1968–1993).

11 *Shlomo Dov Goitein*, Mediterranean trade preceding the Crusades: some facts and problems, in: Diogenes 59:56 (Fall 1967) 47–62; *Armand O. Citarella*, A puzzling question concerning the relations between the Jewish communities of Christian Europe and those represented in the Geniza documents, in: Journal of the American Oriental Society 91 (1971) 390–397.

spread money lending to Gentiles already at the turn of the 10th to the 11th century: *It is forbidden to do as they do in this kingdom, to give at the fair of Cologne one pound of pure silver which is 12* (ounces of silver), *and then to receive in their lodgings in Mainz or upon their return to Worms 13 ounces in coin.*[12] This has nothing to do with money lending. Rather, it is an early form of currency speculation, taking advantage of the price difference between bullion and coined silver and making use of a network of coinless transfer of obligations, in short "dry exchange". Evidenced between Jews as well as with non-Jews, such transactions were important enough to be licensed, surely upon Jewish insistence, in the privilege granted by the bishop of Speyer in 1084[13]. Were this a case of money lending to Gentiles, no medieval Jewish sage would have found reason to interfere. The only reason for Gershom's intervention or for Rashi's quotation was the concern that Jews might obtain forbidden interest from fellow Jews.

Nevertheless, merchants certainly made funds available as loans. Another *Responsum* attributed to Gershom describes two types of debtors: *the violent oppressor* who will recover his pawn without paying interest, and the regular customer, whose pledge can be kept until due interest is paid[14]. The context of such loans is nicely sketched in the opening to yet another *Responsum* by Gershom: *Reuben used to go to many places and to many fiefs distant one or two days from the town where he dwelled; and he used to sell to the lords of the fiefs and buy from them, his regular clientele. And when they had no ready coin they would put in his hand their pawns of silver and gold, and sometimes he would exchange with them merchandise for the cattle that they looted from their enemies…*[15]. This was an environment chronically short of cash, where straightforward loans, delayed payment, and pawns put up as security until completion were all part and parcel of the business of selling merchandise.

Such basic economic facts also had a social aspect. The customers of this trade in goods and money were bishops and priests, in one case an episcopal treasurer, rich ladies up to a queen of Hungary (scholars differ as to her identity), magnates, barons, counts, chatelaines, and lords of villages. In short, these were the upper layers of ecclesiastical and lay society, resident in their palaces in town and in their castles in the countryside. Yet another question addressed to Gershom describes the atmosphere in which Jewish businessmen and Christian customers met: *I have assiduously cultivated his friendship, often lent him money at no interest, and countless times served him in various capacities.*[16] Business was conducted within a context of familiarity, of extended relations with a stock clientele. This is the setting for the social symmetry noticeable even at the eve of the First Crusade (1096)

[12] *Gershom*, no. 29; Germania Judaica I, XXIX–XXX.
[13] *Linder*, 400.
[14] *Zedekiah ben Abraham ha-Rofe*, Sefer Shiboleh ha-Leket, part 2, ed. *M. S. Hasidah* (Jerusalem 1968) 80, no. 45, transl. *Mutius*, I, 70.
[15] *Gershom*, no. 36. The translation of *Agus*, 99, misses the feudal point. This particular case apparently took place in northeastern France, not in Germany.
[16] *Gershom*, 161, transl. *Agus*, 210, no. LXII.

between some Jews and Jewesses called in Hebrew sources "noble", and their Christian counterparts, prelates, aristocrats, and members of the urban patriciate[17]. Only with such patrons in mind did it make sense to design the legal instrument of *Maarufiya* (a term of Arabic derivation), by which the local community gave to a single merchant exclusive access to a potent customer and his household[18]. Simple folk, let alone the poor, are not yet found amongst clients. Instead, they appear as wagoners, craftsmen, and agricultural workers in the employ of Jews. In one case in or near Regensburg they were a pair of professional thieves who provided two rival Jewish "fences" with stolen merchandise[19].

Behind the frequent interference of the sages there lies a major problem besetting business in the 10th and 11th century: the recurrent and apparently vital need to raise substantial capital. The obvious solution, borrowing money from fellow Jewish merchants, ran into the stern biblical prohibition: *Unto a foreigner thou may lend upon interest, but unto thy brother thou shalt not lend upon interest* (Deuteronomy 23:20–21). The mortgaging of agricultural land, much employed by Provencal and Iberian Jews, was of little avail in the north, where Jews lacked widespread landed property, as we shall see. The problem urgently called for a solution, and a number of exceptions came to be permitted by Talmudic scholars. For long-term partnerships in trade ventures, the legal instrument of *Isska* was developed. Very similar to the Italian *commenda* agreement, it guaranteed the silent partner his part of the profits[20]. The regular interest-bearing loan too was legalized, provided the subterfuge of a pawn and a non-Jewish intermediary were employed[21]. Yet another resort was borrowing from well-to-do Gentiles, which was even termed an *old custom*[22]. The sheer amount of *Halakhic* discussion is a conclusive pointer to the widespread need for ready cash, as well as to the fact that Jews indeed took interest from fellow Jews. Another problem was competition in a constricted and highly personalized market, as indicated by the frequent litigation recorded in the sources. When rivalry got out of hand, hatred, violence and the instigation of Christian

[17] *Neubauer, Stern*, in Hebrew on pp. 3, 17, 22, 40, 44, 50–51, in German translation on pp. 86, 101, 116–117, 126, 128, 143, 160, 164, 171, 176, 190. It should be noted that this edition and translation is now superseded by *Eva Haverkamp*, Hebräische Berichte über die Judenverfolgungen während des Ersten Kreuzzugs (Monumenta Germaniae Historica, Hebräische Texte aus dem mittelalterlichen Deutschland I, München 2005).

[18] For the texts see *Agus*, 187–255. For the legal principles see *Irving Agus*, The Heroic Age of Franco-German Jewry (New York 1969) 59–66, and *Shlomo Eidelberg*, "Maarufia" in Rabbenu Gershom's Responsa, in: Historia Judaica 15 (1953) 59–66.

[19] The text, assiduously shunned by earlier Jewish scholars for providing ammunition to anti-Semitic slander, was first published in 1975 (!) by *Abraham Grossman*, The Attitude of the Early Scholars of Ashkenaz towards the Authority of the "Kahal", in: Annual of the Institute for Research in Jewish Law 2 (1975) 195–198 (Hebrew). For a translation see *Mutius*, I, 109–115.

[20] *Soloveitchik*, Pawnbroking 10. For examples of such agreements see *Agus*, nos. XIII–XVII, XIX, XXVIII, LXXVIII, LXXXII, CVII.

[21] *Soloveitchik*, Pawnbroking 25–81.

[22] *Agus*, nos. XXVIII, LXIX, LXXVI, CII; *Mutius*, I, 60, 76; *Soloveitchik*, Pawnbroking 323 and note 51.

authorities could follow, as witnessed for instance by a Hebrew horror tale embellished as an instance of religious persecution and placed in late 10th century France[23]. It is thus not surprising that among the earliest community legislation, there were two ordinances designed to curb the threat of economic anarchy: *Herem ha-yishuv*, which gave the community the right to veto the settlement of newcomers; and the already mentioned *Maarufiya*, by which the community assigned a potent customer to a single merchant.

II. From Traders to Moneylenders: The Central Middle Ages

The sources for the economic history of German Jews increase in volume and detail in the Central Middle Ages, from the late 11th to the end of the 13th century. There is a growing flow of Latin charters, reflecting more settled circumstances and a stronger reliance on written records. Hebrew sources too are more plentiful, as is to be expected in light of the demographic and geographical surge of Jewish life. However, this augmentation has its pitfalls, raising problems of representation. How typical is a sample of Latin charters mainly produced by and for the elite, or of Hebrew *Responsa* recorded in the wake of litigation and doubt as to the norm? The problem is typical to any historical enquiry: how to weigh and balance what is in the record, the tip of the iceberg, as compared to the iceberg itself, the absent commonplace unworthy of recording?

The Central Middle Ages were a time of a commercial revolution, of rapid population growth (including a Jewish one), and of urbanization[24]. One major factor was the overall growth of surface and river trade within continental Europe, on the local, regional, and inter-regional level. Another feature was the emergence of industrial centers and regional specialization in commodities production, most notably in the textile crafts. The task of the merchant and entrepreneur underwent a decisive change, from provisioning a small aristocracy to handling mass consumer goods. The servicing of such huge and growing systems, in size, complexity and capital outlays far surpassing earlier trade structures, was clearly beyond the resources of a numerically still tiny Ashkenazic Jewry. Physical conditions too changed, as the rising tide of enmity turned the traveling Jewish merchant into an endangered species. However, contrary to the assertion frequently put forward by scholars, there is no indication in the sources of a deliberate exclusion of Jews from trade by an emerging Christian merchant class organized in guilds[25].

[23] *A. Haberman* (ed.), Book of Persecutions in Germany and France (Jerusalem 1945/1971 Hebrew) 12.

[24] The classic statement is still *Robert S. Lopez*, The Commercial Revolution of the Middle Ages (Cambridge 1976). For Germany in this period see *Alfred Haverkamp*, Medieval Germany, 1056–1273 (Oxford 1988).

[25] The classic statement is the article of 1875 by *Wilhelm Roscher*, Die Stellung der Juden im Mittelalter, betrachtet vom Standpunkt der allgemeinen Handelspolitik, translated into English by *Shlomo Grayzel* as The Status of the Jews in the Middle Ages Considered from the Standpoint of

Rather, there must have been a strong pull of new opportunities in the sedentary handling and lending of money. Highly significant for our purpose, this was the time when more and more parts of the population became involved, for sustenance and consumer goods, in the market economy and in monetary exchanges[26]. Such economic changes called for huge investments in commodities production and distribution systems. However, apart from the growing urban population, most earnings were still tied to the slow rhythm of agricultural production, where one was paid for one's produce or labor once or twice a year. Even though the papacy, kings and princes were rapidly developing taxation, middling and smaller lords still depended on income from their landed possessions. In addition, the polities of Europe were swept by heightened public consumption and outlays, on the remuneration of administrative personnel, on war overseas and at home, on huge building projects for both religious and military purposes. Thus for example, during the 13th century most German towns constructed new and expensive fortifications[27]. Sheer lavishness too came to the fore, not necessarily because people lost their morals and religion, as preachers and clerics untiringly pointed out, but rather because of the heightened competition between and within the social elites of Europe. While the demand for means of payment surged, the supply side of the monetary system remained in a backward and often anarchic state, with a large number of mints turning out competing and often debased coins. In short, the entire extent of economic, monetary, social, and political development of the Central Middle Ages made for a steady growth in the demand for credit.

Over this period, Jewish trade in northern Europe appears to have diminished, in a course similar to the one effecting Jewish merchants in the Mediterranean south some hundred years earlier[28]. At the same time a remarkably stable perception of the Jew was formed by first French and then other ecclesiastics: the usurer[29]. How accurate was this perception, coming from people intent on moral and religious purposes rather than on economic observation? Overall, it appears to have been warranted by a changing reality, however with significant differences and time lags between the different parts of Europe. In Germany, the move to

Commercial Policy, in: Historia Judaica 6 (1944) 13–26. See also there, on pp. 1–12, the enthusiastic appreciation by *Guido Kisch*, The Jews' Function in the Mediaeval Evolution of Economic Life. For a devastating critique see *Toni Oelsner*, Wilhelm Roscher's Theory and the Economic and Social Position of the Jews in the Middle Ages: A Critical Examination, in: Yivo Annual of Jewish Social Science 12 (1958–9) 176–195.

26 A convincing statement of the tensions and conflicts thus engendered is *Lester K. Little*, Religious Poverty and the Profit Economy in Medieval Europe (Ithaca N.Y. 1978).

27 *Michael Toch*, The Medieval German City under Siege, in: *M. Wolfe*, *I. Corfis* (eds.), The Medieval City under Siege (Woodbridge 1995) 35–48.

28 *Eliyahu Ashtor*, Gli ebrei nel comercio mediterraneo nell'alto medioevo (sec. X–XI), in: Gli ebrei nell'alto medioevo (Spoleto 1980) 401–487. However, as will be demonstrated in my book mentioned in note 7, Ashtor and other scholars highly overestimated Jewish involvement in Mediterranean trade.

29 Its development and modern historiographical offspins are treated in this volume by *Giacomo Todeschini*.

money lending as the main Jewish profession was a long process, beginning in the early 12th century and not completed, by all signs, before the mid-13th century. The initial situation is concisely summed up in a *Responsum* of Elieser ben Nathan of Mainz (died around 1150), where one litigant states: *all Jews live by merchandise and interest and we are no different.* In another place Elieser writes: *just at is allowed to sell to them* (the Gentiles), *it is allowed to give them loans.* Again: ... *because trade serves as our livelihood*[30]. Towards the end of the 12th century, Elieser's son-in-law, Joel ben Yitzhak ha-Levi of Bonn, could still write: *at this time when we have no fields and vineyards and make a living by lending money at interest and buying and selling*[31].

Actually, Joel was not quite correct in his statement. In the 11th century some Jews had indeed possessed vineyards on the Rhine. So did their descendents of the 12th century, on the Rhine and now on the Main River. As earlier, there were some craftsmen working for Jewish and at times for Gentile customers. Jewish agriculturists and craftsmen and their share in the general picture will be treated further below. As earlier, Jews traveled by ship and wagon to the fairs at Cologne, and now to Frankfurt on the Main[32]. Apparently it was still standard procedure, as narrated in the *Book of Pious*, for a merchant to load his wagon with clothes, drive to another town, take lodgings, and open shop[33]. When king Lothair held court in Mainz in 1128, young Jehudah of Cologne, later the convert and autobiographer Herman of Scheda, arrived there with the purpose of selling merchandise, *as all Jews are wont to engage in business*[34]. The same intent brought another young man called Alexander in 1199 to king Philip's camp near Koblenz, and eventually to a violent death. Earlier he had, amongst others, tried his hand selling new wine in the countryside[35]. While inland business trips remain routine, travel abroad becomes definitely sparse in the sources. Jews also settled down as sedentary shopkeepers[36]. This must have entailed a broadening of the clientele beyond the aristocracy, as well as an increasingly anonymous setting for commercial contacts, typically the market place. For the first time we hear of merchants of the two religions coming into conflict. Thus, in 1171 two strange Jews had turned up at the market at Cologne to sell their stock, only to be accused of passing counterfeit money. Put out by a local moneychanger and spread further by the toll officials, this allegation nearly led to a pogrom[37]. Minters, moneychangers, and toll-collectors were right to be apprehensive of Jewish competition, as demonstrated in this volume by Markus Wenninger. These were services riding the crest of the economic modernization, growth, and

30 *Elieser ben-Nathan*, Sefer Raben (Even ha-Ezer), transl. *Hoffmann*, nos. 64, 45, 47.

31 *Dinur*, 248.

32 *Hoffmann*, nos. 51, 52, 53, 56, 57, 61, 80; Germania Judaica I, 107, note 25.

33 *Dinur*, 237.

34 *Hermannus quondam Judaeus*, Opusculum de conversione sua, ed. *G. Niemeyer* (Weimar 1963) 72.

35 *Aronius*, no. 345.

36 *Hoffmann*, no. 83, following *Yitzchak ben Moshe Or sarua*, before 1250.

37 *Neubauer, Stern*, 71–72, 206–209.

commercialization felt, with time lags, all over Europe. The reverse side to this monetary surge was the development, in Germany as well as in other places of Europe, of the stereotype of the Jew as counterfeiter of coins[38].

Both Hebrew and Latin sources leave no doubt to the growing importance of money lending. By the 12th century one can clearly differentiate between trade and credit operations, and loans given against interest are in plain evidence. The clientele is still mainly made up of members of the upper classes, even though by now much extended: archbishops, bishops, abbots, priors, deacons, communities of monks and cathedral priests; kings, dukes, princes, margraves and burgraves, counts, landed proprietors, knights[39]. However, a strong qualification needs to be added here. Latin sources mention details only exceptionally and when grave circumstances are involved, for instance the transfer of landed property, the source of power, or of politically precarious objects put up as pawns, such as precious pieces of the treasury of a cathedral church or abbey[40]. Such sources cannot be expected to wield systematic information. By the 13th century there were already commoners amongst the patrons, and by the early 14th century they made up a significant part of the clientele. The largest numbers were burgers, of practically every more important German town as well as of many smaller ones. There were also peasants, such as the customers of an anonymous Jew active in and around the Bavarian market town of Straubing. His Hebrew list of outstanding debts from the years 1329–1332 provides a cross-section of the more affluent society of the region: lower nobility, burgers of towns and market places, village priests, and, the largest group, peasants and rural artisans[41]. This source and similar ones of the Later Middle Ages invalidate an influential view, namely *that in the entire source material under consideration, reaching up to the 15th century, there is not even a single instance proving or even indicating indebtness of peasants to Jews*[42].

Our sources shed little direct light yet on personal motives for borrowing money. For instance, there is no mention of the expenses occurred by crusaders taking the cross, a matter frequently conjectured by historians to have plunged people into debt. In regard to kings, princes, prelates, and town governments it is safe to infer that many loans and especially more substantial ones were motivated by political necessity. Thus, in 1287 bishop Frederick of Thur, a member of the family of the

[38] *Gerd Mentgen*, Der Münzfrevelvorwurf. Ein Beitrag zur Erforschung antijüdischer Stereotype, in: *A. Giebmeyer, H. Schnabel-Schüle* (eds.), "Das Wichtigste ist der Mensch". Festschrift Klaus Gerteis (Mainz 2000) 291–307.

[39] *Dinur*, 251, 257; *Hoffmann*, nos. 37, 38, 70, 77, 88; *Caro*, I, 349, 439, 441; *Aronius*, nos. 214, 287, 298, 369, 391, 392, 394, 407, 427, 444, 532, 533, 538, 577–581, 594, 619, 628–631, 642, 643, 680, 684, 689, 699, 707, 712, 730, 732. For a regional listing of customers in 13th and early-14th century Alsace see *Mentgen*, 494–502.

[40] For instance *Aronius*, nos. 214, 287, 298, 349, 369, 391, 392, 394, 407; *Caro*, I, 439, 441.

[41] Edited and commented upon by *Toch*, Geld und Kredit. For references to peasant customers in other places, all of them in the early 14th century, see Germania Judaica II, 70, 217, 446, 594, 601, 888.

[42] *Kisch*, 225. His position derived entirely from an inappropriate type of sources, legal texts of urban origin, and was a patent attempt to counter 19th century anti-Semitic apologetics.

counts of Montfort, needed to attend the imperial diet at Würzburg. For this purpose his three brothers borrowed for him the substantial sum of 160 marks from a Jewess, Guta of Überlingen[43]. This was a middling transaction, even though it embroiled the family in years of negotiation and strife. Considerably larger was the sum raised in 1297 by Conrad IV, archbishop of Salzburg, to redeem the valley of Gastein, which one of his predecessors had pawned away almost three centuries earlier[44]. In a complicated arrangement the archbishop borrowed 600 marks silver from a consortium made up of one local Jew, Samson of Mühldorf, and two foreign ones, Hatschim and Jacob of Regensburg. At the top end we find a high-flying banker like Vivelin "the Red", who amongst others lent substantial sums to the Count Palatine of the Rhine and to the archbishop of Mainz[45]. He served as counselor to the archbishop of Trier, with whose Jewish and Christian administrators he jointly carried out numerous financial deals. In addition, he was the principal in a complicated arrangement by which King Edward III of England, in dire need of cash for his military operations in France, raised in 1338/9 the immense sum of 340 000 gold florins. As part of security the great English crown was pawned to the archbishop of Trier, who eventually turned it over to Vivelin.

Outside the elite, the demand for credit by the greater number of commoners has usually been seen by historians as tied to distress: *One went to the usurer only in direst need.*[46] Such a view, clearly conditioned by the moral condemnation of "usury", could detect no redeeming feature or economic contribution in money lending. However, in many documented cases the premise of "direst need" is clearly inapplicable. The Bavarian peasants mentioned above took out most of their loans in the fall; after the harvest was in, when food was plentiful[47]. If hunger does not account for recourse to borrowing, what then does? We return to the general considerations on the need for credit in the expanding economy and society of the Central Middle Ages. Significantly, much of the information on credit in the countryside, indeed on early credit in general, comes from regions that specialized in viticulture. It has been recently suggested that viticulture and its regular need for money inputs provided the initial stimulus for Jews to move from trade to money lending[48]. This was the one agricultural pursuit to be commercialized very early, and Jews were from the beginning significantly engaged in the wine trade (and in

[43] *Caro*, II, 149, 312.
[44] *Eveline Brugger*, "Sechs hundert marchen silbers, di er uns schuldich was um di Gastewn...". Juden als Geldgeber des Salzburger Erzbischofs beim Kauf des Gasteiner Tales, in: Salzburg Archiv 27 (2001) 125–134.
[45] *Gerd Mentgen*, Herausragende jüdische Finanziers im mittelalterlichen Straßburg, in: Hochfinanz im Westen des Reiches 1150–1500, eds. *F. Burgard* et al. (Trier 1996) 75–100.
[46] *Herbert Kellenbenz*, Die Juden in der Wirtschaftsgeschichte des rheinischen Raumes von der Spätantike bis zum Jahre 1648, in: Monumenta Judaica, ed. *K. Schilling* (Köln 1963) I, 216.
[47] *Toch*, Geld und Kredit 514–515. For identical findings from southern France see *R. W. Emery*, The Jews of Perpignan in the 13th Century (New York 1959) 64–65.
[48] *Soloveitchik*, Principles.

wine production – see below). They remained so also in times when they had otherwise largely retreated from commerce.

Information from the largest German town, Cologne, and its sizeable Jewish community illustrates some salient features of the rise of money lending[49]. From the mid-13th century onwards, financiers become identifiable by name. Liverman of Düren, his brother Schoneman, and David of Zülpich, all three residents in Cologne, provided credits to subsequent archbishops of the town, to a count, another noble, a burgrave, a monastery. These were substantial and important men: Hebrew sources call Liverman *Judah the renowned and rich*. He owned five houses in the Jewish quarter of Cologne, Schoneman three and a half. Generations of their family were involved in the running of the community. By 1266, the Jewish bankers of Cologne were important enough for the archbishop to grant them a monopoly, excluding Christian competition from residing in the city. The conditions of this privilege, with other favorable clauses, were cut in a splendid tablet of stone and publicly exhibited outside the cathedral[50].

In many regions professional moneylenders were solely Jews. In others such as the Rhineland and some Alpine districts, there were also foreign Christians active, the so-called Lombards and Cahorsins. However, not only specialists extended credit. Informal arrangements for small credit needs were part of family and neighborhood networks in villages and towns[51]. The lower nobility relied on regional sets of connections for many of their credit requirements, in addition to Jewish and other moneylenders. Christian merchants extended loans for business capital as well as for political purposes, to colleagues, town governments, and kings. Ecclesiastical institutions too were involved in frequent credit operations, which were usually camouflaged as charitable help. Jewish and Christian credit thus fulfilled different economic and social functions, but could also interlock. Jewish financiers would serve as a safety valve and go-between for credit arrangements between Christians. From the 13th century onwards merchants employed a procedure called *Schadennehmen*, literally *to take out* (a loan) *for/against damage*[52]. Faced with a possibly risky debtor in their business deals, Christian merchants would insert an authorization clause in the contract, allowing them to take out in the debtor's name a high interest loan from a Jewish moneylender. In case of default they would collect their debt from the Jew, leaving the debtor saddled with the consequences. Town-governments used the same device to ensure prompt payment of taxes: they

49 For the sources and a detailed exposition on Cologne financiers see *Schmandt*, 75–77.

50 For references and the text see *Schmandt*, 25, 271–272; *Aronius*, no. 718.

51 Cf. *Michael Toch*, Local Credit in an Agrarian Economy: The Case of Bavaria (14th and 15th Centuries), in: *I. Zilli* (ed.), Fra Spazio e Tempo. Studi in Onore di Luigi de Rosa (Naples 1995) I, 793–803; *E. Clark*, Debt Litigation in a Late Medieval English Vill, in: *J. A. Raftis* (ed.), Pathways to Medieval Peasants (Toronto 1981) 247–279.

52 The earliest extant references date to 1257 and 1258: *Aronius*, no. 632; *Schmandt*, 75. For details see *Guido Kisch*, Das Schadennehmen, in: *idem*, Forschungen zur Rechts- und Sozialgeschichte des Mittelalters (Zürich 1980) 296–325.

impounded a valuable belonging to a tax dodger and then satisfied themselves by pawning it to a Jew.

Collateral, the measures taken to secure outstanding debts is a major issue fraught with implications. Most common was the written deed claimable in court (also called charter, instrument, letter of debt, or promissory note) issued by the debtor or by a notary or court of law; warranty (surety) by third party; and the pawn or pledge. There was also a curiously medieval custom called in German *Einlager* (literally "depositing") and in Hebrew *eating on someone as warranty*. Pressure was achieved by lodging on the debtor's account a party in an inn, with their horses in its stable. Both would then merrily eat and drink away, until payment of the debt was effected. This was also practiced between Jews: *Shimon became Reuben's surety to a Gentile and Reuben stipulated with the Gentile that if he delayed payment after a specified date, Shimon would rightfully eat on him. Reuben shall pay for Shimon's standard eating, as Jews eat in a Jewish home, that is a medium and limited eating, since it is the custom of the sons of Abraham, Yitzhak and Jacob to take pity on their brethren ... and not to eat on them cruelly*[53].

Clearly, the type of collateral demanded depended on the trustworthiness of the debtor, of which his social standing was a major component. As evident from the Hebrew record, all forms were employed, separately and in combination, by Jewish lenders[54]. We are told by Ephraim bar Jacob of Bonn that Jewish financiers in France lent *on faith* (*be-amanah*) and thus suffered heavily from the moratorium on debts decreed by the King of France during the Second Crusade[55]. When youthful Jehudah of Cologne failed to secure a pawn in one of his first business deals, *as required by their* (the Jews) *custom*, his elders were scandalized[56]. It follows that loans that relied solely *on faith and belief* were clearly an exception and would be granted only to special customers, the *Maarufiya* treated above[57]. The widespread employment of pawns also points to a certain broadening of the clientele and to a concomitant growing anonymity of the money market. The increasing use of written contracts claimable in court, on the other hand, argues for the integration of credit arrangements into the legal machinery of the period. Even so, this was risky business and things could go very wrong. Rabbi Abraham ben David of Posquières (Southern France, circa 1120 to 1198) had some pertinent advice to investors in the lending business. *And do not lend without a good pledge of gold and silver; and put the money regularly beneath the earth to safeguard from fire and thieves without*

[53] *Maharam*, no. 83. The translation of *Agus*, Rabbi Meir of Rothenburg, his Life and his Works as Sources for the Religious, Legal, and Social History of the Jews of Germany in the 13th Century (Philadelphia 1947/New York 1970) 448, no. 485, flattens the delightful text.

[54] *Hoffmann*, 88–100.

[55] *Neubauer, Stern*, 64,196. The Hebrew term employed does not mean, as translated by *Robert Chazan*, Medieval Jewry in Northern France (Baltimore, London 1973) 34, "by charter", but exactly the opposite.

[56] *Hermannus quondam Judaeus* (above, note 34) 72.

[57] *Hoffmann*, no. 40. The same meaning of dispensing with a pawn appears in contracts between Jews: *Maharam*, nos. 393, 880. For other special treatment see *Shatzmiller*, 99–103.

people knowing about this, so that it shall not be known to thieves and make them think of stealing; and when you receive a pledge of gold and silver conceal it in a secure place beneath the earth. And he (the investor) *shall instruct him* (the agent) *not to take pledges of gold and silver from great townsmen and violent men so that he shall not be forced to return them without security against his will*[58]. Things were done differently in smaller places where everyone knew everyone, like the above-mentioned market town of Straubing in the early 14th century. There, most outstanding loans were not secured by formal measures, but apparently rather by the simple oral promise frowned upon by more circumspect financiers[59].

The employment of pawns as security gave rise to serious tensions. To pawn ecclesiastical utensils endowed with the quality of holiness to the unbelieving Jew was increasingly felt to be sacrilegious. Little less fraught with difficulties was the privileged status granted to Jews (and Lombards) in regard to stolen goods. Civil authorities tried to tread a thin line between the need to deter theft and the wish to promote the smooth performance of the market. Thus it became accepted practice to allow the lender to swear that such pawns had been accepted in good faith as security, rather than acquired as cheap goods of doubtful provenance[60]. Conversely, an increasing range of objects were prohibited as pawns: ecclesiastical utensils; goods whose wet or bloody condition suggested theft or robbery; the weaponry and armor of the members of urban militias; the buckets, axes and shovels kept at different locations in town in case of fire; and a whole range of tools and raw materials essential for the livelihood of artisans. In short, accepting pawns as security could easily develop into pawnbroking, a practice fraught with social problems, as was to become very clear in the Later Middle Ages.

Going by the life-style and status symbols displayed by many Jews, such as housing, servants, clothes, and the jewelry bequeathed in wills, money lending afforded substantial and sometimes opulent rewards, at least to its top practitioners. Another clue is provided by the considerable taxes collected since the 13th century from Jews. The very first extant list of taxes levied by the German emperor on

58 Rabad of Posquières, Responsa, no. 140, in: The Responsa Project (above, note 9).

59 *Toch*, Geld und Kredit 516–520. For identical findings from southern France: *Emery* (above, note 47) 31.

60 The historiography on this topic once more reflects the depths of apologetics Jewish history has been entangled in. Most 19th century scholars saw this privilege as deriving from Jewish law: *Caro*, I 181; Germania Judaica I, XXXI. By the early 20th century anti-Semitic propagandists appropriated this finding, termed it *fence-law* (*Hehlerrecht*), and used it to point an accusing finger. Guido Kisch invested considerable labor to disprove this idea. Betraying a poignant trust in the efficacy of rational argument, he choose this topic to open the first issue (of 1938!) of the journal edited by him in America after his escape from Europe: *Guido Kisch*, The "Jewish Law of Concealment", in: Historia Judaica I (1938) 1–30. After World War II historians were loath to go near anything that might be construed as slanderous to Jews. Kisch's view thus became accepted opinion, despite grave problems in his interpretation of sources. This was finally remedied in 1990 in a perceptive study by *Friedrich Lotter*, Talmudisches Recht in den Judenprivilegien Heinrichs IV.?, in: Archiv für Kulturgeschichte 72 (1990) 23–61. He proved beyond doubt the Talmudic origins of this statute, and thus the early influence of Jews on legislation pertaining to them.

towns and their Jewries (1241) does not include the largest and fiscally most potent communities of Cologne, Mainz, Würzburg, and Regensburg[61]. In the cities that were listed, Jews paid 13% of all the taxes raised, a highly disproportionate share compared to their population numbers. Apparently without causing problems of solvency, the Jewish tax yield in Frankfurt on the Main grew eight-fold between 1241 and 1319[62]. This astonishing fiscal capacity could not have been sustained without the high turnover of lending money against interest. The rising demand for credit in ever more regions and localities, as well as the capability to cater to such needs, thus became the basis for the continuous expansion of Jewish settlement. In turn, such dynamism would have been impossible to maintain without yet another important characteristic of Jewish (and Italian) credit: namely the fact that it enjoyed the explicit support of the powers that be. Bankers depended on government and its agents to carry out their business. They employed the machinery of authority against the borrower to collect debts, foreclose on collateral when the borrower failed, and put pawns up for sale. Despite the odium increasingly attached to money-lending, rulers on all levels put their power – armed, judicial, and legislative – at the disposal of the money-lender. They did so in the name of public order, economic well-being, and of course steadily growing taxes. Such assistance laid civil authorities open to criticism and heavy pressure, especially when combined with accusations of corruption and the taking of bribes. This major contradiction came to beset public attitudes at precisely the point when Jewish (and Italian) money lending was becoming a regular feature in a buoyant market. It became first visible in mid-13th century, when political authorities found it necessary to institute an upper limit on interest rates[63]. Further implications were to become painfully apparent in the Later Middle Ages.

III. Jewish Credit in the Later Middle Ages

There can be no doubt that money lending and credit operations had now become the mainstay of Jewish livelihood in Germany. Rabbi Moses Minz, the foremost *Halakhic* authority of the 15th century, could thus differentiate between *money-lenders and the rest of livelihoods*. Rabbi Joseph Colon (died 1480) put it like this: *His occupation is to lend against interest, and this is the main occupation of Jews that live in these lands*[64]. As evident from numerous agreements and privileges of settlement, by the early 14th century only financiers (and medical doctors, see below) were able to obtain permits of residence in German towns and territories.

[61] MGH, Constitutiones et acta publica imperatorum et regum, III (1980) 1–6, no. 1.

[62] *Karl Bücher*, Die Bevölkerung von Frankfurt am Main im 14. und 15. Jahrhundert. Socialstatistische Studien (Tübingen 1886) 526–601.

[63] *Aronius*, nos. 547, 618.

[64] *Moses Minz*, Responsa (Tel Aviv 1968/69), no. 60; *Joseph Kolon*, Responsa (Jerusalem 1973) no. 132.

Practitioners of any other occupation needed to be included, as household dependents, in the arrangements of licensed moneylenders.

Their activities come into stark relief during the Later Middle Ages, when economic matters are more plentifully treated in the sources. A number of reasons combine to create this state of affairs. Jews had by then become wholly subject to the increasingly well-organized governments of towns and princes, whose administrations were based on written records. The ecclesiastical censure of usury decisively shaped public opinion to stress the social, moral, and spiritual damage caused to Christendom. Established authority and reformers alike shared this groundswell. Precariously balanced against this trend was an ongoing reliance of rulers on Jewish taxes, loans and finances. Lastly, for reasons to be treated below, ever more people were turning to the services of the moneylender. The meeting of these conflicting tendencies generated sustained administrative efforts and legislation to regulate and control the terms of Jewish existence and especially of money lending[65]. This "administrative overload" resulted in a previously unknown wealth of written references to economic matters. Contracts of settlement and legislation specify the conditions under which financiers were allowed to operate. Series of tax-lists help to reconstruct the economic fortunes of individuals, families, and communities over time. Town governments recorded ordinances and other matters pertaining to their Jews in special "Jews Books" (*Judenbuch*) [66]. Civil authorities attempted to compel lenders and borrowers to record their transactions, normally in court registers and, less frequently, in notaries' ledgers. Anti-usury campaigns, periodical confiscations, and the legal squabbling over the spoils made for the recording of Jewish assets, prominently among them due loans, specifying the names of customers, sums and conditions, and the collateral taken as security. As for Jewish writings, legal scholars still devoted much of their time to litigation deriving from economic matters. Finally, from this period we also have a few fragments of account books, usually written in Hebrew.

In contrast to former times, German kings and emperors rarely figure now amongst the customers of Jewish financiers[67]. Only king Ruprecht (1400–1410), whose impecuniousness was proverbial, used their services in a regular manner. In the later 14th century, members of the high nobility – archbishops and bishops, dukes and electoral princes – would still avail themselves routinely of Jewish credit. They did so much less during the 15th century. A similar trend is visible for the next-ranking group of counts and their ecclesiastical equivalents, lesser bishops

[65] For a case study from Nuremberg see *Toch*, *umb gemeyns nutz und nottdurfft willen*. Obrigkeitliches und jurisdiktionelles Denken bei der Austreibung der Nürnberger Juden 1498/99, in: Zeitschrift für historische Forschung 11 (1984) 1–21. For an European overview see *Shatzmiller*, 43–70.

[66] A research project led by Alfred Haverkamp of Trier University is now exploring this genre.

[67] I have used the sources and research literature collected in Germania Judaica III, together with previous work, for a detailed analysis of Jewish livelihoods in the late medieval German empire: *Toch*, Tätigkeit. Unless otherwise indicated, the reader is directed to this study for references. Further insights have been gained from *Andernacht*.

and abbots of monasteries. Of the loans recorded for members of this group, two thirds belong in the second half of the 14th century, only one third in the subsequent hundred years and more until the close of the Middle Ages. Matters of high politics, the financing of war and the acquisition of territories, which had earlier been paramount in the credit needs of the political elite, are now rarely found. The same holds for routine credits taken to fund the running of princely courts. Until the end of the 14th century, the middling and lower nobility of some regions – Austria is an especially well documented case – continued to frequent Jewish moneylenders for their financial conduct, often to finance feuds, raise dowries and inheritance payments, and acquire lands. In other areas credit ties between nobles and Jews had become much weaker. In a similar vein, in the 14th century there were still some town governments, such as Andernach, Basle, or Nuremberg with frequent recourse to Jewish loans to balance their budgets. Others took loans on an intermittent basis when they met unexpected expenditure for political purposes. By the 15th century most towns supported their regular and irregular needs from other sources, especially taxation. The breaking point, in this regard as in others, appears to have been the wholesale liquidation of debts owed to the Jews of a number of important south-German towns. Decreed by King Wenzel in 1385, it was used by some town governments as a powerful political lever in their struggle against the nobility[68]. After that people of the upper classes, the ones in political power, increasingly satisfied their credit needs by recourse to sources other than the Jews. A clear consequence of this process was a lessening of their dependency on Jewish finances and a corresponding loss in the political leverage, always slight, at the disposal of Jews.

In many places, peasants and other inhabitants of the countryside are now found in vast numbers amongst the patrons of money lending. There is not a single town whose citizens and inhabitants did not have frequent recourse to Jewish loans. Detailed inquiries in a number of places have brought out the salient fact that people of the lower classes now replace the more affluent as the main clientele, for instance in a large town such as Nuremberg[69]. This also holds for the smaller towns so typical of the social landscape of the period. For instance, in Bingen on the Rhine a detailed inquiry was undertaken in the year 1427 by the officials of the archbishop of Mainz, the lord of the town, into the indebtness of the people to Jews[70]. In this town of roughly 2500 inhabitants, no less than one hundred and forty-two, men and women, were recorded as owing yet unpaid debts. Amongst them were a chaplain, a toll-official, and the daughter of someone called a lord. However, the vast majority were artisans and other *poor people*. There were altogether 606 yet unpaid

[68] For details see *Toch*, Geldhandel 287.

[69] *Toch*, Geldhandel.

[70] The source for this and the following is a yet unpublished manuscript, first transcribed and utilized by Yacov Guggenheim, in Staatsarchiv Würzburg, catalogue number G 17337, titled: *This is the debt owed by the burghers and poor people* (that is non-citizens) *in Bingen to the Jews*. My thanks go to Yacov for his transcription.

loans with a total of 2270 Gulden, not an exorbitant sum. The arithmetic mean stood at 16 Gulden total per borrower and 70 Gulden total per lender. The average loan was rather small, running in most cases from half a Gulden to ten, with only a small fraction (7%) above that sum. The *common man* and *woman* of Bingen thus had modest credit needs. For some, recourse to the moneylender was a rare or just once occasion. For the majority of customers, however, this was a routine matter. The prize goes to the *son of Arnolt Kemerer* (a man so insignificant to the clerk that his Christian name remained unrecorded), who borrowed the magnificent sum of eight Gulden in 49 transactions from ten different Jews. As an unreliable customer, he had to put up a pawn for every deal. Findings from Frankfurt on the Main and Constance, both mid-sized towns in this period, exhibit a similar trend of widespread and modest credit needs: few loans in sizeable sums and a majority in small ones not exceeding 10 Gulden[71]. They differ from a large town like Nuremberg, where town burgers took out relatively few loans altogether, but with a much larger share of significant sums, 50 and even 100 Gulden and above[72].

There was thus a decisive shift in the make-up of the clientele, less aristocracy, less bourgeoisie, and many more people of the lower middle and lower classes. Accompanying this change was an increasing vulnerability of Jewish money lending to confiscation and legal obstruction, and a diminishing willingness of civil authorities to provide assistance to lenders. The transformation is clearly reflected in the nature of collateral and indicates a darkening cloud of suspicion on both sides of the divide. The simple promise to pay, still found in the early decades of the 14th century in the rural environment of Bavaria, has practically disappeared from the record. Instead, there is a whole arsenal of anticipatory securities: warrantors to stand surety; the promissory note claimable in court; entering the particulars of debts in a notary's register, a court book or other registers kept by political authorities (*Amtsbuch*). As means of pressure on obstinate debtors, especially from the aristocracy, there was still the *Einlager* of eating guests. The main collateral, the pawn or pledge, could take many different forms: designation to proceeds of tolls or tithes; landed property like houses, fields or vineyards, with some aristocratic debtors even whole fortresses, villages or manors; and of course the pawn simple and pure, farm animals, merchandise and stock. Most common were utensils of daily life such as domestic furnishings, furniture, tableware, clothing, textiles, furs, jewelry, weapons, armor, and tools[73]. Nevertheless, in the choice of pledge too Jews came to be increasingly limited. In addition to religious articles or ones per-

[71] *Isidor Kracauer*, Geschichte der Juden in Frankfurt a.M. (Frankfurt 1925) I, 427 (for the year 1389); *idem* (ed.), Urkundenbuch zur Geschichte der Juden in Frankfurt am Main von 1150–1400 (Frankfurt a.M. 1914) 881–906 (for the year 1400); *Hektor Ammann*, Die Judengeschäfte im Konstanzer Ammann-Gerichtsbuch 1423–1434, in: Schriften des Vereins für Geschichte des Bodensees 71 (1952) 44–74 (for the years 1423–1429).

[72] *Toch*, Geldhandel 293–295.

[73] See for instance the lists of pawns confiscated from Regensburg Jews at the time of their expulsion: *K. Matzel*, *J. Riecke*, Das Pfandregister der Regensburger Juden vom Jahre 1519, in: Zeitschrift für Bayerische Landesgeschichte 51 (1988) 767–806.

taining to the defense and safety of the town, many authorities now banned real estate in town and countryside. Such measures, as well as the social change in the clientele, brought about a clear ascendancy of petty movables and personal effects, as amply illustrated by the Bingen document of 1427. There, of a total of 606 credit deals, we have information on the collateral of 371. In 311 cases this was a movable pawn, in 41 cases warranty of third party, in 19 cases an official document signed by the town's jurors (*Schöffenbrief*). There was no landed property, and some deals had to be secured by multiple means. We can thus distinguish an effort by lenders to counter the loss of legal security by turning to tangible assets, the sale of which would offset lost debts. This too was counteracted by the tendency of authorities, visible in many places towards the end of the 15th century, to limit the lender's disposal over forfeited pawns in favor of the debtor. They did so by enforcing the registration of debts, by allowing the debtor extended and repeated terms to redeem the pawn, and by compelling the lender to put up pawns for compulsory sale[74]. Behind these measures one senses one more time the deep uneasiness and resentment that "Jewish usury" aroused.

Going by the many writings and laws produced in the period, the most visible focus for such resentment should be interest. During the 13th to 15th centuries, the idea that Jews took exorbitant interest had become a regular feature of anti-Judaism. Clad into the phrase *servitude of interest* (*Zinsknechtschaft*) by which Jews enslaved Gentiles, it was invoked countless times. Does this image reflect contemporary reality or is it yet another instance of the unceasing polemics characteristic of Christian-Jewish relations? The rich late medieval material allows us to reconstruct the actual interest rates as demanded by lenders and paid by borrowers. One can also determine the level deemed acceptable by political authorities, as expressed in legislation for maximum interest rates. The gist of it is that people of the later Middle Ages paid excessively high interest rates ranging from 24% to 91% per year. These are compound figures aggregated from the totality of recorded instances and thus of course an abstract construct. However, the range of actual interest rates demanded (and sometimes also paid) in Bingen of 1427 exactly fits these composite figures. Actually, there were two different trends, a consistently higher one paid on loans in silver money and a slightly lower one on gold coin. The variation between the two is due to monetary reasons, the fluctuations in the relative price of silver and gold, and to social reasons, the fact that the poor borrowed in silver and the rich in gold. The extreme disparity in rates, ranging from 24% per year to almost four times this amount, 91% per year, points to one further feature heavy with social implications. Poor people tended to take short-term loans that were much more expensive than the longer running credits taken by more affluent (that is, more trustworthy) debtors. Holders of political power borrowed at the cheapest rates. The secular trend was stationary to slightly rising.

[74] For Nuremberg and Göttingen see *Toch, umb gemeyns nutz* (above, note 65) 11–15, and *P. Hoheisel*, Zur jüdischen Pfandleihe im spätmittelalterlichen Göttingen, in: Göttinger Jahrbuch 44 (1996) 107–119.

The same political authorities, princes, prelates and town governments, issued frequent legislation on permissible maximum interest rates[75]. Usually they decreed lower rates for their own citizens and higher or unregulated ones for strangers. Our material documents two parallel and basically stationary trends, with silver being mostly, but not at all points of time, more expensive than gold. As was to be expected, there was a significant gap between effective interest paid and the maximum rates decreed by governments. On the average people paid up to one third more than the upper limit decreed by their rulers. A few important conclusions can be drawn from this fact. For one, it follows that legislation had no or little impact on the market. Its influence should rather be sought in the realm of symbolical representations, the way people felt about things. Secondly, even the moderate interest permitted by authorities was much higher than the one usual in modern times. Different market conditions brought about a different idea of the tolerable and excessively high interest rates were not necessarily considered as such by contemporaries. Going by the voices of the people themselves, for instance the complaints registered in the Bingen document of 1427, customers of Jewish credit were most aggravated by the practice of charging compound interest, which is adding unpaid interest to the capital sum, for which a new interest rate was then computed[76]. Thus it was not "usury" itself – taking interest on loans – that was resented by contemporaries, but rather its abuse. All this is far removed from the intensive arguments on forbidden usury as such that occupied theologians and lawyers of the period and with which they decisively influenced political authorities[77]. Modern historians have mostly turned to their writings for an appreciation of contemporary attitudes. Reading legal norm and religious polemics as economic fact, they appear to be considerably off the mark. A comparison of our German findings to those from other parts of Europe points to a further intriguing fact: official interest rates were lower in Southern Europe (Southern France and Aragon) than in Northern Europe (England and Germany), and highest in Eastern Europe. This parallels a similar difference in effective rates found within Germany, between a lower west-German market and a more expensive Bavarian and Austrian one.

In previous periods, as our inquiry has shown, the reasons for borrowing money were usually connected to the boom conditions of a burgeoning economy and society. This was generally not the case anymore under the adverse circumstances of the Later Middle Ages. One indication is the transformation, sketched above, in the make-up of the clientele. In comparison to earlier times, large numbers of borrowers were by definition poorer and subject to greater hardships in their lives.

[75] For a European overview of official "moderate" interest rates see *Shatzmiller*, 53–54.

[76] For a similar observation from different material see *Markus Wenninger*, Geldkreditgeschäfte im mittelalterlichen Erfurt, in: Erfurt. Geschichte und Gegenwart, ed. *U. Weiß* (Weimar 1995) 439–458.

[77] For such discussions taking place mostly in the learned milieu of university scholars, see also *Wenninger*, Geldkreditgeschäfte (previous note), note 38. See also *M. H. Shank*, „Unless You Believe, You Shall Not Understand". Logic, University and Society in Late Medieval Vienna (Princeton 1988). For a similar argument on the (relative) acceptability of Jewish money lending, as opposed to its unqualified condemnation by the literate, see *Shatzmiller*.

There are also direct indications that penury and poverty now come to the forefront of borrowing. Between the years 1497 and 1501 roughly forty individuals of the agricultural village of Bornheim near Frankfurt on the Main entered into a total of 150 different debts contracted with Jews from Frankfurt[78]. The vast majority of borrowers were simple peasants. Unlike their Bavarian predecessors of the early 14th century, they contracted loans throughout the year, with no particular season standing out. However, an overwhelming percentage of these debts was to be repaid in the fall, from the proceeds of the grain harvest and the vintage, many times directly in agricultural produce. It follows that the peasants of Bornheim, in contrast to their Bavarian predecessors, were able to pay off their debts only after the harvest was in. But even so, in the majority of cases they defaulted, thus leading to protracted litigation and eventually to intervention by the town authorities of Frankfurt. A similar situation of chronic indebtness can be found in many more places, which was indeed one of the grievances forcefully conveyed by German peasants at the time of their great revolt of 1525[79].

Apparently no great changes in the organization of money lending occurred during the one and a half late medieval centuries. Still, we know many more details than in earlier periods. For instance, it was not always money that was lent, but also fruits of the soil such as grains, wine, and flour. More commonly debts were paid back, wholly or partly, in kind. Our Bingen document specifies a whole range of such goods: oil, beer, geese, meat, firewood, wine and oats, as well as transport services of wine to Mainz (30 km distance), of beer to Cologne (125 km distance!), and of firewood in town[80]. Judging by contemporary legislation, this was yet another point of friction, as Jews were forbidden to lend *on the growing grain*. This meant the practice to stipulate repayment of loans in natural produce, at prices fixed before the harvest. Such contracts were considered a device to corner the market in politically sensitive foodstuffs and as speculation on dearth. Neither was deemed acceptable. As we shall see below, in the Later Middle Ages some Jews indeed returned to some degree to sell merchandise, mostly forfeited pawns. They also marketed the produce in kind received in lieu of loans, of which wine was the most usual[81]. However, nowhere did such commerce reach the critical mass that would justify the sinister intentions imputed. Instead, payment in kind should be seen as yet another devise in an economy starved of ready cash.

Mostly, the normal framework for the credit business was the family firm, a single Jew or Jewess (on business-women see Keil in this volume) and their immediate relatives including sons-in-law. According to personal capabilities and resources as well as to location, a wide spectrum emerges. On the lower end, there

[78] *Andernacht*, nos. 2905–2917, 2925, 2932–2934, 2937, 2941–2944, 2948, 2965- 2970, 2973, 2977, 2985, 2986, 2994, 3004, 3016, 3018, 3024–3026, 3042, 3089, 3110, 3120, 3131, 3211.

[79] *H.-J. Gilomen*, Das Motiv der bäuerlichen Verschuldung in den Bauernunruhen an der Wende zur Neuzeit, in: Spannungen und Widersprüche. Gedenkschrift für František Graus, eds. *S. Burghartz* et alia (Sigmaringen 1992) 173–189.

[80] Staatsarchiv Würzburg (above, note 70) 1r, 4v, 5r, 6r, 6v, 10v, 19v, 20r, 20v.

[81] See now *Soloveitchik*, Principles, with abundant quotations, as well as *Mentgen*, 560–574.

were the anonymous Jews of Bingen, their names unknown even to their customers[82]. On the top end we find a man like Jekel of Ulm, later of Nördlingen, Constance and Nuremberg[83]. He did his business together with his sons Menlin, Löw, Isaac, and Fiflin, and his sons-in-law Isaac, son of Vischlin of Strasbourg, and Isaac, son of Rechlin of Reutlingen. Between 1368 and 1402 he was active all over Southern Germany, with family branches in Ulm, Constance, Strasbourg and Reutlingen. For loans to the counts of Werdenberg he received as pledge the town of Langenau and the domain of Albeck, both of which he subsequently sold, on credit, to the town of Ulm. Other customers were the town governments of Nuremberg, Augsburg, and Constance. In 1385, he headed the list of Jewish bankers whose assets had been seized in Nuremberg, with outstanding loans amounting to 15 000 Gulden out of 81 000.

It was not by coincidence that Jeckel first choose Ulm and then Nuremberg as his domicile. These two places were indeed the most important centers of Jewish banking in the second half of the 14th century. Further focal points of supra-local finance were Erfurt, Strasbourg, Cologne, Mainz, Speyer, and Vienna. Towards the end of the 15th century Frankfurt on the Main became increasingly important[84]. The volume of transactions, the composition of the clientele, and the size of the "catchment area" can measure the rank of a place as a financial center. Thus, Nuremberg Jews ministered to an area comprising all Franconia and most of Southern Germany. In contrast, the customers of the Jews of Constance were mostly burgers of the town and of the small towns of the nearer neighborhood, winegrowers on both shores of Lake Constance, and lower nobility of the castles of the region[85]. However, location was not everything and personal circumstances could play a role, as for instance in the case of the important moneylender Hentschlein (grandfather of the scholar Rabbi Israel Isserlein), who resided from 1354 to 1389 in the Austrian town of Herzogenburg[86]. His circle of customers reached as far as Vienna, Regensburg, and Prague, but his small hometown never became a financial center. At the lower end of this hierarchy of financial functions one finds even smaller places, barely townships and mostly villages, were Jews were allowed to settle towards the very end of the period, expressively to provide for the credit needs of the lower nobility, the lords of such places. At the very bottom of the ladder there were Jews like one Abraham, who left in 1450 the town of Lichtenfels in Franconia to settle in Marktgraitz, a market township tucked away in a valley not far away. His few customers came solely from the immediate surroundings of his two domiciles[87]. Thus even in this time of decline, Jewish money lending still reflected a hierarchy of clientele, each with different credit needs.

[82] Staatsarchiv Würzburg (above, note 70) 6v, 7r: "the Jew", "a Jew", "in the house of the Jew".
[83] Germania Judaica III, 1504–1505.
[84] *Toch*, Wirtschaft.
[85] *Ammann*, Judengeschäfte (above, note 71) 43.
[86] Germania Judaica III, entry Herzogenburg.
[87] Germania Judaica III, entry Marktgraitz.

Following a boom after 1350, Jewish finances were badly hit by a series of confiscations of capital and assets, which began in 1375 in Austria and peaked in 1385 in the financial centers of Southern Germany. This started a flight of Jewish capital abroad, mainly to Italy (and thus the beginning of considerable migration of German Jews to Northern Italy). The growing persecutions of the 15th century must have stepped up this process. For the mid-point of the Later Middle Ages, the years around 1426, the total business capital of German Jews has been estimated at one and a half to two million Gulden[88]. This was not more than the assets of the burgers of the three middle-sized towns of Esslingen, Basel, and Constance. It is thus not surprising that German Jews of the Later Middle Ages returned to an increasing involvement in commerce. In many cases, this was a trade in used clothes, gems, furniture, and other utensils of daily life, clearly a by-product of pawnbroking. Towards the end of the Middle Ages such business increased, yet another consequence of the turn towards the pawn described above. In some larger places Jewish brokers, all female, are mentioned, a sign that such trade had reached a certain critical mass. There were also beginnings of a Jewish engagement in the marketing of victuals, cattle, and horses. Trade in wine is of course found in regions of viticulture, such as the Rhineland and Mosel region, Hessen, Alsace, Franconia, and Lower Austria, as well as in some large communities, Nuremberg, Regensburg, and Prague. It was practiced in a highly organized and capital-intensive manner on the eastern fringes of the German Reich, in Styria, Carinthia, Moravia, and Slovenia[89]. Significantly, systematic trade activities (as distinct from trade deriving from pawnbroking) cluster in these eastern regions and especially in Bohemia. They are also found, to a degree, in some smaller places in the west of the country. In the larger towns of the west Jewish traders had no chance against the highly effective lobby of Christian merchants organized in guilds, especially not in the many towns directly ruled by such associations. In the Jewish metropolis of early 16th century Prague, a whole structure of Jewish businesses and shops is found, including dealers in ice, geese, horses, as well as pub keepers[90]. In some places, Heidelberg, Magdeburg, and Neuenburg, Jews served their lords as commercial and financial agents, an early form of *court Jews*. All these are economic patterns that were to become characteristic of the early modern centuries[91].

[88] *Yacov Guggenheim*, Jewish Banks in the German Economy during the First Half of the 15th Century, in: Proceedings of the Ninth World Congress of Jewish Studies. Division B. vol. I (Jerusalem 1986) 121–126 (Hebrew).

[89] See *Herbert Teufel*, Of Wine Growers, Vintners and Wine Dealers. Jews in Agriculture and Viticulture in Moravia during the Sixteenth and Seventeenth Centuries, in: Review of the Society for the History of Czechoslovak Jews 6 (1993/94) 119–131.

[90] *Jan Herman*, Die wirtschaftliche Betätigung und die Berufe der Prager Juden vor ihrer Ausweisung im Jahre 1541, in: Judaica Bohemiae IV/1 (1968) 57–61.

[91] *Toch*, Wirtschaft; *Michael Toch*, Aspects of Stratification of Early Modern German Jewry: Population History and Village Jews, in: *R. Po-chia Hsia*, *H. Lehmann* (eds.), "In and Out of the Ghetto". Jewish-Gentile Relations in Late Medieval and Early Modern Germany (Cambridge 1995) 77–89.

IV. Other Occupations

Around 1503, the German jurist Johannes Purgoldt expanded on statements made almost four hundred years earlier: *Now it is their* (the Jews') *state that they may not own real property in this country, nor own hereditable possessions, because this is not allowed to them. If they had such property, people would damage it; if they work in handicrafts, the guilds and master artisans would not tolerate it, they would not be received into their associations, and the people would not let them work; if they engage in trading, no one would like to buy from them. And therefore must they thus engage in usury, and this is their excuse*[92]. Shaped as it was by religious, literary, and legal concerns, does this recurring image of a very restricted occupational structure reflect historical reality?

Throughout the whole Middle Ages, in Germany as in other parts of Europe, considerable numbers of Jews derived their livelihood by occupations other than commerce or credit. They provided the well off with the conditions necessary to live as Jews in a Jewish community, as well as with some basic amenities. Best known are the rabbis, but there was also a whole range of ritual practitioners, artisans, and providers of varied services, mostly of a menial nature. By numbers the most significant were Jews and Jewesses employed by more affluent co-religionists as manservants, maids, teachers, and religious personnel. These people are the least documented of the Jewish population. One reason for the poor visibility of such humble persons is occupational indistinctness: many of them earned their living by various crafts practiced simultaneously or alternately[93]. This holds also for the Jewish serving classes, as noted in a Hebrew autobiography of 1382: *I settled in Coblence... and served the community as cantor, kosher butcher, examiner* (of food stuffs) *and innkeeper*[94]. Another reason is the insignificance of such mostly indigent persons as taxpayers: there was no reason to list them individually in the records. They became of interest to authorities only when perceived in police terms, as undesirable elements. Following deliberations by the city council of Nuremberg on the need to control its Jewish population, on March 14th 1489, a Sabbath, a clerk entered the synagogue to take down the particulars of the male adults (that is over 13 years old)[95]. Of the male persons present, fourteen percent were community servants and a slightly higher proportion could be identified as house servants and private teachers. Actually, of the fifteen Jewish households of Nuremberg in the year 1489 only one, that of a widow, had no hired help. Similar findings from Osnabrück, Worms, Prague, and Frankfurt on the Main corroborate this basic fact

92 Translated by *Kisch*, 193–194 (with slight emendations by me, M.T.), and quoted, in a different context, by *Shatzmiller*, 96.

93 *H. Swanson*, Medieval Artisans. An Urban Class in Late Medieval England (Oxford 1989).

94 *Israel Yuval*, A German-Jewish Autobiography of the Fourteenth Century, in: Binah 3 (1994) 79–99. See also Germania Judaica III, entries Höchstädt/Donau, Triest, Windecken.

95 *Michael Toch*, Die soziale und demographische Struktur der jüdischen Gemeinde Nürnbergs im Jahre 1489, in: Wirtschaftskräfte und Wirtschaftswege. Festschrift für Hermann Kellenbenz, ed. *J. Schneider*, vol. V (Stuttgart 1981) 82–83.

of Jewish occupational and social structure[96]. Given the peculiarities of the written record, such figures should be understood as the "tip of the iceberg" of an otherwise unrecorded group of Jews and Jewesses of the serving classes, making up close to one third of population numbers.

In contrast to domestics, other non-traders and non-financiers have been of more interest to historians. This again has to do with 19th century polemics and apologetics, and especially with the debate how to "ameliorate the Jews". As part of the emancipation process, a large number of schemes were devised to get the Jews out of finance, trade, and services and into "productive" occupations in agriculture and crafts. Zionism and its tenet of the "return to the soil" are but one offspring of this mindset. Even if not consciously seeking for historical precedent, the figure of the sturdy Jewish peasant, a human type purportedly in balance with his surroundings, has fascinated historians. However, he is very hard to find in the sources. As quoted above, there are clear testimonies, penned by Jews and non-Jews from the 12th century onwards, against agricultural pursuits. What do other types of sources have to say on Jewish agriculturists and on farmland held by Jews?

In the early period, in Latin sources there are but two concrete instances of such agricultural property[97]. The first in or near Metz (before 945) was a vineyard and the second one near Regensburg (before 981) might have been one as well. In both cases the property had already passed from Jewish into Christian hands. A third text, the privilege accorded in 1090 by emperor Henry IV to a number of Jews of Speyer, guaranteed the *properties that they possess in hereditary rights, in open grounds, in houses, in gardens, in vineyards, in fields, in slaves, or in other properties, mobile and immobile*[98]. This is the usual enumeration of all legal forms of ownership, and might or might not indicate that Jews of Speyer indeed owned agricultural land. In short, in the early period there is little evidence that German Jews possessed significant landed property beyond vineyards, in contrast to southern France and to a lesser extent to northern France[99]. Such (relative) dearth is corroborated by the Hebrew sources. Of the questions addressed to Gershom ben Jehudah "Light of the Exile" on the possession, mortgaging, and inheritance of agricultural land, not one can be identified as coming from Germany. More frequent in *Halakhic* sources are references to vineyards and wine production, but here too the context is mostly a commercial one, of the transport and sale of wine

[96] Germania Judaica III, entries Osnabrück, Worms; *G. Wolf*, Zur Geschichte der Juden in Österreich. I. Verzeichniß der Prager Juden, ihrer Frauen, Kinder und Dienstboten im Jahre 1546, in: Zeitschrift für die Geschichte der Juden in Deutschland 1 (1887) 176–189; *Andernacht*, nos. 344, 1766.

[97] *Aronius*, nos. 126, 135.

[98] *Linder*, 394.

[99] See *Bernard Blumenkranz*, Cultivateurs et vignerons juifs en Bourgogne du IXe au XIe siècles, in: *idem*, Juifs en France. Ecrits dispersés (Paris 1989) 89–99; *Norman Golb*, The Jews in Medieval Normandy (Cambridge 1998) 552–553. I am now in the process of integrating the Latin sources with the Hebrew ones, with fascinating results.

produced by Jews[100]. From the 12th century onwards, the possession of vineyards is more often mentioned[101]. In some cases, Jewish owners were personally involved in wine production, for instance Isaac bar Joel ha-Levi and Judah, both of Mainz, killed in 1146 by crusaders while gathering the grapes[102]. Their participation in the work process was required by religious law in order to make the wine potable by observing Jews. Such properties are also found in the Later Middle Ages, indicating an ongoing concern for the production of kosher wine[103]. In 1374, we learn that the Jews of Vienna were freed from taxes on two kinds of wine: on their *pauwein*, wine produced by themselves, and on wine received in payment for loans[104]. The latter appears in many places in sizeable quantities and was clearly funneled into trade. The same applies for wine grown in vineyards in Jewish possession but worked by non-Jews[105]. In many cases these must have been holdings put up as collateral for loans.

In the 10th/11th century there are only dim references to other agricultural pursuits[106]. Later, landed property that was not vineyards becomes somewhat more common. In mid-13th century Austria two Jewish officials in ducal service received possession (or the right of usage, the source is somewhat uncertain) of sixteen feudal estates. As in other more modest cases, their title to the land was most probably acquired when lenders defaulted on their loans[107]. This was clearly the instance in one of Meir ben Barukh's (the Maharam of Rothenburg, ca. 1220–1293) *Responsa*, where a village and the enjoyment of its harvest were handed over by the debtor to a consortium of Jewish lenders for a number of years. However, yet another *Responsum* tells of a Jewish landowner who arranged with a Christian peasant, clearly his dependent, to exchange fields and oxen. In another case two Jewish brothers went to court over intermingling fields possessed by them[108]. In the Later Middle Ages there are further indications for some Jews making a living by agriculture[109]. Clearly, the working of fields, unlike vineyards, remained an isolated occurrence, and most of the property reported in the sources was forfeited collateral from credit operations. Real change appears only at the very end of our period, when a

[100] *Agus*, nos. LXXXIV, CII, CXXXV, CLXXXIV, CCLXXIII; *Mutius* I 70–75, 83, 88, 100–2, 110; II, 28, 73, 76–77, 82, 84, 86, 105, 119; *Aronius*, no. 170. On the ritual problems of wine production, the real reason for its frequent mention in the sources, see *Soloveitchik*, Principles.

[101] For references see *Soloveitchik*, Principles, as well as Germania Judaica II, 344, 801, 837, and *Aronius*, nos. 317, 336, 371, 404.

[102] *Neubauer, Stern*, 191.

[103] Germania Judaica III, entries Bohemia, Austria, Konstanz, Kitzingen; *Stewart Jenks*, Judenverschuldung und Verfolgung von Juden im 14. Jahrhundert: Franken bis 1349, in: Vierteljahrschrift für Sozial- und Wirtschaftsgeschichte 65 (1978) 349; *Mentgen*, 557–560, as well as a sizable amount of Hebrew sources, for instance *Israel Isserlein*, Sepher Terumath ha-Deshen (Warsaw 1882) no. 329.

[104] *Mentgen*, 558.

[105] *Aronius*, no. 336.

[106] *Agus*, nos. CXXXIX, CCLXXXIII.

[107] *Aronius*, nos. 627, 349, 360, 361, 364, 375, 442.

[108] *Maharam*, nos. 997, 452, 640.

[109] Germania Judaica III, entries Pardubitz, Spandau, Sezemitz, Wildberg, Winterbach.

complex economic structure developed in the rural communities and small towns centered on Frankfurt on the Main[110]. The village Jews of these places worked small plots for their own provision. Their main livelihood however was a combination of money lending, the peddling of urban craft goods in the countryside, and the supply of rural products to Frankfurt. As a by-line they also provided the Jewish community of that town with kosher meat and wine. By the 16th century they were raising considerable quantities of livestock, as indicated by frequent conflicts with their Christian neighbors over grazing rights.

The agricultural nexus holds an important implication of social history. In medieval society, work in agriculture and indeed life in the countryside was held to be socially and culturally demeaning. Town-dwelling Jews also held to this attitude, nicely expressed in a *Responsum* by Meir ben Barukh of Rothenburg, where a woman categorically states: *it never entered my mind to live in a village without Minyan* (orderly religious services) *and prayer*[111]. When Jews became socially degraded at the end of the Middle Ages, when they turned from town-dwellers into village Jews, one begins to find agricultural pursuits similar to surrounding society. It was then that the stereotype of the itinerant Jew, the cattle-dealer and peddler, arose. The major exception to the degrading aspect of rural occupations is viticulture, for its ritual feature of the provision of kosher wine, as well as an important source of merchandise for entrepreneurs.

The Torah is being fulfilled in Ashkenaz more than in other countries because they take interest from the Gentiles and do not need to work in crafts, and therefore they have leisure to study the Torah. This is one more dictum by a late medieval Rabbi, Joseph ben Moses (died after 1488), indicating the supreme value put on religious studies[112]. Does it also indicate, as it purports to, the absence of Jewish men and women making a living from crafts? In the early period there are only faint indications: Gershom ben Jehudah refers to a man who depended for his livelihood on the bakery oven owned and operated by him[113]. Other texts of the 11th century, on a goldsmith, on horse shooing, and on the repairing of vessels, can be understood to refer to Jewish craftsmen working for internal needs[114]. By the 12th/13th centuries, some craftsmen catering for Jewish and at times for Gentile customers can be more clearly made out[115].

More substantial information becomes known in the Later Middle Ages, mostly from urban sources[116]. In many cases, one learns of crafts practiced by Jews only

110 *Michael Toch*, Die ländliche Wirtschaftstätigkeit der Juden im frühmodernen Deutschland, in: *M. Richarz*, *R. Rürup* (eds.), Jüdisches Leben auf dem Lande. Studien zur deutsch-jüdischen Geschichte (Berlin 1997) 59–67; *Toch*, Wirtschaft.

111 *Maharam*, no. 1006.

112 *Joseph ben Moshe*, Leket Joscher, ed. *J. Freimann*, part I (Berlin 1903) 119, paragraph B.

113 *Agus*, no. XLIX.

114 *Agus*, nos. CXXII, CCLXXVI.

115 *Dinur*, 223, 225, 229; *Aronius*, no. 305; *Maharam*, nos. 677, 856.

116 For details and references see *Michael Toch*, Geldleiher und sonst nichts? Zur wirtschaftlichen Tätigkeit der Juden im deutschen Sprachraum des Spätmittelalters, in: Tel Aviver Jahrbuch für deutsche Geschichte 22 (1993) 117–126; *Toch*, Tätigkeit; *Mentgen*, 579–585.

when political authorities prohibited such activity, mostly after pressure by crafts guilds. At the very end of the Middle Ages, the strong current against Jewish money lending also led to some attempts to "ameliorate the Jews" by forcing them to earn a living by the sweat of their brow. Thus, in 1497 the bishop of Strasbourg allowed one Jew to settle in the village of Schäfersheim, provided he refrained from lending money to the bishop's subjects and dealt only in window glazing, production of playing cards, or sword-cutling. The range of crafts evident in late-medieval Germany is quite impressive and was mostly geared towards a general, non-Jewish, clientele. In the leather branch there were producers of bags and purses, belts, saddles, sheats, maybe also of bellows, as well as furriers and cobblers. In textiles, there were weavers, dyers, tailors and (female) producers of veils. In the metal crafts one finds knife grinders and comparatively numerous sword cutlers and goldsmiths. Apparently, Jews were also drawn towards somewhat artistic occupations, as producers of playing cards (among them a woman of Worms) and of dice, illuminators, printers, and bookbinders. There were makers of *shofaroth* and, in Prague, a manufacturer of mousetraps, brewers, a distiller of spirits, a miller, a turner, and a bricklayer. Glaziers, mentioned in eight different places, were apparently a Jewish profession. The bishop of Strasbourg was thus right on the mark: glaziers, painters of playing cards and cutlers were indeed the most common crafts for Jews. The highest concentration is found in Bohemia, especially in Prague, while the German west has only isolated instances, most probably because of the opposition of craft guilds that there were much more powerful.

Jewish entrepreneurs, engineers, and proprietors of exotic expertise provide an intriguing chapter of occupational history. It opens with a somewhat enigmatic reference of Ibrahim ibn Jacub, the Jewish traveler from Cordoba (before 970), to a salt refinery situated on the river Saale and worked by Jews. This allusion, outlandish as it might be, returns almost 300 years later, when a Latin source mentions at the very same place, near Halle on the river Saale, the Jewish member of a consortium engaged in salt refinery[117]. This is the only source from the central Middle Ages, but later meticulous bookkeeping by princely and town administrations produces a rich harvest of information on Jewish technical expertise[118]. Usually we learn of these individuals when they are being rewarded: for disclosing the secrets of an unspecified *art* (in Frankfurt in 1454 this meant *the strange art* of blowing up fortifications); for the production of guns, gunpowder and other military equipment; for building mills and the model of a mill; for drainage work and the laying of pipes; for employment in minting, mining and the working of precious metals. In 1455, one Michael served landgrave Ludwig I of Kassel as alchemist. Another practitioner of the occult was less lucky: a Jew who had dabbled in Nuremberg a few years earlier in alchemy of silver and gold was branded on forehead and cheeks and expelled from town. Such people led a mobile existence, moving from one

[117] *Aronius*, nos. 131, 447.

[118] For details and source references see *Toch*, Tätigkeit; *M. Ginsburger*, Les juifs et l'art militaire au moyen âge, in: Revue des études juives 88 (1929) 156–166.

place to the other, as migrants and by the invitation of rulers, even to localities were the Jews had previously been expelled.

Medicine is among the earliest occupations mentioned for Jews in Europe, and this holds also for Germany[119]. From the *Book of Pious* one learns of the use of medical handbooks already in the 12th/13th century. Though no hard information is available, such instruction manuals might well be the link between Jewish practitioners in the north of Europe and the much more highly developed medical culture in the south. Substantial information again becomes available in the Later Middle Ages. The most remarkable fact is the widespread reliance of rulers – kings, princes, and town governments – on Jewish doctors. They were retained both on a permanent basis and from case to case. From such employment records we learn that between 1350 and 1520 over 160 Jewish physicians, surgeons and other medical practitioners known by name were active in Germany. Their actual number might well have been larger. Significantly, they are also found in regions that by then had been altogether emptied of Jews, such as the Netherlands, the German northwest, today's Switzerland and Bavaria. Their expertise was important enough to overcome the extremely strong anti-Jewish feelings rampant in these regions.

Physicians were probably the most mobile element of the Jewish population. They moved from place to place, but also from culture to culture. A Moses traveled from Rome to Aschaffenburg and then to Frankfurt on the Main, where he was employed as town surgeon and pioneered the treatment of syphilis. Feifel, *traveler and surgeon from the holy city of Jerusalem*, reached amongst other places also Prague, where he became personal physician to king Wenzel. However, he also worked as kosher butcher[120]. Since the early Middle Ages, doctors were apparently especially prone to convert to Christianity, maybe because of their proximity to rulers and of the considerable rewards offered to them. In the Later Middle Ages this included the bestowal of academic titles and, in at least one case, ennoblement[121]. These were dignities no normal Jews could aspire to. Jewish medicine also included humble dispensers of medicine and ointments, simple surgeons, a sizable number of specialists in ophthalmology and dentistry, and women practicing general medicine as well as midwifery. There were veterinary surgeons, for instance Ytzinger the Young of Kronberg, who *for his art* was allowed in 1486 by the archbishop of Mainz to settle in a small town on the Rhine. There was also that one *blind baptized Jew, who dabbled in quack medicine* and was expelled from Frankfurt on the Main in 1497[122]. Still, Jewish medicine was not wholly directed towards the outside world. In 1364 a Rabbi Lebelang proposed to establish a hospice for

[119] For the following see *Toch*, Tätigkeit; *Joseph Shatzmiller*, Doctors and Medical Practice in Germany around the Year 1200, in: Journal of Jewish Studies 33 (1982) 583–593; *Mentgen*, 585–591.

[120] Germania Judaica III, entries Frankfurt/Main, Prague.

[121] *Markus Wenninger*, Zur Promotion jüdischer Ärzte durch Kaiser Friedrich III., in: Aschkenas 5 (1995) 413–424; *Gerd Mentgen*, Die mittelalterliche Ärzte-Familie "Gutleben", in: Zeitschrift für Geschichte des Oberrheins 139 (1991) 79–93.

[122] *Andernacht*, no. 2896.

Jewish lepers in Weinheim near Heidelberg (where centuries later Martin Buber lived). Possibly his plan, a remarkable exercise in community solidarity, was realized to some measure. Rainer Barzen is further elaborating on the topic in this volume.

To sum up: There was always a sizable stratum of "lower-class" Jews and Jewesses employed in the service sector of the communities and of affluent families. However, our examination has found the traditional picture of the preponderance of trade, and later of money-lending, largely valid. Such occupations certainly provided the basis for Jewish existence, in the sense that its practitioners were the ones whose economic activities answered to the demands of the market-place. As such, they were of use to the authorities as highly significant taxpayers. They were also the ones in full view of Christian society, with all that entailed for the shaping of the image of the Jew. As traders, Jews were certainly not as all-important as has been claimed. As money-lenders, they fulfilled a more significant role in the economy and society, alongside other people and institutions engaged in extending credit. As for the impact of economics on broader history: I see the turn to money lending as one growing influence, amongst other factors, on the increasingly negative image that German society, as that of other European ones, came to hold of and apply to the Jews.

Index

Bearbeitet von Anna Gutgarts

Schriften des Historischen Kollegs: Kolloquien

1 *Heinrich Lutz* (Hrsg.): Das römisch-deutsche Reich im politischen System Karls V., 1982, XII, 288 S. ISBN 3-486-51371-0 *vergriffen*

2 *Otto Pflanze* (Hrsg.): Innenpolitische Probleme des Bismarck-Reiches, 1983, XII, 304 S. ISBN 3-486-51481-4 *vergriffen*

3 *Hans Conrad Peyer* (Hrsg.): Gastfreundschaft, Taverne und Gasthaus im Mittelalter, 1983, XIV, 275 S. ISBN 3-486-51661-2 *vergriffen*

4 *Eberhard Weis* (Hrsg.): Reformen im rheinbündischen Deutschland, 1984, XVI, 310 S. ISBN 3-486-51671-X

5 *Heinz Angermeier* (Hrsg.): Säkulare Aspekte der Reformationszeit, 1983, XII, 278 S. ISBN 3-486-51841-0

6 *Gerald D. Feldman* (Hrsg.): Die Nachwirkungen der Inflation auf die deutsche Geschichte 1924–1933, 1985, XII, 407 S. ISBN 3-486-52221-3 *vergriffen*

7 *Jürgen Kocka* (Hrsg.): Arbeiter und Bürger im 19. Jahrhundert. Varianten ihres Verhältnisses im europäischen Vergleich, 1986, XVI, 342 S. ISBN 3-486-52871-8 *vergriffen*

8 *Konrad Repgen* (Hrsg.): Krieg und Politik 1618–1648. Europäische Probleme und Perspektiven, 1988, XII, 454 S. ISBN 3-486-53761-X *vergriffen*

9 *Antoni Mączak* (Hrsg.): Klientelsysteme im Europa der Frühen Neuzeit, 1988, X, 386 S. ISBN 3-486-54021-1

10 *Eberhard Kolb* (Hrsg.): Europa vor dem Krieg von 1870. Mächtekonstellation – Konfliktfelder – Kriegsausbruch, 1987, XII, 216 S. ISBN 3-486-54121-8

11 *Helmut Georg Koenigsberger* (Hrsg.): Republiken und Republikanismus im Europa der Frühen Neuzeit, 1988, XII, 323 S. ISBN 3-486-54341-5

12 *Winfried Schulze* (Hrsg.): Ständische Gesellschaft und soziale Mobilität, 1988, X, 416 S. ISBN 3-486-54351-2

13 *Johanne Autenrieth* (Hrsg.): Renaissance- und Humanistenhandschriften, 1988, XII, 214 S. mit Abbildungen ISBN 3-486-54511-6

14 *Ernst Schulin* (Hrsg.): Deutsche Geschichtswissenschaft nach dem Zweiten Weltkrieg (1945–1965), 1989, XI, 303 S. ISBN 3-486-54831-X

15 *Wilfried Barner* (Hrsg.): Tradition, Norm, Innovation. Soziales und literarisches Traditionsverhalten in der Frühzeit der deutschen Aufklärung, 1989, XXV, 370 S. ISBN 3-486-54771-2

16 *Hartmut Boockmann* (Hrsg.): Die Anfänge der ständischen Vertretungen in Preußen und seinen Nachbarländern, 1992, X, 264 S. ISBN 3-486-55840-4

17 *John C. G. Röhl* (Hrsg.): Der Ort Kaiser Wilhelms II. in der deutschen Geschichte, 1991, XIII, 366 S. ISBN 3-486-55841-2 *vergriffen*

Schriften des Historischen Kollegs: Kolloquien

18 *Gerhard A. Ritter* (Hrsg.): Der Aufstieg der deutschen Arbeiterbewegung. Sozialdemokratie und Freie Gewerkschaften im Parteiensystem und Sozialmilieu des Kaiserreichs, 1990, XXI, 461 S. ISBN 3-486-55641-X

19 *Roger Dufraisse* (Hrsg.): Revolution und Gegenrevolution 1789–1830. Zur geistigen Auseinandersetzung in Frankreich und Deutschland, 1991, XX, 274 S. ISBN 3-486-55844-7

20 *Klaus Schreiner* (Hrsg.): Laienfrömmigkeit im späten Mittelalter. Formen, Funktionen, politisch-soziale Zusammenhänge, 1992, XII, 411 S. ISBN 3-486-55902-8

21 *Jürgen Miethke* (Hrsg.): Das Publikum politischer Theorie im 14. Jahrhundert, 1992, IX, 301 S. ISBN 3-486-55898-6

22 *Dieter Simon* (Hrsg.): Eherecht und Familiengut in Antike und Mittelalter, 1992, IX, 168 S. ISBN 3-486-55885-4

23 *Volker Press* (Hrsg.): Alternativen zur Reichsverfassung in der Frühen Neuzeit? 1995, X, 254 S. ISBN 3-486-56035-2

24 *Kurt Raaflaub* (Hrsg.): Anfänge politischen Denkens in der Antike. Die nahöstlichen Kulturen und die Griechen, 1993, XXIV, 461 S. ISBN 3-486-55993-1

25 *Shulamit Volkov* (Hrsg.): Deutsche Juden und die Moderne, 1994, XXIV, 170 S. ISBN 3-486-56029-8 *vergriffen*

26 *Heinrich A. Winkler* (Hrsg.): Die deutsche Staatskrise 1930–1933. Handlungsspielräume und Alternativen, 1992, XIII, 296 S. ISBN 3-486-55943-5 *vergriffen*

27 *Johannes Fried* (Hrsg.): Dialektik und Rhetorik im früheren und hohen Mittelalter. Rezeption, Überlieferung und gesellschaftliche Wirkung antiker Gelehrsamkeit vornehmlich im 9. und 12. Jahrhundert, 1997, XXI, 304 S. ISBN 3-486-56028-X

28 *Paolo Prodi* (Hrsg.): Glaube und Eid. Treueformeln, Glaubensbekenntnisse und Sozialdisziplinierung zwischen Mittelalter und Neuzeit, 1993, XXX, 246 S. ISBN 3-486-55994-X

29 *Ludwig Schmugge* (Hrsg.): Illegitimität im Spätmittelalter, 1994, X, 314 S. ISBN 3-486-56069-7

30 *Bernhard Kölver* (Hrsg.): Recht, Staat und Verwaltung im klassischen Indien/ The State, the Law, and Administration in Classical India, 1997, XVIII, 257 S. ISBN 3-486-56193-6

31 *Elisabeth Fehrenbach* (Hrsg.): Adel und Bürgertum in Deutschland 1770–1848, 1994, XVI, 251 S. ISBN 3-486-56027-1

32 *Robert E. Lerner* (Hrsg.): Neue Richtungen in der hoch- und spätmittelalterlichen Bibelexegese, 1996, XII, 191 S. ISBN 3-486-56083-2

33 *Klaus Hildebrand* (Hrsg.): Das Deutsche Reich im Urteil der Großen Mächte und europäischen Nachbarn (1871–1945), 1995, X, 232 S. ISBN 3-486-56084-0

Schriften des Historischen Kollegs: Kolloquien

34 *Wolfgang J. Mommsen* (Hrsg.): Kultur und Krieg. Die Rolle der Intellektuellen, Künstler und Schriftsteller im Ersten Weltkrieg, 1995, X, 282 S. ISBN 3-486-56085-9 *vergriffen*

35 *Peter Krüger* (Hrsg.): Das europäische Staatensystem im Wandel. Strukturelle Bedingungen und bewegende Kräfte seit der Frühen Neuzeit, 1996, XVI, 272 S. ISBN 3-486-56171-5

36 *Peter Blickle* (Hrsg.): Theorien kommunaler Ordnung in Europa, 1996, IX, 268 S. ISBN 3-486-56192-8

37 *Hans Eberhard Mayer* (Hrsg.): Die Kreuzfahrerstaaten als multikulturelle Gesellschaft. Einwanderer und Minderheiten im 12. und 13. Jahrhundert, 1997, XI, 187 S. ISBN 3-486-56257-6

38 *Manlio Bellomo* (Hrsg.): Die Kunst der Disputation. Probleme der Rechtsauslegung und Rechtsanwendung im 13. und 14. Jahrhundert, 1997, X, 248 S. ISBN 3-486-56258-4

39 *František Šmahel* (Hrsg.): Häresie und vorzeitige Reformation im Spätmittelalter, 1998, XV, 304 S. ISBN 3-486-56259-2

40 *Alfred Haverkamp* (Hrsg.): Information, Kommunikation und Selbstdarstellung in mittelalterlichen Gemeinden, 1998, XXII, 288 S. ISBN 3-486-56260-6

41 *Knut Schulz* (Hrsg.): Handwerk in Europa. Vom Spätmittelalter bis zur Frühen Neuzeit, 1999, XX, 313 S. ISBN 3-486-56395-5

42 *Werner Eck* (Hrsg.): Lokale Autonomie und römische Ordnungsmacht in den kaiserzeitlichen Provinzen vom 1. bis 3. Jahrhundert, 1999, X, 327 S. ISBN 3-486-56385-8

43 *Manfred Hildermeier* (Hrsg.): Stalinismus vor dem Zweiten Weltkrieg. Neue Wege der Forschung / Stalinism before the Second World War. New Avenues of Research, 1998, XVI, 345 S. ISBN 3-486-56350-5

44 *Aharon Oppenheimer* (Hrsg.): Jüdische Geschichte in hellenistisch-römischer Zeit. Wege der Forschung: Vom alten zum neuen Schürer, 1999, XII, 275 S. ISBN 3-486-56414-5

45 *Dietmar Willoweit* (Hrsg.): Die Begründung des Rechts als historisches Problem, 2000, VIII, 345 S. ISBN 3-486-56482-X

46 *Stephen A. Schuker* (Hrsg.): Deutschland und Frankreich. Vom Konflikt zur Aussöhnung. Die Gestaltung der westeuropäischen Sicherheit 1914–1963, 2000, XX, 280 S. ISBN 3-486-56496-X

47 *Wolfgang Reinhard* (Hrsg.): Verstaatlichung der Welt? Europäische Staatsmodelle und außereuropäische Machtprozesse, 1999, XVI, 375 S. ISBN 3-486-56416-1

48 *Gerhard Besier* (Hrsg.): Zwischen „nationaler Revolution“ und militärischer Aggression. Transformationen in Kirche und Gesellschaft während der konsolidierten NS-Gewaltherrschaft 1934–1939, 2001, XXVIII, 276 S. ISBN 3-486-56543-5

Schriften des Historischen Kollegs: Kolloquien

49 *David Cohen* (Hrsg.): Demokratie, Recht und soziale Kontrolle im klassischen Athen, 2002, VI, 205 S. ISBN 3-486-56662-8

50 *Thomas A. Brady* (Hrsg.): Die deutsche Reformation zwischen Spätmittelalter und Früher Neuzeit, 2001, XXI, 258 S., ISBN 3-486-56565-6

51 *Harold James* (Hrsg.): The Interwar Depression in an International Context, 2002, XVII, 192 S., ISBN 3-486-56610-5

52 *Christof Dipper* (Hrsg.): Deutschland und Italien, 1860–1960. Politische und kulturelle Aspekte im Vergleich, 2005, X, 284 S. ISBN 3-486-20015-1

53 *Frank-Rutger Hausmann* (Hrsg.): Die Rolle der Geisteswissenschaften im Dritten Reich 1933–1945, 2002, XXV, 373 S. ISBN 3-486-56639-3

54 *Frank Kolb* (Hrsg.): Chora und Polis, 2004, XVIII, 382 S. ISBN 3-486-56730-6

55 *Hans Günter Hockerts* (Hrsg.): Koordinaten deutscher Geschichte in der Epoche des Ost-West-Konflikts, 2004, XVIII, 339 S. ISBN 3-486-56768-3

56 *Wolfgang Hardtwig* (Hrsg.): Utopie und politische Herrschaft im Europa der Zwischenkriegszeit, 2003, IX, 356 S. ISBN 3-486-56642-3

57 *Diethelm Klippel* (Hrsg.): Naturrecht und Staat. Politische Funktionen des europäischen Naturrechts (17.–19. Jahrhundert) (mit Beiträgen von H. Brandt, W. Brauneder, W. Demel, Ch. Dipper, M. Fitzpatrick, S. Hofer, S. Rus Rufino, W. Schmale, J. Schröder, D. Schwab, B. Stollberg-Rilinger) 2006, XI, 231 S. ISBN 3-486-57905-3

58 *Jürgen Reulecke* (Hrsg.): Generationalität und Lebensgeschichte im 20. Jahrhundert, 2003, XV, 300 S. ISBN 3-486-56747-0

59 *Klaus Hildebrand* (Hrsg.): Zwischen Politik und Religion. Studien zur Entstehung, Existenz und Wirkung des Totalitarismus. Kolloquium der Mitglieder des Historischen Kollegs, 23. November 2001, 2003, XIV, 155 S. ISBN 3-486-56748-9

60 *Marie-Luise Recker* (Hrsg.): Parlamentarismus in Europa. Deutschland, England und Frankreich im Vergleich, 2004, XVIII, 232 S. ISBN 3-486-56817-5

61 *Helmut Altrichter* (Hrsg.): GegenErinnerung. Geschichte als politisches Argument im Transformationsprozeß Ost-, Ostmittel- und Südosteuropas (mit Beiträgen von H. Altrichter, C. Bethke, K. Brüggemann, V. Dumbrava, R. Eckert, U. von Hirschhausen, J. Hösler, I. Ivelijć, W. Jilge, C. Kraft, H. Lemberg, R. Lindner, B. Murgescu, A. Nikžentaitis, A. Pók, H. Sundhaussen, S. Troebst, M. Wien) 2006, XXII, 326 S. ISBN 3-486-57873-1

62 *Jürgen Trabant* (Hrsg.): Sprache der Geschichte, 2005, XXIV, 166 S. ISBN 3-486-57572-4

63 *Anselm Doering-Manteuffel* (Hrsg.): Strukturmerkmale der deutschen Geschichte des 20. Jahrhunderts (mit Beiträgen von E. Conze, A. Doering-Manteuffel, M. Geyer, H.-G. Haupt, H. James, G. Koenen, D. van Laak, M. Niehuss, L. Raphael, J. Reulecke, J. Rückert, M. Ruck, A. von Saldern, A. Schildt, A. Wirsching, M. Zimmermann) 2006, VIII, 273 S. ISBN 3-486-58057-4

Schriften des Historischen Kollegs: Kolloquien

64 *Jan-Dirk Müller* (Hrsg.): Text und Kontext: Fallstudien und theoretische Begründungen einer kulturwissenschaftlich angeleiteten Mediävistik (mit Beiträgen von G. Althoff, H. Bleumer, U. von Bloh, U. Friedrich, B. Jussen, B. Kellner, Ch. Kiening, K. Krüger, St. G. Nichols, P. Strohschneider, Ch. Witthöft) 2007, XIII, 272 S. ISBN 3-486-58106-5

65 *Peter Schäfer* (Hrsg.): Wege mystischer Gotteserfahrung. Judentum, Christentum und Islam / Mystical Approaches to God. Judaism, Christianity, and Islam (mit Beiträgen von W. Beierwaltes, P. Dinzelbacher, R. Elior, A. M. Haas, M. Himmelfarb, P. Schäfer, G. G. Stroumsa, S. Stroumsa) 2006, X, 164 S. ISBN 3-486-58006-X

66 *Friedrich Wilhelm Graf* (Hrsg.): Intellektuellen-Götter. Das religiöse Laboratorium der klassischen Moderne (mit Beiträgen von C. Arnold, K. Große Kracht, H. Haury, G. Hübinger, V. Krech, Ch. Nottmeier, M. Pyka, A. Reuter, U. Sieg) (in Vorbereitung)

67 *Werner Busch* (Hrsg.): Verfeinertes Sehen. Optik und Farbe im 18. und frühen 19. Jahrhundert (mit Beiträgen von U. Boskamp, W. Busch, E. Fioretini, J. Gage, B. Gockel, U. Klein, C. Meister, J. Müller-Tamm, A. Pietsch, H. O. Sibum, M. Wagner, M. Wellmann) 2008, X, 228 S. ISBN 978-3-486-58490-5

68 *Kaspar von Greyerz* (Hrsg.): Selbstzeugnissse in der Frühen Neuzeit. Individualisierungsweisen in interdisziplinärer Perspektive (mit Beitägen von J. S. Amelang, P. Becker, M. Christadler, R. Dekker, S. Faroqhi, K. v. Greyerz, V. Groebner, G. Jancke, S. Mendelson, G. Piller, R. Ries) 2007, VII, 201 S. ISBN 978-3-486-58236-9

69 *Wilfried Hartmann* (Hrsg.): Recht und Gericht in Kirche und Welt um 900 (mit Beiträgen von C. Cubitt, R. Deutinger, S. Hamilton, W. Hartmann, E.-D. Hehl, K. Herbers, W. Kaiser, L. Körntgen, R. Meens, H. Siems, K. Ubl, K. Zechiel-Eckes) 2007, IX, 249 S. ISBN 978-3-486-58147-8

70 *Heinz Schilling* (Hrsg.): Konfessioneller Fundamentalismus. Religion als politischer Faktor im europäischen Mächtesystem um 1600 (mit Beiträgen von R. Bireley, H.-J. Bömelburg, W. Frijhoff, A. Gotthard, H. Th. Gräf, W. Harms, Th. Kaufmann, A. Koller, V. Leppin, W. Monter, B. Roeck, A. Schindling, W. Schulze, I. Tóth, E. Wolgast) 2007, XI, 320 S. ISBN 978-3-486-58150-8

71 *Michael Toch* (Hrsg.): Wirtschaftsgeschichte der mittelalterlichen Juden. Fragen und Einschätzungen (mit Beiträgen von D. Abulafia, R. Barzen, A. Holtmann, D. Jacoby, M. Keil, R. Mueller, H.-G. von Mutius, J. Shatzmiller, M. Toch, G. Todeschini, M. Wenniger) 2008, X, 218 S. ISBN 978-3-486-58670-1

72 *Tilman Nagel* (Hrsg.): Der Koran und sein religiöses und kulturelles Umfeld (in Vorbereitung)

73 *Karl-Joachim Hölkeskamp* (Hrsg.): Eine politische Kultur (in) der Krise? Die „letzte Generation" der römischen Republik (mit Beiträgen von H. Beck, F. Bücher, J.-M. David, E. Flaig, K.-J. Hölkeskamp, T. Hölscher, M. Jehne, R. Morstein Marx, W. Nippel, U. Walter, G. Zecchini) (in Vorbereitung)

Schriften des Historischen Kollegs: Kolloquien

74 *Karl Schlögel* (Hrsg.): Mastering Space. Raum und Raumbewältigung als Probleme der russischen Geschichte (in Vorbereitung)

75 *Aloys Winterling* (Hrsg.): Zwischen Strukturgeschichte und Biographie. Probleme und Perspektiven einer römischen Kaisergeschichte (Augustus bis Commodus) (mit Beiträgen von Chr. Bruun, R. Haensch, O. Hekster, R. van den Hoff, M. Hose, Ch. Ronning, D. Schnurbusch, G. Seelentag, D. Timpe, U. Walter, A. Winterling, Chr. Witschel, R. Wolters, M. Zimmermann) (in Vorbereitung)

76 *Rüdiger vom Bruch* (Hrsg.): Die Berliner Universität im Kontext der deutschen Universitätslandschaft nach 1800, um 1860 und um 1910 (mit Beiträgen von Th. Becker, H.-W. Hahn, N. Hammerstein, W. Höflechner, P. Lundgreen, Ch. E. McClelland, M. Middell, W. Müller, W. Neugebauer, R. C. Schwinges, M. Stickler) (in Vorbereitung)

77 *Christoph Buchheim* (Hrsg.): Europäische Volkswirtschaften unter deutscher Hegemonie 1938–1945 (mit Beiträgen von St. Andersen, J. Balcar, M. Boldorf, J. Catalan, H. James, H. Joly, S. Kudrjaschow, K. Oosterlinck, J. Scherner, H. Wixforth) (in Vorbereitung)

78 *Klaus Schreiner* (Hrsg.): Heilige Kriege. Religiöse Begründungen militärischer Gewaltanwendung: Judentum, Christentum und Islam im Vergleich. Kolloquium der Mitglieder des Historischen Kollegs, 7.–9. November 2007 (mit Beiträgen von W. Eck, F. W. Graf, H. G. Hockerts, H.-Chr. Kraus, H. Maier, T. Nagel, A. Oppenheimer, R. Schieffer, H. Schilling, L. Schmugge, K. Schreiner, D. Willoweit) (in Vorbereitung)

79 *Jörg Fisch* (Hrsg.): Selbstbestimmung und Selbstbestimmungsrecht: Errungenschaft der Moderne oder kollektive Illusion? Self-Determination and the Right of Self Determination: Achiverment of Modernity or Collective Illusion? (in Vorbereitung)

80 *Georg Schmidt* (Hrsg.): Die deutsche Nation im frühneuzeitlichen Europa. Politische Ordnung und kulturelle Identität? (in Vorbereitung)

81 *Albrecht Cordes* (Hrsg.): Eine Grenze in Bewegung. Öffentliche und private Justiz im Handels- und Seerecht (in Vorbereitung)

Sonderveröffentlichungen

Horst Fuhrmann (Hrsg.): Die Kaulbach-Villa als Haus des Historischen Kollegs. Reden und wissenschaftliche Beiträge zur Eröffnung, 1989, XII, 232 S. ISBN 3-486-55611-8

Lothar Gall (Hrsg.): 25 Jahre Historisches Kolleg. Rückblick – Bilanz – Perspektiven, 2006, 293 S. ISBN 3-486-58005-1

Oldenbourg

Schriften des Historischen Kollegs: Vorträge

1 *Heinrich Lutz:* Die deutsche Nation zu Beginn der Neuzeit. Fragen nach dem Gelingen und Scheitern deutscher Einheit im 16. Jahrhundert, 1982, IV, 31 S. *vergriffen*

2 *Otto Pflanze:* Bismarcks Herrschaftstechnik als Problem der gegenwärtigen Historiographie, 1982, IV, 39 S. *vergriffen*

3 *Hans Conrad Peyer:* Gastfreundschaft und kommerzielle Gastlichkeit im Mittelalter, 1983, IV, 24 S. *vergriffen*

4 *Eberhard Weis:* Bayern und Frankreich in der Zeit des Konsulats und des ersten Empire (1799–1815), 1984, 41 S. *vergriffen*

5 *Heinz Angermeier:* Reichsreform und Reformation, 1983, IV, 76 S. *vergriffen*

6 *Gerald D. Feldman:* Bayern und Sachsen in der Hyperinflation 1922/23, 1984, IV, 41 S. *vergriffen*

7 *Erich Angermann:* Abraham Lincoln und die Erneuerung der nationalen Identität der Vereinigten Staaten von Amerika, 1984, IV, 33 S. *vergriffen*

8 *Jürgen Kocka:* Traditionsbindung und Klassenbildung. Zum sozialhistorischen Ort der frühen deutschen Arbeiterbewegung, 1987, 48 S. *vergriffen*

9 *Konrad Repgen:* Kriegslegitimationen in Alteuropa. Entwurf einer historischen Typologie, 1985, 27 S. *vergriffen*

10 *Antoni Mączak:* Der Staat als Unternehmen. Adel und Amtsträger in Polen und Europa in der Frühen Neuzeit, 1989, 32 S. *vergriffen*

11 *Eberhard Kolb:* Der schwierige Weg zum Frieden. Das Problem der Kriegsbeendigung 1870/71, 1985, 33 S. *vergriffen*

12 *Helmut Georg Koenigsberger:* Fürst und Generalstände. Maximilian I. in den Niederlanden (1477–1493), 1987, 27 S. *vergriffen*

13 *Winfried Schulze:* Vom Gemeinnutz zum Eigennutz. Über den Normenwandel in der ständischen Gesellschaft der Frühen Neuzeit, 1987, 40 S. *vergriffen*

14 *Johanne Autenrieth:* „Litterae Virgilianae". Vom Fortleben einer römischen Schrift, 1988, 51 S. *vergriffen*

15 *Tilemann Grimm:* Blickpunkte auf Südostasien. Historische und kulturanthropologische Fragen zur Politik, 1988, 37 S.

16 *Ernst Schulin:* Geschichtswissenschaft in unserem Jahrhundert. Probleme und Umrisse einer Geschichte der Historie, 1988, 34 S. *vergriffen*

17 *Hartmut Boockmann:* Geschäfte und Geschäftigkeit auf dem Reichstag im späten Mittelalter, 1988, 33 S. *vergriffen*

18 *Wilfried Barner:* Literaturwissenschaft – eine Geschichtswissenschaft? 1990, 42 S. *vergriffen*

Schriften des Historischen Kollegs: Vorträge

19 *John C. G. Röhl:* Kaiser Wilhelm II. Eine Studie über Cäsarenwahnsinn, 1989, 36 S. *vergriffen*

20 *Klaus Schreiner:* Mönchsein in der Adelsgesellschaft des hohen und späten Mittelalters. Klösterliche Gemeinschaftsbildung zwischen spiritueller Selbstbehauptung und sozialer Anpassung, 1989, 68 S. *vergriffen*

21 *Roger Dufraisse:* Die Deutschen und Napoleon im 20. Jahrhundert, 1991, 43 S.

22 *Gerhard A. Ritter:* Die Sozialdemokratie im Deutschen Kaiserreich in sozialgeschichtlicher Perspektive, 1989, 72 S. *vergriffen*

23 *Jürgen Miethke:* Die mittelalterlichen Universitäten und das gesprochene Wort, 1990, 48 S. *vergriffen*

24 *Dieter Simon:* Lob des Eunuchen, 1994, 27 S.

25 *Thomas Vogtherr:* Der König und der Heilige. Heinrich IV., der heilige Remaklus und die Mönche des Doppelklosters Stablo-Malmedy, 1990, 29 S. *vergriffen*

26 *Johannes Schilling:* Gewesene Mönche. Lebensgeschichten in der Reformation, 1990, 36 S. *vergriffen*

27 *Kurt Raaflaub:* Politisches Denken und Krise der Polis. Athen im Verfassungskonflikt des späten 5. Jahrhunderts v. Chr., 1992, 63 S.

28 *Volker Press:* Altes Reich und Deutscher Bund. Kontinuität in der Diskontinuität, 1995, 31 S.

29 *Shulamit Volkov:* Die Erfindung einer Tradition. Zur Entstehung des modernen Judentums in Deutschland, 1992, 30 S. *vergriffen*

30 *Franz Bauer:* Gehalt und Gestalt in der Monumentalsymbolik. Zur Ikonologie des Nationalstaats in Deutschland und Italien 1860–1914, 1992, 39 S.

31 *Heinrich A. Winkler:* Mußte Weimar scheitern? Das Ende der ersten Republik und die Kontinuität der deutschen Geschichte, 1991, 32 S. *vergriffen*

32 *Johannes Fried:* Kunst und Kommerz. Über das Zusammenwirken von Wissenschaft und Wirtschaft im Mittelalter vornehmlich am Beispiel der Kaufleute und Handelsmessen, 1992, 40 S.

33 *Paolo Prodi:* Der Eid in der europäischen Verfassungsgeschichte, 1992, 35 S.

34 *Jean-Marie Moeglin:* Dynastisches Bewußtsein und Geschichtsschreibung. Zum Selbstverständnis der Wittelsbacher, Habsburger und Hohenzollern im Spätmittelalter, 1993, 47 S.

35 *Bernhard Kölver:* Ritual und historischer Raum. Zum indischen Geschichtsverständnis, 1993, 65 S.

36 *Elisabeth Fehrenbach:* Adel und Bürgertum im deutschen Vormärz, 1994, 31 S.

Schriften des Historischen Kollegs: Vorträge

37 *Ludwig Schmugge:* Schleichwege zu Pfründe und Altar. Päpstliche Dispense vom Geburtsmakel 1449–1533, 1994, 35 S.

38 *Hans-Werner Hahn:* Zwischen Fortschritt und Krisen. Die vierziger Jahre des 19. Jahrhunderts als Durchbruchsphase der deutschen Industrialisierung, 1995, 47 S.

39 *Robert E. Lerner:* Himmelsvision oder Sinnendelirium? Franziskaner und Professoren als Traumdeuter im Paris des 13. Jahrhunderts, 1995, 35 S.

40 *Andreas Schulz:* Weltbürger und Geldaristokraten. Hanseatisches Bürgertum im 19. Jahrhundert, 1995, 38 S.

41 *Wolfgang J. Mommsen:* Die Herausforderung der bürgerlichen Kultur durch die künstlerische Avantgarde. Zum Verhältnis von Kultur und Politik im Wilhelminischen Deutschland, 1994, 30 S.

42 *Klaus Hildebrand:* Reich – Großmacht – Nation. Betrachtungen zur Geschichte der deutschen Außenpolitik 1871–1945, 1995, 25 S. *vergriffen*

43 *Hans Eberhard Mayer:* Herrschaft und Verwaltung im Kreuzfahrerkönigreich Jerusalem, 1996, 38 S.

44 *Peter Blickle:* Reformation und kommunaler Geist. Die Antwort der Theologen auf den Wandel der Verfassung im Spätmittelalter, 1996, 42 S.

45 *Peter Krüger:* Wege und Widersprüche der europäischen Integration im 20. Jahrhundert, 1995, 39 S.

46 *Werner Greiling:* „Intelligenzblätter“ und gesellschaftlicher Wandel in Thüringen. Anzeigenwesen, Nachrichtenvermittlung, Räsonnement und Sozialdisziplinierung, 1995, 38 S.

Schriften des Historischen Kollegs: Dokumentationen

1 Stiftung Historisches Kolleg im Stifterverband für die Deutsche Wissenschaft: Erste Verleihung des Preises des Historischen Kollegs. Aufgaben, Stipendiaten, Schriften des Historischen Kollegs, 1984, VI, 70 S., mit Abbildungen *vergriffen*

2 Theodor-Schieder-Gedächtnisvorlesung: Horst Fuhrmann, Das Interesse am Mittelalter in heutiger Zeit. Beobachtungen und Vermutungen – Lothar Gall, Theodor Schieder 1908 bis 1984, 1987, 65 S. *vergriffen*

3 Leopold von Ranke: Vorträge anläßlich seines 100. Todestages. Gedenkfeier der Historischen Kommission bei der Bayerischen Akademie der Wissenschaften und der Stiftung Historisches Kolleg im Stifterverband für die Deutsche Wissenschaft am 12. Mai 1986, 1987, 44 S. *vergriffen*

4 Stiftung Historisches Kolleg im Stifterverband für die Deutsche Wissenschaft: Zweite Verleihung des Preises des Historischen Kollegs. Aufgaben, Stipendiaten, Schriften des Historischen Kollegs, 1987, 98 S., mit Abbildungen

5 Theodor-Schieder-Gedächtnisvorlesung: Thomas Nipperdey, Religion und Gesellschaft: Deutschland um 1900, 1988, 29 S. *vergriffen*

6 Theodor-Schieder-Gedächtnisvorlesung: Christian Meier, Die Rolle des Krieges im klassischen Athen, 1991, 55 S. *vergriffen*

7 Stiftung Historisches Kolleg im Stifterverband für die Deutsche Wissenschaft: Dritte Verleihung des Preises des Historischen Kollegs. Aufgaben, Stipendiaten, Schriften des Historischen Kollegs, 1991, 122 S., mit Abbildungen *vergriffen*

8 Stiftung Historisches Kolleg im Stifterverband für die Deutsche Wissenschaft: Historisches Kolleg 1980–1990. Vorträge anläßlich des zehnjährigen Bestehens und zum Gedenken an Alfred Herrhausen, 1991, 63 S.

9 Theodor-Schieder-Gedächtnisvorlesung: Karl Leyser, Am Vorabend der ersten europäischen Revolution. Das 11. Jahrhundert als Umbruchszeit, 1994, 32 S.

10 Stiftung Historisches Kolleg im Stifterverband für die Deutsche Wissenschaft: Vierte Verleihung des Preises des Historischen Kollegs. Aufgaben, Stipendiaten, Schriften des Historischen Kollegs, 1993, 98 S., mit Abbildungen

11 Theodor-Schieder-Gedächtnisvorlesung: Rudolf Smend, Mose als geschichtliche Gestalt, 1995, 23 S.

12 Stiftung Historisches Kolleg im Stifterverband für die Deutsche Wissenschaft: Über die Offenheit der Geschichte. Kolloquium der Mitglieder des Historischen Kollegs, 20. und 21. November 1992, 1996, 84 S.

Vorträge und Dokumentationen sind nicht im Buchhandel erhältlich;
sie können, soweit lieferbar, über die Geschäftsstelle des Historischen Kollegs (Kaulbachstraße 15, 80539 München) bezogen werden.

Schriften des Historischen Kollegs: Jahrbuch

Jahrbuch des Historischen Kollegs 1995:

Arnold Esch
Rom in der Renaissance. Seine Quellenlage als methodisches Problem

Manlio Bellomo
Geschichte eines Mannes: Bartolus von Sassoferrato und die moderne europäische Jurisprudenz

František Šmahel
Das verlorene Ideal der Stadt in der böhmischen Reformation

Alfred Haverkamp
„... an die große Glocke hängen". Über Öffentlichkeit im Mittelalter

Hans-Christof Kraus
Montesquicu, Blackstone, De Lolme und die englische Verfassung des 18. Jahrhunderts

1996, VIII, 180 S. 4 Abb. ISBN 3-486-56176-6

Jahrbuch des Historischen Kollegs 1996:

Johannes Fried
Wissenschaft und Phantasie. Das Beispiel der Geschichte

Manfred Hildermeier
Revolution und Kultur: Der „Neue Mensch" in der frühen Sowjetunion

Knut Schulz
Handwerk im spätmittelalterlichen Europa. Zur Wanderung und Ausbildung von Lehrlingen in der Fremde

Werner Eck
Mord im Kaiserhaus? Ein politischer Prozeß im Rom des Jahres 20 n. Chr.

Wolfram Pyta
Konzert der Mächte und kollektives Sicherheitssystem: Neue Wege zwischenstaatlicher Friedenswahrung in Europa nach dem Wiener Kongreß 1815

1997, VI, 202 S. 1 Abb. ISBN 3-486-56300-9

Schriften des Historischen Kollegs: Jahrbuch

Jahrbuch des Historischen Kollegs 1997:

Eberhard Weis
Hardenberg und Montgelas. Versuch eines Vergleichs ihrer Persönlichkeiten und ihrer Politik

Dietmar Willoweit
Vom alten guten Recht. Normensuche zwischen Erfahrungswissen und Ursprungslegenden

Aharon Oppenheimer
Messianismus in römischer Zeit. Zur Pluralität eines Begriffes bei Juden und Christen

Stephen A. Schuker
Bayern und der rheinische Separatismus 1923–1924

Gerhard Schuck
Zwischen Ständeordnung und Arbeitsgesellschaft. Der Arbeitsbegriff in der frühneuzeitlichen Policey am Beispiel Bayerns

1998, XXI, 169 S. ISBN 3-486-56375-0

Jahrbuch des Historischen Kollegs 1998:

Peter Pulzer
Der deutsche Michel in John Bulls Spiegel: Das britische Deutschlandbild im 19. Jahrhundert

Gerhard Besier
„The friends ... in America need to know the truth ..."
Die deutschen Kirchen im Urteil der Vereinigten Staaten (1933–1941)

David Cohen
Die Schwestern der Medea. Frauen, Öffentlichkeit und soziale Kontrolle im klassischen Athen

Wolfgang Reinhard
Staat machen: Verfassungsgeschichte als Kulturgeschichte

Lutz Klinkhammer
Die Zivilisierung der Affekte. Kriminalitätsbekämpfung im Rheinland und in Piemont unter französischer Herrschaft 1798–1814

1999, 193 S. 5 Abb. ISBN 3-486-56420-X

Schriften des Historischen Kollegs: Jahrbuch

Jahrbuch des Historischen Kollegs 1999:

Jan Assmann
Ägypten in der Gedächtnisgeschichte des Abendlandes

Thomas A. Brady
Ranke, Rom und die Reformation: Leopold von Rankes Entdeckung des Katholizismus

Harold James
Das Ende der Globalisierung? Lehren aus der Weltwirtschaftskrise

Christof Dipper
Helden überkreuz oder das Kreuz mit den Helden. Wie Deutsche und Italiener die Heroen der nationalen Einigung (der anderen) wahrnahmen.

Felicitas Schmieder
„... von etlichen geistlichen leyen wegen". Definitionen der Bürgerschaft im spätmittelalterlichen Frankfurt

2000, VI, 199 S. 7 Abb. ISBN 3-486-56492-7

Jahrbuch des Historischen Kollegs 2000:

Winfried Schulze
Die Wahrnehmung von Zeit und Jahrhundertwenden

Frank Kolb
Von der Burg zur Polis. Akkulturation in einer kleinasiatischen „Provinz"

Hans Günter Hockerts
Nach der Verfolgung. Wiedergutmachung in Deutschland: Eine historische Bilanz 1945–2000

Frank-Rutger Hausmann
„Auch im Krieg schweigen die Musen nicht". Die ‚Deutschen Wissenschaftlichen Institute' (DWI) im Zweiten Weltkrieg (1940–1945)

Ulrike Freitag
Scheich oder Sultan – Stamm oder Staat? Staatsbildung im Hadramaut (Jemen) im 19. und 20. Jahrhundert

2001, VI, 250 S. 16 Abb. ISBN 3-486-56557-5

Schriften des Historischen Kollegs: Jahrbuch

Jahrbuch des Historischen Kollegs 2001:

Michael Stolleis
Das Auge des Gesetzes. Materialien zu einer neuzeitlichen Metapher

Wolfgang Hardtwig
Die Krise des Geschichtsbewußtseins in Kaiserreich und Weimarer Republik und der Aufstieg des Nationalsozialismus

Diethelm Klippel
Kant im Kontext. Der naturrechtliche Diskurs um 1800

Jürgen Reulecke
Neuer Mensch und neue Männlichkeit. Die „junge Generation" im ersten Drittel des 20. Jahrhunderts

Peter Burschel
Paradiese der Gewalt. Martyrium, Imagination und die Metamorphosen des nachtridentinischen Heiligenhimmels

2002, VI, 219 S. 16 Abb. ISBN 3-486-56641-5

Jahrbuch des Historischen Kollegs 2002:

Wolfgang Reinhard
Geschichte als Delegitimation

Jürgen Trabant
Sprache der Geschichte

Marie-Luise Recker
„Es braucht nicht niederreißende Polemik, sondern aufbauende Tat."
Zur Parlamentskultur der Bundesrepublik Deutschland

Helmut Altrichter
War der Zerfall der Sowjetunion vorauszusehen?

Andreas Rödder
„Durchbruch im Kaukasus"? Die deutsche Wiedervereinigung und die Zeitgeschichtsschreibung

2003, VI, 179 S. 2 Abb. ISBN 3-486-56736-5

Schriften des Historischen Kollegs: Jahrbuch

Jahrbuch des Historischen Kollegs 2003:

Jochen Martin
Rom und die Heilsgeschichte. Beobachtungen zum Triumphbogenmosaik von S. Maria Maggiore in Rom

Jan-Dirk Müller
Imaginäre Ordnungen und literarische Imaginationen um 1200

Peter Schäfer
Ex oriente lux? Heinrich Graetz und Gershom Scholem über den Ursprung der Kabbala

Anselm Doering-Manteuffel
Mensch, Maschine, Zeit. Fortschrittsbewußtsein und Kulturkritik im ersten Drittel des 20. Jahrhunderts

Bernhard Löffler
Öffentliches Wirken und öffentliche Wirkung Ludwig Erhards

2004, VI, 205 S. 20 Abb. ISBN 3-486-56843-4

Jahrbuch des Historischen Kollegs 2004:

Wolfgang Frühwald
„Wer es gesehen hat, der hat es auf sein ganzes Leben". Die italienischen Tagebücher der Familie Goethe

Kaspar von Greyerz
Vom Nutzen und Vorteil der Selbstzeugnisforschung für die Frühneuzeithistorie

Friedrich Wilhelm Graf
Annihilatio historiae? Theologische Geschichtsdiskurse in der Weimarer Republik

Werner Busch
Die Naturwissenschaften als Basis des Erhabenen in der Kunst des 18. und frühen 19. Jahrhunderts

Jörn Leonhard
Der Ort der Nation im Deutungswandel kriegerischer Gewalt: Europa und die Vereinigten Staaten 1854–1871

2005, VI, 182 S. 9 Abb. ISBN 3-486-57741-7

Schriften des Historischen Kollegs: Jahrbuch

Jahrbuch des Historischen Kollegs 2005:

Michael Mitterauer
Europäische Geschichte in globalem Kontext

Michael Toch
Das Gold der Juden – Mittelalter und Neuzeit

Heinz Schilling
Gab es um 1600 in Europa einen Konfessionsfundamentalismus? Die Geburt des internationalen Systems in der Krise des konfessionellen Zeitalters

Wilfried Hartmann
„Sozialdisziplinierung" und „Sündenzucht" im frühen Mittelalter? Das bischöfliche Sendgericht in der Zeit um 900

Peter Scholz
Imitatio patris statt griechischer Pädagogik. Überlegungen zur Sozialisation und Erziehung der republikanischen Senatsaristokratie

2006, VI, 190 S. 17 Abb. ISBN 978-3-486-57963-5

Jahrbuch des Historischen Kollegs 2006:

Klaus Hildebrand
Globalisierung 1900. Alte Staatenwelt und neue Weltpolitik an der Wende vom 19. zum 20. Jahrhundert

Karl-Joachim Hölkeskamp
Pomp und Prozessionen. Rituale und Zeremonien in der politischen Kultur der römischen Republik

Tilman Nagel
Verstehen oder nachahmen? Grundtypen der muslimischen Erinnerung an Mohammed

Karl Schlögel
Moskau 1937. Eine Stadt in den Zeiten des Großen Terrors

Claire Gantet
Seele und persönliche Identität im Heiligen Römischen Reich, ca. 1500 – ca. 1750. Ansätze zu einer kulturellen Wissenschaftsgeschichte

2007, VI, 211 S., 7 Abb. ISBN 978-3-486-58036-5

Schriften des Historischen Kollegs: Jahrbuch

Jahrbuch des Historischen Kollegs 2007:

Luise Schorn-Schütte
Kommunikation über Politik im Europa der Frühen Neuzeit. Ein Forschungskonzept

Christoph Buchheim
Der Wirtschaftsaufschwung im Deutschland der NS-Zeit

Jan-Otmar Hesse
„Ein Wunder der Wirtschaftstheorie". Die „Amerikanisierung" der Volkswirtschaftslehre in der frühen Bundesrepublik

Aloys Winterling
Cäsarenwahnsinn im Alten Rom

Christoph H. F. Meyer
Maßstäbe frühmittelalterlicher Gesetzgeber. Raum und Zeit in den Leges Langobardorum

Rüdiger vom Bruch
Vom Humboldt-Modell zum Harnack-Plan. Forschung, Disziplinierung und Gesellung an der Berliner Universität im 19. Jahrhundert

2008, 267 S., 3 Abb. ISBN 978-3-486-58489-9

Bei Fragen zur Produktsicherheit wenden Sie sich bitte an:
If you have any questions regarding product safety,
please contact:

Walter de Gruyter GmbH
Genthiner Straße 13
10785 Berlin
productsafety@degruyterbrill.com